Innovation Markets and Competition Analysis

NEW HORIZONS IN COMPETITION LAW AND ECONOMICS

Series Editor: Steve Anderman, *Professor of Law, University of Essex, UK*

This series has been created to provide research based analysis and discussion of the appropriate role for economic thinking in the formulation of competition law and policy. The books in the series will move beyond studies of the traditional role of economics – that of helping to define markets and assess market power – to explore the extent to which economic thinking can play a role in the formulation of legal norms, such as abuse of a dominant position, restriction of competition and substantial impediments to or lessening of competition. This in many ways is the *new horizon* of competition law policy.

US antitrust policy, influenced in its formative years by the Chicago School, has already experienced an expansion of the role of economic thinking in its competition rules. Now the EU is committed to a greater role for economic thinking in its Block Exemption Regulations and Modernisation package as well as possibly in its reform of Article 82. Yet these developments still raise the issue of the *extent* to which economics should be adopted in defining the public interest in competition policy and what role economists should play in legal argument. The series will provide a forum for research perspectives that are critical of an unduly-expanded role for economics as well as those that support its greater use.

Titles in the series include:

Antitrust, Patents and Copyright
EU and US Perspectives
Edited by François Lévêque and Howard Shelanski

Innovation Markets and Competition Analysis
EU Competition Law and US Antitrust Law
Marcus Glader

Innovation Markets and Competition Analysis

EU Competition Law and US Antitrust Law

Marcus Glader

Associate, Cleary Gottlieb Steen & Hamilton LLP, Brussels, Belgium

NEW HORIZONS IN COMPETITION LAW AND ECONOMICS

Edward Elgar
Cheltenham, UK • Northampton, MA, USA

Published by
Edward Elgar Publishing Limited
The Lypiatts
15 Lansdown Road
Cheltenham
Glos GL50 2JA
UK

Edward Elgar Publishing, Inc.
William Pratt House
9 Dewey Court
Northampton
Massachusetts 01060
USA

Reprinted 2014

A catalogue record for this book is available from the British Library

Library of Congress Cataloguing in Publication Data

Glader, Marcus, 1972–
Innovation markets and competition analysis: EU competition law and US antitrust law / by Marcus Glader.
p. cm – (New horizons in competition law and economics series)
Includes bibliographical references and index.
1. Antitrust law—United States. 2. Antitrust law—European Union countries. 3. Competition. I. Title. II. New horizons in competition law and economics.

K3850.G58 2006
343.24′0712—dc22

2005057450

FSC
www.fsc.org
MIX
Paper from responsible sources
FSC® C013056

ISBN 978 1 84542 607 1

Typeset by Cambrian Typesetters, Camberley, Surrey
Printed and bound in Great Britain by TJ International Ltd, Padstow, Cornwall

Contents

Acknowledgments

This book is based on my doctoral thesis, which was defended in December 2004. While I have revised certain sections, this does not constitute a complete update. The book was substantially completed before I joined Cleary Gottlieb Steen & Hamilton LLP and does not represent the view of the firm or any of its clients.

There are several people and institutions to whom I would like to express my gratitude for their support in the process of writing this book.

Encouraged by Professor Ingemar Ståhl, I was fortunate to spend a year in Hamburg and Aix-en-Provence earning a European Master in Law and Economics. Along with deeper insights in economics and public policy came a particular interest in competition law. As it turned out, during my time abroad, Professor Hans Henrik Lidgard resumed a position at the Faculty of Law in Lund. Our continued cooperation has been of a disparate nature and of great value both professionally and privately. A particular appreciation also goes to Associate Professor Katarina Olsson, Professors Aleksander Peczenik, Lars Gorton and Birgitta Nyström for reading and commenting on manuscripts and giving encouragement at various stages.

I had the privilege of spending five inspiring months at the European Commission. Apart from providing me with the opportunity to work in a very dynamic unit of DG Competition, I would like to thank the former Head of Unit Luc Gyselen and Director Sven Norberg for their involvement in this book.

Although very challenging, the public defence of my doctoral thesis was indeed constructive and much rewarding. For this memorable event I owe my formidable opponent Dr John Temple Lang.

I am grateful to the Swedish Competition Authority and the Council for Competition Research for financially backing up my PhD project. Finally, I would like to express my gratitude to the research foundation of Awapatent AB for its generous contribution for the publishing of this book.

Marcus Glader
Brussels, September 2005

Abbreviations

CFI	Court of First Instance
DG	Directorate General (European Commission)
DOJ	Department of Justice (United States)
EC	European Community
ECJ	European Court of Justice
ECR	European Court Reports
Ed., Eds	Editor, editors
EEA	European Economic Area
EEC	European Economic Community
ETSI	European Telecommunication Standards Institute
EU	European Union
F.2d, F.3d	Federal Reporter
F.Supp.	Federal Supplement
FDA	Federal Drug Administration
Fed. Reg.	Federal Register
FTC	Federal Trade Commission
GNP	Gross National Product
IP, IPR	Intellectual Property, Intellectual Property Right
JV	Joint Venture
OECD	Organisation for Economic Co-operation and Development
OEM	Original Equipment Manufacturer
OFT	Office of Fair Trading (United Kingdom)
OJ	Official Journal of the European Union (Official Journal of the European Communities prior to 1 February 2003)
R&D	Research and Development
SSNIP	Small but Significant Non-transitory Increase in Price
TTBER	Transfer of Technology – Block Exemption Regulation
US	United States, United States Report
USC	United States Code
USCCAN	United States Code Congressional and Administrative News
WL	Westlaw

Official documents

EU

Council Regulations and Directives

Commission Regulations and Notices

US

Cases

EUROPEAN COURT OF JUSTICE

COURT OF FIRST INSTANCE

European Commission

US SUPREME COURT

US CIRCUIT COURTS

US District Courts

DEPARTMENT OF JUSTICE

FEDERAL TRADE COMMISSION

1. Introduction

1.1 THE SUBJECT

This book explores the standards for the protection of competition in the innovation process in American antitrust law and European competition law, respectively. The development and current state of the relevant legal frameworks are described and analysed, and the results evaluated with regard to underlying economic rationale of the law. Suggestions for further development and clarification are presented and potential future applications discussed.

The single most notable doctrinal development in the area of protecting competition in the innovation process is the introduction of the 'Innovation Market' concept, developed in US antitrust policy in the 1990s. Consequently, the innovation market concept serves as a concrete point of departure for this work. Nonetheless, in order to analyse the boundaries of the innovation market approach and its relationship to other market definitions and other tools for analysing the innovation process, the scope of the investigation has gradually grown. Moreover, since the limits of the different legal concepts and doctrines are imprecise and the same transaction may have effects on multiple 'relevant markets', it is appropriate to highlight the interplay and limitations between product markets, technology markets and innovation markets.

1.2 THE ANTITRUST LAW CONCEPT OF INNOVATION MARKETS

The logic behind the concept of defining relevant markets as a basis for a competition law analysis is to identify the competitive restraints (in terms of competitors and competing products) that might reasonably discipline a firm by exerting competitive pressure. The innovation market concept can thus be seen as resulting from a concern that antitrust analysis had been limited to analysing competition in current markets where products and technologies are traded. The concept entails the delineation, for purposes of antitrust analysis, of an upstream market for innovation efforts (typically R&D programmes). The US 1995 Antitrust Guidelines for the Licensing of Intellectual Property provide the following description.

> An innovation market consists of the research and development directed to particular new or improved goods or processes, and the close substitutes for that research and development. The close substitutes are research and development efforts, technologies, and goods that significantly constrain the exercise of market power with respect to the relevant research and development, for example by limiting the ability and incentive of a hypothetical monopolist to retard the pace of research and development. The Agencies will delineate an innovation market only when the capabilities to engage in the relevant research and development can be associated with specialized assets or characteristics of specific firms.[1]

In other words, a market is defined for such research as aims either to improve currently existing products, or, more characteristically, to develop a completely new product for which no product market may yet exist. Consequently, such a market normally consists of the R&D for a specific product or process and relevant substitutes for this R&D (often in terms of competing R&D programmes).

In Europe, a less formalized methodology has been applied where the Commission analyses competition in R&D of certain products. Commenting on the European practices, John Temple Lang (at the time Director at DG Competition) asserted that, '[i]f there is a "market for R&D", it is only if companies are selling the service of providing R&D to other companies. That is a present service, and it is not the same as the question of whether R&D activities for the researcher's own use is a good measure of future market power.'[2] He nevertheless maintained that the Commission may consider whether a merger or agreement is likely to 'restrict substantially competition in R&D' and that this is something different from the potential competition approach.[3] Contrasting the US method of identifying competing R&D directed towards a particular good in situations where the innovation is associated with specialized assets or the characteristics of specific firms, he claimed that the European approach focuses on competition in R&D where competition between the relevant firms 'is the leading research in the field, is directed specifically towards producing or improving the same product or process, and is associated with specialized R&D programmes of those firms'.[4] He believed the American approach might be broader, but usually not significantly different.

Elsewhere the Commission has stated that, in the light of the uncertainties surrounding concentration and innovation, it does not apply competition

1 The US 1995 Antitrust Guidelines for the Licensing of Intellectual Property, §3.2.3.

2 Temple Lang, John, 'European Community Antitrust Law: Innovation Markets and High Technology Industries', 20 *Fordham International Law Journal* 717, 764f. (1997).

3 Ibid., pp. 760f.

4 Ibid.

policy to innovation markets *directly*. However, the Commission uses the innovation market concept to base its decision on likely effects for the market of the future products involved.[5]

In *Ciba-Geigy/Sandoz* (EU 1996),[6] some competitors had pointed out to the European Commission that there was a trend towards commissioning firms to carry out R&D. The Commission noted that 'some do not see research and development as a separate market. This is evidently based essentially on the fact that research and development, at least by pharmaceutical undertakings engaging in research, is still carried out predominantly for in-house purposes.'[7] The Commission did however assess relevant R&D 'in terms of its importance for future markets', that is, where no product has yet been introduced.[8] In *GlaxoWellcome/SmithKline Beecham* (EU 2000) under the 'future market' heading, the Commission asserted it had to assess 'the impact of the transaction on existing markets and on R&D markets'.[9] Also in *Upjohn/Pharmacia* (EU 1995)[10] the Commission repeatedly referred to R&D markets.

In the 2001 Guidelines on Horizontal Cooperation, the Commission briefly expanded on its approach to innovation competition (competing R&D efforts), thereby moving towards a formalization of its methodology.[11] These guidelines label product markets and technology markets as 'existing markets'. Rather than referring R&D competition analysis to 'future markets', the guidelines address 'competition in innovation' and 'R&D efforts'. The guidelines also make reference to the 'innovation market', referring to the previously defined R&D efforts. The 2004 EU Technology Transfer Guidelines take the final step and formally include innovation markets as a third kind of relevant market, besides product and technology markets.[12]

In spite of the ambiguous categorizations, the term 'innovation market' will here be used for both the EU and the US methodologies used to analyse the impact of transactions with reference to the structure and competitive conditions in R&D.

---

5 OECD, 'Application of Competition Policy to High Tech Markets', *OECD Working Papers*, Series Roundtables on Competition Policy no. 9, Paris, 1997, p. 90.

6 Case No IV/M.737 – *Ciba-Geigy/Sandoz* (1996) OJ L 201/1 (1997).

7 Ibid., §43.

8 Ibid., §44.

9 Case No COMP/M.1846 – *Glaxo Wellcome/SmithKline Beecham* (2000), §174.

10 Case No IV/M.631 – *Upjohn/Pharmacia*, OJ C 294/9 (1995).

11 Guidelines on the applicability of Article 81 of the EC Treaty to horizontal cooperation agreements, OJ C 3/2 (2001).

12 Guidelines on the application of Article 81 of the EC Treaty to technology transfer agreements, §25, OJ C 101/2 (2004).

Outside the US and EU guidelines' definitions of innovation markets, innovation issues can still be central. Notably, diminished competition in innovation can be suspected even though the relevant market may be better defined by the characteristics of existing products (rather than by R&D projects directed toward future products). There is thus a large overlap between a doctrine for analysing potential competition in relation to existing markets, and what would be expressed as innovation market competition. As will be seen, doctrinal labelling does not necessarily change the underlying analysis. In order to find an appreciable reduction in potential competition, the analysis would often have to include the same parameters as an innovation market analysis – and thus share many of the same difficulties.

Moreover, innovation-related cases frequently turn on conduct involving intellectual property rights. Various IPR practices, such as creation of patent pools or amalgamation of important patent portfolios, are particularly likely to affect innovation and markets in a context that is larger than a particular future product by influencing a number of future product developments and markets.

Since in all these cases some analysis must be conducted regarding the terms and conditions for innovation, their inclusion in the analysis allows for a general grasp of antitrust policy in this field, with a view to providing an adequate systemization and evaluation of the subject area.

1.3 BACKGROUND

In order to put the legal standards and developments in this field in a broader context, it is appropriate to consider first why competition policy might be concerned with innovation at all and should even think of acting to protect competition in the innovation process.

The central position of innovation and dynamic efficiency in achieving continuous economic growth and welfare in society has been acknowledged, not only by economists, but also, to an increasing extent, by public policy makers. A desire to foster competition and support a market environment that spurs entrepreneurial and innovative activities naturally has implications for antitrust enforcement. By recognizing the dynamics of technological development as both a source of competition and as a means to compete and by assessing market transactions with a view to the dynamics of market processes, antitrust authorities can affect competition and consumer welfare in the long run. Apart from other dynamic aspects of technological development, in many modern markets today's conditions for R&D and innovation will be a determinant for tomorrow's product market competition. This relationship must thus also be addressed when assessing the competitive nature and effects of market transactions and corporate behaviour.

Usually, competition fosters efficiency at all levels: product development, production and distribution. There may be no real way of distinguishing between competition in innovation and competition in resale. Nevertheless, the primary means for a market actor to attract business – to compete – may differ from case to case, the obstacles to competition may be of various origins, and the primary effect of lessened competition may vary. In order to analyse the effects of a transaction or business behaviour in a way which correctly reflects the consumer welfare aspects at stake, account must be taken of the underlying conditions for competition and the possible consequences of the market practice in question.

When the ability to compete rests largely on the ability to bring attractive products and services to the market, itself dependent on successful product development, there may be little to stop market entry. With a high pace of technological development and current technologies soon becoming obsolete, innovation generally opens up opportunities for new competitors and products. It thus constitutes a primary means of both competition between current market participants and entry, imposing a serious threat on incumbent firms. Where technological development is difficult to control, there is little possibility for actors to maintain current market positions with less than efficient performance. If a particular firm is dominant at any time, this is presumably the product of superior efficiency and it will be continuously contested by others who strive to become the market leader through successful innovation. In such a case, the role of competition law is diminished as the market forces single out inefficient actors and strategies.

However, high-tech markets, although R&D intense, frequently display substantial barriers to entry, as a consequence of which incumbent firms may have considerable advantages. These barriers to entry, relating to R&D or to access to markets for the resulting products, often have some relationship to intellectual property rights, yet the mechanisms by which entry is impeded vary considerably between industries.

In some markets, patents effectively foreclose competition even in the medium or long term. The availability of technological alternatives in a specific market may be limited and a patent or a patent portfolio, for example, covering a chemical compound or a gene sequence, may confer substantial market power on the owner of this key asset.

Other barriers such as very high fixed costs and large commercial risks serve to make entry less attractive. This is even more apparent in industries like the pharmaceutical industry with long R&D cycles where product development is contingent on authority approval. Although heavily R&D intense and equipped with sophisticated underlying technologies, new actors and products emerge rather slowly.

In some industries innovation is closely connected to production and marketing, with tight feedback mechanisms and information flow going between the level of R&D, the actual manufacturing of products and interaction with the customers. Combined with large economies of scale in production and other entry barriers at the level of the finished products, innovation is restricted to a small number of actors.

In other industries, technology is more heterogeneous and the capabilities for technological development are more readily available. But, even here, dominance in one product generation may nevertheless give exclusive access and control over crucial inputs to the next generation, allowing dominance and market power to be maintained. For example, market power due to control of a technology that has become a standard may be very hard to dislodge. Customers may have invested heavily in current technology standards and would face considerable switching costs, creating lock-in effects. Moreover, network effects are a common phenomenon in many high-tech markets; here a particular customer cannot readily switch to an alternative product if this is not compatible with the current standard. Innovation aspects arise at both the 'architectural' (standard) level and the 'modular' level (the various parts or sub-systems which a standard comprises), and raises questions, *inter alia,* about standard setting and access to set standards.

These diverse entry barriers may enable market participants successfully to affect their competitive environment through strategic action and to exercise market power to the detriment of consumer welfare. A currently dominant market actor may have incentives to reduce the output of the R&D process, in terms of new or improved products, in order to extract more profits from the current product generation. This could, for example, be achieved by acquiring competing products under development, artificially reducing consumer choice. Another example would be the creation of bottlenecks operated to create or perpetuate dominance. Such a bottleneck could be created through the joint formation of a patent portfolio as a result of which potential actors in a market would be dependent on a licence in order to pursue R&D effectively, in the end resulting in restricted choice and more expensive products. Similarly, an established standard to which an entrant would need access could effectively foreclose more efficient competitors.

Some of these actions, such as horizontal mergers on a concentrated market, will be of a kind familiar to antitrust analysis. Others may be more novel, for example certain exclusionary practices in relation to intellectual property rights or standards, with the potential of driving more efficient firms out of the market. In any event, since innovation remains a primary means and force of competition, key issues in competition analysis, not least the analysis of entry conditions, clearly relate to the innovation process. Although the legal framework is flexible and its commitment to economic rationality probably makes the law in principle able to cope with new issues in new settings, it is crucial for courts and antitrust authorities to frame the analyses in a way that reflects the competitive nature of the market and correctly identifies and then remedies unjustifiable practices and consequences.

This is all the more important bearing in mind the fact that mergers and joint ventures often generate substantial efficiencies. Likewise, the creation of an intellectual property right ('IPR') portfolio or the acquisition of a potential entrant may be beneficial to society. The coordination of complementary resources and know-how, sharing of risks, minimization of spending, reduction of transaction costs and so on typically enhance the chances of efficient technological progress, to the benefit of consumers. By the same token, standards usually confer considerable benefits on consumers, achieving compatibility between a great variety of components and systems.

Traditionally, however, antitrust policy has been concerned with competition in markets for existing products and services. Admittedly, antitrust analysis often incorporates the conditions for entry onto the market of new products and actors, but the economic foundations for antitrust law can be traced to microeconomic perceptions where price is the main variable of competition and where the ideal market presumes homogeneous products and commonly known and available technology. The incumbent market actors' relative shares of the production and distribution of goods are still the general basis for deciding whether a market practice will lead to a restriction of competition. Moreover, anti-competitive effects are typically expressed as the ability to exercise market power by charging prices that exceed those a competitive market would support.

A competition policy focusing too narrowly on market shares and pricing strategies may protect consumer welfare less effectively, getting the trade-off skewed between short- and long-run benefits. The incentives for investment and risk, not least in the development of new and improved products and services, as well as the strategies for lowering risks and making R&D efforts more efficient, must be acknowledged if markets and competition are to evolve dynamically. This is especially the case for areas where antitrust enforcement interacts with the realm of intellectual property rights, what may seem intuitively attractive in the short run may in reality not further consumer welfare in the long run. Moreover, current market shares, prices and profit levels may say little about the true level of competition. Particularly in high-tech markets, dominance and high profits are not necessarily signs of ineffective competition. Rather, such conditions are generally the result of an efficiently and successfully conducted enterprise.

Even if a dynamic perspective is taken and competition policy intends to assess and protect competition in the innovation process, it may still have a variety of objectives. Since future product market conditions are frequently determined by the current conditions for R&D, the objective of maintaining alternative R&D sources could merely be the protection of competition for (the resulting) future products. However, competition policy could also take an independent interest in competition in R&D, if this is considered necessary in order for participants to have incentives to invest in and, as energetically as possible, pursue R&D, thereby enhancing the potential for fast and innovative product and technology introductions. At the same time, an objective could be to allow integration or cooperation that increase efficiency in the innovation process. By the achieving of scale efficiencies, synergetic effects, avoiding wasteful duplication and so on, consumers would then benefit through an increased pace of innovation and low R&D expenditure.

These aims are not necessarily in conflict – at least to some extent, they are likely to be achieved simultaneously. But, depending on the closer objectives, the demands on policy makers, competition authorities and courts will be changed, in terms of the required level of information, their analytical skills and their forecasting abilities. Questions thus arise regarding the manner in which antitrust law can incorporate dynamic considerations in its analyses. Particularly when one considers the murky theoretical and empirical evidence regarding the links between market structures, R&D competition and innovation efficiencies, the boundaries of public intervention may therefore deserve scrutiny.

1.4 ECONOMICS AND LAW

Since this is a book on competition law, the extensive use of economic sources and reasoning may deserve some further comment. Economic analysis of law is a discipline that has been growing during the last decades and which today includes studies of many aspects of law. Economics may, among other things, help to structure and explain the underlying problems that regulatory frameworks aim to manage. A better understanding of the stakes involved, such as conflicting interests, incentive structures and information asymmetries, is essential for comprehending legal structure and function. Moreover, legal rules typically provide incentives or disincentives for the subjects to act in different ways. Since microeconomics is about choices, and these choices are affected by changes in the relative attractiveness of the available options, economic analysis may predict the response of actors. The consequences of different rules or policies can thereby be assessed, in terms both of effectiveness in fulfilling its purposes and of the risk and magnitude of unintended effects. Account may also be taken of the costs sustained in connection with the enforcement of, and compliance with, the policy in question.

In few other areas of law are economic considerations so central to legal analysis as in antitrust law. Not only can economics provide insights regarding the various problems in the functioning of markets which give rise to antitrust law, but enforcement of the legal provisions also necessitates economic analysis at some level.

The basic legal provisions in this field are typically short, but far-reaching, leaving a large margin for interpretation. From a quick glance it is clear that economic analysis is necessary in order to determine their scope. Legal prerequisites such as 'distortion of competition', 'restraint of trade', 'limit or control markets' or 'substantially lessen competition' indicate that economic considerations are part of the legal framework. While such considerations are considered in court precedents, competition authorities' implementing guidelines and so on, economic analysis is also mandated in assessing the legality of specific transactions or business practices. Taken together, this is why former Commissioner Mario Monti can explain the convergence in the authorities' legal analysis of cases, by the use of the same microeconomic analytical tools.[13]

Considering the purpose of the law, it is clear that in both the EU and the US the underlying aim is to protect consumer welfare. Although the scope and exclusivity of the welfare goal is the object of some discussion, it is a well-recognized fact that American antitrust enforcement, especially after the 'Chicago revolution', has narrowed and tightened its objectives to become more efficiency-oriented. The former Assistant Attorney General for the Antitrust Division, Joel I. Klein, asserts that the Chicago School's basic focus on consumer welfare is the key to sound antitrust analysis.[14] It is further stated that, '[e]ssentially, these laws prohibit business practices that unreasonably deprive consumers of the benefits of competition, resulting in higher prices for inferior products and services'.[15] Klein's successor in that position, R. Hewitt Pate, explained certain developments in antitrust case law by referring to the

---

[13] Monti claims that, despite differences in both the language and the practical enforcement of the laws, the European and US standards are nowadays largely consistent. It is moreover emphasized that the key reasons for overcoming formal and practical differences is agreement on the ultimate purpose of competition policy – ensuring consumer welfare – and the fact that the agencies have 'in spite of the different legal instruments at our disposal, been using the same micro-economic analytical tools'. *Convergence in EU–US Antitrust Policy Regarding Mergers and Acquisitions: An EU Perspective,* speech at UCLA Law First Annual Institute on US and EU Antitrust Aspects of Mergers and Acquisitions, Los Angeles, 28 February 2004, available at http://www.europa.eu.int/comm/competition/speeches/ (last visited 3 March 2005).

[14] Klein, Joel I., *A Stepwise Approach to Antitrust Review of Horizontal Agreements*, address before the American Bar Association, Washington, DC, 7 November 1996, available at http://www.usdoj.gov/atr/public/speeches/0979.htm (last visited 3 March 2005).

[15] U.S. Department of Justice, *Antitrust Enforcement and the Consumer*, available at www.usdoj.gov/atr/public/div_stats/1638.htm (last visited 3 March 2005).

US Supreme Court as being '[d]isciplined by a concern for economic efficiency'. He noted that '[t]he lesson is that legal systems that permit evolution through the development of precedent in case law, as both the US and EU systems do, can transform their competition policy to reflect sound economic understanding as such understanding develops'.[16]

In the European context, the Community is founded on objectives declared in the EC Treaty. These objectives include 'sustainable and non-inflationary growth, a high degree of competitiveness' and 'the raising of the standard of living and quality of life' to be achieved through 'an open market economy with free competition, favouring an efficient allocation of resources'.[17] Commissioner Monti summarized the Treaty as acknowledging 'the fundamental role of the market and of competition in guaranteeing consumer welfare, in encouraging the optimal allocation of resources, and in granting to economic agents the appropriate incentives to pursue productive efficiency, quality, and innovation'.[18] The European Commission and the US agencies 'share a common fundamental vision of the role and limitations of public intervention. We both agree that the ultimate purpose of our respective intervention in the marketplace should be to ensure that consumer welfare is not harmed'.[19] According to recently issued Commission guidelines, '[t]he objective of Article 81 is to protect competition on the market as a means of enhancing consumer welfare and of ensuring an efficient allocation of resources'.[20]

Now, another overriding aim of the EC Treaty is the integration of the European common market. Although tensions may arise, especially in the short term, between a welfare-oriented application of Articles 81 and 82 and the aim of integrating European markets, this conflict should not be over-

---

16 Pate, R. Hewitt, *The Common Law Approach and Improving Standards for Analyzing Single Firm Conduct,* address before the Thirtieth Annual Conference on International Antitrust Law and Policy Fordham Corporate Law Institute, New York, 23 October 2003, available at www.usdoj.gov/atr/public/speeches/202724.htm (last visited 3 March 2005).

17 Articles 2, 4 and 98 of the EC Treaty.

18 Monti, Mario, *European Competition Policy for the 21st Century,* speech at The Fordham Corporate Law Institute, 28 Annual Conference on International Antitrust Law and Policy, 20 October 2000, available at http://www.europa.eu.int/comm/competition/speeches/ (last visited 3 March 2005).

19 Monti, Mario, *Convergence in EU–US Antitrust Policy Regarding Mergers and Acquisitions: An EU Perspective,* speech at UCLA Law First Annual Institute on US and EU Antitrust Aspects of Mergers and Acquisitions Los Angeles, 28 February 2004, available at http://www.europa.eu.int/comm/competition/speeches/ (last visited 3 March 2005).

20 Guidelines on the application of Article 81(3) of the Treaty, §13, OJ C 101/97 (2004).

estimated.[21] And there is much evidence to suggest that market integration nowadays is underplayed in comparison to efficiency considerations.[22] Moreover, since the core of this book does not concern market allocation issues, any such friction will not be of significance to the discussion.

Also at the international level, within the framework of the OECD, it is maintained that '[t]he promotion of efficiency is generally regarded as the most fundamental goal of competition law and policy. . . . [C]ompetition law and policy is generally used to promote the overall economic welfare of society by preventing harmful distortions of the process by which consumer demand is expressed and satisfied'.[23]

The important role of economics in antitrust law does not, however, mean that the legal framework, or the outcome of the specific cases, should always correspond to the solutions preferred by a unanimous body of economists. First of all, competition law is more than a practical incarnation of economic theory. For example, complex principles relating to the rule of law in general apply to competition law like any other field of law. The legal framework must be predictable and just (regardless of the fact that predictability can easily be analysed in economic terms). Moreover, economic theory and subsequent

---

21 Successful and sustainable market integration must generally allow efficient business conduct. Efficient management is in turn spurred by international competition and opportunities to expand beyond national borders. Possible tensions may arise, particularly in the short run, for example in contractual restraints regarding product market sales (for example, territorial exclusivity, customer allocation, parallel trade and so on).

22 Potential tensions between efficiency and market integration could arise in the field of vertical restrictions, which typically are analysed with a view to potential market foreclosure, yet the European Commission's Guidelines on Vertical Restraints, *OJ C 291/1* (2000), include the following passage (§7): 'The protection of competition is the primary objective of EC competition policy, as this enhances consumer welfare and creates an efficient allocation of resources. In applying the EC competition rules, the Commission will adopt an economic approach which is based on the effects on the market; vertical agreements have to be analysed in their legal and economic context. . . . Market integration is an additional goal of EC competition policy. Market integration enhances competition in the Community. Companies should not be allowed to recreate private barriers between Member States where State barriers have been successfully abolished.'

Moreover, in the words of the Guidelines on the application of Article 81(3) of the Treaty, *supra*, note 20, §13: 'Competition and market integration serve these ends [consumer welfare and efficient allocation of resources] since the creation and preservation of an open single market promotes an efficient allocation of resources throughout the Community for the benefit of consumers.'

23 OECD, *OECD Global Forum on Competition – Preventing Market Abuses and Promoting Economic Efficiency, Growth and Opportunity*, 2004, p. 41. Available at www.oecd.org/dataoecd/13/42/27892500.pdf (last visited 11 October 2004).

analyses are heterogeneous. Different theories and models focus on different problems, are built on diverging assumptions, emphasize different economic consequences and reach a variety of conclusions. Finally, for the effectiveness of the legal system, not all kinds of questions are open to case-by-case analysis of economic consequences at the margin. For example, authorities and courts can adopt standards for analysis (such as methods to define a relevant market), formulate presumption rules (such as high market shares being an indicator of market power) and even condemn certain practises as per se prohibited (normally if they would very seldom be justifiable on closer analysis). Even if the development of legal standards is largely influenced by experience and economic thinking, '[w]here economics leaves off, law and policy must take over, to craft *workable* rules or presumptions', based on likely consequences.[24]

Court precedents, agency decisions, policy statements, doctrine and so on are thus important instruments for providing guidance as to the interpretation of the legal prerequisites: the analyses that have been performed and the arguments that have been recognized. A strong argument in antitrust cases will find support in various sources, including widely accepted economic theory, and needs a properly executed analysis, combining law and economics.

In the area of antitrust law, the interpretation of the US Sherman Act and Clayton Act and the EC Treaty has changed and developed significantly over the decades. Such changes can be the result of different influences, but three factors stand out when explaining historical policy changes.[25] First, industries and markets continuously change, not least owing to technological development, changing the underlying structures and problems facing antitrust law. Second, a political system that is receptive to a new approach may arise, which will therefore be in line with overall social thought and values. Third, developments in economic thinking have improved the understanding of the economic consequences of different business practices and the flaws and merits of public intervention.

Taken together, this has all had an impact on the method used for the research behind this book. In order to comprehend and describe the development and state of relevant legal frameworks it has been helpful to consider both theoretical and empirical findings concerning innovation as a force in the economic system and as a determinant for success in the market, and hence as a determinant for competition (and dominance) on various levels. This contemporary economic discussion is summarized in Chapter 2, which also

---

24 Pate, *supra*, note 16.

25 Baker, Jonathan B., 'A preface to Post-Chicago antitrust', in Cucinotta, Antonio, Pardolesi, Roberto & Van den Bergh, Roger (eds), *Post-Chicago Developments in Antitrust Law*, Edward Elgar, Cheltenham, 2002, pp. 68f.

includes economic growth issues and different efficiency concepts in order to understand what is decisive for consumer welfare. Moreover, various sources of technological development are depicted and individual actors' incentives and abilities discussed to provide more relevant background. The characteristics of the market and competition processes represent the context in which the legal frameworks operate and must be understood. On this basis different analytical approaches are presented and relevant implications for the execution of antitrust policy are highlighted.

The economic background discussion is necessary for the subsequent analysis of the legal standards, which incorporates considerations of economic origin. The analysis of statutes, policy documents and case law is joined by economic insights and the results are evaluated with regard to the economic rationale of the law. The inclusion of economic considerations is useful for structuring the analysis and for evaluating the legal material, possibly providing arguments for or against certain policy options.

1.5 PREVIOUS WORKS

At a general level there is a whole range of research and literature relevant to this area of study, such as the importance of innovation to economic growth, theory and empirical findings regarding the innovation process, public policy and innovation, competition law objectives and developments, case law commentaries and so on. A wide range of books and articles in the fields of law and economics has therefore been reviewed. Since innovation-related issues, not least the intersection between intellectual property rights and antitrust law, are an area of research that occupies an impressive group of authors (mostly of articles), a major problem has been one of selection and digestion.

Although the intersection between intellectual property and antitrust law, and the plentiful issues that arise in this field, have been widely analysed from many different angles, the innovation market approach is seldom commented on more than briefly. However, the development of the concept in the US, and its application in early practice, was followed by a rather short but intense discussion in the mid-1990s which has been helpful in framing important questions. This debate will be summarized in Chapter 3, together with some more recent commentaries.

Apart from the above-mentioned early policy discussion, the innovation market concept is often commented upon from similar economic standpoints, often without much analysis of actual legal implementation. As for case law commentaries, on the other hand, these seldom analyse the legal practices with a view to locating the underlying doctrinal issues. One exception is Lawrence

B. Landman, who made valuable contributions in analysing legal practices in Europe and the US in the 1990s.[26] John Temple Lang, in a comprehensive article, has also combined case law analysis with broader policy discussions in this field.[27] Other works of particular importance are Alan S. Gutterman's comparative study of US and EU policy for licensing and R&D collaboration and two articles by former FTC officials concerning innovation issues and American antitrust law.[28]

Taking advantage of the existing doctrinal discussions, the contribution of this book is to update the field of research in light of new developments and to broaden and deepen the categorization and analysis of the innovation market area. A better understanding and increased coherency should thereby be achieved with regard to recent legal developments, economic insights and to antitrust policy at large. The analysis presented will thus both provide systematization of the subject area and make suggestions for limiting principles to make the legal implementation more predictable and transparent.

1.6 OUTLINE

In Chapter 2, current economic thinking is examined. The overriding purpose is to learn more about efficiency concepts and consumer welfare, to explore factual characteristics of market and competition processes and contrast different analytical approaches, and, finally, to present some policy implications regarding competition in the innovation process.

In Chapter 3, the policy development in the EU and the US regarding innovation-related competition concerns is examined, primarily through early case law and more recent policy statements. Through legislative acts and other

---

26 Landman, Lawrence B., 'Innovation and the Structure of Competition', 81 *Journal of the Patent and Trademark Office Society* 728 (1999); 'The Economics of Future Goods Markets', 21 *World Competition – Law and Economics Review* 63 (1998); 'Innovation Markets in Europe', 19 *European Competition Law Review* 21 (1998); 'Competing in the Global Pharmaceutical Industry: Innovation and Future Potential Competition', 2 *The Journal of Biolaw & Business* 29 (1998).

27 Temple Lang, *supra*, note 2.

28 Gutterman, Alan S., *Innovation and Competition Policy: A Comparative Study of the Regulation of Patent Licensing and Collaborative Research & Development in the United States and the European Community,* Kluwer Law International, London, 1997; Tom, Willard K. & Newberg, Joshua A., 'Antitrust and Intellectual Property: From Separate Spheres to Unified Field', 66 *Antitrust Law Journal* 167 (1997); Gilbert, Richard J. & Tom, Willard K., 'Is Innovation King at the Antitrust Agencies? The Intellectual Property Guidelines Five Years Later', 69 *Antitrust Law Journal* 43 (2001).

policy documents, analytical frameworks have evolved in which innovation is a central element for the antitrust analysis. The chapter also summarizes important commentaries on central issues in these frameworks.

This leads up to Chapter 4, which is an examination of case law, an extensive study which puts into practice the methodological frameworks previously elaborated. The purpose of the case law investigation is to structure and present cases where EU and US competition authorities have addressed and assessed potential negative effects from lessened competition in the innovation process. The relevant case law largely covers mergers, but it also considers some joint ventures, agreements relating to intellectual property (such as acquisition and pooling of patents) and cases concerning abuse of dominance. With the current practices categorized on the basis of factual background, relevant questions regarding market definitions, subsequent competition analysis, remedy choices and so on are handled.

The analysis of the previous chapters is brought together into a synthesis in Chapters 5 and 6. These chapters aim both at a critical analysis of what the law is and to say something about the consequences of this. Suggestions for modifications of and clarifications in legal policy are presented. Based on this analysis, Chapter 7 presents central elements of a policy for innovation competition, which should be coherent but also nuanced and properly limited in its scope. Finally, the presentation is completed by some concluding remarks in Chapter 8.

2. Economics, innovation and competition

2.1 BACKGROUND

Innovation is a major factor behind economic growth and is increasingly shaping market conditions and affecting market participants' behaviour. Competition policy continues to play an important role in regulating markets and promoting welfare, but changing market characteristics increasingly affect the correct assessment of various practices.

Recent antitrust cases have provoked diverse opinions regarding the scope of antitrust law and its execution by the antitrust authorities. When decision making is based on analysis of both current structures and future developments in dynamic environments, there is concern about the limits of authorities' ability correctly to apprehend, assess and regulate market behaviour. On the other hand, when decision making refrains from such an analysis, or makes too limited an analysis, the policy may be seriously criticized for not factoring in important aspects of the market process.

Whether an antitrust authority will allow a certain transaction or behaviour could depend on whether economic welfare, on balance, is likely to be enhanced or diminished. In both US and EU competition policy, this goal is not indifferent as to whose welfare is enhanced. In both jurisdictions, consumers are favoured. This means that a fair share of the resulting benefits from a scrutinized operation must end up with consumers. In most cases, this consumer criterion will not differ from a pure efficiency criterion. A passing on of resulting benefits to consumers is generally accomplished as long as effective competition remains on the market.

More importantly, economic welfare cannot be restricted to pure price concerns. In the words of Robert H. Lande, consumers want many things from the economy, including optimal levels of quality, variety, and safety.[1] But economic efficiency is a heterogeneous concept, which can be divided into

---

1 Lande, Robert H., 'Proving the Obvious: The Antitrust Laws Were Passed to Protect Consumers (Not Just to Increase Efficiency)', 50 *Hastings Law Journal* 959, 962f. (1999).

allocative efficiency, production efficiency, innovation (or, dynamic) efficiency, and transactional efficiency.[2] The most important type of economic efficiency, in terms of significance for societal wealth in the long run – innovation efficiency – is however also the least measurable, even ex post. It requires comparison and evaluation, in the particular case, of actual and hypothetical situations with regard to uncertain innovation.

Although many studies have been conducted, evidence is largely inconclusive regarding what market structures and concentration levels best encourage R&D and innovation, what a socially optimal rate of technological progress would be and, generally, what is the precise correlation between R&D and innovation.[3] It is probably fair to say that innovation is generally best promoted neither by unthreatened monopolistic enterprises nor by a totally atomistic market structure. Nevertheless, the conclusion must be that more precise generalizations are very difficult to make.[4]

An unthreatened current monopolist may thus have less incentive to develop new technology than an actor facing competition, since the monopolist at best will replace his monopoly with another. On the other hand, the notion of a perfectly competitive market does not consider the introduction of new products and technologies, and is dependent on conditions that cancel out the incentives for incurring sunk costs of innovation investment.

In an antitrust analysis, dynamic and static efficiencies can be at odds with each other, representing a trade-off between short-term and long-term consumer interests. This highlights the difference between an ex ante and an

---

2 Allocative and production efficiencies can be denoted static efficiency whereas innovation efficiency is dynamic. Allocative efficiency is realized when resources in society are allocated to those who value them most in terms of willingness to pay. Production efficiency relates to the most cost-effective use of means of production available under existing technology. Innovation efficiency relates to production, development and diffusion of desirable new products and processes. Transactional efficiencies relate to least expensive means of carrying out transactions. See Brodley, Joseph F., 'The Economic Goals of Antitrust: Efficiency, Consumer Welfare, and Technological Progress', 62 *New York University Law Review* 1020, 1025f. (1987); Kolasky, William J. and Dick, Andrew R., *The Merger Guidelines and the Integration of Efficiencies into Antitrust Review of Horizontal Mergers*, 2002, available at http://www.usdoj.gov/atr/hmerger/11254.pdf (last visited 3 March 2005).

3 Bork, Robert H., *The Antitrust Paradox – A Policy at War With Itself*, The Free Press, New York, 1978/1993, p. 132. Bork argues that, since technological progress requires the use of resources and we do not know the willingness to pay for progress (the price), we do not know the 'proper' rate of progress and we should consequently not give the matter any weight in antitrust analysis. See also Landman, Lawrence B., 'The Economics of Future Goods Markets', 21 *World Competition – Law and Economics Review* 63 (1998).

4 Scherer, Frederic M., 'Antitrust, Efficiency, and Progress', 62 *New York University Law Review* 998, 1010f., 1019 (1987).

ex post analysis. Although fierce price competition (static efficiency), after the innovative activity has been undertaken, would benefit consumers, ex post profitability is necessary for the ex ante investment to take place at all. Typically, innovative activity is undertaken with a view to obtaining the future power to charge prices that reward the risks and investments incurred – thus in pursuit of some market power and allegedly monopolistic profits. However, without more, these profits are monopolistic only if compared to the hypothetical equilibrium achieved under perfect competition. Such a standard cannot serve as a regulatory goal, particularly considering industries where large sunk costs are inherent and pricing at marginal cost would be a short way to bankruptcy. Moreover, entry onto the market may occur if entrants believe sunk costs may be covered in the future. If so, there may be little to stop entry, and excessive prices will be eliminated by competition, although prices will still remain at a level where costs are covered. Under these conditions, sunk costs and pricing over marginal cost do not imply monopoly or market power for the incumbents. Incumbent firms and potential entrants counterbalance such power, while considering the cost structure and the prospects of pricing at a level to allow recouping.

In many markets, profits levels are increasingly determined by the ability to compete in innovation and performance. To offer entirely new products or improved versions has become vital. This means that price is no longer the primary means of competition. Still, innovation affects not only product quality, but also efficiency in production processes, implying reduced production costs. Moreover, the dynamics of innovation may still lead to competition at the product market level. Although high prices may be charged for new and improved products, slightly inferior or older products often compete vigorously in price. Hence, if the market is truly dynamic and a continuous line of new products is to be expected, competition in the future product market is maintained or even improved. Even if a technological leader becomes a dominant actor on the market, a dynamic environment nevertheless implies that others who strive to attain this position through successful innovation will continuously contest the market leader. This all benefits society at large and, in the end, consumers.

In reality however, entry onto many of the innovative markets is not so swift and easy that incumbent successful firms will lack possibilities for exercising market power. Market structures where the R&D process is very lengthy, risky and expensive, where technological opportunities are relatively limited,[5] where highly specialized competence is needed, intellectual property

[5] Sometimes owing to narrow product segments with little opportunity for demand substitution, for example in pharmaceutical markets the number of competing technologies available for each specific medical diagnosis may be limited, even though the industry at large is displaying seemingly infinite technological opportunities.

rights are important, or other important entry barriers exist,[6] are particularly sensitive from an antitrust perspective. Despite the fact that success may be determined by successful innovation in these markets, the number of potential actors may be limited at the same time as mergers and collaborations may enhance efficiency in reducing expenditure and joining together complementary assets and skills.

Particularly in industries dominated by a number of large corporations, innovation tends to become routine, subject to the same corporate structures for analysis, decision making and control as any other part of the corporation.[7] It should not come as a surprise if R&D decisions are part of the overall strategic action plan prevalent in oligopolistic, yet possibly competitive, industries.

Competition policy may have different interrelated objectives and ambitions when it comes to competition in innovation. It could focus primarily on product markets, but still be interested in currently undertaken R&D. Through investigation of proposed mergers and the like, it could act to maintain some competing lines of R&D in order to maintain competition in the exploitation of the R&D results (competing future products or technologies). Intervention would then only occur where the future product market situation is established with some required level of certainty. A reasonably competitive product market could also increase the likelihood of continued future pressure to compete through innovation.

However, competition policy could also see an independent value in innovation competition, if such competition is deemed likely to enhance market actors' incentives and abilities to engage in efficient innovation. This could also allow for something of a portfolio theory in R&D, particularly since some R&D programmes will fail. The more paths, the greater the likelihood of some competing successes. Also, if an evolutionary perspective is taken on technological change, variety in R&D will increase the likelihood of a variety of R&D results, and thereby an open-ended range of possible future technological advances in various fields. At the same time, since innovation does consume resources, it cannot be maximized: investment decisions must be derived from some market demand. Also, the output from innovation in an area cannot simply be imputed to the level of R&D invested. There is a decreasing margin to R&D investment, particularly since competing R&D projects typically involve some duplication. Moreover, the unification of assets and competencies may be necessary to increase efficiency in R&D.

---

6 For example regulatory approval processes and asymmetrical capital costs from imperfect capital markets.

7 See, for example, Baumol, William J., *The Free-Market Innovation Machine: Analyzing the Growth Miracle of Capitalism*, Princeton University Press, Princeton, 2002.

Such transactions may create investment incentives and increase the success rate and quality of innovation through scale economies, synergy effects, reductions of costs and risks, and so on.

All this is of course important when considering the appropriate level of governmental interference. Should antitrust policy act aggressively to maintain certain market structures and forbid certain behaviour, in the belief that, thereby, market performance is likely to be most favourable to society? Or are markets generally best left to themselves, largely limiting the monitoring to cartel behaviour and competition-eradicating mergers where instant price increases and output restrictions are certain? Alternatively, is it possible to carve out some middle ground but still maintain transparency and predictability?

In order to put some flesh on the bones for the coming analysis, an overview of current theoretical and empirical findings will be provided. More particularly this chapter will (a) present the possible heterogeneity of 'consumer welfare' as a criterion for analysis, rather than a narrowly construed efficiency criterion; (b) appraise the value of a dynamic view of competition which puts technological development at the centre; (c) highlight differences between a static, but very sophisticated, microeconomic model of a market and more dynamic economic market models taking factual market circumstances into account; (d) display difficulties and limitations in a more dynamically oriented market analysis; (e) present rudimentary, but central, indications for antitrust policy, and (f) provide the foundation for a critical analysis of current legal standards and tendencies as well as a *de lege ferenda* discussion.[8]

2.2 INNOVATION AND ECONOMIC WELFARE

The predominant role of innovation and technological change in the achievement of economic wealth is both hard to estimate precisely and to overrate. Empirical research early indicated the important role of 'technical improvement' in achieving increased outputs.[9] By the mid-50s, Nobel Laureate Robert Solow formalized the empirical findings and concluded that technological change is the major factor behind the majority of economic growth (in one

---

[8] This chapter partly builds on a previous article, Glader, Marcus, 'Innovation Economics and the Antitrust Guidelines on Horizontal Co-operation', 24 *World Competition – Law and Economics Review* 513 (2001).

[9] See Nelson, Richard R., 'The Agenda for Growth Theory: A Different Point of View', 22 *Cambridge Journal of Economics* 497, 501f. (1998), referring to Abramovitz, Moses, 'Economics of Growth', in Haley, Bernard F. (ed.), *A Survey of Contemporary Economics,* Vol. II, Richard D. Irwin Inc., Homewood, 1952.

study by Solow estimated at 87.5 per cent).[10] The very high share of growth attributed to innovation in the early estimations has been reduced in more recent studies.[11] Many empirical studies have been conducted, but these are associated with various imperfections, which make an exact assessment of the contribution to society from innovation difficult.

The following example, regarding productivity in the US, gives an idea of the impact of technological progress on society. Between 1955 and 1970, the output (productivity) per labour hour in the US increased at an average rate of 2.54 per cent per year. Between 1970 and 1985 the rate dropped to 1.17 per cent per year. Had the former rate of increased productivity continued, and assuming the same number of labour hours to be employed, the GNP in the business sector would have been 22.7 per cent higher in 1985 than it actually was. In money, that would have corresponded to $771 billion.[12]

2.2.1 Traditional Growth Theory

The traditional neoclassical models that Solow and others use do not consider the causes of technological changes, they merely deal with the rate of change and estimate its value to society.[13] In this growth theory, built on decreasing returns on capital, perfect competition, perfect knowledge and exogenous technology, the emphasis is put on the accumulation of capital.

If an economy has a low capital–labour ratio (little capital compared to labour) the marginal product of capital (the return of an invested € compared to a labour hour) will be high. If part of the income generated by investments is saved, the bulk of capital will rise. Over time the capital–labour ratio will rise and the marginal product of capital will decrease. Eventually, the savings generated by capital accruing will equal the amount necessary to replace worn-out machines and equip new workers. At this point the economy cannot grow any more simply by accumulating capital. Technological change, however, increases the marginal productivity of capital (and labour), spurring savings and investments, which raise the volume of capital. A larger volume

---

10 Solow, Robert, 'Technical Change and the Aggregate Production Function' 39 *Review of Economics and Statistics* 312, 316f. (1957), see also 'A Contribution to the Theory of Economic Growth', 70 *Quarterly Journal of Economics* 65 (1956).

11 Mainly because quality estimations of factor inputs have been incorporated into the analysis: Grossman, Gene M. & Helpman, Elhanan, *Innovation and Growth in the Global Economy*, MIT Press, Cambridge, Mass., 1991, p. 6.

12 Scherer, *supra*, note 4, p. 1001.

13 Cameron, Gavin, *Innovation and Growth: A Survey of the Empirical Evidence*, Nuffield College, Oxford, 1998, p. 4, available at http://hicks.nuff.ox.ac.uk/users/cameron/papers/empiric.pdf (last visited 3 March 2005).

of capital reduces the marginal productivity of capital, and investments fall. The rate of growth decreases until a new technological change occurs.

Decreasing returns implies that more than capital accumulation is needed for continuous growth. That can only be the creation of technological change (and to some extent growth in population). According to the model, such technological progress is, like population growth, assumed to be exogenous to the growth process, which is why only capital accumulation is determined endogenously.[14] The method used to account for growth is thus to measure factor accumulation (capital and labour) and then impute the expansion of output to the accumulated inputs. The part of output growth that cannot be attributed to input accumulation, the 'Solow residual', is ascribed to technological progress.[15]

2.2.2 Endogenous Growth Theory

This traditional approach, highlighting issues of private and public spending and saving (capital accumulation), had something of a comeback during the 1980s, but has since then gradually been replaced or supplemented by another theory, denoted 'endogenous growth theory' or sometimes 'new growth theory'. The new theory suggests that the traditional macroeconomic policy prescriptions miss the central question, since '[n]either adjustments to monetary and fiscal policy, nor increases in the rate of savings and capital accumulation can by themselves generate persistent increases in standards of living'.[16] Instead, the crucial task is to create an institutional environment that supports technological change.[17] Paul Romer exemplifies this by supposing that there had been no innovation and no technological change during the 19th century: if we continued to accumulate human capital in the form of high school and college education and physical capital in the form of sailing ships, water wheels and ox carts, in the end we had to admit that we have little use of one more college graduate who is employed in driving one more ox cart.[18]

---

[14] Ahn, Sanghoon & Hemmings, Philip, 'Policy Influences on Economic Growth in OECD Countries: An Evaluation of the Evidence', *Economics Department Working Papers*, no. 246, OECD, 2000, pp. 7f. Ahn and Hemmings also briefly describes the production function on which the Solow model centres, Y = F(K,AL), where *Y* is output, *K* is capital and *AL* is the labour force measured in efficiency units, which incorporates both the amount of labour and the productivity of labour as determined by the available technology.

[15] Grossman & Helpman, *supra*, note 11, p. 6.

[16] Romer, Paul M., 'Beyond Classical and Keynesian Macroeconomic Policy', *Policy Options*, July–August 1994, available at www.stanford.edu/~promer/policyop.htm (last visited 11 October 2004).

[17] As a consequence, the regulatory task also includes resisting impeding change even when such change causes temporary disruption.

[18] Ibid.

With endogenous growth theory, technological progress is no longer taken to be a fixed rate, fallen like 'manna from heaven'. Rather it is endogenously influenced, a result of the efforts and investments of individuals and firms. An economy cannot grow simply by accumulating capital goods, as capital (human or physical) accumulation runs into the limits of diminishing returns and it is not realistic to simplify the analysis by assuming perfect allocation of resources in society (such as perfect competition). In the endogenous growth theory, capital incorporates not only physical and human capital but also the accumulation of knowledge, assumed to be the basis of technological progress.[19]

Because new knowledge cannot be perfectly patented or kept secret, a natural externality may be assumed. Creation of new knowledge by one firm is assumed to have an effect on the production possibilities of other firms.[20] However, there is a crucial difference between the two public good aspects of new discoveries: non-rivalry and non-excludability.[21] Information is a public good in the sense that it is non-rival, that it is possible for everybody to use the same information at the same time. But as far as the other criterion for a public good is concerned – non-excludability – economically important discoveries usually do not meet this criterion.[22] Rather, they are partially excludable or excludable for some period of time, not least because they are under the control of the people or firm behind the discovery, perhaps backed up by the legal system.[23] Since the use of some particular information has no opportunity cost, a firm that can control access to a discovery earns monopoly profits when commercializing the information at a price higher than zero. New technology is largely developed in view of the prospect of such profit and it is this quest for new profit that makes long-term growth feasible.

By incorporating knowledge in what is denoted as capital, the model can assume output to vary proportionally or even increasingly with the amount of

---

19 Ahn & Hemmings, *supra*, note 14, pp. 9f. The production function used in explaining endogenous growth theory, therefore, is $Y = AK$ where Y is output, K is capital and A is a constant.

20 Romer, Paul M., 'Increasing Returns and Long-Run Growth', 94 *Journal of Political Economy* 1002, 1003 (1986).

21 Non-rivalry in consumption means that the consumption of the good by one person does not limit the consumption of another. Non-excludability means it will be impossible or prohibitively costly to exclude anyone from consumption. Since non-paying consumers are hard to exclude, there is an appropriation problem, and markets consequently tend to underproduce the good.

22 Romer, Paul M. 'The Origins of Endogenous Growth', 8 *Journal of Economic Perspectives* 3, 13 (1994).

23 Romer, Paul M. 'Endogenous Technological Change', 98 *Journal of Political Economy* S71, S74 (1990).

capital since knowledge may be assumed to be a production input with increasing marginal productivity.[24] However, investments in knowledge production face diminishing returns, that is, given a stock of knowledge at a point in time, doubling the inputs into research (assumed to be the source of new knowledge) will not double the amount of new knowledge produced.[25]

There is some empirical evidence in support of the endogenous growth model. First, growth over time is not decreasing, but continuously increasing. Secondly, there is not a convergence in different countries' growth rates, as suggested by the older neoclassical model.[26] Endogenous growth theory has had an impact in public policy discussions.[27] A simple reason for this is that, when the analysis explicitly assumes that new goods can be introduced into the economy, we can ask ourselves how policy affects the aggregate rate of innovation.[28] It thus becomes a policy maker's challenge to create incentives to innovate and compete. The answers tend to suggest environments characterized by open trade of goods and ideas and economic structures that support autonomy and entrepreneurship. Subsidies for education and research may help, especially if there are developed linkages between academia and the private sector.[29]

2.2.3 Criticism and Conclusions

Endogenous growth theory and the neoclassical tradition[30] that it is built upon have been criticized for lacking a number of vital components. Even if the new growth theories have gained in realism through the incorporation of certain

---

24 Romer, *supra*, note 20, pp. 1002f.

25 Ibid., p. 1003.

26 See e.g. Grossman, Gene M. & Helpman, Elhanan, 'Endogenous Innovation in the Theory of Growth', 8 *Journal of Economic Perspectives* 23 (1994); '. . . growth rates appear to be increasing not only as a function of calendar time but also as a function of the level of development' Romer, *supra*, note 19, p. 1012.

27 See, for example, Ahn & Hemmings, *supra*, note 20, pp. 6 *et seq.*, providing a short review of recent literature on economic growth.

28 Romer, Paul M., 'New Goods, Old Theory, and the Welfare Costs of Trade Restrictions', 43 *Journal of Development Economics* 5 *et seq.* (1994).

29 Romer, *supra*, note 16.

30 It is an ambition of the neoclassic tradition to express economic problems and solutions in precise mathematical terms. Economic theory was thereby formalized and gained mathematical sophistication. A microeconomic perspective in economics was introduced, focusing on the choices of individuals in the economy. These choices are analysed in terms of marginal utilities and marginal costs. Since the marginal utility of some activity is assumed to be decreasing, the interaction between marginal utility and marginal cost will, given some additional assumptions, result in equilibrium. This is, for example, the basis for the theory of the equilibrium of demand and supply.

features of innovation into the formal theory, these features have been generally known for a long time. That technological change is largely endogenous, technology is at least partly proprietary, market structures supporting technological advance are not perfectly competitive and externalities and economies of scale are involved, and so on, are hardly new insights.[31] Empirical scholars have long stressed these notions, and others.[32]

It has been pointed out that it is of particular importance to complete the picture by focusing on 'background' factors behind growth.[33] First, growth models must be able to treat innovation essentially as a disequilibrium process, focusing on the nature of technology and the process driving technological change. Secondly, it should be realized that the abilities of specific firms, and the activities they conduct, largely determine technological success. Thus, rather than the neoclassical view of firms as black-box production functions, the organization and strategies of firms should be highlighted. The firms must be seen as the key actors in the economy. The effectiveness of firms (and other organizations) is thus of central importance. This leads to the third area that should be highlighted, which is the wide range of institutions affecting the innovation process.[34] Institutions can be defined as 'rules of the game'[35] (including the institutions enforcing the rules). Patent, antitrust and liability laws, as well as various other regulations and less formalized norms and customs, unsurprisingly influence the behaviour of the actors. The importance of this institutional environment, supporting and constraining industry, should be realized.

In conclusion, growth theory gives some general indications of the sources of economic growth. Innovation is important to welfare and public policy may influence an institutional environment that supports dynamic markets and organizations while spurring competition and investments in innovation. Antitrust policy with its goal of economic welfare should therefore be sensitive to its impact on the innovation process. However, the theory does not further investigate the actual mechanisms of innovation and does not provide guidance about market characteristics and competition mechanisms, the impact of different legal and organizational institutions and so on. For antitrust policy, such implications generally do not follow from macroeconomic sketches, but from sound appreciation of microeconomic conditions.

31 Nelson, *supra*, note 9, p. 498.

32 For example, the early contribution by Abramovitz, *supra*, note 9.

33 Nelson, *supra*, note 9, pp. 499, 508 *et seq.*

34 Ibid.

35 See North, Douglass, *Institutions, Institutional Change and Economic Performance*, Cambridge University Press, 1990.

2.3 INNOVATION AND COMPETITION

2.3.1 Static and Dynamic Efficiency

The predominating point of departure when discussing competition and economic efficiency is the model of perfect competition. In this equilibrium, resources are allocated and used optimally in a static sense. All gains of trade are exhausted by use of the market forces and price equals marginal cost (allocative efficiency). Moreover, all producers make use of existing technologies in an efficient way in order not to make losses (production efficiency). Not only microeconomic textbooks but also traditional antitrust analysis is built on this neoclassic view of markets. To realize this Pareto-optimal equilibrium of perfect competition, a number of assumptions must be fulfilled.[36] There must be a large number of independent buyers and sellers whose individual transactions are relatively small compared to the total quantity traded on the market, consumers must be perfectly informed about the products, prices and so on and act rationally using this information to maximize their preferences given their budget constraints. Also the producers must have perfect information and thus maximize their profits using perfect production functions that rule out increasing returns if they were to change scale or technology. No individual, neither producer nor consumer, can be strong enough to exercise market power, that is to influence price and output by his or her own behaviour. Transactions on the market must be costless and, finally, no externalities may exist.

The diametrical opposite to perfect competition is the monopoly. In the same tradition, the efficiency losses incurred by the pricing and production decisions taken by a profit-maximizing monopolist create the picture of inefficiency. It is of course generally acknowledged that many of the conditions for perfect competition are never fully achievable, which is why the state of perfect competition is never realized in real life. Rather than using the model as a real policy guideline in itself, it is maintained that perfect competition should be seen as a yardstick with which to judge other market structures.[37] The welfare gains demonstrated in the model indeed underpin much of current antitrust law. It is realized that deviations from the model may produce distortions in allocative and production efficiency.

---

[36] See Viscusi, W Kip, Vernon, John M. & Harrington Jr., Joseph E., *Economics of Regulation and Antitrust,* MIT Press, Cambridge Mass., 1995, p. 73; Gellhorn, Ernest & Kovacic, William E. *Antitrust Law and Economics,* 4 edn, West, St. Paul, 1994, pp. 52 *et seq.*

[37] Van Cayseele, Patrick & Van den Bergh, Roger, 'Antitrust Law', in Bouckaert, Boudewijn & De Geest, Gerrit (eds), *Encyclopedia of Law and Economics, Volume II. Civil Law and Economics,* Edward Elgar, Cheltenham, 2000, pp. 470, 485.

The static model is built on given technologies, homogeneous products and price as the number one means of competition. It is a snapshot market theory, where neither history nor future exists. In all markets, a genuine welfare analysis should take into account developments over time, above all the introduction of new products and technologies into the economy. Particularly when a market is characterized by heavy fixed costs in R&D, continuous developments in products and production processes, and innovation as the primary weapon in competition, the presumptions behind the static model correspond hardly at all to reality.

Moreover, innovation is closely related to what would be considered a 'market failure' in the static model of perfect competition. The innovation process both generates and is influenced by uncertainty, particularly regarding behaviour of other individuals and firms. In a fundamental way innovation is inherently connected to asymmetric information. In fact they are two sides of the same coin. Since innovation is induced by, and inseparable from, information asymmetries, working against optimal market solutions in the static sense, innovation and Pareto-optimality are incompatible.[38]

For the purposes of antitrust analysis, the trade-off between dynamic and static efficiency is central. Continuous technological change confers a wide range of positive effects on society. Production costs for new and old products are lowered, product quality and performance is improved and product assortments are broadened. Thus dynamic efficiency represents the generation of economically desirable new products and production processes and requires that resources be used in an efficient way in this process.[39] However, contrary to the static efficiency case, a formalized market model for achieving dynamic (innovation) efficiency does not exist.

It is widely recognized that the driving force behind such a process is the quest for profits. There must be proper incentives for market actors to invest in risky, often long-term, innovation. The marginal cost pricing in the model of perfect competition would in practice mean that large sunk costs incurred in the process never would be recouped. Yet the opposite of perfect competition, the monopoly, may also lack proper incentives to engage in development and dissemination of new technology.[40]

But if a company may, through innovation, achieve or maintain a position that would enable it to recoup investments made and to provide a fair risk

---

[38] Metcalfe, Stan, 'The Economic Foundations of Technology Policy: Equilibrium and Evolutionary Perspectives', in Stoneman, Paul (ed.), *Handbook of the Economics of Innovation and Technological Change*, Blackwell Publishers, Oxford, 1995, pp. 412f.

[39] See, e.g., Brodley, *supra*, note 30, pp. 1025f.

[40] See section 2.3.3. below.

premium, it would have the necessary incentives. High market shares and even temporary monopolies may then be seen as the result of successful management and product development, hence superior efficiency, rather than an indication of a market failure. What would have been considered supracompetitive profits in the model of perfect competition might thus be seen as a reward for success, necessary to give ex ante incentives to take innovative risks. In fact, these rewards constitute the fuel that keeps markets running at a high rate of development.

Technological change creates pressure on all market actors. Not even a dominant firm can afford to lag behind in an innovative and cost-reducing environment. On a truly dynamic market, such a firm would quickly lose its position if unsuccessful in constant product and process development. Competition is still vital for market performance; not primarily static price competition between producers of homogeneous goods, but rather dynamic innovation competition between actual or potential developers of new and improved goods. In such a dynamic model, anti-competitive market power would primarily consist in the power to control and possibly reduce the continuous development of products and technologies.

Conclusions

As seen, economic efficiency is a heterogeneous concept. The most robust microeconomic theory with relevance to antitrust is the neoclassical price theory. This theory, and particularly the notion of perfect competition, has had a great impact on the shape of competition policy. Nevertheless, this theory is built on critical assumptions that are not met in reality, which is why the model works as a yardstick at best. Further, in terms of importance to welfare in society at large, and also to consumers, dynamic efficiencies are more significant. Where technological change is important, the traditional equilibrium model is of limited applicability: 'competition in R&D *necessitates* imperfect competition in product markets'.[41] Although some other form of analysis is required, robust models which illustrate and measure dynamic efficiency do not exist.

2.3.2 Sources of Innovation

Entrepreneurs and business opportunities

Technological change is thus hard to squeeze into models that describe and explain markets and market behaviour in terms of equilibrium. Evolutionary theory does not seek to describe firm behaviour in optimizing terms but rather

---

[41] Dasgupta, Partha & Stiglitz, Joseph, 'Uncertainty, Industrial Structure, and the Speed of R&D', 11:1 *Bell Journal of Economics* 1, 27 (1980).

in terms of differences – how firms employ different technologies with different efficiencies and improve them at different rates over time.[42] A focus on a dynamic market process instead of perceived ideal end states is closely associated with the Austrian School of economics.[43] Joseph Schumpeter long ago maintained that technological progress was the main source of competition and singled out the role of the entrepreneur in that process.[44] Through innovations in organization, processes or products, the entrepreneur is able to respond to an unmet need, a previously forgone demand. This can take the form of a completely new product or an improvement in existing products and production processes. Driven by a profitable opportunity, the entrepreneur fills the important role of exploiting differences in price, quality, technology and so on. The entrepreneur thereby keeps the market forces rolling, which stimulates the continuous development of competition and markets. Thus the focus is far from an equilibrium state in perfect conditions where no entrepreneurial profits exist; rather it is on the very dynamic incentive mechanism of as yet unexploited gains of trade waiting to be exploited. In the Austrian view there is an open-endedness to the situation, a prospect of unquantifiable profits motivating the entrepreneur, and making it impossible to ascertain the amount of return that is adequate to elicit a given level of entrepreneurial activity. Therefore not even persistently high profits can be taken as a sign of monopoly.[45]

Schumpeter also distinguishes invention from innovation (and the inventor from the entrepreneur) and stresses the role of the entrepreneur in transforming invention into innovation.[46] Innovation is a non-linear, dynamic, interactive and complex process that transforms an invention into marketable products. Realizing and exploiting such a business opportunity is often

---

42 Metcalfe, *supra*, note 38, p. 410.

43 Three major developers and proponents of the Austrian tradition can be distinguished. While all adhere to a similar dynamic market perception, Joseph A. Schumpeter put forward theories on 'the process of creative destruction', an evolutionary, entrepreneurial, process in which markets are constantly restructured by innovation, Ludwig von Mises (*Human Action*, Yale University Press, New Haven, 1949) emphasized the crucial role of entrepreneurial profit-seeking speculation, and Friedrich A. Hayek (*Individualism and Economic Order*, Routledge and Kegan Paul, London, 1949) described the process as one of mutual learning of market participants' attitudes and plans.

44 Schumpeter, Joseph A., *The Theory of Economic Development: an inquiry into profits, capital, credit, interest, and the business cycle*, Cambridge, Mass., 1934.

45 Ellig, Jerome, 'Industrial Organization', in Boettke, Peter J. (ed.), *The Elgar Companion to Austrian Economics*, Edward Elgar, Aldershot, 1994, pp. 244–8.

46 In these early Schumpeterian theories, the inventor and the process of invention in itself are outside the role of, exogenous to, the entrepreneur. It is the exploitation of inventions that is mostly considered.

rewarded by a temporary monopoly. In this process markets will be affected and established structures will be changed. Therefore innovation is much more important to understand than equilibrium.

It may be argued that technological progress is driven by science, independent of economic incentives. But this is neither the view of scholars of industrial innovation, nor the conclusion of many studies of particular industries and technological developments.[47] It is apparent from empirical studies of historically important innovations that they were stimulated by 'a costly problem to be solved or a potentially profitable opportunity to be seized'.[48] Empirical studies also suggest a positive and strong relationship between R&D and productivity growth.[49] This indicates that a notion of innovation as a result of profit opportunities is apt. It is, therefore, emphasized that the innovation process is mainly guided by market forces and that commercial exploitation and dissemination of scientific ideas almost always requires substantial investments.[50]

Large firms and routinization

Innovation driven by striving entrepreneurs, constantly reacting to business opportunities, embodying the market's trial and error process in their attempts to outperform incumbent firms and rivals with new and improved technologies, products, organizations and so on is only part of the story. In later works by Schumpeter,[51] the technological and scientific (R&D) efforts and investments by, often, large corporations are taken into account. Arguably, large firms can realize economies both in scale (large sales volumes to spread R&D costs) and scope (positive spillovers between different research programmes) in R&D. Moreover, larger firms could reduce risk by diversification, entering into a larger number of R&D projects. If capital markets were imperfect, large firms with market power could also secure finance for risky R&D investments.[52]

---

[47] Grossman & Helpman, *supra*, note 26, pp. 26f. Examples referred to by Grossman and Helpman stem from machine tools, aircraft, synthetic chemicals, metallurgy, semiconductors and so on.

[48] Schmookler, Jacob, *Invention and Economic Growth,* Harvard University Press, Cambridge, 1966, p. 199.

[49] Ahn, Sanghoon, 'Competition, Innovation and Productivity Growth: A Review of Theory and Evidence', *Economics Department Working Papers,* no. 317, OECD, 2002, p. 14.

[50] Grossman & Helpman, *supra*, note 11, pp. 4f.; Grossman & Helpman, *supra*, note 26, pp. 25f.

[51] Schumpeter, Joseph A., *Capitalism, Socialism, and Democracy,* 2nd edition, Harper & Brothers, New York, 1947.

[52] Ahn, *supra*, note 49, pp. 7, 10.

Similar to the Schumpeterian focus on large firms as major sources of innovation, fierce innovation competition among large high-tech firms in oligopolistic markets is seen by William J. Baumol as a major innovation factor and wealth creator.[53] Looking at many of the high-tech markets (computers, pharmaceuticals, telecom and so on) the market participants are not primarily entrepreneurs in small new firms. According to Baumol, many of these markets display imperfect but effective competition. Although firms price their products above marginal costs, this seldom implies monopoly; rather, many of these markets can be very competitive. The primary weapon in this competition is innovation, which has replaced price as 'the name of the game'.

A central element in Baumol's theories is routinization of R&D investments. To large high-tech firms, in markets with a range of rival firms active in innovation, R&D investments are just like any other investment.[54] Market forces pressure firms to systematize the innovation process in order to minimize uncertainty and chance in that process; this becomes a regular and ordinary component in the firms' activities.[55] This also implies that firms cannot, ex ante, expect higher returns on R&D investments compared to other kinds of investments. If entry to innovation is free, firms must optimize their R&D investments in order to survive on the market. Heads of R&D departments compete for internal funding with equivalent managers in production, marketing and so on. The management then decides, using reported prospective innovations and the corresponding plans from other parts of the firm, which investments to make. Moreover, R&D departments are frequently given assignments on innovations needed in order to launch new or improved products and processes.

> This is not the realm of the unexpected, of the unrestricted exercise of imagination and boldness that is the essence of entrepreneurship. It is, rather, the domain of memorandums, rigid cost controls, and standardized procedures, which are the hallmark of trained management.[56]

Even if firms cannot expect more than normal profits from their investments in innovation, it does not mean that this will be the result. Some firms are more successful than others, thanks to skill or luck, and will as a consequence earn more profit than others. Just as in any other part of business life, survival and

---

53 Baumol, *supra*, note 7.

54 Already Schumpeter noted that '[i]nnovation itself is being reduced to routine. Technological progress is increasingly becoming the business of teams of trained specialists who turn out what is required and make it work in predictable ways'; *supra* note 51, p. 132.

55 Baumol, *supra*, note 7, pp. 4, 11, 30 *et seq*.

56 Ibid., p. 36.

success is determined by relative superiority compared to rivals. And just like any other part of business, the surrounding markets (securities, finance and so on) closely monitor the innovation aspects of the high-tech firms and react on how well the firms match the expectations. News of delays or negative test results in the development and launch of new products and processes is quickly reflected in share prices. This further demonstrates the level of routine characterizing the whole process.

Synthesis

There is no clear indication that large firms in general should be more efficient innovators. Large firms may, for example, experience managerial slack as the organization grows. Also the incentives of individual scientists and entrepreneurs become attenuated as their ability to capture benefits from their efforts diminishes. Recent reviews of the literature on empirical studies suggest strongly that the hypothesis of large firms being significantly more active in innovation cannot be supported. Rather, some studies indicate that both very small firms and very large firms account for a disproportionately large share of innovations.[57]

Oligopolistic competition among large high-tech firms, where R&D investment is routine, adds an important element to the picture. However, it does not diminish the role of smaller entrepreneurial firms. Empirical evidence confirms that leading firms prefer other forms of innovation to those chosen by challengers, aspiring to preserve their position rather than fundamentally change the market. Ground-breaking new technology may be an attractive aim for small fringe players or larger firms acting outside their normal specialization.[58] Quantum leaps in technological development remain unpredictable and are often the deed of the imaginative entrepreneur.

The entrepreneur thus continues to play a very important role as a major supplier of revolutionary new ideas. After successful innovation, entrepreneurs often transform their businesses into larger companies and routinize their innovation, for example focusing on improvements, new uses and enhanced attributes.[59] Such incremental cumulative innovation is still very important in terms of the benefits to society.

Thus both large and small firms play important roles as providers of essential inputs in the innovation machinery of a knowledge-based society. The conditions under which they operate, their incentives and behaviour – not least

---

[57] Ahn, *supra*, note 49, pp. 10, 14f.

[58] Rubinfeld, Daniel L. & Hoven, John, 'Innovation and Antitrust Enforcement', in Ellig, Jerry (ed.), *Dynamic Competition and Public Policy,* Cambridge University Press, 2001, p. 75.

[59] Baumol, *supra*, note 7, p. 21.

the connections between the two groups – are important factors in producing innovation. Small firms play an important role in preparing innovations that are then developed and fully exploited by large firms, a sequential characteristic of R&D and innovation.[60] They can be in direct competition with one another or they can cooperate, but they nonetheless provide complementary features to the innovation process.

Capabilities, resources and strategies

Dynamic theories do not merely focus on firm sizes but also on other properties of the firm. For example, the firm may be seen as a body based on organisational knowledge that is constantly updated and accumulated. Such a process of using resources to learn or acquire new knowledge is fundamental to economic growth. The accumulated, firm-specific, knowledge earns a rent that may be considered the rationale of the firm.[61] Market success depends on the extent of this learning compared to that of rivals, which further establishes the connection to Schumpeter and evolutionary perspectives. The adaptive learning behaviour involved in generating and applying new technology is at the centre of the analysis.[62] In such a disequilibrium theory, the firm continuously goes through creative, analytical and operational steps, and accumulates experience, which is fed back into the creative, innovative process. The transaction costs of holding a company together in such an experimentally organized economy are the costs of this learning. If you learn less than your competitors, you lose and the firm will break up.[63]

Competitive advantage can thus be regarded as the core of the market process. Moreover, such an advantage cannot be limited to resources, but must include the capabilities of the firm, as contrasted with its competitors, to utilize resources to achieve innovations, quality and other efficiencies.[64] Along this line of thinking, a product market outlook may not be the most

---

60 See Sylos-Labini, Paolo, 'Capitalism, Socialism, and Democracy and Large-Scale Firms', in Scherer, Frederic M. & Perlman, Mark (eds), *Entrepreneurship, Technological Innovation, and Economic Growth – Studies in the Schumpeterian Tradition,* The University of Michigan Press, Ann Arbor, 1992, pp. 58f.; Scherer, Frederic M., *Industrial Market Structure and Economic Performance,* Rand McNally, Chicago, 1980, p. 416.

61 Eliasson, Gunnar, 'Business Competence, Organizational Learning, and Economic Growth: Establishing the Smith–Schumpeter–Wicksell (SSW) Connection', in Scherer, Frederic M. & Perlman, Mark (eds), *Entrepreneurship, Technological Innovation, and Economic Growth – Studies in the Schumpeterian Tradition,* The University of Michigan Press, Ann Arbor, 1992, pp. 253f.

62 Metcalfe, *supra*, note 38, p. 410.

63 Eliasson, *supra*, note 61, pp. 261 *et seq.*

64 Porter, Michel E., *Competitive Advantage: Creating and Sustaining Superior Performance*, Free Press, New York, 1985.

appropriate for competition analysis. If the firm is seen as a portfolio of core competencies and disciplines, inter-firm competition, as opposed to inter-product competition, is essentially concerned with the acquisition of skills. Product-based advantages at a given time may provide little insight into this learning process, where knowledge is acquired and skill is built.[65]

If success and profits are the result of such inter-firm superiority, it is necessary to analyse firms' resources and capabilities, both tangible and intangible assets. These are the units at a firm's disposal when implementing its strategies. In order to explain the profits of superior resources and capabilities it must be assumed that such assets are not homogeneously distributed across competing firms and that they have some degree of immobility;[66] in other words, that such differences and advantages are not quickly imitated or substituted.

If a firm's assets are valuable, rare and costly to imitate, the firm may have a lasting competitive advantage and earn great profits. However, this advantage may be changed, owing to the introduction of new technologies or changes in consumer preferences. If the assets are valuable and rare but not costly to imitate, a firm will have a short-lived competitive advantage during which profits will be made. If the assets are valuable but neither rare nor costly to imitate, the firm will only be in competitive parity.[67]

Interorganizational linkages

When firms are no longer perceived as black-box production functions as in the neoclassical theory and when it is realized that firms' resources and competencies are at the heart of the innovation process, various forms of inter-firm exchanges can more clearly be understood. Firms do not only learn from their own experience. Several studies stress the importance of external sources of various kinds: customers, suppliers, licensors, licensees, competitors, universities and so on.[68]

In older perceptions, the innovation process is seen as a fairly predictable linear process. Starting from basic research it extends over more specialized R&D, design and production to end with marketing, sales and services.[69] The

---

[65] Hamel, Gary, 'Competition for Competence and Interpartner Learning within International Strategic Alliances', 12 *Strategic Management Journal* 83 (1991).

[66] Barney, Jay B., 'Competence Explanations of Economic Profits in Strategic Management: Some Policy Implications', in Ellig, Jerry (ed.), *Dynamic Competition and Public Policy,* Cambridge University Press, 2001, p. 48.

[67] Ibid., p. 51.

[68] Freeman, Chris, 'The Economics of Technical Change', 18 *Cambridge Journal of Economics* 463, 470 (1994).

[69] Jorde, Thomas M. & Teece, David J., 'Innovation and Cooperation: Implications for Competition and Antitrust', 4(3) *Journal of Economic Perspectives* 75, 77 (1990).

theory of innovation as a vertical process may today still be apt to describe how innovation occurs in some scale-intensive industries,[70] but is inappropriate for many other innovative industries. In more recent theory, innovation is rather seen as a simultaneous process with tight linkages and feedback mechanisms within firms, between firms and between firms and other institutions.[71] Such a flow of information, a continuous feedback mechanism, sheds new light on the organizational requirements for innovation industries. Hence much innovation today requires horizontal as well as vertical linkages.[72] It furthermore implies new patterns of technology transfer and rent dissipation between different actors in the process. Restrictive contracts governing access to complementary assets and inputs may thus enable firms to innovate efficiently.

Empirically, globalized competition and market opportunities have also meant new sources of innovation. Business strategies have become outward-oriented, seeking a wider variety of sources for new technology and innovative concepts, outside the particular firm. Wider diversity of knowledge requirements and more complex technology frontiers imply a need for networks and openness.[73] Not surprisingly, the number of networks and strategic alliances between firms is growing rapidly, especially in information technology, biotechnology and advanced material industries.[74] The number of new strategic alliances rose during the period 1989–99, from just over 1000 in 1989 (around 860 of these were cross-border alliances) to 7000 in 1999 (cross-border: 4400).[75] The share of patents that have a foreign co-inventor almost doubled both in the EU and in the US between the periods 1985–7 and 1993–5.[76] By these trends it is clear that companies believe that key know-how is increasingly international.[77]

With the view of the firm as a portfolio of core competencies, strategic alliances have specific attributes. The alliance may be a way of trading access to another's skills. Naturally the consequences of alliance building between

---

70 Jorde, Thomas M. & Teece, David J. 'Innovation, Cooperation, and Antitrust', in Jorde, Thomas M. & Teece, David J. (eds), *Antitrust, Innovation, and Competitiveness,* Oxford University Press, New York, 1992, p. 48.

71 Jorde & Teece, *supra*, note 69, p. 77.

72 Jorde & Teece, *supra*, note 70, p. 49.

73 OECD, *A New Economy?: The Changing Role of Innovation and Information in Growth*, Paris, 2000, p. 37.

74 OECD, *Globalisation of Industrial R&D: Policy Issues,* Paris, 1999, p. 13. About 65 per cent of those alliances involved two partners from different countries.

75 Nam-Hoon Kang & Kentaro Sakai, 'International Strategic Alliances: Their Role In Industrial Globalisation', *STI Working Paper* 2000/5, OECD, Paris, 2000, pp. 7f.

76 OECD, *supra*, note 73, pp. 37 *et seq.*

77 OECD, *supra*, note 74, p. 13.

actual or potential competitors may be sensitive for antitrust analysis, but very much so also for the firms involved. A firm that fails to outlearn its partner may first become dependent and then redundant within the partnership, and competitively vulnerable outside it.[78]

The positive aspects of cooperation are not limited to sophisticated variables of interorganizational learning and sharing of competencies. Within the field of industrial organization, various scholars have devoted attention to more general effects of R&D cooperation. Divided into broad categories, such benefits could relate to ex ante R&D incentives, economies of joint research and ex post dissemination of the results.[79] As noted before, regarding the resulting intangible benefits from research activities, information and knowledge, there are spillover effects to the rest of the economy. And, even if intellectual property rights protect innovators, there will often be leaks due to employee mobility, reverse engineering and security failure, and so on, which may result in competitors' free-riding. In addition, a large part of know-how cannot be protected, given current systems of intellectual property rights. Spillovers that reduce the returns of the R&D investment and benefit rivals naturally negatively affect the incentives for it. A joint venture may therefore substantially improve ex ante incentives for R&D activity and investment.[80]

As for the R&D undertaken, cooperation may increase R&D efficiency – hence the value of the money spent – by exploiting synergies, joining complementary technologies and techniques among the parties. When each party has its own special skills and experiences, teamwork potentially produces a cross-

---

78 Hamel, *supra*, note 65, p. 84. Control in an alliance by being ahead in developing competencies can bring control over standards and the evolution of technology, but also price and performance advantages. Hamel quotes one senior manager of an international partnership: 'Friendship is friendship, but competition is competition. Competition is the future and that is R&D', p. 89.

79 Grossman, Gene M. & Shapiro, Carl, 'Research Joint Ventures: An Antitrust Analysis' 2 *Journal of Law, Economics and Organization* 315, 321 *et seq.* (1986); Glader, Marcus, 'Research and Development Cooperation in European Competition Law', *CFE Working Paper Series,* no. 6, 2000; available at: http://www.cfe.lu.se/CFEWP/WP.html (last visited 11 October 2004); OECD, *Competition Policy and Joint Ventures,* Paris 1986, pp. 19f.; Kattan, Joseph, 'Antitrust Analysis of Technology Joint Ventures: Allocative Efficiency and the Rewards of Innovation', 61 *Antitrust Law Journal* 937, 939 *et seq.* (1993).

80 D'Aspremont, Claude & Jacquemin, Alexis, 'Cooperative and Noncooperative R&D in Duopoly with Spillovers', 78(5) *American Economic Review* 1133 (1988); Katz, Michael L. 'An Analysis of Cooperative Research and Development', 17 *Rand Journal of Economics* 527 (1996); Leahy, Dermot & Neary, J. Peter, 'Public Policy Towards R&D in Oligopolistic Industries', 87(4) *American Economic Review* 642 (1997); Petit, Maria Luisa & Tolwinski, Boleslaw, 'R&D cooperation or competition?', 43 *European Economic Review* 185 (1999).

fertilization of ideas. Cooperation may allow smaller players to attain a minimum efficient scale of R&D, allow the parties to share substantial risks and more generally avoid wasteful duplication of R&D efforts. This last may, though, at some point conflict with the evolutionary idea of variety: too much collaboration risks stifling diversity of research, thereby leading to a narrow range of R&D outcomes and possible applications at the same time as the R&D race for superior competitiveness becomes limited. 'Inevitably evolutionary processes are inefficient . . . so-called static inefficiencies are the necessary cost of sustaining requisite variety and they must be incurred if economic systems are to develop and evolve.'[81]

The third benefit of joining up in R&D would be to enhance ex post dissemination of the results. The public good aspects of innovation, and the related problems of trading R&D results, can result in an insufficient spreading of information in the market. Under these circumstances, cooperation in R&D among parties interested in commercializing the expected results can be seen as an ex ante licensing agreement, which may reduce problems of asymmetric information and risks of opportunism, thereby allowing for a wider dissemination of the results.

Many of these benefits are common, at least to some degree, to the different mechanisms by which R&D efforts are combined. The choice of structure for achieving the parties' goals, ranging from full mergers, via complex contractual joint venture or alliance arrangements to licence agreements of a more simple kind, depends markedly on the relative needs for exchange, risks of opportunism, costs of monitoring and so on.

Conclusions

It is worth emphasizing the important role of both small and big companies in the innovation process and the conditions for cooperation and competition. Smaller challengers may invoke ground-breaking innovations as a way to change the state of the art in the market.

Expansion in R&D-intense markets takes place through a spectrum of interorganizational structures and transactions: 'While vertical growth, typically via acquisitions, is of course still common, large firms often "partner", via a dizzying array of organizational forms, with small firms steeped in new technologies. Joint ventures, R&D partnerships, corporate venture capital, spinoffs, startups, licensing deals, and "out-sourcing" arrangements (that is, purchase of components formerly manufactured in-house) – all forms of 'strategic alliance' have been adopted widely in recent years.'[82]

81 Metcalfe, *supra*, note 38, pp. 415f.

82 Merges, Robert P., *Intellectual Property Rights, Input Markets, and the Value of Intangible Assets*, University of California at Berkeley, 1999, p. 3.

In order to understand the competition process where the firm is no black box, competition is dynamic, future product generations are hard to predict and firms' strategies go beyond the positioning of particular products, it may be appropriate to have firms' core competencies as a point of departure rather than product markets. That may hold for both fast-moving industries such as software and telecom and areas where the R&D process is more long-term, such as biotech and pharmaceuticals.

2.3.3 Market Structure and Innovation

Monopoly and competition

The discussion about which market structures would be most conducive to innovation usually starts from the two contrasting perspectives of Joseph Schumpeter and Kenneth Arrow. Schumpeter put forward the theory that large firms would be superior providers of innovation, basically for two reasons.[83] First, large companies have the financial resources necessary to invest in costly and uncertain R&D and they can realize important economies of scale in research. With diversified product lines, they would also be able to exploit unexpected R&D results in a way that a small company would not. Secondly, large firms in monopolistic markets would be able to appropriate the benefits from the innovative effort, and thereby finance continued R&D with the monopoly profits accrued.

Arrow, on the contrary, emphasizes the role of competition as a spur to innovation.[84] Particularly where intellectual property rights protect resulting products, he showed that a monopolist would have fewer incentives to innovate than would a company that faced competition. Even if the patented product is supposed to create market power for the company that introduces it, the monopolist will only replace its current product and not gain any relative market power. In addition, if the market is not (at least potentially) competitive, the monopolist will not be punished for unsuccessful R&D.

If potential competition is introduced, the level of risk will affect the incentives for a monopolist to engage in R&D. If, with a high degree of certainty, innovation follows from investments in R&D and the firm which invests most in R&D will consequently be the first to innovate, investment in innovation becomes similar to bidding at an auction.[85] Under such conditions, an

---

83 Schumpeter, *supra*, note 51.

84 Arrow, Kenneth J. 'Economic Welfare and the Allocation of Resources for Inventions', in Nelson, R. (ed.), *The Rate and Direction of Inventive Activity*, Princeton University Press, 1962.

85 Bergman, Mats, *Potential Competition: Theory, empirical evidence and legal practice*, The Swedish Competition Authority, 2002, p. 24.

incumbent monopolist will have more to lose from entry than a potential entrant will gain. The monopolist will thus have incentives to spend more on R&D in order to maintain its monopoly, since the sum of profits in a duopoly will be lower than the monopoly profits.[86] On the other hand, if R&D involves a high risk and innovation is dramatic, in the sense that the new product will capture a large share of the market, entrants will have the larger incentive to engage in R&D. Since the incumbent firm will invest only to keep entrants out, whereas the entrant has the additional incentive to reduce entry time, the latter will spend more on R&D. For incremental improvements in existing products, the monopolist will still have superior incentives.

F.M. Scherer and David Ross investigated the pace of development and the level of competition.[87] In a model of two firms engaging in R&D for a new product, they show that, when the incumbent firm has an advantage from the fact that it is already present on the market (reputation, distribution network and so on) and thus may be able to capture more of the resulting sales if the products are introduced simultaneously, firms will increase the speed of development when competition is on the horizon. A small entrant firm will have more to gain from being first with the new product, if that allows the firm to capture some important fraction of the incumbent's larger sales. In this situation, the incumbent firm, which does not want to force the pace, will realize that losing the race will incur large losses in sales and it will thus accelerate its R&D. With an increasing number of incumbent firms, accelerated product R&D will follow up to the point where the smaller market shares yield revenues insufficient to cover the R&D costs. In this model, too many firms may then reduce the speed of development.

Empirically, Scherer and Ross found support for their theory that competition stimulated R&D up to a certain level. In particular, when the technological opportunities were rich and technological change could be rapid and unexpected, providing large benefits for the innovator, rivalry was a stimulant. They found an 'inverted-U' relationship, suggesting that the R&D/sales ratios peaked when the four-firm concentration ratio (the share of the four largest firms) reached 50–55 per cent. Further increases in concentration tended to lessen R&D spending. More recent studies have supported such a relationship, while others found that it disappeared when inter-industry differences were included.[88]

---

86 Ibid. See Gilbert, Richard J. & Newbery, David M.G., 'Preemptive Patenting and the Persistence of Monopoly', 75 *American Economic Review* 514 (1982).

87 Scherer, Frederic M. & Ross, David, *Industrial Market Structure and Economic Performance* Houghton Mifflin, Boston, 1990, pp. 635 f.

88 Aghion, Philippe *et al.*, 'Competition and innovation: an inverted U relationship' *NBER Working Paper*, no 9269, 2002. Available at: http://www.nber.org/papers/w9269 (last visited 3 March 2005); Ahn, *supra*, note 49, p. 15.

Game-theoretical models, of various kinds, can help predict and explain firms' incentives and strategic actions with regard to R&D investments, if tailored to the particular situation. The result of such models is generally dependent on the structure and nature of the market, the R&D to be conducted and the investment to be made, varying if the firms are pursuing different paths of research or rather are competing for the same innovation (a patent race), the level of spillovers, whether investment decisions are repeated and so on. The assumptions underlying a particular model are therefore crucial both for its realism and for its results.[89]

Despite the sensitivity of game-theoretical models to the case-specific circumstances in which they are applied, the models of innovation illustrate two important incentives for R&D investments. The first is the profit incentive, which represents the increase in profits that would result from successful innovation, compared to the situation if the firm did not innovate, other things being equal. The prospect of increased profits thus provides incentives for a stand-alone decision to invest in R&D. The second is the competitive threat, representing the loss of competitiveness, and thus the difference in profits, if a firm does not innovate and a competitor does. This dimension highlights the strategic interaction involved in innovation. Innovation may be important, not only in isolation, but as part of a strategic competitive game.[90]

Oligopolies

As previously mentioned, oligopolistic competition between large firms is an important source of innovation. Of interest in the discussion on market structure and innovation are mechanisms to reduce the risk of R&D investments, particularly as they relate to structure and investment levels. According to Baumol, oligopolistic firms reduce the risks involved in such investments in at least two different ways.[91]

In the oligopolistic competition process, market participants may achieve temporary equilibrium in innovation investments for some time. The firms' investment decisions correspond to the pricing decisions that occur in oligopolistic markets, where kinked demand curves may imply temporary price equi-

---

89 Dasgupta & Stiglitz, *supra*, note 41; Leahy & Neary, *supra*, note 80; Wickelgren, Abraham L., 'Innovation, market structure and the holdup problem: investment incentives and coordination', 22 *International Journal of Industrial Organization* 693 (2004).

90 Europe Economics, *The Development of Analytical Tools for Assessing Market Dynamics in the Knowledge Based Economy*, Annex to Draft Final Report: Literature Review (2003) p. 8; available at http://europa.eu.int/comm/enterprise/library/lib-competition/doc/analytical_tools_annex.pdf (last visited 3 March 2005).

91 Baumol, *supra*, note 7, pp. 32 *et seq.*

libria. If a firm lowers prices it may expect its rivals to do the same in order not to lose sales, and the result will hurt all firms involved. A costly price war may even result. But if the firm decides to increase prices, it may very well be rational for the rivals not to react but to benefit from increased sales. In the same way, innovative firms may face kinked profit curves in R&D investment. If a firm increases its R&D investment levels, market participants are likely to follow. However, decreases are more difficult to realize since it may be profitable to continue at prior levels if competitors reduce R&D output. From time to time the equilibrium breaks down, for example if a player finds it too profitable to forgo the chance to raise its R&D level. The same may apply where a new player enters the market with a particular new potential. Such breakdowns are likely to occur if there arises a highly promising project which could result in a major technological breakthrough and large profits. The R&D level will then be raised until a new, higher, equilibrium is reached. Such 'stochastic shocks' thus stimulate increased spending in a stepwise manner.[92]

This model assumes something like the law of large numbers. Although an R&D project is surrounded by great uncertainty as to costs, time and value, the firms must be so large that the number of projects in which they are involved makes the overall value of their R&D moderately predictable. Moreover, the firms' reactions are not to be influenced by possible differences among them and their managers. There is also an assumption that firms are perfectly informed about the R&D spending of the rivals.[93] Even if these assumptions may not be fully realized in reality, the model seems appropriate enough to demonstrate the possible impact of interdependence in oligopolistic markets.

The second way that firms reduce uncertainty is by coordinating their behaviour. Through the formation of JVs, by technical cooperation and licensing, perhaps within strategic alliances, market participants reduce the risk of being outperformed by rivals and also reduce costs of innovation. The growing importance of strategic alliances mentioned earlier and recent merger waves may be taken as a sign of this.

Potential competition and barriers to entry

The important role of potential entrants as an important source of competition has already been highlighted, for example in giving incumbents incentives to engage in R&D. In the light of the ambiguous relationship between innovation and market concentration and the inherent nature of disequilibrium in dynamic competition, the role of potential competition may nonetheless deserve some further comment.

92 Ibid., pp. 33, 46.
93 Ibid., p. 46.

According to the contestable market theory, even a monopolist can be disciplined by the threats of potential competition. In a perfectly contestable market, an incumbent monopoly firm is not able to misuse its position, since entry would occur if the firm did not behave efficiently.[94] In high-tech industry in particular it is often claimed that competition primarily occurs *for* the market rather than *in* the market, implying that the most successful innovator becomes the market leader for some time. The most obvious example is industries with a high degree of network effects, where competition largely takes place at an early stage and an early technological lead may lead to dominance. However, general R&D competition to develop the 'killer' product or service will also have this property of competition for the market rather than performance in an already existing market.[95] Competition for markets may, to different degrees, be found in computer software and hardware industries, communication networks, mobile telephony, biotechnology and pharmaceuticals.[96]

In such markets, competition largely relates to the potential introduction of new products and technologies. As for all potential competition, the level and effectiveness of such competition is closely related to entry conditions. In the information-based economy, where knowledge represents an increasing share of the value of products and services and where innovation and performance are major competitive attributes, markets display an array of different entry barriers as well as possibilities for incumbents to deter entry. Network effects, key intellectual property rights, essential research tools, regulatory delays, large sunk costs, high risks and so on are present and will naturally limit the scope and timeliness of entry.

The existence and level of potential competition is not mirrored in concentration ratios, which is why empirical evidence based on such variables may be flawed. Nevertheless, also empirically, the importance of technological newcomers is highlighted, with the message that efficient industry performance may very much be dependent on modest entry barriers.[97]

Reward for innovation

The problem of excessive competition is a problem of appropriation of the resulting benefits. Evidently, the innovator needs some mechanism in order to recoup the risky investments incurred. Temporary monopolies with high profitability as rewards for successful innovation are something rather different

94 Bergman, *supra*, note 85, p. 11.

95 Evans, David S. & Schmalensee, Richard, 'Some Economic Aspects of Antitrust Analysis in Dynamically Competitive Industries', *NBER Working Paper*, no. 8268, 2001, p. 2.

96 Ibid., p. 6.

97 See Scherer & Ross, *supra*, note 87, p. 660.

from incumbent firms with substantial and shielded monopoly power and too little incentives for innovation. Even disciples of the Austrian school would reluctantly agree that in the latter case there could be a case for public intervention, while still maintaining that the prospect of large profits will induce entry through innovation by others.[98]

As with all investment decisions, enforceable property rights (including the intellectual) or availability of strategies and structures that enable firms to appropriate a return from their investment, are likely to be key factors.[99] In relation to this, Edmund Kitch's arguments for broad patent rights should be highlighted. In this view, patents are prospects of developing a particular technological possibility, with a potential of enhancing efficiency in innovation, rather than exclusivity for a particular market application seen as a reward. Broad patent rights granted early in the R&D process, that is, upstream from the commercial application, will allow the innovator to reap the benefits needed in order to induce proper R&D investments. Also, such rights would reduce duplicative R&D, as subsequent developers would have to turn to the patent holder for licences.[100] Other arguments for broad patent rights are based on the fact that the commercial value of the initial innovation may be far less than that of subsequent applications and improvements induced by the innovation. To provide proper incentives for the initial innovation, the innovator should be allowed to appropriate a fair part of its value to the next generation.[101] This is also reflected in arguments for public funding

---

[98] Audretsch, David B., Baumol, William J. & Burke, Andrew E., 'Competition Policy in Dynamic Markets', 19 *International Journal of Industrial Organization* 613, 619 (2001); Kirzner, Israel M., *How Markets Work: Disequilibrium, Entrepreneurship and Discovery,* London, 1997, p. 62: 'The *only* government action needed to ensure the dynamically competitive character of market activity is to remove all such government-created obstacles. The market itself is unable to erect such obstacles against entrepreneurial entry. Collusion among 'dominant' firms in an industry (unless it takes the form of effectively monopolising the control of essential scarce resources), while it may appear to be effective in keeping up prices is incapable of preventing entry.'

[99] See e.g. Jorde, Thomas M. & Teece, David J. 'Introduction', in Jorde Thomas M. & Teece, David J. (eds), *Antitrust, Innovation, and Competitiveness,* Oxford University Press, New York, 1992, p. 6.

[100] Kitch, Edmund W., 'The Nature and Function of the Patent System', 20 *Journal of Law and Economics* 265, 276 (1977).

[101] Cooter, Robert & Ulen, Thomas, *Law and Economics*, 3rd ed Reading, Mass., Addison-Wesley, 2000, pp. 126f.; Scotchmer, Suzanne, 'Standing on the Shoulders of Giants: Cumulative Research and the Patent Law', 5 *Journal of Economic Perspectives* 29 (1991); Scotchmer, Suzanne, 'Protecting Early Innovators: Should Second-Generation Products Be Patentable?', 27 *Rand Journal of Economics* 322 (1996); Chang, Howard F., 'Patent Scope, Antitrust Policy, and Cumulative Innovation', 26 *Rand Journal of Economics* 34 (1995).

for basic research, as an alternative solution to the problem of underproduction.[102]

Advocates of more narrow patents argue that holders of broad patent rights will tend to slow down research rather than control it in the efficient ways suggested by Kitch.[103] They also point out that duplicative R&D is far from being a social waste in all cases. Often, parallel research follows different paths and leads to different resulting innovations. Although duplication of R&D expenditure will entail costs to society – a static inefficiency, if you will – the result of diverse research is likely to create variety in the research output that is beneficial in a dynamic perspective. Moreover, when R&D can be expected to result in large benefits, competition will not reduce its ex ante incentives. In addition, as noted in the previous section, the monopoly firm may not be the most efficient manager of research, implying that competition in R&D will avoid technological opportunities being overlooked and will spur R&D performance.[104] Finally, considering the initial arguments of Arrow concerning the lack of incentive for monopolists to invest in R&D (or engage in licensing of its intellectual property) and to create a substitute for its own monopoly, the proper level of competition seems hard to solve theoretically. There is also empirical support for the argument that a leading firm owning basic patents controlling development in an industry is likely to slow down innovation.[105] Competition is thus prescribed for swift and continued development.

In the patent system there is thus an inherent conflict in supporting the 'first', initial, invention in an area, and simultaneously giving incentives for later innovation. Initial research is likely to be more basic whereas subsequent development is more directed to the applications that may be derived from it.[106] To give incentives for initial, risky, basic research, typically opening up new areas where it is uncertain what the future will hold in terms of

---

[102] See Rai, Arti K., 'Fostering Cumulative Innovation in the Biopharmaceutical Industry: The Role of Patents and Antitrust', 16 *Berkeley Technology Law Journal* 813, 819 footnote 24 (2001).

[103] Merges, Robert P. & Nelson, Richard R., 'Market Structure and Technical Advance: The Role of Patent Scope Decisions', in Jorde, Thomas M. & Teece, David J. (eds), *Antitrust, Innovation, and Competitiveness,* Oxford University Press, New York, 1992, p. 185; Merges, Robert P. & Nelson, Richard R., 'On the Complex Economics of Patent Scope', 90 *Columbia Law Review* 839 (1990).

[104] See Scherer & Ross, *supra*, note 87, p. 644.

[105] Merges, Robert P. & Nelson, Richard R., 'Market Structure and Technical Advance: The Role of Patent Scope Decisions', in Jorde, Thomas M. & Teece, David J. (eds), *Antitrust, Innovation, and Competitiveness,* Oxford University Press, New York, 1992, pp. 201 *et seq.*

[106] Barton, John H., 'Patents and Antitrust: A Rethinking in Light of Patent Breadth and Sequential Innovation', 65 *Antitrust Law Journal* 449, 453 (1997).

marketable products, broad patent coverage would be preferable. At the same time the risk of later anti-competitive behaviour is often larger with this kind of exclusivity. Not only may the initial patent cover various future products, possibly developed by an array of companies, but essential research tools may also be in the exclusive hands of the initial inventor. Barton provides an example with a patent on a biological receptor of importance to schizophrenia.[107] The receptor is unlikely to constitute a product in itself, but is an important tool for research regarding this disease. It may be that various products could be produced, marketed and used without infringing the patent, but the work of developing these products would not be possible without access to the patent. The initial inventor may have limited incentives to cooperate with subsequent innovators. In the case where the initial patent covers future products resulting from follow-on research, a licence could be negotiated ex ante, before any investments are made into R&D. But situations are likely to arise ex post, after investment in R&D has been made, where an innovator is forced to seek a licence from a holder of basic patents in order to market his product. In this situation, the initial inventor is in a formidable bargaining position. The stronger the position conferred by broad patents, the greater the ability to control development in that industry.[108]

Yet, if narrow patents are not sufficiently tied to marketable products or processes that are their end result, another negative effect can appear. With numerous stakeholders in upstream technologies, coordination problems and holdout positions may arise. Well-recognized are the problems arising from non-existent, ill-defined or inadequately upheld property rights, leading to an over-use of scarce resources in the 'tragedy of the commons'. Where defined property rights exist but are fragmented, the result may be underuse of the protected technologies as the coordination problems of navigating through the patent thicket become too burdensome. Heller and Eisenberg use such a theory in the context of patents on short fragments of human genes and give a name to this kind of result: ' "the tragedy of the anticommons" refers to the more complex obstacles that arise when a user needs access to multiple patented inputs to create a single useful product. Each upstream patent allows its owner to set up another tollbooth on the road to product development, adding to the cost and slowing the pace of downstream biomedical innovation'.[109]

Finally, it should be highlighted that, for many industries, empirical evidence shows that the strongest incentive for innovation may not be intellectual property right protection. While this is an important strategic tool

---

107 Ibid., pp. 451, 453 *et seq.*

108 Ibid., 453f.

109 Heller, Michael A. & Eisenberg, Rebecca S., 'Can Patents Deter Innovation? The Anticommons in Biomedical Research', 280 *Science* 698, 699 (1998).

which may add value, many industries rely more heavily on other business strategies as ways of appropriating the value of R&D. In one comprehensive study of 130 industry sectors, patents were regarded as highly effective means of appropriating returns in only five industries, such as the drug, organic chemistry and pesticide industries.[110] Recent reports enforce the observation that patents are not among the major mechanisms of appropriation in many industries.[111] Generally industry is shown to put a higher value on business strategies such as being first with an innovation and exploiting a lead-time, secrecy, sales and service efforts, and manufacturing capabilities, than it does on patents.[112] Patents seem to be important value-adders, for example, in blocking competitors or inducing negotiations for (often royalty-free) cross-licences, but only a minority of firms considers them crucial. Scherer concludes that research in this area shows that the basic incentive for R&D in many industries is not patent protection but competition: 'If you don't keep running on the treadmill, you're going to be thrown off.'[113]

In the light of this, patent protection should not be overestimated as a determinant of R&D and innovation. Nonetheless, R&D and commercialization conditions vary greatly between industries. Long, expensive, sequential research cycles, perhaps contingent on regulatory milestone approvals as in the pharmaceutical industry, naturally significantly reinforce the role of intellectual property rights. Relatively low manufacturing know-how and relatively unimportant first-mover advantages also fortify these property rights.[114] Still, even in industry groups where patents are considered an important mechanism for helping appropriation, such as drugs and medical equipment, other mechanisms were deemed at least as effective.[115]

---

110 Federal Trade Commission, *Anticipating the 21st Century, Competition Policy in the New High-Tech, Global Marketplace*, Staff Report, 1996, Volume 1, Chapter 6, pp. 6f., referring to Levin, Richard C. *et al.*, 'Appropriating the Returns from Industrial R&D', *Brookings Papers on Economic Activity*, 3, 783, 795f. (1987).

111 Cohen, Wesley M., Nelson, Richard R. & Walsh, John P., 'Protecting Their Intellectual Assets: Appropriability Conditions and Why U.S. Manufacturing Firms Patent (or Not)', *NBER Working Paper,* no. 7552 (2000), available at http://papers.nber.org/papers/W7552.pdf (last visited 3 March 2005).

112 Cohen, Wesley M. & Levin, Richard C. 'Empirical Suggestions of Innovation and Market Structure', in: Schmalensee, Richard & Willig, Robert D. (eds), *Handbook of Industrial Organization,* North-Holland, Amsterdam, 1989, pp. 1059, 1092f.

113 Federal Trade Commission, *supra*, note 110, Volume 1, Chapter 6, p. 8.

114 See Gutterman, Alan S., *Innovation and Competition Policy: A Comparative Study of the Regulation of Patent Licensing and Collaborative Research & Development in the United States and the European Community*, Kluwer Law International, London, 1997, pp. 42f.

115 Cohen et al., *supra*, note 111.

Technology trading

Technology markets, where intellectual property is traded through licensing, may alleviate negative effects by limiting foreclosure that is not even in the interest of the IPR owner. This facilitates the commercialization of patents for wider spectra of uses and may prevent broad patent rights locking potential innovators out. Well functioning technology markets may also help overcome the inefficiencies linked to fragmented property rights.

Since it is seen that cutting-edge competences and technologies are internationally and institutionally scattered, patents along with technology markets could facilitate trade in these inputs (technology and knowledge). Incentives to develop these inputs would be spurred and they would be disseminated in the society, thus stimulating further innovation. With disseminated inputs for current and future products, the risk of technological entry barriers that seriously impede market entry could also be diminished.

Where numerous IPR licenses would be needed for any company to develop and market attractive products, patent pools are an often deployed institution. Where patent pools are most significant, covering whole industries, they are often preceded by standard setting, establishing the basic technological rules of the game and allowing for interoperability. In such a situation a patent pool alleviates the anticommons problem that otherwise would easily have impeded the development of products meeting the standard.

Conclusions

Since technological opportunities, the character of innovation and the mechanisms of appropriation vary largely from industry to industry, the general conclusion is that general conclusions do not offer much guidance. All in all, proper R&D incentives require at least some potential competition. In a stable monopoly position, the incentives for R&D are limited. Further, Schumpeter's argument that large firms will have the resources needed for R&D investments is weakened when capital markets can be expected to function well. Nevertheless, innovation also requires mechanisms of appropriation, cooperation and integration. At the same time, multiple sources of R&D could be beneficial to innovation, particularly where it is unknown which innovation strategy will be the most successful one, allowing for the market's trial and error process to choose the winner.

Conditions for market entry are central to any competition analysis. High protection for incumbent firms may naturally reduce competitive pressure and thereby also reduce incentives to keep the innovation trail going. Dominant firms may have an interest in keeping things the way they are. Entry barriers imply some foreclosure of potential entrants to current markets, but they may also stifle the possibility of developing markets or even creating new ones.

The scope of patent protection is likely to spur different kinds of incentives.

Roughly, broad patents are more likely to spur a race to be the first in a new area, by granting a wider area of exclusiveness to the owner. At the same time foreclosure problems arise, not least for parties interested in developing similar technologies, new or improved applications and so on. A narrower patent is likely to stimulate research of a complementary and cumulative nature. Nevertheless, fragmented property rights, particularly if they cover upstream inputs to research and product development may create substantial coordination problems and blocks. Regardless of such patent law choices, well-functioning technology markets tend to lessen the negative consequences.

Summing up the discussion, it seems that '[w]hat is needed for rapid technical progress is a subtle blend of competition and monopoly with more emphasis on the former than the latter, and with the role of monopolistic elements diminishing when rich technological opportunities exist'.[116]

2.4 IMPLICATIONS FOR ANTITRUST POLICY

2.4.1 The Harvard School and the SCP Paradigm

The first framework of economic theory with real impact on antitrust policy came in the 1950s with the so-called 'Harvard School'. It was within this school that Joe S. Bain introduced the Structure–Conduct–Performance (SCP) paradigm.[117] In this, causation runs from structure to conduct to performance. Structural conditions such as concentration, technology and preference structures determine the conduct of the market participants, such as decisions on prices, R&D and advertising. These decisions determine the performance of the market, measured in different ways, such as consumer benefits, employment, price stability and technological advancement. Government policy at large, including antitrust laws, regulations, taxes and so on, which affects conditions on the market, consequently affects industry performance.[118] The main challenge facing the theory was to determine the more exact relationships between market structure and market performance in order to figure out what structures were most favourable to society. Through the years numerous empirical studies were conducted. When analysing performance, quantifiable static variables (profits and consumer surplus) were addressed through

116 Scherer & Ross, *supra*, note 87, p. 660.

117 See Bain, J.S., *Barriers to New Competition*, Harvard University Press, Cambridge, 1956, see also Mason, Edward S., 'Price and Production Policies of Large Scale Enterprises', 29 *American Economic Review* 61 (1949). The SCP paradigm is often referred to as the origin of industrial economics.

118 Van Cayseele & Van den Bergh, *supra*, note 37, p. 485.

measurement of the rate of return and price–cost margins (differences between price and marginal cost). In the end conclusions were linked to market structures such as four-firm concentration ratios (CR4), eight-firm concentration ratios (CR8) or the Herfindal–Hirschman Index (HHI). The role of the authorities was consequently to preserve a market structure giving rise to workable competition and they were granted substantial discretion in determining and enforcing that ambition.

Many of these notions still appear in competition law, at least to the extent that concentration ratios constitute prima facie evidence of market power, defined as the power to raise prices and decrease output. This also creates a link to the model of perfect competition. Concerning European enforcement, it has been noted that '[t]he influence of the perfect competition model on competition policy is reflected in the competition authorities' strong focus on market shares (rather than barriers to entry) and their support for small and medium-sized firms'.[119]

2.4.2 The Chicago School and Efficiency Orientation

The SCP paradigm was reversed in what later came to be called the Chicago School.[120] The Chicagoans hold that conduct and performance determine market structure. The approach is a reappraisal of price theory, and it uses microeconomic tools to create a valid economic theory. It intends to do more than merely explain empirical statistics. The static approach of the Harvard School is replaced by the more dynamically oriented view that the rational conduct of a firm, inherent in profit maximization, will be competitive and may make markets correct their own failures. According to the Chicago School, the objective of the authorities is limited to productive and allocative efficiency, and competition policy should consequently not hamper profit maximization but only proscribe inefficient conduct which alone harms consumer welfare.

Many of the empirical studies on which the Harvard School relied were criticized; in particular, the correlation between profits and concentration was distrusted. Furthermore, even if such correlation could be shown, it ignored the question of the origin of concentration and the profit rate. In the Chicago view, concentration is usually the result of superior efficiency. The winners on the markets are the most efficient firms, which thus grow more rapidly, get

[119] Ahlborn, Christian, Evans, David S. & Padilla, Atilano Jorge, 'Competition Policy in the New Economy', 22 *European Competition Law Review* 156, 160 footnote 27 (2001).

[120] See Bork, *supra*, note 3. This frequently quoted work offers a comprehensive overview of the Chicago School doctrine.

larger market shares and make high profits. Concentration is not a problem, it is only monopoly or cartelization, that is, collusive price increases and output restrictions, that should be a concern.

In the new line of thought, it was claimed that many restrictive practices, such as exclusive distribution and resale price maintenance, could be efficient answers to market failures, such as free-riding. In the Chicago approach, vertical restraints are presumed to be competitive improvements of distribution and hardly ever anti-competitive. Predation is not seen as a major antitrust problem, since it will only rarely be profitable. Normally, the predator would simply benefit consumers if he engaged in sales below costs and would have little chance of recouping the losses incurred.

The Chicago School did not only confine the raison d'être of antitrust law to efficiency. It also defined the efficiency goal negatively, only condemning conduct that would be proved inefficient by giving rise to artificial price increases and output limitations. Taken together with a presumption that markets work well and are more reliable than individuals (thereby stressing the risk of inefficiencies from public decisions), the scope for intervention was effectively narrowed.[121]

The Chicago School has had a great impact on American antitrust execution from the early 1980s, when antitrust theory was revolutionized, above all in merger control and the treatment of vertical restraints. A strong faith in the market and a notion that public market intervention often does more harm than good coincided with political conservatism in the Reagan administration. Nevertheless, in European competition policy too, the reception of Chicago thinking is noticeable, particularly in the revised policy on vertical arrangements.

The pure version of static analysis has been updated and supplemented with doctrines of potential competition and entry analysis, adding more long-term aspects to the antitrust framework. However, while the Chicago School acknowledges that consumer welfare consists partly of technological progress, for antitrust purposes the welfare orientation is oriented towards allocative efficiency. Innovation activities are largely ignored, or they are presumed to have some pro-competitive end since the competitive market will sort out inefficient conduct.[122] As technological progress requires the use of resources and we cannot measure the willingness to pay (the price) for progress, we consequently

---

121 Fox, Eleanor M. 'Post-Chicago, Post-Seattle and the Dilemma of Globalization', in Cucinotta, Antonio, Pardolesi, Roberto & Van den Bergh, Roger (eds), *Post-Chicago Developments in Antitrust Law*, Edward Elgar, Cheltenham, 2002, p. 78.

122 Flynn, John J., 'Antitrust Policy, Innovation Efficiencies, and the Suppression of Technology', 66 *Antitrust Law Journal* 487, 493 (1998).

do not know the 'proper' rate of progress. Hence technological progress should not be an independent goal for antitrust, and should not be given weight as such in antitrust analysis.[123]

2.4.3 Post-Chicago Developments

Thanks to the theoretical and judicial revolution created by the Chicago School, research in various fields has been stimulated. This has spurred the development of a range of theories in the post-Chicago era. For example, recent theories of industrial organization further enforce the more nuanced view of vertical and horizontal restraints, implying that integration is only problematic where the market structure in the specific case would support strategic behaviour.[124] A more robust theory of industrial organization has thus been developed. In the 'new' industrial organization theory, it is understood that the causational flows are not unidirectional (SPC paradigm) and that structure and conduct affect one another. Firms do not merely act in response to external conditions, they also try to act strategically in order to shape their environment, to modify market structures and their competitors' conduct.[125] Consequently, new industrial organization theory uses game theory extensively and has also developed an understanding of the endogenous forces affecting market concentration.[126] It is realized that the strategic actions of market participants may affect market structure through creation of entry barriers, changes in technology and so on. The consideration of such qualitative aspects has reinforced competition policy notions that measurement of (relative) market shares cannot be equated with market power or even dominance, above all not without analysis of potential competition.

The Chicago theory has been exposed to criticism, primarily aimed at its underlying theoretical assumptions. The conclusions derived from formal microeconomic theory have been taken to task for not fully appreciating the effects of practices in the real world. For example, relaxing the common microeconomic assumption of perfect information, it becomes important to model approaches that can handle and distinguish cases of incomplete and asymmetric information. If, furthermore, one acknowledges that corporate

---

123 Bork, *supra*, note 3, p. 132.

124 See Williamson, Oliver E., 'Antitrust Policy', in *The New Palgrave – A directory of Economics,* Stockton Press, New York, 1987; Tirole, Jean, *The Theory of Industrial Organization,* MIT Press, Cambridge, Mass., 1988; Viscusi *et al.*, *supra*, note 36.

125 Jacquemin, Alexis, *Theories of Industrial Organisation and Competition Policy: What are the Links?*, working paper, European Commission, Forward Studies Unit, 2000, p. 11.

126 Audretsch et al., *supra*, note 98, pp. 613f.

conduct does not necessarily aim simply at maximized profits in the short run, and relaxes assumptions of perfect capital markets, the scope for various predatory behaviours is significantly extended.[127]

Moreover, as underlying market structures and competition strategies develop, market analysts are forced to develop their analytical tools. With markets becoming more complex, as a result of geographical expansion, technological development, inter-firm alliances and other governance structures, new thinking and analysis is needed to provide more accurate results.

Relevant areas where post-Chicago thinking has made appreciable contributions include analysis of the unilateral effects of horizontal mergers and the scope for anti-competitive foreclosure. The latter typically involves a dominant firm refusing access or charging a higher price to some actual or potential competitor. When a clearly dominant firm evidently raises its rivals' costs, there is a normative suggestion that, in non-marginal cases, inquiry into possible business justifications should be made. If, on the other hand, the foreclosure is small, alternatives can be developed or, if the practice results in substantial efficiencies, the judiciary should favour non-liability.[128]

US merger control has traditionally focused on the prevention of post-merger problems of collusion or oligopoly. The treatment of unilateral effects where, post-merger, a firm will be able to raise prices or otherwise behave inefficiently, has however been described as one of the more useable and robust contributions of the post-Chicago development.[129] This is a less revolutionary thought in EU merger control (albeit not based on the same economic foundations). Mergers between sellers of differentiated products may be particularly sensitive, but in other contexts too, evidence of market power may trump inferences from market share statistics. Also

---

127 Disner, Eliot G. 'The Chicago School Meets the Real World', 25-Mar *Los Angeles Lawyer* 14 (2002). Disner refers to the 'Silicon Valley School', personified by a former congressman representing the Silicon Area of California, Tom Campbell, a PhD from the University of Chicago, now a Stanford professor. Campbell was the director of the FTC's Bureau of Competition during the Reagan era and has been one of the strongest proponents of the Chicago approach. Having met frequently the countless small high-tech firms in his constituency, he has changed his attitude, particularly towards predatory behaviour, realizing the problem is real and significant. He has publicly stated his support for governmental action in a recent predation case (*United States v. AMR Corporation*) and also indicated that today he might have decided a specific predation case (*Business Electronics*) from his time at the FTC differently.

128 Hovenkamp, Herbert, 'The Reckoning of Post-Chicago Antitrust', in Cucinotta, Antonio, Pardolesi, Roberto & Van den Bergh, Roger (eds), *Post-Chicago Developments in Antitrust Law*, Edward Elgar, Cheltenham, 2002, pp. 16f.

129 Ibid., p. 20.

the innovation market concept itself may be attributed to this expanded line of analysis.[130]

Post-Chicago developments can be traced in American case law. Often highlighted, and criticized, decisions indicating such a development include the 1992 Supreme Court judgment in *Kodak*[131] where the Court accepted a theory of 'installed base opportunism' whereby Kodak could possibly charge monopoly prices in the market for spare parts, without being dominant in the market for photocopiers. Among other things the Court pointed to the possibility that customers, when purchasing photocopiers, were unable to calculate and compare long-term costs including future spare parts and risked being locked in later on. The Court thus dismissed the assumption that customers are always sufficiently well informed. Other cases in this category include affirming exclusionary practices in vertical settings such as in *Microsoft*[132] and *Intel*.[133] Still, agency representatives of the current administration have aired some disgruntlement with these cases.[134]

In Europe, where the reception of Chicago School thinking has been less dramatic, it is harder to ascribe developments in case law to a post-Chicago trend. Nevertheless, since post-Chicago theories are prepared to relax theoretical microeconomic assumptions when they seem to be contradicted in practice (alternatively, they work with a more complex set of assumptions) and extend the welfare criterion beyond allocative efficiencies, thereby extending the range of anti-competitive outcomes, post-Chicago thinking seems more

---

130 Baker, Jonathan B., 'A Preface to Post-Chicago Antitrust', in Cucinotta, Antonio, Pardolesi, Roberto & Van den Bergh, Roger (eds), *Post-Chicago Developments in Antitrust Law*, Edward Elgar, Cheltenham, 2002, p. 70. The legal and economic principles behind this concept, and the continued debate and criticism thereof, will be handled in Chapter 3.

131 *Eastman Kodak Co. v. Image Technical Services*, 504 U.S. 451 (1992).

132 *United States v. Microsoft*, 253 F.3d 34 (D.C. Cir., en banc), cert. denied, 534 U.S. 952 (2001).

133 *Intel Corporation*, Docket No. 9288 (1999). Both cases will be analysed later on. For further discussion and case references on the reception of post-Chicago thinking, see Fox, *supra*, note 121; Hovenkamp, *supra*, note 128; Lopatka, John E. & Page, William H., ' "Obvious" Consumer Harm in Antitrust Policy: the Chicago School, the Post-Chicago School and the Courts', in Cucinotta, Antonio, Pardolesi, Roberto & Van den Bergh, Roger (eds), *Post-Chicago Developments in Antitrust Law*, Edward Elgar, Cheltenham, 2002.

134 Regarding the Intel case see Muris, Timothy J., 'The FTC and the Law of Monopolization' 67 *Antitrust Law Journal* 693, 718 (2000); and regarding Microsoft: Pate, Hewitt R., *Antitrust in a Transatlantic Context – From The Cicada's Perspective*, address at 'Antitrust in a Transatlantic Context' Conference, Brussels, Belgium, 7 June 2004; available at http://www.usdoj.gov/atr/public/speeches/203973.pdf (last visited 11 October 2004).

readily acceptable to EU competition policy as executed by the Commission and the community courts.

While recognizing that antitrust law to a large extent remains within the realm of Chicagoan thinking and that the post-Chicago criticism is largely 'internal',[135] much seems to favour making use of the advances in the field, including industrial organization (including game theory and transaction cost economics) when discussing antitrust analysis of structures outside traditional markets and perceptions and conduct associated with competitive means other than price setting. Modern industrial organization theorists, just like many economists in other fields, emphasize dynamics both for competition and for consumer welfare. This could unite the theoretical achievements of the Chicago approach with current real world observations and analytical developments. Consumer welfare is the ultimate aim of antitrust policy, and competition in the innovation process a central process by which it is achieved.

Yet it should be borne in mind that, even if economic thinking leads to new insights, more complex economics and more complex market analysis make antitrust law messier.[136] It is relevant to ask what economic insights are transformable into appropriate constructive policy. Alternatively, is a benign simplified version (based on Chicago School orthodox thinking) necessarily a second best choice? Application of a more detailed theory by authorities and courts may be burdensome and lead to increased unpredictability, opaqueness and erroneousness.[137] If one thing is certain, it is that substantial legal uncertainty does not favour efficient markets.

On the other hand, simplifications with reference to legal certainty may give rise to false impressions, misleading certainty. It has been pointed out that a preference for seemingly 'simple rules', such as the use of market shares to create safe harbours, often veils inherent problems, such as the paramount importance of correctly determining the relevant market in the first place.[138]

---

135 Baker, *supra*, note 130, p. 70.

136 Hovenkamp, *supra*, note 128, p. 5.

137 'So the test for a post-Chicago economic model is not merely whether it discovers an anticompetitive strategy that Chicago School theory had not. Policy makers must also be able to devise rules that will recognize such strategies without an unacceptably high incidence of false positives, and then produce remedies that are not more socially costly that the evils they correct. Measured by this test, post-Chicago economics has had only limited success' (Hovenkamp, *supra*, note 128, p. 21).

138 Van den Bergh, Roger, 'The Difficult Reception of Economic Analysis in European Competition Law', in Cucinotta, Antonio, Pardolesi, Roberto & Van den Bergh, Roger (eds), *Post-Chicago Developments in Antitrust Law*, Edward Elgar, Cheltenham, 2002, pp. 46 *et seq.*

2.4.4 Competition Policy and Innovation Industries

From a practical point of view, the execution of antitrust law lies in the handling of individual situations. There has been lively discussion regarding the appropriateness of applying antitrust laws to dynamic industries where innovation is at the centre. The Microsoft case highlighted differences among commentators in the view of competition law and the role of the authorities. Regardless of diverging opinions in specific cases and different perspectives on the general level of public intervention, there seems to be strong support, among both economists and antitrust lawyers, for continued antitrust enforcement along well-established basic frameworks and principles.[139]

In the *Microsoft* case the Court of Appeals (D.C. Cir. 2001) addressed the difficulties posed by innovative markets.[140] On the theoretical level, regarding the application of old doctrines to firms competing in dynamic technological markets, the court found no consensus among commentators whether and to what extent the monopolization doctrine should be amended.[141] Confronted with Microsoft's suggestion that monopoly power in software industry should be supported by direct evidence (such as low R&D investments and high prices) rather than market structure, the court decided that it was correct to apply a structural approach (including entry analysis) in order to determine the competition the company faced in the short term.[142] As to the practical difficulties faced in this kind of case the court noted:[143]

> By the time a court can assess liability, firms, products and the marketplace are likely to have changed dramatically. This, in turn, threatens enormous practical difficulties for courts considering the appropriate measure of relief in equitable enforcement actions, both in crafting injunctive remedies in the first instance and reviewing those remedies in the second. Conduct remedies may be unavailing in such cases, because innovation to a large degree has already rendered the anti-competitive conduct obsolete (although by no means harmless).
>
> We do not mean to say that enforcement actions will no longer play an important role in curbing infringements of the antitrust laws in technologically dynamic markets, nor do we assume this in assessing the merits of this case. Even in those cases where forward-looking remedies appear limited, the Government will

---

139 See, for example, OFT, *Innovation and Competition policy*, Economic Discussion Paper 3, Report prepared for the Office of Fair Trading by Charles River Associates, 2002, pp. 59 *et seq.*, 137 *et seq.* presenting a survey of renowned commentators representing different perspectives of antitrust theory.

140 *United States v. Microsoft*, 253 F.3d 34 (D.C. Cir., en banc), cert. denied, 534 U.S. 952 (2001).

141 253 F.3d 34, 49.

142 253 F.3d 34, 56f. This thus without prejudice to the subsequent analysis of whether the various investigated practices in the market in fact were anti-competitive.

143 253 F.3d 34, 49.

> continue to have an interest in defining the contours of the antitrust laws so that law-abiding firms will have a clear sense of what is permissible and what is not. And the threat of private damage actions will remain to deter those firms inclined to test the limits of the law. In technologically dynamic markets, however, such entrenchment may be temporary, because innovation may alter the field altogether.

Commentators frequently point out that antitrust analysis must be tailored to the situations in which it is applied. Changing underlying market structures and technological environments combined with new ways for firms to affect structure and performance suggest that the traditional concepts must also be developed and adapted to new situations.

Very high sunk costs and low marginal costs generally imply highly concentrated markets, with price discrimination and high margins to recover the sunk costs. It is essential that these effects of the cost structure in the market are interpreted correctly, particularly since the antitrust authorities are traditionally concerned with all the three characteristics.[144] Since the driving motor of many innovative markets is the prospect of large market shares and high profits, it is important that industries and transactions are analysed on a case-by-case basis. If the process of achieving these positions and profits is open and competitive and if no artificial barriers are created to prevent or deter potential contestants, competition authorities should rely on market forces.

Conversely, for the dynamic process to work there is need for competition on the merits. Schumpeter relies on the potential entrant with a superior product or organization. The role of the antitrust authorities would then be to take action against strategic behaviour which aims at controlling the process or excluding possibilities for potentially superior competitors. Antitrust authority officials have also highlighted this:

> The most obvious criticism of antitrust enforcement as applied to high-tech industries starts with the notion that these are fast-moving industries in which today's technology is quickly outmoded, opening the way for new competitors to overturn the dominance of incumbents. If those generalizations were uniformly true of high-tech markets, then surely antitrust enforcement would be less important. . . . Of course, experience shows that this caricature of high-tech markets is true in some cases and false in others. For example, even in an innovation-driven market, dominance in one generation may enable a firm to gain exclusive control over critical inputs, such as software applications, allowing monopoly power to be carried over from generation to generation regardless of the relative superiority or inferiority of the incumbent's later generation products. In addition, large sunk costs, high risks, and other entry barriers may mean that while product characteristics change rapidly, the identity of the dominant players may be unchanging for long periods of time. . . . Regulatory barriers, as in the need for FDA approval of pharmaceuticals, may

---

144 OFT, *supra*, note 139, p. 3.

> mean that new entrants arrive only very slowly regardless of the sophistication of the underlying technology. And, of course, patents or other intellectual property may play a role – not as something for antitrust to condemn, but as a fact of life in a particular market, like economies of scale or large sunk costs, that makes entry unlikely, slow, or insufficient.[145] (Footnotes omitted)

The static framework of analysis, regarding both market definition and market share analysis, will not solve the issue of market power by itself. Analysis of dynamic competition requires evidence of investment patterns in the development of new products, the control of critical assets and the beliefs of the participants and informed observers about the nature and pace of innovation and so on.[146] In the newer theory it is recognized that firm capabilities are central and that market performance is as much influenced by variations in the abilities of firms to exploit profit opportunities as it is by variations in the availability of profit opportunities.[147]

Where competition largely takes place *for* the market, concentration will occur. From an antitrust perspective, the interesting question is whether a transaction, such as a merger, will change the identity of the winner of the market battle to the detriment of consumers, or is likely to slow down the timing of innovation or significantly reduce incentives to innovate.[148] It has also been noted that for many markets a test of whether competition will be substantially lessened may be better than focusing on 'dominance', since the market may be dominated by one company anyway. For mergers in the new economy, the argument continues, the question is whether a merger will strengthen or weaken competition in the process of determining the dominant firm.[149]

Issues related to intellectual property appear frequently in the innovation context. Various market arrangements will reduce blocking effects, allow combination of complementary assets, and achieve synergies and other forms of efficiencies. Against this, IPR strategies include various means of coordination between competitors, of monopolization and of deterrence.

Former DOJ-officials Gilbert and Tom note that, despite substantial differences between intellectual property and other forms of property, the authorities have declared that they are, for antitrust analysis, essentially comparable. They continue, '[o]ne might expect the agencies to take a similar approach to

145 Baer, William J. & Balto, David A., 'Antitrust Enforcement and High-Technology Markets', 5 *Michigan Telecommunication Technology Law Review* 73, 75 (2001).

146 Evans & Schmalensee, *supra*, note 95, p. 47.

147 Audretsch *et al.*, *supra*, note 98, p. 623.

148 OFT, *supra*, note 139, p. 7.

149 Ibid.

whether antitrust should be different in high-technology markets: to treat competitive markets as generally conducive to innovation and to deal with factors, such as technological change, high fixed costs, knowledge spillovers, and network effects on a case-by-case basis, rather than through the broad generalizations either of the Schumpeterian hypothesis or of the arguments for stricter scrutiny.'[150]

Meanwhile, competition law analysis needs to be transparent and predictable so that market participants can organize their business efficiently and have the confidence to cooperate and invest. This is particularly important in a regime where substantial responsibility is put on market actors to assess the legality of their own practices.

Finally, the perception that the traditional antitrust framework should also be applied to innovation-intense markets, albeit with appropriate customization, has also been highlighted by an OECD roundtable discussion in June 2002. The need for customization was particularly noted for 'defining markets and assigning market shares; assessing the significance of changes in market structure; giving proper weight to benefits consumers reap through innovation; assessing the ability of merging parties to exclude or restrict competitors; and designing appropriate remedies'.[151]

The remainder of this book is devoted to analysing the transformation of this theory into practice.

---

[150] Gilbert, Richard J. & Tom, Willard K., 'Is Innovation King at the Antitrust Agencies? The Intellectual Property Guidelines Five Years Later', 69 *Antitrust Law Journal* 43, 47 (2001).

[151] OECD, *Merger Review in Emerging New Innovation Markets*, Paris, 2003, p. 8.

3. Policy developments

3.1 INTRODUCTION

This chapter will describe the general development of a dynamic view of antitrust law analysis in the US and the EU. Significant early antitrust case law is presented where courts have been active in emphasizing, and possibly assessing, future market developments. Sometimes the terms under which new products and processes are created and the availability to market participants of new technologies had to be considered, since this seriously affects the level and nature of competition. The case law presented gives only a sketchy outline of the area under investigation: competition in the innovation process. Regulations and policy documents are next discussed; these further elaborate on market definition issues with regard to R&D and technology dimensions of competition law analysis. Through such instruments, analytical frameworks have evolved in which innovation constitutes a central element for antitrust analysis. The emphasis throughout is on the innovation market concept, but product and technology market issues are also covered.

3.2 DYNAMIC ANTITRUST ASSESSMENT

3.2.1 Present and Future Market Conditions

Formally, US antitrust policy has never been confined to merely assessing the instantaneous effects of a transaction on current markets. In *FTC v. Procter & Gamble Co.*,[1] the Supreme Court held that the standard of Section 7 of the Clayton Act – testing whether a merger might substantially lessen competition – requires 'a prediction of the merger's impact on competition, present and future'.[2]

---

1 *Federal Trade Commission v. Procter & Gamble Co.*, 386 U.S. 568 (1967).

2 The Supreme Court furthermore stated: 'Section 7 of the Clayton Act was intended to arrest the anticompetitive effects of market power in their incipiency. The core question is whether a merger may substantially lessen competition, and necessarily requires a prediction of the merger's impact on competition, present and future. [. . .] The section can deal only with probabilities, not with certainties. [. . .] And there

Later, in *United States v. General Dynamics Corp.*,[3] the government challenged a merger between two coal producers, based on statistical evidence supporting 'undue concentration'. The Supreme Court held, however, that the District Court was justified in its finding that other pertinent factors affecting the industry and the specific firms mandated a conclusion that no substantial lessening of competition occurred or was threatened. In the particular case, changes in the coal industry since World War II were highlighted. The analysis included, among other things, how coal was increasingly sold on long-term requirement contracts, under which coal producers promised to meet the requirements for a specific period of time and at predetermined prices. This significantly limited the availability of 'spot' purchases on the open market. As the specific producer's coal reserve prospects were 'unpromising', past production was of little significance and the acquired firm was a far less significant factor in the coal market than the Government contended or the statistics seemed to indicate.[4]

In line with this and other cases, courts and agencies implementing antitrust law moved away from a merely static policy to reviewing whether the transaction (often a merger) would reduce future competition in a relevant market, analysing likely effects on entry, prices, quality and so on and whether these effects might be outweighed by efficiencies.[5] Hence market shares may be indicators of market power 'but only a further examination of the particular market – its structure, history and probable future – can provide the appropriate setting for judging the probable anti-competitive effect'.[6] In *United States v. Siemens Corp.*,[7] it was concluded that the market concentration ratio or percentages may not accurately depict the economic characteristics of competition in relatively new, volatile and competitive markets. Conversely, if current market shares alone do not suggest anti-

---

is certainly no requirement that the anticompetitive power manifest itself in anticompetitive action before 7 can be called into play. If the enforcement of 7 turned on the existence of actual anticompetitive practices, the congressional policy of thwarting such practices in their incipiency would be frustrated', 386 U.S. 568, 577.

3 *United States v. General Dynamics Corp.*, 415 U.S. 486 (1974).

4 415 U.S. 486, 489–503.

5 Dahdouh, Thomas N. & Mongoven, James F., 'The Shape of Things to Come: Innovation Market Analysis in Merger Cases', 64 *Antitrust Law Journal* 405 (1996).

6 *Brown Shoe Co. v. United States,* 370 U.S. 294, 322 n. 38 (1962).

7 *United States v. Siemens Corp.*, 621 F.2d 499, 506 (2d Cir. 1980) referring to *United States v. Black & Decker Mfg*, 430 F.Supp. 729 (D.Md. 1976). See also Gutterman, Alan S., *Innovation and Competition Policy: A Comparative Study of the Regulation of Patent Licensing and Collaborative Research & Development in the United States and the European Community,* Kluwer Law International, London, 1997, p. 335.

competitive effects, the analysis may have to go on to include other, future-oriented factors.[8]

The inclusion of these dynamic aspects is also part of European Competition Law. Market shares are seen as an important starting point in assessing dominance and market power, but must be supplemented by other aspects.[9] In a result similar to the outcome of *US v. General Dynamics Corp.*,[10] the European Commission cleared the *ABB/BREL* merger, focusing on the 'degree of competition likely to exist for future contracts', without paying too much attention to current market shares. In this case, market shares in the market for locomotives and rolling stock fluctuated wildly from year to year as a small number of manufacturers competed for a few high value contracts.[11]

Although a market share exceeding 40 per cent of the relevant market is regarded as an indication of a dominant position, not only the market position of other competitors but also conditions for entry in the market may affect the assessment.[12] In *Tetra Pak/Alfa Laval*, a market share of 90 per cent was a 'very strong indicator' of a dominant position, but the Commission noted that in 'certain rare circumstances' such a market share does not necessarily result in dominance. Particularly low entry barriers, combined with a heterogeneous market character with growth, innovation and technological change, may result in market shares providing no indication of market power.[13] In *Mannesmann/Hoesch*, the Commission concluded that high market shares represented 'an important factor as evidence of a dominant position provided they not only reflect current conditions but are also a reliable indicator of future conditions'.[14]

3.2.2 Potential Competition

> It must also be stressed that the examination of conditions of competition is based not only on existing competition between undertakings already present on the rele-

8 See however *SCM Corp. v. Xerox Corp.*, 645 F.2d 1195 (2d Cir. 1981), where the court would not impose liability for patent acquisitions if the relevant product market did not exist at the time of the acquisitions. The judgement has been criticized for focusing on the wrong question, see e.g. Tom, Willard K., 'The 1975 Xerox Consent Decree: Ancient Artifacts and Current Tensions', 68 *Antitrust Law Journal* 967, 976 (2001).

9 See e.g. European Commission, *Tenth Report on Competition Policy*, 1981.

10 *United States v. General Dynamics Corp.*, 415 U.S. 486 (1974).

11 Case No IV/M.221 – *ABB/BREL*, OJ C 142 (1992).

12 See European Commission, *supra*, note 9, §150.

13 Case No IV/M.68 – *Tetra Pak/Alfa Laval*, OJ L 290/35 (1991). Cook, C.J. & Kerse, C.S., *E.C. Merger Control*, 3rd edn, Sweet & Maxwell, London, 2000, p. 153.

14 Case No IV/M.222 – *Mannesmann/Hoesch*, OJ L 114/34 (1992), §61.

> vant market but also on potential competition, in order to ascertain whether, in the light of the structure of the market and the economic and legal context within which it functions, there are real concrete possibilities for the undertakings concerned to compete among themselves or for a new competitor to penetrate the relevant market and compete with the undertakings already established.[15]

In the light of these remarks by the Court of First Instance, it is clear that theories that focus on potential competition are useful in analysing both immediate and near-future competition effects. It needs to be assessed whether parties to an agreement or practice, even though not currently competing on a product market, could become competitors on that market and whether the integration negatively affects that potential. The future state of competition in the market may thereby be altered. Moreover, potential competitors often play an important role in preventing inefficient conduct by incumbent firms. Sometimes the threat of entry only has to be latent in order to discipline markets.

Particularly under US antitrust law, it is therefore appropriate to distinguish between an actual potential competition theory and a perceived potential competition theory. If, for example, an incumbent firm merges with a firm that, absent the merger, would have entered the market, either de novo or through a smaller – toehold – acquisition, this might lessen actual potential competition. In order to have an anti-competitive effect 'the market would have to pose sufficient anti-competitive proclivities and have a sufficient shortage of potential entrants such that the loss of an opportunity to enhance competition would be worrisome'.[16] In other words, in our merger case, the US Agencies would have to show (1) a highly concentrated market, (2) difficult entry, (3) the proposed merger between an incumbent firm and a company which would, but for the acquisition, have entered the market as a competitor in the near future.[17]

For a perceived potential competition case it must be shown that, in addition to a highly concentrated market, the non-incumbent company is (1) perceived by incumbent firms as a potential independent entrant, and (2) has had a tempering effect on the competitive conduct of incumbent firms.[18]

Assessing the level of potential competition in a market naturally involves

---

[15] Joined Cases T-374/94, T-375/94, T-384/94 and T-388/94, *European Night Services v. Commission*, ECR II-3141 (1998), §137.

[16] Areeda, Philip & Kaplow, Louis, *Antitrust Analysis: Problems, Texts, Cases*, 5th edn, Aspen Law & Business, New York, 1997, p. 881.

[17] See *Bendix Corp.*, Docket no. 8739 (1970).

[18] See e.g. Hoerner, Robert J. 'Innovation Markets: New Wine in Old Bottles?', 64 *Antitrust Law Journal* 49, 56 (1995); *United States v. Falstaff Brewing Corp.*, 410 U.S. 526 (1973).

analysing the conditions for entry onto the market in terms of motivations and barriers. The prospect of entry may save a transaction that otherwise would have been considered restrictive of competition, if current market participants are thereby denied the incentives and abilities to exercise market power. Incumbent firms may on the other hand have advantages over potential entrants, for example if they have access to resources that are not available to the entrant (perhaps owing to key IPRs or legal restrictions on entry) or strategic advantages from being established (capital requirements, goodwill, brand loyalty, advertising, distribution systems and so on). One may also analyse whether the incumbent firms may act strategically to deter entry (predatory pricing, refusals to supply and so on).[19]

The US authorities will assess whether entry will be timely, likely and sufficient to prevent competitive harm from a merger. It is often considered that entry should be possible within a period of two years if it is to be taken into account when assessing the future effect of a transaction.[20]

As under American law, European law considers whether potential competition might discipline incumbent market actors within a reasonable time period and also whether entry is affected by a certain transaction. Naturally, the analysis of potential future market developments must be substantiated and reasonably certain in order to be accepted. Regarding the time period within which a new entry should be possible in order to discipline incumbent firms, some cases and authority guidelines suggest a two-year period similar to the American standard.[21] However, the European authorities probably do not operate under the same firm rule expressed in the US Merger Guidelines.

3.2.3 R&D and Technology Issues

Closely related to potential competition and entry conditions are conditions relating to development of new products and processes and availability to the market participants of relevant technologies. Innovation and technology licensing aspects are often decisive for firms' abilities to compete successfully, whether being already present on the market or a potential entrant. In R&D intense industries in particular parties may, through mergers, joint ventures, licensing arrangements or unilateral behaviour, affect competitive conditions in relation to R&D and licensing. By limiting or controlling competition in

---

19 Cook & Kerse, *supra*, note 13, pp. 159f.

20 US 1992 Horizontal Merger Guidelines, §3.2.

21 Cook & Kerse, *supra*, note 13, p. 154; Guidelines on the assessment of horizontal mergers under the Council Regulation on the control of concentrations between undertakings, OJ C 31/5 (2004), §§58 *et seq.*, 74; EU Guidelines on Vertical Restraints, OJ C 291/1 (2000), §§26, 126.

R&D or between competing technologies, long-term competition in the market may be diminished.

In *FTC v. PPG Industries*[22] the FTC contested the merger between two competitors in the 'high-tech' market for aircraft transparencies which would leave only two major actors in that market. PPG was the world's largest producer of *glass* aircraft transparencies (windows, windshields and canopies) whereas Swedlow was the largest *acrylic* aircraft transparencies producer. PPG and Swedlow maintained that they did not compete, because their businesses were largely complementary. But the evidence suggested that they in fact were competitors. Swedlow and PPG had already been invited to compete for orders and PPG officials testified that neither glass nor acrylic technology alone would be able to meet the demands of the near future. The Court concluded that competition between PPG and Swedlow existed 'not only in bidding but at the proposal stage when airframe designers receive proposals from manufacturers offering different materials and at the stage of research and development as transparency manufacturers try to influence airframe customers about types of transparencies for future generations of aircraft'.[23]

It was impossible to calculate market shares and HHI[24] for the high technology market since that market was growing rapidly and market shares would depend on the future success of the companies in the upcoming biddings. However the court noted that there before the merger appeared to be only three fully capable firms, which indicated that the HHI would be very high. The Court of Appeals (Judge Bork) granted the FTC's request for preliminary injunction.

Regarding competition, inter-firm collaboration and R&D, both the US Agencies and the European Commission have taken a fairly favourable view of such operations. The European Commission in 1968 issued a notice[25] where it was declared that pure research and development cooperation generally do not restrict competition, particularly if the parties remain free to pursue their own R&D and there are no restrictions regarding the use of the results.

In *Eurogypsum*[26] appearing at the same time as the notice, the Commission approved industry-wide research that was performed by a trade association in the plaster and gypsum industry. Important to this case was that all results were available to all members, the members remained free to carry out their own R&D, there were no discriminatory conditions restraining entry to the

---

22 *Federal Trade Commission v. PPG Industries, Inc.*, 789 F.2d 1500 (D.C. Cir. 1986) (Bork, J.)

23 Ibid., p. 1505.

24 The Herfindahl–Hirschman Index (HHI) is used to measure market concentration, and is calculated by summing the squares of the market shares held by the respective firms. For example, an industry consisting of two firms with market shares of 70 per cent and 30 per cent has an HHI of $70^2 + 30^2$, or 5800.

25 Notice concerning agreements, decisions and concerted practices in the field of cooperation between enterprises, OJ C 75/3 (1968).

26 Case No IV/26352 – *Eurogypsum* OJ L 57/9 (1968), CMLR. D1 [1968].

association and the results were published widely.[27] However, in *Henkel/Colgate*,[28] the Commission held that Article 81(1) could apply to a more narrowly based R&D collaboration. In the specific case, the two parties had a strong position on an oligopolistic market with great technological homogeneity and large entry barriers (particularly 'intensive and costly advertising'). Possible market expansion was dependent on successful innovation, making 'competition in the field of research extremely important'.[29] The agreement was considered appreciably to restrict such competition between the parties, but the Commission exempted the agreement under 81(3) since it contained no restrictions on access to results, or production and distribution of the products. Also an agreement between an electrical transmission systems producer and a bus manufacturer to make a new type of electrically powered bus was found to restrict competition although the agreement 'was likely to increase the possibility of a useful result being obtained'.[30] Certain ancillary restrictions (particularly a non-compete clause covering the field of the agreement, exclusive supplies of complementary production inputs and limits on the number of buyers of the new electrical propulsion system) were exemptible under Article 81(3).

In a rare case from the US, *United States v. Automobile Mfrs. Ass'n.*,[31] the DOJ challenged an agreement among four car manufacturers and their trade association.

> The firms were collaborating regarding the development of a new pollution control device. The complaint alleged a broad set of horizontal agreements, *inter alia,* restricting the dissemination of information regarding relevant R&D, joint assessment of the value of patent rights on such devices held by third parties, and preventing individual statements towards governmental regulatory agencies with power to issue emission standards or regulations for new cars.[32] The government however alleged that agreement in fact was a conspiracy under §1 of the Sherman Act, which would delay the development, manufacture and installation of this device. The case was settled with a consent decree.
>
> The device had been mandated by the state of California, giving the manufacturers five years to comply. The manufacturers jointly addressed the state declaring the impossibility to develop such a device in the given time. Nevertheless, another

27 European Commission, *First Report on Competition Policy,* 1972, p. 46; Korah, Valentine, *R&D and the EEC competition rules. Regulation 418/85*, ESC, Oxford, 1986, p. 13.

28 Case No IV/26917 – *Henkel/Colgate,* OJ L14/14 (1972); European Commission, *supra*, note 206, p. 47.

29 European Commission, *supra*, note 27, p. 47.

30 Case No IV/23077 – *Acec-Berliet,* OJ L 201/7 (1968). European Commission, *supra*, note 27, pp. 48f.

31 *United States v. Automobile Mfrs. Ass'n*, 307 F.Supp. 617 (C.D. Cal. 1969).

32 See Dahdouh & Mongoven, *supra*, note 5, p. 426.

> manufacturer produced a device within a year and twelve months thereafter, all of the manufacturers had developed and installed similar devices.[33]

This case suggests that R&D collaboration is not always set up in order to speed up innovation or make R&D more efficient in other ways. In this case the parties jointly stalled the development of a particular device. At the same time, it is in a situation where the product development to be undertaken is dictated by public regulation, not by market demand.

3.3 INNOVATION AND TECHNOLOGY IN THE GUIDELINES

Guidelines have become much used by US and EU competition authorities for communicating their outlook on the state of competition policy in different areas. This kind of policy document is a way of summing up recent executive decisions and court rulings, elucidating established methods and principles in contemporary law and providing a methodological framework for antitrust analysis. Yet it is also a way of influencing legal practice, pushing antitrust policy in the desired direction, so that it better reflects the needs of industry and markets, developments in economic thinking, as well as executive preferences of a practical or even a political character.[34] Since the methodologies described have not necessarily been tested and accepted by courts, it may be wise to take a careful attitude in the interpretation of authority guidelines. All the same, guidelines are important for the development and execution of competition policy for a number of reasons. First of all, the authorities only actually review a tiny fraction of all market transactions. In turn, only a fraction of the matters reviewed go to court. The most important effect of competition policy is hence preventive, controlling certain kinds of business behaviour without competition authorities ever being actively involved.

---

[33] Widnell, Nicholas A., 'The Crystal Ball of Innovation Market Analysis in Merger Review: An Appropriate Means of Predicting the Future?', 4 *George Mason Law Review* 369 (1996).

[34] For example, the current FTC chairman Timothy J. Muris, claims the 1968 Merger Guidelines 'took a formative first step toward rationalizing merger policy that faced a danger of becoming completely detached from any sound conception of economics. Though modest in retrospect, [the] self-limiting guidelines were revolutionary when adopted, in part because they refused to push enforcement policy to the limits the courts had established'. *Improving the Economic Foundations of Competition Policy,* Remarks at George Mason University Law Review's Winter Antitrust Symposium, Washington, D.C., 15 January 2003: available at http://www.ftc.gov/speeches/muris/improveconfoundatio.htm (last visited 11 October 2004).

Guidelines are a useful tool for influencing firms' and lawyers' assessments. Moreover, although these policy documents are not binding on the courts, their credibility and importance have grown as courts actually make use of, and even cite, various guidelines.[35] At any rate, they are likely to constrain the authorities by which they have been issued.

One area where guidelines have served to establish notions is in the delimitation of relevant markets. Since the market definition sets the agenda for subsequent analysis, the outcome of the analysis may vary considerably through variations in the way the market is delimited.

A significant, and subsequently well-recognized, development in the method of defining markets came through the US DOJ 1982 Merger Guidelines. The Head of the DOJ Antitrust Division, William Baxter, designed a test for assessing which products in fact compete with each other, that is, whether products may be considered as substitutes for each other, and thereby together constitute a relevant product market (or goods market). According to the test, such a market comprises the product or group of products a hypothetical profit-maximizing monopolist would have to control in order to impose a 'small but significant and nontransitory increase in price' (the SSNIP test). The agencies consider the likely reaction of buyers (demand-side substitution) to a hypothetical price increase. The resulting market comprises the products which the buyers consider substitutable. This test has also been adopted by the European Commission for the definition of relevant markets.[36]

The 1982 Merger Guidelines marked the start of aligning antitrust policy with contemporary economic thinking – a symbol of the impact of Chicago School thinking (see Chapter 2).

More recent antitrust guidelines in the US have considered a focus on existing product markets as providing too narrow an approach for appreciating all the competitive effects of a transaction. Therefore it is mandated that effects on relevant technology markets and innovation markets at times must also be analysed. Relevant to this development was the National Cooperative Research Act (NCRA)[37] of 1984, in which Congress declared that to the extent R&D joint ventures create anti-competitive risks they would most likely come

35 See e.g. Joined Cases T-374/94, T-375/94, T-384/94 and T-388/94, *European Night Services v. Commission,* ECR II-3141 (1998) §§102, 137. Also US courts occasionally refer to FTC/DOJ Guidelines, which can be seen as a sign of increased influence, see e.g. *In re Papst Licensing, GmbH Patent litigation*, 2000 WL 1145725 (E.D.La Aug. 11, 2000).

36 Commission Notice on the definition of the relevant market for the purposes of Community competition law, OJ C 372/5 (1997).

37 H.R. Conf. Rep. No. 98–1044, 9th Conq., 3d Sess. at 10 (1984), reprinted in 1984 USCCAN 3131, 3134–35.

from effects on competition in properly defined R&D markets.[38] Since 1993, when the Act as amended became the NCRPA, the National Cooperative Research and Production Act,[39] registered ventures' competitive effects are to be assessed under the rule of reason 'in properly defined relevant research, development, product, process and service markets'.[40]

In Europe too, recent guidelines have expanded on the differences between product markets, technology markets and innovation markets (sometimes referred to as Competition in Research and Development). This development will be described in the following sections.

3.3.1 US 1992/1997 Horizontal Merger Guidelines

The Horizontal Merger Guidelines, issued by the DOJ and the FTC in 1992, in fact are rather silent on how to handle market dynamics or competition in the innovation process. They do, however, make reference to the necessity of applying the standards for antitrust analysis in a reasonable and flexible way, precisely because historical evidence may provide an incomplete answer to the forward-looking merger inquiry.[41] Recent or current changes in the market conditions, such as by way of a new important technology, may affect the significance of historical market shares.[42] They also indicate the possibility that market shares may be altered by a new technology that will not be available to all market participants.

More importantly, in 1997, the fourth section of the guidelines, dealing with the appraisal of efficiencies, was revised. Efficiencies are considered important to the merger analysis, being the primary benefit that could stem from such a transaction, thereby enhancing the firm's ability and incentive to compete, which may result in lower prices, improved quality, enhanced service or new products.

To be taken into account, efficiencies must be merger-specific, that is, likely to be achieved through the merger, but unlikely to be achieved without it or some arrangement having similar anti-competitive effects. It is up to the firms to substantiate their claims in a way that makes it possible for the authorities to verify the likelihood and size of resulting benefits. Moreover, the efficiencies that are taken into account must not result from anti-competitive

38 OECD, 'Application of Competition Policy to High Tech Markets', *OECD Working Papers*, Series Roundtables on Competition Policy no. 9, Paris, 1997, p. 12.

39 15 USC §§4301–6.

40 15 USC §4302. In June 2004 the NCRPA Act was extended to include standards development organizations (SDOs).

41 US 1992 Horizontal Merger Guidelines, §0.

42 Ibid., §1.521.

output reductions (that is, savings due to fewer products and services). Naturally, efficiencies are difficult to prove and measure, but, if the transaction is likely to achieve merger-specific and determinable (pro-competitive) efficiencies, the authorities may conclude that the merger is not likely to create anti-competitive net effects (such as a price increase) in the relevant market. Naturally, the greater the negative effects expected, the greater must the offsetting efficiencies be. According to the guidelines, efficiencies are therefore likely to be important when the negative effects are rather small, and they will almost never justify a merger to monopoly or near-monopoly.

While different kinds of efficiencies can be considered, some are inherently harder to establish. Accordingly, the guidelines state that efficiencies relating to R&D are potentially substantial, but less susceptible to verification, and may be the result of anti-competitive output reductions. By comparison, marginal cost reductions in production, resulting from two production facilities merging to one, can usually be verified and found to be merger-specific. One may expect that, if efficiencies are crucial to the outcome of a merger investigation, they will more often relate to the production process.

3.3.2 US 1995 Licensing Guidelines

The 1995 Antitrust Guidelines for the Licensing of Intellectual Property are probably the most concrete expression of paradigm shift in the antitrust outlook towards IPRs. As such they are also important to the development of a more dynamic view of markets and antitrust analysis overall, and not just to IPRs. These guidelines handed out the final blow to the restrictive practices in the 1960s and 1970s, the era of the so-called '9 no-nos.'[43] During this period, antitrust law was particularly concerned with, and deemed unlawful, contractual obligations that seemed to limit competition in the patented technology.

By comparison, the 1995 guidelines are founded on the notion that IPR

[43] The notion of the 9 no-nos was expressed by Deputy Assistant Attorney Bruce B. Wilson in *Patent and Know-How License Agreements: Field of Use, Territorial, Price and Quantity Restriction*', Address Before the Fourth New England Antitrust Conference (Nov. 6, 1970) and included tying of unpatented supplies, mandatory grant-backs, post-sale restrictions on resale by purchasers of patented products, tie-outs (competition clauses), a licensee veto power over the licenser's grant of further licences (exclusive licensing), mandatory package licensing, compulsory payment of royalties in amounts not reasonably related to sales of the patented product, restrictions on sales of unpatented products made by a patented process, and specifying prices licensee could charge upon resale of licensed products. For a concise yet comprehensive treatment of antitrust policy and the intersection with intellectual property see Tom, Willard K. & Newberg, Joshua A., 'Antitrust and Intellectual Property: From Separate Spheres to Unified Field', 66 *Antitrust Law Journal* 167, 225f. (1997).

laws and antitrust laws have the common purpose of promoting innovation and enhancing consumer welfare. Based on this premise, the guidelines embody three general principles:[44]

1. for the purpose of antitrust analysis, the Agencies regard intellectual property as being essentially comparable to any other form of property;
2. the Agencies do not presume that intellectual property creates market power in the antitrust context; and
3. the Agencies recognize that intellectual property licensing allows firms to combine complementary factors of production and is generally pro-competitive.

In more practical terms, these principles mean that there is nothing mysterious about IPRs and, just like transactions relating to any other kind of property, it is for the authorities to show that an anti-competitive effect is likely to result. Moreover, a careful investigation and analysis of available substitutes must be conducted to assess potential market power, and finally, cooperation that may seem horizontal at first glance in fact ought to be analysed as vertical, for example when a licensee competitor would not have access to an equivalent technology without the licence agreement.

A rule of reason approach is applied to investigate the real consequences of an agreement, unless 'a restraint's nature and necessary effect is so plainly anticompetitive', that a per se methodology may be applied.[45] If less dramatic anti-competitive effects are likely to result, the investigation must go on to cover potential efficiencies. A qualitative assessment is thus conducted to establish whether the pro-competitive effects outweigh any negative consequences. Efficiencies may relate to the combination of patents or other IPRs of a complementary nature, allowing for efficient product development and synergy effects to be realized. As in the merger guidelines, restrictions on competition must be necessary to attain the efficiencies, that is, the efficiencies should not be attainable through less restrictive means (such as type of restraint or time).

The guidelines take a positive stance towards licensing, emphasizing the importance of intra-brand competition. Accordingly, a licensor does not have

44 US 1995 IP Guidelines, §2.0.

45 A truncated rule of reason can also be applied. If, for example, parties agree to pool competing patents and agree on royalties charged to third parties, such an arrangement may achieve efficiencies and is thereby not per se illegal. But it may be easy to conclude large anti-competitive effects, and so the transaction cannot be justified. In such an event, a truncated rule of reason is applied where the agencies do not have to go into further detail.

to create competition in its own technology. An IPR holder may thus practically limit a licensee's use of a licensed technology in the same manner that the patentee would have been able to, had he chosen to commercialize his technology in-house. Anti-competitive effects may occur when the licence agreement extends the area of exclusivity of the intellectual property, for example through tie-ins where the licensor, dominant in the market for a particular product, extends this dominance to another area by bundling the two products (such as a package of two different licences, one for which competing alternatives exist). Also, in exclusive agreements between competitors with market power, negative effects from extending exclusivity are more likely to occur. This could result in price coordination, lower production levels, foreclosure, delay of innovations and product introductions.

Grantbacks, by which the licensee agrees to offer its improvements to the licensed technology to the licensor, is a common kind of restraint which has a significant impact on the innovation process.[46] This may be a way of sharing risks and promoting the development and diffusion both of the initial innovation and of subsequent improvements, hence a pro-competitive tool. But grantbacks may nonetheless also limit the incentives for the licensee to invest in further development of the licensed technology, particularly if the obligation is exclusive. To evaluate both the licensee's incentives and the likely effect on the market, it is therefore necessary to analyse the level of competition between substitutable technologies. But not only the existing alternatives matter; just as important may be the level of competition in R&D for the improving of existing technologies and for the development of new technologies.

In order to fully appreciate these kinds of concerns, the guidelines elaborate a concept of three different relevant markets. *Goods* markets analysis includes the products of each participant and is conducted in accordance with the 1992 Horizontal Merger Guidelines. A goods market consequently consists of substitutes, and is delineated to include the product or group of products for which a hypothetical profit-maximizing monopolist likely would impose at least a 'small but significant and nontransitory increase in price' (the SSNIP test again).

Technology markets may be delineated when intellectual property is marketed separately from the products in which they are used.[47] The technology market consists of the intellectual property that is licensed and its close substitutes: the technologies or goods that constrain the exercise of market power of the licensed IPR, and may thus provide the basis for assessing the competitive effects of a licensing agreement.

---

46 US 1995 IP Guidelines, §5.6.

47 Ibid., §3.2.2.

The guidelines provide the following definition of an *innovation* market:

> An innovation market consists of the research and development directed to particular new or improved goods or processes, and the close substitutes for that research and development. The close substitutes are research and development efforts, technologies, and goods that significantly constrain the exercise of market power with respect to the relevant research and development, for example by limiting the ability and incentive of a hypothetical monopolist to retard the pace of research and development. The Agencies will delineate an innovation market only when the capabilities to engage in the relevant research and development can be associated with specialized assets or characteristics of specific firms.[48]

Through these guidelines, the innovation market approach had thus been institutionalized. The antitrust authorities did not, however, confine the use of the innovation market analysis to licensing practices.[49] The introduction of the formalized innovation market approach, and the early application thereof, was followed by a debate on the theoretical and practical content, applicability and appropriateness of the innovation market analysis, a debate to which we will return later on.

3.3.3 The Gilbert & Sunshine model

US Department of Justice officials Richard J. Gilbert and Steven C. Sunshine promoted this innovation market approach as a way to analyse the consequences of a transaction for innovation efforts, which, according to them, is hard to do if the analysis is restricted to existing product markets.[50] Moreover, they outlined important elements of the innovation market approach as applicable to mergers, R&D joint ventures and other arrangements. Matching the general product market methodology of the 1992 Horizontal Merger Guidelines, the innovation market approach included assessments of market concentration, competitive effects on incentives to invest in R&D and efficiencies resulting from a combination of R&D activities. Their model incorporated a number of stages.[51]

First is identification of overlapping R&D activities that may lead to improved products or processes, in order to establish whether the outcome can have a significant impact in relevant downstream product markets, as a precondition for including the R&D activities in a relevant innovation market.

---

48 Ibid., §3.2.3.

49 See Gilbert, Richard J. & Sunshine, Steven C., 'Incorporating Dynamic Efficiency Concerns in Merger Analysis: The Use of Innovation Markets', 63 *Antitrust Law Journal* 569 (1995).

50 Ibid., p. 570.

51 Ibid., pp. 594 *et seq.*

Second is identification of alternative sources of R&D, that is, R&D activities that are reasonable substitutes (directed to particular new products and processes) for the activities of the merging firm. These sources should be the firms that possess the capabilities (scientific skills and equipment) to supply these activities, rather than an attempt to categorize each activity separately. It may include both firms that possess the necessary specialized assets for R&D and those that could be expected to acquire those assets within a reasonably short time in response to a small but significant and non-transitory reduction in R&D.

Third is evaluation of actual and potential competition from downstream products. In addition to competition from alternative technologies, a reduction in R&D may be unprofitable for a hypothetical monopolist because of actual and potential competition from downstream products. Innovation allows the firm increased shares and profits on downstream markets, and the loss of competitive opportunity following a reduction in R&D may exceed any savings in R&D expenditures.

Fourth is assessment of the increase in concentration in R&D and competitive effects on investment in R&D. A relevant innovation market is established when the analysis identifies the set of R&D activities from which a hypothetical monopolist would profit by a small but significant and non-transitory reduction in R&D. After defining the innovation market, the analysis must consider whether the firms' share of R&D is sufficient to affect the total level of R&D in that market, and whether there are any particular factors that affect the likelihood of impact on competition. The proper measure of innovation activity will depend upon individual circumstances such as expenditures on R&D leading to the relevant new products or processes, the level of activity (such as production) or the level of assets.

The last stage is assessment of R&D efficiencies. It is not sufficient to end the evaluation with a determination only of the likelihood that the combination will reduce R&D effort. Since the relevant competitive concern is whether the combination will have an adverse impact on innovation – for which R&D is only an input – the analysis must consider whether the transaction results in efficiency benefits that enhance the likelihood or value of innovation. The potential for exploiting complementary R&D assets and scale economies in R&D as well as for eliminating redundant R&D programmes must be assessed.

3.3.4 US 2000 Competitor Collaboration Guidelines

In 1995, the FTC held comprehensive hearings on global and innovation-based competition. One result of this, apart from the testimonies given, was a staff report presented in 1996.[52] This report concluded that it was necessary to improve the clarity of the antitrust treatment of joint ventures, through the issuance of guidelines. This happened in 2000 when joint FTC and DOJ Antitrust Guidelines for Collaboration Among Competitors were presented.

According to these guidelines, certain types of agreements, especially among competitors, are so likely to have detrimental effects on competition and so unlikely to bring benefits that they are per se prohibited, whereas agreements that cannot be presupposed to have these negative effects are analysed under a rule of reason. Since most R&D agreements are pro-competitive, they will typically be analysed under the rule of reason, in order to determine their overall competitive effect on price, output, quality, service and innovation.[53]

Further, even the kind of agreements that otherwise might be considered as per se illegal are to be analysed under a rule of reason provided they are reasonably related to an efficiency-enhancing integration of economic activity, and reasonably necessary to achieve the pro-competitive benefits.[54] An R&D collaboration extending to joint production and even distribution of the developed products is therefore normally analysed under the rule of reason.

Rule of reason analysis is said to be flexible, focusing on the relevant factors that may be determinative for competition in the specific case. The analysis thus depends on the nature of the agreement and the market circumstances.[55]

Agencies' interest in R&D collaborations ultimately aims to investigate whether the parties may exercise market power to reduce the level of innovation, leading to fewer or no products for consumers to choose from, lower-quality products, or products that reach consumers more slowly than they otherwise would. Furthermore, according to the guidelines, R&D collaboration may also reduce the number of independent competitors in the market for the goods, services or production processes derived from the R&D collaboration, and thereby lead to higher prices or reduced output, quality or service.

Of central importance is whether a transaction increases the ability or incentive to reduce R&D efforts, for example by slowing down the pace. Such conditions may particularly arise when parties 'already possess a secure source of market power over an existing product and the new R&D efforts might cannibalize their supracompetitive earnings' and when 'R&D competition is confined to firms with specialized characteristics or assets, such as

---

52 Federal Trade Commission, *Anticipating the 21st Century – Competition Policy in the New High-Tech, Global Marketplace*, Staff Report, 1996.

53 US 2000 Competitor Collaboration Guidelines, §§1.2, 3.31(a).

54 Ibid., §1.2.

55 Ibid.

intellectual property, or when a regulatory approval process limits the ability of late-comers to catch up with competitors already engaged in the R&D'.[56]

Methodologically, the 2000 Collaboration Guidelines borrow from the 1995 IP Guidelines. In their analysis, the Agencies will identify and assess the effects in all relevant product and geographic markets that may be affected.[57] The relevant markets will include the markets in which the parties' joint operations occur or operate and may include additional markets in which any participant is an actual or potential competitor. The Agencies typically distinguish between goods markets, technology markets and innovation markets.

Often the effects of R&D collaboration on innovation will only be analysed as a separate competitive effect when analysing the relevant product (goods or technology) market. However, when the effects on innovation may not be adequately addressed through such analysis, an innovation market will be defined and analysed in accordance with the IP Guidelines. An innovation market consists of the research and development directed to particular new or improved goods or processes and the close substitutes for that research and development. Just as in licensing cases, the use of innovation markets is limited to cases where capabilities to engage in the relevant research and development are associated with specialized assets or characteristics of specific firms.

3.3.5 EU 1984 and 2000 R&D Block Exemptions

The block exemptions issued by the European Commission are general exemptions according to Article 81(3) of the Treaty, for specified groups of agreements. The applicability of these exemptions is ordinarily based on the parties' market shares on current product markets.[58] The first block exemption for categories of R&D agreements, issued in 1984,[59] was no exception and applied, under certain conditions, to R&D agreements where the parties' currently combined production of the products capable of being improved or replaced by the contract products (that is, current product market) did not exceed 20 per cent of the market. If the parties jointly were to distribute the products, the relevant market cap was 10 per cent. Where the parties were non-competitors in current product markets, the exemption was generally

56 Ibid., §3.31 (a).

57 Ibid., §3.32.

58 The Regulations also provide other important conditions, e.g. black-listed provisions which, if included, will render the agreement outside the scope of the exemption.

59 Commission Regulation (EEC) No 418/85 of 19 December 1984 on the application of Article 85(3) of the Treaty to categories of research and development agreements. Amended by Commission Regulation (EEC) No 151/93 of 23 December 1992.

applicable. The exemption lasted for the duration of the R&D programme and, in cases where the results were jointly exploited, five years from the time the products were put on the common market or as long as the parties did not control more than 20 per cent of the relevant market. This meant that, when the R&D was directed towards completely new products, the block exemption applied regardless of the structure of competition in the specific R&D sector. However, the block exemption provided the Commission with the possibility of withdrawing the benefits of the regulation where an agreement was found incompatible with the conditions of Article 81(3). That could, for example, be the case for an agreement that, owing to limited available research capacity, substantially restricted the scope for third parties to carry out R&D in the relevant field.[60] Whether an agreement could be disallowed because of too little competition among too few independent R&D sources is unclear.

In November 2000, the Commission issued a new block exemption[61] for R&D agreements. The ambition was to create a regulation that both ensured effective protection of competition and at the same time provided adequate security for undertakings. The Commission states that, below a certain level of market power, it can, in general, be presumed that the positive effects of R&D will outweigh any negative effects on competition.[62] The market power in question refers to product markets and the regulation consequently maintains the system of excluding from the automatic exemption agreements between competitors in the market for the products capable of being replaced or improved by the contract products. In the new block exemption the combined market share must not exceed 25 per cent when the agreement is entered into. For collaboration between non-competitors there is no market cap. Where the parties jointly exploit the results, the exemption continues to apply seven years after the introduction of the products on the common market or as long as the parties' sales do not exceed 25 per cent of the market in total. The regulation also specifies certain other conditions which must be fulfilled and provisions which may not be included for the exemption to apply.

The Commission or, nowadays, a national competition authority, may still revoke the application of the block exemption for agreements that, in the specific case, has effects which are incompatible with Article 81(3).[63] In addi-

---

60 Article 10(a) of the Regulation.

61 Commission Regulation (EC) No 2659/2000 of 29 November 2000 on the application of Article 81(3) of the Treaty to categories of research and development agreements.

62 Preamble 5 of the Regulation.

63 For the powers of national authorities see Council Regulation (EC) No 1/2003 of 16 December 2002 on the implementation of the rules on competition laid down in Articles 81 and 82 of the Treaty, Articles 5, 11 and Preamble 10.

tion to the examples already given in the 1984 regulation, the Commission has added that this may particularly arise where 'the existence of the research and development agreement would eliminate effective competition in research and development on a particular market'.[64] Through this addition to the new block exemption there is now something of an 'R&D market escape' for the European antitrust authorities, in cases where the parties, although not being competitors or not having substantial market shares on current product markets, risk eliminating effective competition in R&D. This amendment, although not likely to be frequently employed, is interesting in the innovation market context, particularly in the light of the new guidelines for horizontal collaboration, to which we now turn.[65]

3.3.6 EU 2001 Horizontal Cooperation Guidelines

In January 2001, the European Commission issued a notice, the Horizontal Cooperation Guidelines,[66] with the purpose of providing an analytical framework for the most common types of horizontal cooperation. The guidelines should be seen as a more generally applicable complement to the R&D block exemption regulation, which should aid market actors in assessing whether their business arrangements violate community competition law or not.

According to the Commission, the key to defining relevant markets when assessing R&D agreements is to identify those products, technologies or R&D efforts that will act as a competitive constraint on the parties.[67] Very much like their American equivalents, the European guidelines distinguish between competition on existing markets (products and technology markets) and competition in innovation (R&D efforts).

> R&D cooperation may not – or not only – affect competition in existing markets, but competition in innovation. This is the case where cooperation concerns the development of new products/technology which either may – if emerging – one day replace existing ones or which are being developed for a new intended use and will therefore not replace existing products but create a completely new demand. The effects on competition in innovation are important in these situations, but can in some cases not be sufficiently assessed by analysing actual or potential competition in existing product/technology markets.[68]

---

64 Article 7(e) of the Regulation.

65 All European block exemptions contain some right for the Commission to revoke the exemption on certain grounds in a specific case, but that has not yet happened in practice under any block exemption.

66 Commission Notice – Guidelines on the applicability of Article 81 of the EC Treaty to horizontal cooperation agreements, OJ C 3/02 (2001).

67 Ibid., §43.

68 Ibid., §50.

Whether emphasis will be put on effects on existing markets or pure R&D efforts will depend on the objective of the specific R&D agreement. Where, for example, R&D is directed towards slight improvements or variations, such as new models of certain products, possible effects concern the market for existing products only. On the other hand, innovation may result in an entirely new product that creates its own new market.[69] In such cases, the Commission considers existing markets relevant only if they are somehow related to the innovation in question. Instead an assessment of the effects of the cooperation on innovation should, if possible, be made. However, most cases probably fall in between these extremes, particularly when R&D is directed towards products that will replace existing products over time. As a consequence, analysis of both existing markets and the impact on innovation will often be called for.[70]

When a specific R&D analysis is necessary, the Commission distinguishes between two cases, depending on the nature of the innovative process in the given industry. In the first scenario, the innovation process is well structured and transparent, so that it is possible at an early stage to identify relevant R&D poles. This could, for example, be possible when assessing collaboration in the pharmaceutical industry. In the other scenario, probably typical of many innovative industries, the industry is not clearly structured enough to allow identification of credible competing R&D poles. In these cases the Commission will not, 'absent exceptional circumstances', attempt to assess the impact of a given R&D cooperation on innovation, but will limit the assessment to related product and technology markets.

If R&D in the specific industry is structured in an identifiable and assessable way (scenario one), the relevant boundaries of R&D must be determined in order to say something about the effects on innovation of a specific collaboration. The guidelines offer the following formula for an innovation market (§51):

> R&D poles are R&D efforts directed towards a certain new product or technology, and the substitutes for that R&D, that is R&D aimed at developing substitutable products or technology for those developed by the cooperation and having comparable access to resources as well as a similar timing. In this case, it can be analysed if after the agreement there will be a sufficient number of R&D poles left. The starting point of the analysis is the R&D of the parties. Then credible competing R&D poles have to be identified. In order to assess the credibility of competing poles, the following aspects have to be taken into account: the nature, scope and size of possible other R&D efforts, their access to financial and human resources, know-how patents, or other specialised assets as well as their timing and their capability to

[69] The Commission gives the example of a new vaccine for a previously incurable disease, §43.
[70] Ibid.

> exploit possible results. An R&D pole is not a credible competitor if it can not be regarded as a close substitute for the parties' R&D effort from the viewpoint of, for instance, access to resources or timing.

When the relevant R&D sources are defined the question arises of how to assess their competitiveness and the impact of the transaction under investigation. Whether a concentration in R&D is problematic or unacceptable should depend on the credibility and relative importance that can be attributed to the competing programmes.

Formally, the European Guidelines address the analysis of competition in innovation equivalent to the more regular product market analysis. Consequently the analysis should, if required in the specific case, be included in the overall analysis of an agreement's concordance with Article 81. As a general rule of EU Competition law, an agreement violating Article 81(1) may not receive an exemption under 81(3) if the parties are afforded the possibility of eliminating competition in respect of a substantial part of the products (or technologies) in question. The guidelines addresses this issue in the innovation context and §71 states:

> Where as a consequence of a R&D agreement an undertaking is dominant or becoming dominant either on an existing markets or with respect to innovation, such an agreement which produces anti-competitive effects in the meaning of Article 81 can in principle not be exempted. For innovation this is the case, for example, if the agreement combines the only two existing poles of research.

3.3.7 EU 2004 Horizontal Merger Guidelines

Following the adoption of a new Merger Regulation in January 2004,[71] the European Commission issued a set of guidelines relating to it.[72] While the new Merger Regulation amends the 'substantive test', that is, the legal prerequisite for deeming a merger incompatible with the common market, the Commission maintains the differences are not so significant that past case law can no longer be taken fully into account.[73] The guidelines set out to explain the analytical framework within which the Commission will assess concentrations between parties that are actual or potential competitors in the relevant market.[74] Equivalent guidelines for vertical and conglomerate mergers are awaited.

---

[71] Council Regulation (EC) No 139/2004 of 20 January 2004 on the control of concentrations between undertakings, OJ L 24/1 (2004).

[72] Guidelines on the assessment of horizontal mergers under the Council Regulation on the control of concentrations between undertakings, OJ C 31/5 (2004).

[73] Ibid., §4.

[74] The term 'concentration' used in the Merger Regulation covers various types of transactions such as mergers, acquisitions, takeovers and certain types of joint ventures.

When the Commission investigates a proposed transaction, it will first define the relevant product and geographical markets and thereafter make a competitive assessment of the merger. As regards the first step, the definition of markets, the guidelines offer no surprises. Apart from stating that '[t]he main purpose of market definition is to identify in a systematic way the immediate competitive constraints facing the merged entity', the guidelines refer to the Commission's Notice on the definition of the relevant market.[75]

For the rest, it is the competitive assessment that is covered. Here, two things stick out regarding analysis of competition in the innovation process. First, §38:

> In markets where innovation is an important competitive force, a merger may increase the firms' ability and incentive to bring new innovations to the market and, thereby, the competitive pressure on rivals to innovate in that market. Alternatively, effective competition may be significantly impeded by a merger between two important innovators, for instance between two companies with 'pipeline' products related to a specific product market. Similarly, a firm with a relatively small market share may nevertheless be an important competitive force if it has promising pipeline products.

This section should be read in conjunction with the section on barriers to entry, which highlights the possibility of incumbents enjoying technical advantages, such as preferential access to essential facilities, natural resources, innovation and R&D, or IPRs.[76] Such obstacles to newcomers are considered capable of making it difficult for any firm to compete successfully. Also 'other factors', such as economies of scale and scope and access to important technologies, is included here.

3.3.8 EU 2004 Technology Transfer Block Exemption and Guidelines

In December 2001, the Commission presented an evaluation report regarding its policy in the field of technology licensing.[77] According to the report, the block exemption in force at the time followed a legalistic approach that was previously also found in the field of vertical and horizontal agreements. Depending on rather formal requirements, various contractual clauses were

---

75 Commission's Notice on the definition of the relevant market for the purposes of Community competition law, OJ C 372/5 (1997).

76 Ibid., §71 (b).

77 Commission Evaluation Report on the Transfer of Technology – Block Exemption Regulation N° 240/96, Technology Transfer Agreements under Article 81, available at www.europa.eu.int/comm/competition/antitrust/technology_transfer/en.pdf. (last visited 3 March 2005).

listed as white (harmless), grey (suspected) or black (prohibited) – sometimes without these distinctions making economic sense. The focus was moreover mainly on intra-brand competition and market integration. The old approach was therefore considered a legal straitjacket which could discourage the dissemination of technologies and deter efficiency-creating transactions. An overhaul of the block exemption was therefore initiated to make it more consistent with other recent policy reforms.

In April 2004, a new block exemption regulation for technology transfer agreements (TTBER) was presented, along with supplementing guidelines.[78] The application of the TTBER is limited by thresholds for the parties' combined market shares: 20 per cent for agreements between competitors and 30 per cent for agreements between non-competitors. These market caps must be satisfied vis-à-vis both relevant product markets and relevant technology markets. Regarding product markets, both actual and potential competitors fall under the criterion of 'competing undertakings' whereas only actual competitors are considered competing undertakings when dealing with technology markets.[79]

If the parties do not exceed the market thresholds, their licensing agreements are automatically exempted provided that they do not contain any of the 'hardcore' restraints listed. The restraints applicable depend on whether the agreements are between competitors or non-competitors.[80] The hardcore restraints are broadly defined, but the regulation also lists important exceptions to these restraints which effectively increase the scope of the exempted area. For example, allocation of markets or customers is prohibited between competitors, but it is permitted to limit a licensee's use of the technology to a certain field or product market, to restrict active and/or passive sales by the licensee and/or the licensor into the exclusive territory or to the exclusive customer group reserved for the other party in non-reciprocal agreements.

In addition there is another list of clauses that will not be automatically exempted, and which thus require an individual assessment. Even if such a clause is included, the block exemption can be applied to the rest of the agreement.[81] If an agreement falls outside the scope of the block exemption, for example because of too high market shares, or if it contains a 'hardcore' restriction, it will have to be assessed on an individual basis under Article 81.

78 Commission Regulation (EC) No 772/2004 of 27 April 2004 on the application of Article 81(3) of the Treaty to categories of technology transfer agreements, OJ L 123/11 (2004); Commission Notice – Guidelines on the application of Article 81 of the EC Treaty to technology transfer agreements, OJ C 101/2 (2004). The guidelines serve the purpose of providing guidance for the application of the block exemption and for agreements that fall outside the exemption.

79 Article 1.1.h.

80 Article 5.

81 Article 6.

Particularly regarding technology markets, the market share threshold could have very significant consequences. If a firm decides that licensing would be a profitable way of commercializing its technology, and thus licensed the technology to a non-competitor, a 30 per cent market cap could easily be reached if little comparable licensing were currently undertaken in the specific industry. The TTBER partly solves the problem by calculating market shares, not by the ratio of total licensing revenues, but by the 'combined market share on the relevant product market(s) of the contract products manufactured or provided by the licensor and its licensees'.[82] Thus the share of the technology market is calculated 'on the basis of sales of products incorporating the licensed technology on downstream product markets'.[83] All sales on the product market are included and thereby also technologies that are exclusively used for captive production.

A remaining problem would arise in the common case where licensing takes place before any product has reached the market. If the licensor's technology is the first among possibly substitutable technologies to give rise to a good or service which actually reaches the market, the licensor will be attributed the entire technology market.[84] This holds even if other technologies have been licensed and products are in the pipeline but not yet on the market. Similarly, the applicability of the block exemption could vary with the success on the product market of other licensees to the technology, whose sales will add on to the licensor's technology market share. Continuous re-evaluation will be called for.[85]

This suggests an increased interplay between reliance on the block exemption and individual analysis in accordance with the guidelines. In this respect, agreements falling outside the scope of the TTBER may be analysed differently. According to the EU 2004 Technology Transfer Guidelines '[o]utside the safe harbour of the TTBER potential competition on the technology market is taken into account'.[86] In other words, potential competitors on a technology

---

[82] Article 3.3.

[83] EU 2004 Technology Transfer Guidelines, §23.

[84] Ibid., §70: 'In the case of new technologies that have not yet generated any sales, a zero market share is assigned. When sales commence the technology will start accumulating market share.' The Guidelines also acknowledge that market shares may not always be a good indication of the strength of the technology, why an individual assessment, *inter alia,* will have regard to the number of independent technologies: §§24, 131.

[85] See TTBER Article 8 regarding consequences of increased market shares for the applicability of the block exemption.

[86] EU 2004 Technology Transfer Guidelines, §66, also stating that, if the parties in an individual assessment are considered potential competitors on the technology market, this will not lead to the application of the hardcore list for agreements between competitors in the TTBER.

market may also be treated as competitors in an individual analysis. Moreover, the market is defined by the licensed technology and those other technologies to which customers could switch in response to a small but significant price increase. Market shares are assigned on the basis of each technology's share of the total licensing revenues in that market. Nevertheless, since it is acknowledged that (downstream) product market competition may constrain (upstream) technology market licensors, the methodology used in the TTBER may be applied as a supplement in individual cases.[87] In such a case, an increase in upstream royalties, making the resulting products less competitive, would cause the licensor to lose sales.[88]

On a general level the guidelines view IPRs and licensing positively. It is asserted that there is no inherent conflict between IP laws and competition law, they are complementing rather than competing areas of law, sharing the same basic objectives of promoting consumer welfare and efficient allocation of resources.[89] Innovation is regarded as 'an essential and dynamic component of an open and competitive market economy'. Since IPRs encourage investments in developing new or improved products and competition does the same by putting pressure on firms to innovate, they are both 'necessary to promote innovation and ensure a competitive exploitation thereof'.[90]

For the practical execution of competition law, this means that an ex ante perspective must be taken, not focusing on what the level of competition will be when all investments are made but rather trying to maintain the incentive to innovate, why 'the innovator not be unduly restricted in the exploitation' of IPRs that have turned out successful. Just as with the American approach, IPRs are not considered a presumption for market power and licensing is generally regarded as pro-competitive, even if it contains restrictions on the licensor or licensee. Restrictions of competition are likely when some party obtains or increases market power.

At the same time it is clear that the European Commission cares both for inter-technology competition (between competing technologies) and intra-technology competition (between companies using the same technology). According to the guidelines, two questions frame the analysis:[91] (1) does the

---

[87] See below, section 5.3.2.

[88] EU 2004 Technology Transfer Guidelines, §23.

[89] Regarding this relationship see Lidgard, Hans Henrik, *Parallellhandel: Konsumtion av immaterialrätt i Europa och USA*, Norstedts Juridik, Stockholm, 2002, pp. 242 *et seq.*; Korah, Valentine, 'The Interface Between Intellectual Property and Antitrust: The European Experience', 69 *Antitrust Law Journal* 801 (2002).

[90] EU 2004 Technology Transfer Guidelines, §7.

[91] Ibid., §12.

licence agreement restrict actual or potential competition that would have existed without the contemplated agreement, and (2) does the agreement restrict actual or potential competition that would have existed in the absence of the contractual restraint(s)?

The first question regards inter-technology competition and the answer will be dependent on the strength and competitive relationship of the parties, the likelihood of foreclosure of third parties and so on. The second question aims at intra-technology competition and is dependent on whether the parties have restricted competition further than would have been necessary. This is not a subjective test but an assessment of what restrictions firms generally consider necessary if they are to conclude the agreement in question.

As regards market definitions, the guidelines explain that technology is an input, and licensing can therefore affect competition both in the input market and in output markets. Therefore both technology markets and product markets will be delineated. Moreover, some licence agreements may affect innovation markets (§25):

> In analysing such effects, however, the Commission will normally confine itself to examining the impact of the agreement on competition within existing product and technology markets. Competition on such markets may be affected by agreements that delay the introduction of improved products or new products that over time will replace existing products. In such cases innovation is a source of potential competition which must be taken into account when assessing the impact of the agreement on product markets and technology markets. In a limited number of cases, however, it may be useful and necessary to also define innovation markets. This is particularly the case where the agreement affects innovation aiming at creating new products and where it is possible at an early stage to identify research and development poles. In such cases it can be analysed whether after the agreement there will be a sufficient number of competing research and development poles left for effective competition in innovation to be maintained.

3.4 EARLY DEBATE ON THE INNOVATION MARKET APPROACH

The formulation and early application by the US authorities of the innovation market analysis was greeted with a fair share of scepticism. The application to merger control in particular, by far the most widely used application, caused substantial concern. An illustrative example was the *Antitrust Law Journal*'s symposium, 'A Critical Appraisal of the "Innovation Market" Approach', in which these issues were treated in several articles.

In one of these articles, George Hay points out that, even though traditional merger analysis has featured static analysis of price and output where innovation has not played a central role, innovation has been part of the background against which merger policy has been developed.[92] Although scholars and policy makers have been sensitive to the possibility that a more permissive attitude could be beneficial to spur international competition and R&D incentives, the problem has been that the links between concentration and R&D or concentration and innovation have always been murky. Hay does not wish to argue with the assertion that antitrust analysis ought to be more concerned with innovation, but rather how innovation ought to affect the antitrust analysis and whether new tools are required.[93] When innovation is evolutionary, Hay sees no reason why the traditional analysis (including the potential competition doctrine) is inadequate.[94] When innovation is aiming at completely new products the relevant antitrust market could be either a future product market or an innovation market. The factual basis for both approaches is the belief that the merging parties would be significant independent sellers in the product market.[95] Whether the merger takes place at the R&D or production and sales stage is of no great importance. In addition, if a certain product innovation is patentable, only one of the firms could act in the product market anyway. Finally, there is, according to Hay, no sound theoretical reason why the merging firms should reduce combined R&D or, if they did, that such a reduction would be a bad thing.[96]

Richard Rapp develops similar views. He finds the innovation market approach in most applications superfluous and merely a new way of talking about potential competition. In some other cases 'it represents a leap into the unknown, with a potential for harm to economic welfare as great as any potential benefit'.[97] According to Rapp the utility of the approach is contingent on the validity of two statements, with little support in fact or theory, namely (1), an increase in R&D concentration is likely to reduce the amount of R&D undertaken, and (2) reducing the amount of R&D is likely to diminish innovation.[98] Evidence on the links between concentration and R&D levels is inconclusive and there is a lack of deterministic relationship between R&D expenditure and innovation.[99] R&D can often be duplicative and wasteful and there is no principled way to distinguish good R&D reductions from bad

92 Hay, George A., 'Innovations in Antitrust Enforcement', 64 *Antitrust Law Journal* 7, 9 (1995).

93 Ibid., p. 11.

94 Ibid., p. 14.

95 Ibid., p. 15.

96 Ibid., p. 16.

97 Rapp, Richard T., 'The Misapplication of the Innovation Market Approach to Merger Analysis', 64 *Antitrust Law Journal* 19, 20 (1995).

98 Ibid., pp. 26f.

99 Ibid., pp. 27 *et seq.*

ones.[100] Rather, Rapp argues, the analysis set forth in the 1992 Horizontal Merger Guidelines, which includes potential competition, supply response and entry analyses, suffices to cover dynamic effects.[101] Where the innovation market approach seems most apt – in cases where no product yet exists – the application of the approach is also the most dangerous, raising the risk of bad and unpredictable agency decisions.[102]

Richard Brunell notes that there may be more agreement than meets the eye on how mergers involving R&D should be treated. Starting with the NCRA of 1984, old and new policy makers seem to agree that very high market shares in R&D may raise serious anti-competitive concerns in a way that moderate or high concentration does not and that mergers may be allowed even if they leave only a handful of players in the innovation market. The real debate, according to Brunell, seems to be in the facts, not the theory, and whether the facts are in fact determinable.[103]

Apart from the criticism from economic and practical viewpoints, some commentators, among them Robert J. Hoerner, have asserted that innovation markets do not involve a 'line of commerce' in the wording of §7 of the Clayton Act as R&D normally is not traded on a market.[104]

In addition to, or as a development of, the early discussions, Lawrence B. Landman has brought the debate forward.[105] Landman asserts that, although the US Agencies claim to find and regulate an innovation market, in reality they cannot, and do not, do so. No authority can define a market where competition is the product. By requiring divestitures, licences and so on the authorities do not ensure that the specific firms, or any other firms, innovate. They do not act to keep competing R&D programmes because that in itself implies more growth in the economy. They act to preserve competition in

---

100 Ibid., pp. 33 *et seq.* Rapp gives an example with GM's R&D and investment programme. GM spent $67.2 billion in excess of depreciation in the 1980s and produced a firm with a total ending value of equity of $26.2 billion. The entire equity value of Toyota and Honda in 1985 totalled $21.5 billion. See Jensen, Michael C., 'The Modern Industrial Revolution, Exit, and the Failure of Internal Control Systems', 48 *Journal of Finance* 831, 858 (1993).

101 Ibid., p. 40.

102 Ibid., pp. 45 *et seq.*

103 Brunell, Richard M., 'Editor's Note', *64 Antitrust Law Journal* 1, 5f. (1995).

104 Hoerner, *supra*, note 18, pp. 50–55.

105 Landman, Lawrence B., 'Innovation and the Structure of Competition', 81 *Journal of the Patent and Trademark Office Society* 728 (1999); 'The Economics of Future Goods Markets', 21 *World Competition – Law and Economics Review* 63 (1998); 'Innovation Markets in Europe', 19 *European Competition Law Review* 21 (1998); 'Competing in the Global Pharmaceutical Industry: Innovation and Future Potential Competition', 2 *The Journal of Biolaw & Business* 29 (1998).

future goods markets. While preserving competition in future markets they hope that competition will spur innovation.[106] The agencies cannot follow either the IP Guidelines or the Gilbert & Sunshine model for a number of reasons. For one thing, they would require the agencies to measure market power in the innovation market by reference to ability to reduce R&D spending. It is not even known whether an innovation market monopolist generally would reduce R&D investments.[107] The agencies would also have to consider if and how the transaction would improve innovation efficiencies. Moreover, potential innovation market competitors that might in future engage in R&D aiming at the same product market cannot be identified. According to Landman, what the authorities can do, and are doing, is to define those R&D programmes that, if successful, would allow for the development of the same future product. Similarly in Europe, although the European Commission officials claim they act to preserve competition in R&D, they only act when it is probable that the transaction will lead to dominance in the future product market.

Reference has already been made to John Temple Lang's commentary on European standards in the 1990s.[108] He maintained that '[i]f there is a "market for R&D", it is only if companies are selling the service of providing R&D to other companies. That is a present service, and it is not the same as the question of whether R&D activities for the researcher's own use is a good measure of future market power.'[109] Even if the Commission did not define innovation markets, Temple Lang acknowledged that, where the parties were leading competitors in research directed towards the same goal, it in fact assessed whether a transaction would restrict competition in R&D. Since improved R&D may be accepted as a benefit of cooperation and mergers, it should be possible to recognize the reverse as an anti-competitive effect. For example, the creation of incentives not to invest in R&D would be an anti-competitive effect to be taken into account.[110] The question is rather how to take such dynamic aspects into account. Temple Lang points to various factors that would warrant caution on trying to deploy 'non-static'

---

106 Landman, Lawrence B., 'The Economics of Future Goods Markets', 21 *World Competition – Law and Economics Review* 63, 84f. (1998).

107 Landman, Lawrence B., 'Competing in the Global Pharmaceutical Industry: Innovation and Future Potential Competition', 2 *The Journal of Biolaw & Business* 29, 34 (1998).

108 See section 1.1.3.

109 Temple Lang, John, 'European Community Antitrust Law: Innovation Markets and High Technology Industries', 20 *Fordham International Law Journal* 717, 764f. (1997).

110 Ibid., pp. 760ff

competition analysis.[111] The uncertainties in conducting dynamic antitrust analysis necessitate a case-by-case or at least industry-by-industry approach and limit the notion of antitrust analysis based on R&D considerations.

Apart from the early American debate and the works presented here, the innovation market approach has been commented on subsequently, often from similar starting-points. Innovation is central in many modern markets but the closer application of antitrust policy to it may often raise many difficult issues about market structures, incentives and R&D levels.[112] Even today, many economists take a sceptical stance towards the innovation market concept. As an example, in a recent report to the National Bureau of Economic Research, Dennis W. Carlton and Robert H. Gertner maintain that a concept that considers innovation markets separately from standard product markets, and blocks mergers which significantly increase concentration in R&D, is dependent on three propositions for which there is no general or empirical support: first, that reducing R&D expenditure is undesirable; second, if there are fewer firms performing R&D, there will be less aggregate R&D and fewer new products; and third, it is possible to determine that there are not enough other firms to perform R&D and develop future products to compete with the future products to be developed by the merged firm.[113]

A recent report on Multiparty Licensing, delivered by Charles River Associates on behalf of the European Commission, comments on the innovation market approach in the following words: 'We are not particularly comfortable with the idea of an innovation market – a pure market in R&D, as against a product market in which innovation is a significant feature of competition – as there are quite serious conceptual problems associated with attempting to apply conventional competition analysis to pure R&D activity.'[114] It is nevertheless admitted that '[i]f product markets cannot be defined because it is not clear from the nature of the innovation what products might be developed, but

111 Ibid., pp. 763, 767f. Temple Lang points, inter alia, at the imprecise relationship between R&D spending, innovation and competition, differences in how technological development occurs in different industries, the difficulties in predicting the success of particular R&D projects and the importance of not penalizing firms for investing heavily in R&D.

112 See e.g. OECD, *supra*, note 38; OFT, *Innovation and Competition policy*, Economic Discussion Paper 3, Report prepared for the Office of Fair Trading by Charles River Associates, 2002.

113 Carlton, Dennis W. & Gertner, Robert H., *Intellectual Property, Antitrust and Strategic Behavior*, NBER Working Paper, No 8976 (2002), p. 10; available at www.nber.org/papers/w8976 (last visited 3 March 2005).

114 Charles River Associates, *Report on Multiparty Licensing*, Report to the European Commission, (2003), p. 47; available at http://europa.eu.int/comm/competition/antitrust/legislation/multiparty_licensing.pdf (last visited 3 March 2005).

it is apparent that there will be a reduction in the level of rivalry in a market that involves R&D, then it may be necessary and desirable to analyse the relevant innovation market'.[115] It is stressed that in these rare instances the tools applied to ordinary markets cannot be applied blindly.[116] Similar conclusions are presented in a report prepared for the Commission by Europe Economics, arguing that a key drawback of the innovation market concept is that it tries to analyse innovation in competition in the same way as product market competition is assessed.[117]

Against this background it is time to analyse relevant case law to see how innovation analysis is conducted, particularly the practical implementation of the innovation market concept.

115 Ibid., p. 48

116 OFT, *supra*, note 112, p. 135.

117 Europe Economics, *The Development of Analytical Tools for Assessing Market Dynamics in the Knowledge Based Economy*, Report to the European Commission, (2003), p. 57; available at http://europa.eu.int/comm/enterprise/library/lib-competition/ doc/analytical_tools_final_report.pdf (last visited 3 March 2005).

4. Innovation analysis in practice

4.1 INTRODUCTION

This chapter will present and analyse cases in which potential negative effects relating to competition in the innovation process have been addressed and assessed. Such analysis has been most widely performed in the field of merger control, but the case presentation also comprises some joint ventures, agreements relating to intellectual property (such as acquisition and pooling of patents) and abuses of dominance. In spite of the predominance of merger cases amongst the analysed cases, it should be possible, as former FTC officials Gilbert and Sunshine have suggested,[1] to draw general conclusions applicable also to other fields.

The chapter focuses on the delineation of markets; when, how and what potential anti-competitive effects and pro-competitive benefits are identified on these markets; and finally what remedies are typically being used to overcome any unacceptable effects. The practical handling by the authorities of these specific issues will be presented and briefly analysed in this chapter. A deeper and more generally applicable analysis is presented in the following chapters.

4.2 INNOVATION ANALYSIS IN VARIOUS CONTEXTS

At the outset it can be noted that few cases concern themselves exclusively with innovation effects. Whether dealing with mergers, joint ventures, technology transfers or other practices, competition analysis of various kinds is frequently brought into play. Some cases do relate more explicitly to the innovation process and the terms and conditions for future competition in that process. But the conditions for innovation may be relevant also where the overall analysis addresses competition between current or future products. Depending on the particular setting, the method of analysis may differ. Even in the same case, innovation analyses may be conducted in different manners,

1 See section 3.3.3, the Gilbert & Sunshine model.

and for different primary purposes. Such differences reflect an adequate 'methodological relativism', to which there should probably also be added elements of inconsistency and discrepancy.

More specifically, analysis of the competitive aspects of R&D can relate to an identified existing product market. In such cases, the innovation analysis is part of, or supplements, a prospective competition analysis of that market. In practice, the authorities sometimes equate the R&D potential with the capabilities of incumbent firms and the terms of competition between them on the market for current products. Hence no further elaboration regarding specific R&D programmes is conducted. In other cases, R&D programmes are assessed more carefully. These different analyses sometimes aim at predicting competition effects on product markets (existing or potentially existing), but may also explicitly address a transaction's likely impact on performance in innovation itself.

In more 'orthodox' innovation market cases (following the guidelines), the analysis departs from identifying the competing R&D programmes directed towards a specific range of future products. Relevant existing R&D alternatives are identified and assessed. The impact of the transaction on incentives and abilities to engage in innovation is analysed, together with the effects on third parties. On this basis, conclusions regarding innovation competition may be presented. Yet also when an innovation market analysis is being conducted, the conditions for innovation often explicitly underpin conclusions regarding the likely impact on competition in future product markets.

A limited number of cases analyse innovation conditions in a more general sense. Reviewed are transactions combining R&D assets, access to which is crucial in order to act in the R&D process or crucial to the commercialization of resulting products (and thereby crucial for the incentive to conduct R&D at all). Typically, intellectual property rights, sometimes combined with other assets, are in issue. Merging such assets may seriously affect the incentives for and abilities of actual or potential participants to act in the R&D process.

4.3 INDUSTRY BIAS

In order to analyse competition in the innovation process, and to predict future effects, the conditions for innovation must be reasonably transparent and foreseeable. As will become apparent in this chapter, transactions in the pharmaceutical, medical equipment and biotechnological industries are the classic fields for innovation analysis in antitrust. Here the R&D cycles are long and rather transparent and are also closely linked to important IPRs. This opens the path for strategic behaviour which may affect competition negatively.

In markets where innovation takes frequent and unpredictable turns, and product developments are concealed and rapid, R&D aspects may influence the regular product market assessment, but have little stand-alone value. In this kind of market, innovation is a phenomenon that tends to make public intervention superfluous, since it is difficult, even for a current monopolist, to exercise any power over the innovation process. Yet both inside and outside pharmaceutical and the like markets, other structural phenomena and entry barriers, such as network effects,[2] industry standards and key technologies, can create a competition structure relating to innovation that is more predictable and thus more conducive both to strategic action by market participants and to antitrust analysis.

4.4 CATEGORIZATION OF CASE LAW

In order to structure the presentation and analysis, the cases will be divided into five categories. Although no categorization is flawless, it will help in distinguishing important aspects of the competition law analysis.

4.4.1 Innovation in Existing Markets

The first category relates to transactions undertaken between actors active on a concentrated product or technology market where innovation is an important aspect of competition. Interesting questions in this category of cases relate, inter alia, to the kind of circumstances under which innovation becomes a relevant parameter and whether the innovation analysis aims primarily at considering effects on innovation or rather constitutes a means to predict the level of future competition in the product or technology market. A related question concerns the definition of markets: under what circumstances may innovation analyses be performed as part of the relevant product market and when will a particular innovation market analysis seem warranted?

4.4.2 Potential R&D Entrants

A second category of cases relates to transactions between incumbent market participants and potential entrants. Entry may be dependent on successful innovation and entrants may significantly alter the competitive environment

---

[2] Network effects imply that a good or service becomes more valuable to the buyer, the more users the good or service already has. Computer software, telephone and other communication systems are classical examples of network industries.

through the introduction of a new product. Entry itself, and the conditions under which it takes place, may therefore be largely determined by the prevailing conditions in R&D. Various transactions may thus affect the incentives and abilities for subsequent product development, both by incumbents and by entrants, which in the longer run will be determinant for the nature and number of products and the level of competition on the market. The limits and merits of potential competition doctrines pose interesting questions, especially concerning the issue of market definition.

4.4.3 Competition for Future Products

A third category of cases may be distinguished where a transaction relates to R&D conducted for a future product or technology market, that is, alternative R&D sources for particular products or technologies. These are instances where neither of the parties, nor, typically, anyone else, is currently marketing a product that will be a close competitor to the products or the processes under development. The result may be an entirely new product that will create its own demand and market. Or it could be a next-generation product, which to a large extent renders current products obsolete or otherwise changes the current market boundaries in a significant way. It may be possible, depending on the circumstances to assess the future potential of R&D undertaken today and predict the transaction's competitive effects on the continued development and commercialization of the products involved.

4.4.4 General R&D Competition

A fourth category comprises upstream transactions in R&D with a potential of creating and developing various technologies and products, potentially belonging to different downstream markets. The relevant R&D may be structured in a way that makes it possible to assess the broader innovation effects for these markets although the 'identity' and characteristics of the downstream markets may be largely unknown at the time of the analysis. Often it is the combination of some vital R&D assets that is crucial here. Holders of such assets may be able to create bottlenecks and control the development of various markets. In some instances, mergers and joint ventures that combine important IPR portfolios have therefore been analysed from a broader perspective where product markets or innovation markets (defined as competing R&D programmes for specific future products) are inadequate tools to address important competition issues. Similar analyses may be performed when assessing innovation aspects of patent pools.

4.4.5 Unilateral Conduct

The first four categories primarily deal with the effects of mergers and other agreements between participants in various markets. Although the innovation market approach was developed to address the dynamic effects of such transactions, innovation analysis may also be important when assessing the effect of powerful market actors' unilateral conduct. Just as with bilateral or multilateral agreements, it may be relevant to analyse effects on incentives and abilities to engage in R&D. The treatment of this category of cases will not be exhaustive, in the sense that many questions that relate particularly to unilateral conduct must be left out. The factual, legal and economic disparity makes the area impossible to cover in a systematic way within the scope of this book. Rather, the cases presented will serve to complete the picture of innovation analysis in the light of some recent case law. As will be seen, notions from the previous four categories are also reflected in these cases. Even if a monopoly or a dominant position relates to a situation of current market power, conduct may relate to R&D entrants, the development of a new market or even effects on a variety of future markets.

4.5. INNOVATION IN EXISTING MARKETS

4.5.1 Innovation: a Relevant Market or Feature of a Market?

The delimitation of a particular market for innovation was expanded upon by the US Department of Justice in *United States v. General Motors Corp.*[3] (1993) concerning a proposed sale of General Motor's Allison Division to the German firm ZF Friedrichshafen.

> GM and ZF were the two largest producers of medium and heavy automatic transmissions in the world. ZF was dominant in Europe while GM was dominant in the US. The parties were actual competitors only in some bus and truck transmission product markets in the US. In the complaint, the DOJ defined the following markets in which the acquisition was alleged to reduce competition: the US markets for production and sale of transmissions for transit buses and for heavy refuse trucks, respectively (the relevant product markets) and the worldwide market for technical innovation in the design, development and production of medium and heavy automatic transmissions for commercial and military vehicles (the relevant innovation market).

[3] *United States v. General Motors Corp.*, Civ. No. 93-530 (D. Del. filed Nov. 16, 1993).

In other words, even though the parties did not compete on many of the different product markets in the US, the excessive concentration was believed to threaten innovation. The DOJ was concerned that the firms would control most of the worldwide assets, including large-scale specialized production assets, necessary for innovation in these automatic transmissions. Innovation required constant feedback from production experiences and GM and ZF were the only firms with the necessary production capacity. GM and ZF produced 89 per cent of such automatic transmissions sold worldwide at the time.[4] Moreover, in the past, innovation had largely occurred when the two companies continuously leapfrogged each other.[5] The effect of stifled innovation would consequently have affected not only the product markets on which they were actual competitors but, more importantly, on all other product markets where the improvements would have been implemented. The proposed acquisition was abandoned.

What makes the GM case special is that the concept of a market for competing technical innovation solves a problem facing the antitrust authority: the parties were competing on the same geographical markets to a very small extent only. Analysing an ordinary product market (transmissions for transit buses and for heavy refuse trucks) gave too narrow an assessment of the effects of the merger, in comparison to the impact predicted after delineating an innovation market.

Although geographical market limitations played a particular role in GM, similar reasoning, alleging a specific effect on competition in innovation, can be found in various cases through the years. One example is *United States v. Flow International* (DOJ 1994) regarding water jet pumps.[6] In a more recent

---

4 In fact, the Department of Justice stated that '[b]ecause of the importance of production and customer experience in the innovation process, market shares in the Innovation Market can be approximated by the number of units produced worldwide by each manufacturer of medium and heavy automatic transmissions for commercial and military vehicles. Using this measure and transmission data generated by Allison and ZF, Allison has over 75 percent of the Innovation Market and ZF has approximately 14 percent': Complaint §42.

5 Tom, Willard K. & Newberg, Joshua A., 'Antitrust and Intellectual Property: From Separate Spheres to Unified Field', 66 *Antitrust Law Journal* 167, 225f. (1997).

6 In *United States v. Flow International Corp and Ingersoll-Rand Co.*, Civ. 94-71320 (E.D. Mich. filed April 14, 1994), the DOJ alleged harmed competition in the relevant markets of ultra-high pressure water jet intensifier pumps and their innovation. The two major makers of these pumps would together control 90 per cent of the relevant product market but were also specifically alleged to compete in innovation leading to 'new and improved waterjet pumps, nozzles, cutting heads, abrasive delivery systems, and components such as seals and check valves'. The parties were very dominant in the product market and the DOJ consequently found it necessary to protect competition both in the product market and in the development and improvement of technology. This merger was abandoned too.

case, *United States v. Halliburton*[7] (1999), the DOJ sought to block the proposed merger between two companies in the market for 'logging-while-drilling' (LWD) tools and services. An important basis for the intervention was the claim that a slower rate of innovation could otherwise be expected.

> LWD techniques are particularly important for companies engaged in offshore drilling for oil and gas. Sensors in the tools provide information during the drilling, concerning the formation that is being drilled, the existence of oil, the possibilities for extraction and so on. Apart from the value of the information, the fact that it is delivered while drilling makes it possible to make adjustments at the same time. No realistic substitutes for LWD services existed in offshore drilling.[8]
>
> The companies were two among four competitors in the US market for offshore LWD tools and services: Dresser, the second largest, and Halliburton the fourth, respectively accounting for 27 and 18 per cent of total revenues. The merger would result in an increase of HHI by almost 1000 points to approximately 3600.
>
> Entry onto the market was difficult, time-consuming and costly. To provide a full range of LWD tools would take years and require large investment and extensive testing. It would be important to establish a lofty reputation, particularly considering the great losses sustained by the customers in the event of tool failure. All four companies were active in extensive engineering programmes for devising new LWD tools and improving existing products. Experience, considerable R&D activity and global business activity characterised the actors on the market. According to the DOJ, successful innovation was unlikely to come from a firm lacking the scale, scope, revenue base and reputation of the incumbent firms.[9]
>
> The DOJ concluded that no domestic or foreign firm would be able to enter or expand in the LWD services to thwart a price increase or prevent a slowdown or lessening in innovation. According to the complaint, the increased concentration and elimination of one competitor was likely to result both in a price increase and in an innovation slow-down.[10]
>
> A settlement was reached, stipulating the divestiture of Halliburton's LWD business as a going concern, including, inter alia, R&D equipment and laboratory records, worldwide royalty-free IPR licences and sublicences and so on.

A common theme in these cases is the suggestion that further concentration in the oligopolistic structure of the market will lead to reductions in innovation. The innovation market is thus the R&D conducted by the incumbent firms.

---

7 *United States v. Halliburton Company and Dresser Industries, Inc.*, Civ. No 98-CV-2340 (April 1, 1999).

8 The Department of Justice concluded that LWD constituted a separate market, since customers facing a small but significant and nontransitory price increase would not substitute (SSNIP test). See complaint §14.

9 See complaint, §§20–22.

10 Since the merger would remove 'one of only a few significant suppliers from an already concentrated market', it would also make an increase in price 'through anti-competitive coordination by the few remaining firms easier and more likely'. See complaint §24.

With reference to the established R&D activities and heavy entry barriers, but without any further identification of R&D programmes or specific assets, the general risk of strategic behaviour or collusion suffices to enjoin the proposed transaction.[11] The incumbent parties in these oligopolistic markets are often in a unique position to conduct R&D with a view to improving the specialized products they manufacture.[12] The prediction of both potential price increases and innovation decreases largely share the same underlying analysis. The authorities maintain that lack of competition leads to negative consumer effects at various levels.

The European Commission also considers innovation as both a consumer value to be protected and a source of competition. In Europe those aspects are often analysed within the product market in question, without a separate innovation market being argued for.

> *Crown Cork & Seal / CarnaudMetalbox*[13] (EU 1995) concerned the merger between two large manufacturers active in the packaging industry. One relevant product market, among others, affected by the merger, was the market for tinplate aerosol cans in the EU.
>
> Based on users' and competitors' statements about lack of substitutability, the Commission found metal aerosol cans to be distinct from other alternative packaging, primarily owing to the technical inadequacies of other possible alternatives. The vast majority of tinplate aerosol can users would not consider switching to aluminium cans even in the case of a significant price increase in tinplate cans. Tinplate cans were considerably less expensive (price differences varying between 5 and 200 per cent) and hence used in industrial and household applications, whereas aluminium cans were typically used in personal care products such as pharmaceuticals and perfumes. Tinplate and aluminium had distinct uses with no substitution. As only marginal imports into the EEA took place and as the product was relatively sensitive to proximity of supply, the relevant geographical area was considered to be the EEA.
>
> The new entity would be very dominant in the market. The merger would leave them with a market share of 60 to 70 per cent, with the closest competitor at 18 per cent and the remaining approximately 20 per cent of the market dispersed among small local competitors.[14] Other factors, such as excess capacity, were also investigated. A decisive aspect for this case was the concentration of know-how, R&D and technology in the two companies.[15]
>
> Know-how played an important role in the ability to compete, particularly for

---

11 In GM/ZF specific assets were identified, consisting of large-scale specialized production assets.

12 Kattan, Joseph, 'After the IP Guidelines: Trends in Intellectual Property Antitrust Enforcement, 11 *Antitrust* 26, 27. (Summer, 1997).

13 Case No IV/M.603 – *Crown Cork & Seal/CarnaudMetalbox*, OJ L 75/38 (1995).

14 §55.

15 §61.

> certain quality variables in the production process. The largest customers saw CarnaudMetalbox as a high-quality innovative supplier while Crown Cork was making efforts to achieve the same level of quality. Together the two firms were seen as the innovative force in a market experiencing 'a fast-moving and costly evolution in technology and know-how'.[16] Possessing and updating state-of-the-art know-how was thus 'a primary factor driving competition in the market'. That driving force was dependent on the parties. CarnaudMetalbox, considered the technology-wise most advanced firm, forced other competitors, particularly Crown Cork, to follow up and develop their technologies.
>
> No other supplier on the market was financially strong enough to develop new technology apart from Crown Cork and CarnaudMetalbox. Even if the market was not stagnant, entry was considered to be costly, difficult and unlikely. The Commission consequently found that the merger would create a dominant position in the relevant market. Nevertheless, the Commission approved the merger subject to undertakings where Crown Cork, for example, agreed to divest substantial parts of its aerosol businesses as a going concern and to provide licences, technical assistance and so on.

Innovation seems to be an integral part of competition in the particular market in this case. It was historically spurred by the competition between the merging parties, and the incentives for continued innovation were therefore specifically highlighted. In this, it resembles the DOJ decision concerning *GM/ZF* (DOJ 1993). Where appropriate, the European Commission does consider the incentives and abilities for continued R&D investments and innovation in mergers between incumbent firms.[17] A potential drawback, or at least risk, in analysing innovation aspects as part of the defined product market could be too narrow a point of departure. It is not certain that parties currently active in the particular product market under investigation – in the Crown Cork decision, the tinplate aerosol market – are necessarily the only ones that carry out relevant technical development. It may very well be that other (potentially competing) technologies are being developed elsewhere.

To distinguish cases where innovation concerns have been treated as a factor in product market competition from cases where innovation has been treated as an independent competition consideration is not easy.

Montedison[18] (FTC 1995) concerned the proposed formation by Montedison and Shell Petroleum of a joint venture, Montell, which would merge the majority of the two companies' worldwide polyolefin business.

---

16 Ibid.

17 See e.g. Case No IV/M.623 – *Kimberly-Clark/Scott Paper,* OJ L 183/1 (1996), §§48, 161–5, regarding toilet tissue; Case No IV/M.214 – *Du Pont/ICI,* OJ L 7/13 (1992), §47, regarding nylon carpet fibres; and Case No COMP/M.2220 – *General Electric/Honeywell* (2001), §§347, 384, 417, 418, regarding aviation engines.

18 *Montedison S.p.A.*, File No. 941-0043 (Jan. 11, 1995) consent order involving divestiture.

Even though the venture excluded Shell's US subsidiary, Shell Oil, and that company's R&D and technology licensing business, the FTC alleged that the joint venture would lead to the combination of the two companies' worldwide production, R&D, and licensing of polypropylene technology.

> The FTC analysed the effects on polypropylene (PP) markets and a polypropylene technology licensing market. In production and sale, the relevant products were different PP resins and catalysts necessary for the production of the resin. However, the FTC was also concerned with PP technology as such and the market for licences for this technology (including licences for catalysts). Geographically the markets for production and sale of polypropylene resins included the United States and Canada. For catalysts and PP technology licences, the relevant geographical area comprised the whole world.[19]
>
> Montedison was the market leader in each of the relevant markets, particularly in technology licensing, where it had coordinated its business with Mitsui. Together their PP technology accounted for over 50 percent of production capacity built or projected to be built under technology licences. Furthermore Montedison and Mitsui catalysts accounted for over 55 percent of world production of PP catalysts.
>
> Shell was the second largest producer of these resins and catalysts in the world and a leader in catalyst technology. The company was engaged in R&D and licensing of PP technology together with Union Carbide: it combined its catalysts with Union Carbide's process technology. The two companies' licences accounted for over 30 percent of capacity built or projected to be built pursuant to technology licences. Consequently, Montedison and Shell together controlled over 80 percent of completed and projected additions to capacity pursuant to technology licences. In the total technology market, i.e. including the in-house technologies of companies not active in licensing, the parties accounted for over 70 percent of built or projected capacity.
>
> Moreover, the long time lags in R&D, the required technological expertise and large sunk costs combined with patent obstacles, made entry very hard. The FTC concluded that the proposed joint venture would increase concentration and eliminate actual competition between the parties in all the relevant markets, create shared interests and result in spillover effects on competition outside the joint venture. In addition, the incentives for technology licensing would be diminished and the price of licences increased, whereas innovation would be reduced.
>
> The long and very complex consent order required, *inter alia,* Shell to divest its interests in the joint venture with Union Carbide and prohibited Montedison and Montell from sharing in royalties from future technology licences granted by Mitsui.

As seen, this is an example of innovation concerns expressed as a part of the anti-competitive effects in the relevant markets. The case has been promoted as an innovation market case, but the way it reads suggests rather that innovation aspects were not separately analysed but just formed an aspect of the current technology market.

---

[19] Complaint, §§9–15.

The European version of the case, *Shell/Montecatini,* (EU 1994)[20] was analysed under the merger regulation, since the cooperation constituted a full-function joint venture. The European Commission also defined and analysed both upstream and downstream markets – a polypropylene (PP) technology market and a polypropylene product market. The technology market was delineated similarly to a product market, by investigating demand substitution. On the PP technology market, the PP manufacturers demanded a technology package consisting of a polymerization process and a catalyst, which had become the standard procedure for PP technology licensing. The relevant market for technology was therefore restricted to packages of 'process-and-catalyst' technology. In addition, the PP technologies had developed considerably since the 1950s. The relevant market for PP technology was therefore defined more precisely to include advanced technology only.[21] Geographically the relevant market for PP production and sale was confined to Western Europe, primarily because of transportation costs. The technology market was considered worldwide. The possible additional costs of choosing a licensor outside the geographical area of the licensee, such as costs of licensor's technical personnel during start-up and subsequent support, did not seem substantially to deter licensees from choosing such licensors.[22]

As seen in the FTC decision above, the PP technologies of the two JV parents – Shell's Unipol technology and Montedison's Spheripol technology – together accounted for most of the technology market (according to the Commission, some 50–75 per cent, excluding licences to the licensor's own plants or joint ventures). Shell would be the industrial leader of the JV, which would develop and market Montedison's Spheripol technology, while Shell would provide the catalyst used in the Unipol technology package.[23] The rivalry between Spheripol and Unipol was considered the main source of competition on the market. The Commission concluded that, subsequent to the concentration, these two technologies would no longer be sufficiently independent of each other.[24]

In reaching its conclusions, the Commission especially highlighted the fact that Spheripol and Unipol seemed to be the technologies that best combined the elements that industry considered vital, when selecting technology. They had the best track record and a wide geographical and technical coverage. The large number of licences provided revenues for R&D efforts and the large amount of already installed capacity tended to reinforce the market situation since industry had disincentives to switch to alternative technology providers. Furthermore, Montedison's patent situation was particularly strong, being the owner or coowner of all major patents for the basic invention as well as subsequent improvements in catalysts, constituting a major barrier to entry. For this, and a number of additional reasons, competitors and newcomers were not considered likely to be able to restrain the market power of the two leading technologies. The two largest competitors each accounted for some 10–25 per cent and one of these, Mitsui, was already engaged in collaboration with Montedison. Although other technologies existed, these could hardly compare with Spheripol and

---

20 Case No IV/M. 269 – *Shell/Montecatini*, OJ L 332/48 (1994).
21 Decision, §§41–3.
22 §§46–51.
23 §58.
24 §60.

> Unipol.[25] There were a number of companies engaged in R&D in the PP sector, but the research often focused on product differentiation, not the development of new products or processes that would displace the current ones. However, a number of companies were also engaged in work on a new generation of catalysts, metallocenes, with at least five to seven years before full commercialization. The fact that a new generation of catalysts was being developed did not affect the Commission's competition assessment, 'since the potential of metallocenes cannot be precisely determined and in any case it is not expected to be fully exploited in the short to medium term.'[26]
>
> In the end the Commission concluded that the JV would create a dominant position, significantly impeding competition in the technology market. They ordered Montedison to transfer to a subsidiary (Technipol) all Montedison's worldwide PP technology licensing businesses, including intellectual property rights, R&D staff and facilities, and a pilot plant for development and testing. Technipol would be a separate, full-functioning company, under sole Montedison control, independent of any Shell interest, and capable of conducting PP technology businesses on a continuing, viable and competitive basis and with the resources necessary to continue independent PP technology development.[27]

Again, the Commission does not seem to have focused on specific R&D efforts regarding the particular technologies. Rather, R&D is relevant as an aspect of competition in the technology market. If the technology market remained competitive, it could induce technological development by both by licensors and licensees.[28] It can also be noted that the European Commission did consider the impact of a new generation of catalysts, but it also limited its time frame to the short to medium term. Finally, it is noteworthy that, although the FTC case is promoted as an innovation market case, the American version does not mention let alone assess the potential introduction of metallocenes.

Recently, the FTC intervened in the proposed acquisition by *GenCorp's* (FTC 2004)[29] subsidiary Aerojet of Atlantic Research Corporation ('ARC'), in order to protect competition for various in-space propulsion thrusters – engines used to manoeuvre spacecrafts once the launch vehicle has delivered them to the upper atmosphere.

> More particularly, the FTC delineated four separate thrusters markets, depending on

---

25 §§32, 61–84.

26 §§30, 85.

27 §§6, 102, 116.

28 Lawrence B. Landman concludes that 'the Commission focused on the polypropylene technology market, including innovation in this market': 'Innovation Markets in Europe', 19 *European Competition Law Review* 21, 24 (1998). Landman also notes that the FTC remedy was stronger and rendered the Commission's order superfluous, and the Commission later allowed Montedison's technology licensing back into the joint venture.

29 *GenCorp Inc.*, Docket No. C-4099, File No. 031 0152, (October 15, 2003).

> the primary use (whether used to transport the spacecraft to its orbit or to control its position while in orbit) and on fuel source (different fuel systems varying in suitability depending on purpose). For the customers, the decision as to what kind of thrusters to use would be based, *inter alia,* on the nature and length of the space mission and the features of the spacecraft. Price differences between different types of thrusters would however be a relatively modest factor in this engineering decision. Consequently, the customers would not be likely to switch to any other thruster type, if faced with a 5 to 10 per cent price increase.
>
> In three of the four markets the two firms were 'the only two significant suppliers' and the acquisition would result in a near monopoly.[30] In the fourth, ARC was the leading supplier with 'essentially [. . .] a monopoly position' for many customers (including US governmental customers) but with Aerojet, having substantial expertise, being considered a likely and effective potential competitor.[31]
>
> Entry was unlikely, not, apparently, primarily because of intellectual property hurdles, but rather owing to the difficult, expensive and time-consuming process of R&D, production and testing. Moreover, for a successful entry, expertise would need to be developed and the developed products would need a 'heritage': a successful track record of use in space.
>
> The markets were defined to include 'research, development, manufacture and sale' of the different thrusters. Since the merger would either create a 'virtual monopoly' or reduce 'actual potential competition' in each of the defined markets, the FTC concluded that the merger would substantially increase the likelihood that Aerojet would exercise unilateral market power, reduce incentives to improve service or product quality, or pursue further innovation. Also the likelihood that US commercial, civil and defence customers would pay higher prices would increase. The FTC thus ordered the divestiture of ARC's in-space propulsion business.

Interestingly, the geographical scope of the market was limited to the US. US export regulations,[32] which made it burdensome and time-consuming for US customers to buy foreign thrusters, combined with the national security issues arising in many governmental space programmes, meant that foreign suppliers were not considered effective competitors for most US customers.[33] Hence 'a handful' of foreign thruster suppliers were not taken into account. All in all, it seems reasonable to assume that innovation was part, but not an independent aspect, of maintaining competition in four narrow, highly specialized and price-inelastic markets where the government, in different roles, is the major customer.

It may be questioned to what extent such geographical limitation is tenable. As a parallel, the DOJ recently lost one of the rare, litigated, merger cases, *United States v. Oracle Corp.* (N.D. Cal. 2004).[34] The case concerned the

---

30 Complaint, §7.

31 Complaint, §8.

32 Particularly the International Traffic in Arms Regulations.

33 Complaint, §6 and Analysis to Aid Public Comment, p. 3.

34 *United States v. Oracle Corporation*, Case No. C 04-00807 VRW, (N.D. Cal. Sept. 9, 2004).

hostile takeover by Oracle of its competitor PeopleSoft, both being engaged in enterprise application software (EAS).[35] Within this broader area the DOJ argued for narrower defined markets, more particularly delineating high function (tailored for large corporations) human resource management and financial management systems in the United States. Apart from failing to prove the existence of this narrowly construed product market, the DOJ was also unable to prove that these high-tech markets should be geographically confined to the US. The court found the market to be worldwide.[36]

4.5.2 Vertical and Horizontal Effects

As explained in Chapter 2, the innovation process is not best characterized as a linear process. Rather, there are important feedback mechanisms flowing between research, development, manufacture and marketing. Control of a link in this chain may therefore imply indirect control, or at least influence, over the innovation process.[37] Such concerns were aired regarding the sale of certain semiconductor business assets from *Digital*[38] to Intel (FTC 1998). Although Digital retained its key technology, which it also planned to continue developing, the FTC acted to prevent negative effects on innovation.

In 1997 Digital filed a lawsuit alleging that Intel had infringed ten patents held by Digital in its manufacture and sales of Pentium processors. Intel filed countersuits claiming breach of secrecy obligations and patent infringements. In a proposed settlement of all pending litigation, the two companies agreed, *inter alia,* that Digital should sell the business and operations used to produce semiconductors, including Digital's Alpha microprocessors. Intel would produce and supply the Alpha processors exclusively to Digital, but Digital was not prevented from entering into similar agreements with other manufacturers for the procurement of these products. Digital would retain its IPRs, design assets and R&D capacity for Alpha architecture, but broad cross-licences were granted in order to settle the pending litigation.

According to the FTC, one relevant market to analyse was the manufacture and sale of all general-purpose microprocessors. Another separate market comprised the manufacture and sale of high-performance, general-purpose microprocessors capable of running Windows NT. In addition to these product markets, the FTC alleged that innovation in the design and development of high-performance, general-purpose microprocessors constituted a separate market. The geographical market was the world.[39]

---

35 EAS includes software applications that automate the business data processing for managing a range of enterprise activities – business intelligence, human resources, financial systems, customer relations, supply chains, product life cycles etc.

36 Decision, p. 138.

37 This was also highlighted in *GM/ZF* (DOJ 1993) above.

38 *Digital Equipment Corporation,* Docket No. C-3818, (1998).

39 Complaint, §§11–14.

Intel was dominant on the two product markets with 90 per cent of dollar sales and 80–85 per cent of unit sales. In both markets Digital represented 1 per cent of dollar sales and other competitors were also very small compared to Intel. In the high-performance segment Digital's Alpha processors and Intel's Pentium processors were probably the only viable alternatives for computer manufacturers. Entry conditions were difficult. The development of a high-performance processor would require at least four years of engineering and investments exceeding $250 million. In addition, to equip a fabrication facility of sufficient scale would cost approximately $1.6 billion. The alternative of contracting with an existing manufacturer would also be costly and time consuming. Network effects created a Catch 22: an entrant would need simultaneously to secure a large number of users to attract software developers and secure support from software developers so as to attract users. Also, very large sales volumes would be required to succeed in obtaining Windows NT support which would be needed to make the processor compatible with this crucial operating system.

The FTC alleged that the transaction would reduce competition between Intel and Digital in the sales of processors and other products to computer manufacturers. Intel would hire current Digital personnel and Digital would be less likely to maintain its sales forces. In addition, concentration 'in the relevant innovation market', where Digital and Intel were the most significant players, would increase significantly.[40] Although Digital was comparatively small, its Alpha technology represented the largest threat to Intel's dominance. It was acknowledged as the fastest and best performing microprocessor in the world. Putting Digital's supply of Alpha processors solely in the hands of Intel would give Intel the opportunity to delay the production, impede the development of new generations, and otherwise undermine the competitiveness of Alpha processors. In particular, there was a risk that Intel would not provide the coordination between design and manufacturing necessary for the development process. All in all, the agreement was likely to create uncertainty regarding the future viability of Alpha. Intel's market power would thereby be increased, which would most likely lead to increased prices and reduced quality and innovation.

The FTC sought to remedy this by ensuring alternative sources for development, manufacture and sales of Alpha products. Digital was thus required to enter into, or extend, certain licensing agreements with Advanced Micro Devices and Samsung Electronics for the Alpha architecture, to enable these firms to develop products, 'Alpha-derivative innovations', based on the Alpha technology. Moreover, Digital was to begin the process of certifying IBM as an additional manufacturer.[41]

It is thus clear that the FTC will not automatically accept any patent infringement settlements, even if the competitors 'only' enter into vertical arrangements.[42] The strategic effects on continued innovation were highlighted and

40 Analysis to Aid Public Comment.

41 This Consent Order was modified in February 2000, after Compaq had acquired Digital, since AMD declined Compaq's offer of a licence and there were no viable substitute licensees for Alpha microprocessor technology. By that time Compaq was not dependent on Intel for its supplies of Alpha microprocessors.

42 For further discussion on horizontal and vertical effects see *Intel* (1999), section 4.9.1, below.

remedied. It could also be noticed that the remedy imposed obligations on Digital, although the competition issues arose from a strengthening of Intel's dominance.

The European Commission assessed similar vertical and horizontal innovation aspects under Article 81, the matter arising from a complex joint venture arrangement.

In *Optical Fibres* (EU 1986),[43] the American manufacturer of optical fibres, Corning, entered into different joint ventures with three large European cable makers for production of such fibres. Corning was a dominant player in the production of optical fibres but also a principal technology provider, offering licences to other manufacturers throughout the world. The European cable makers were established suppliers of the PTTs[44] in their respective countries: the United Kingdom, Germany and France. The cooperation between Corning and important cable makers was essential for its penetration of the EEC market, considering that Corning was a new entrant in the telecommunications market facing strong local purchasing policies from most European PTTs. Moreover, although Corning was active in production of optical fibres and dominant in licensing the optical fibre technology, it had, at the time of the agreements, no experience of cable manufacturing. The cooperation with the cable manufacturers was thus of a complementary nature. Further, the agreements did not foreclose market access by third parties, the parents were free to engage in independent R&D of optical fibres and there was no obligation to grant exclusive licences to Corning for improvements and innovations. The Commission therefore concluded that the agreements did not directly restrict or distort competition between Corning and its partners.[45]

However, in the relationship between the joint ventures there were substantial competition concerns. The joint ventures producing and marketing optical fibres were direct competitors and were now acting in a network of closely interrelated agreements with a common technology provider in an oligopolistic market.[46]

The manufacturers remained free to make active and passive sales into each other's territories, but in countries where Corning had an exclusive licensee, only passive sales were permitted. Corning had interests, through joint ventures, subsidiaries and licensees in several Member States. Moreover, Corning was represented in the joint ventures, both financially and through key personnel. Also, the joint ventures depended fully on Corning's technology and Corning's willingness to supply them with its most up-to-date technology. This technological dependence meant that Corning could coordinate the competitive relationship between the joint ventures. The joint ventures were also obliged to grant back, on a non-exclusive basis, any improvements and innovations to the technology. This led the Commission to conclude that '[u]nlike independent licensees which often develop licensed technology in different directions, the joint ventures in this case will follow the same technological development. This uniform technological development

[43] Case No IV/30.320 – *optical fibres*, OJ L 236/30 1986.

[44] The national posts and telecommunication undertakings or authorities.

[45] §§46, 47.

[46] §§48, 52.

substantially reduces competition between the joint ventures because technology is a key element in competition between optical fibre producers.'[47]

The Commission still found that most of these restrictions, although severe, were indispensable for the attainment of the benefits of the arrangement, allowing the rapid transfer to Europe of a fast moving technology. Some restrictions, especially regarding the exclusivity of sales, were modified.

The Commission thus regarded innovation competition as central on this high-tech market and found that the joint ventures thus restricted competition since no party to them could gain a competitive advantage through independent innovation. An important means of competition between the national JVs would be eliminated when innovation was thus coordinated, thereby having a negative effect on future innovation incentives.

4.5.3 Acquisitions in Adjacent Markets

Tetra Laval/Sidel[48] (CFI 2002) is a noteworthy case, first of all because it involves a conglomerate merger blocked by the competition authorities, secondly as their decision was litigated and overturned by the European Court of First Instance (CFI) and thirdly since it involved court analysis of incentives for future innovation.

The case is most famous for the Commission's conclusion that the acquisition by Tetra Laval of Sidel would enable Tetra Laval to lever its dominance in liquid food carton packaging (where it was the world leader) into the market for SBM[49] machines used in the production of plastic PET bottles (where Sidel was a significant player). The Commission's conclusions regarding these conglomerate effects were overturned by the CFI. The Commission also argued that the merger would strengthen Tetra's dominance in carton packaging.

Although carton and PET packaging did not belong to the same market, the Commission forecast a substantial growth in the PET market, particularly in the use of PET bottles for sensitive products currently distributed in cartons. By acquiring a significant player in this neighbouring market, the Commission argued, a source of significant competition would be eliminated. Such a lessening of potential competition from the PET market would result in Tetra having an incentive not to cut prices and to stop innovating on the carton markets.

In this regard, the CFI found that in order for the Commission to rely on the reduction of potential competition, even of competition which will otherwise tend to grow (that is the PET market), 'the factors which it identifies to show the

---

[47] §50.

[48] Commission Decision, Case No COMP/M.2416 *Tetra Laval/Sidel* (2001); Case T-5/02, *Tetra Laval v. Commission,* ECR II-4381 (2002).

[49] SBM is the abbreviation for Stretch Blow Moulding.

strengthening of a dominant position must be based on convincing evidence'.[50] Tetra's dominance was an important factor, but not sufficient in itself to justify that the position would be strengthened by any reduction in potential competition. The court found the forecasted PET growth to be exaggerated. Moreover, as for Tetra's future conduct it had not been established that, in the event of a reduction of competitive pressure from the PET markets, it would maintain prices and stop innovating. The court stressed that competition on the aseptic carton markets took place largely through innovation, but it had not been shown that Tetra would have incentives to stop innovating due to reduced competitive pressure from the PET markets. Rather innovation seemed to emanate from the demand of consumers of carton-packed products. Besides, since the carton markets were very profitable, the merged entity would probably have incentives to keep carton consumers from substituting PET packaging. Finally, it would probably benefit Tetra's competitors, although currently small, if Tetra stopped innovating.

It is therefore apparent that the CFI too will not refrain from analysing incentives for future innovation. The competition authority must however be careful not to find effects on innovation based on too schematic an analysis. Innovation effects must be substantiated in accordance with the same legal standards as other anti-competitive effects. When new technology will have repercussions on a neighbouring market where competition is currently severely restrained, in terms of market convergence and growing competition, a claimed lessening of this growing competition *and the effects on the adjacent market* must both be clearly established.

Relevant to this finding would seem to be that Sidel was not dominant in the PET packaging market which made it impossible for the merged entity to control the growing competition from this market.

4.5.4 Product Variety, Innovation Pace and Quality

The benefits of competition in the innovation process, providing the market participants with incentives to conduct their product development actively and efficiently, may have different benefits for customers. An ambition to foster various aspects of innovation was apparent when the DOJ in 1998 acted to prevent the merger between Lockheed Martin and Northrop Grumman (DOJ 1998).[51]

According to the complaint, the parties were the only competitors for an array of electronics systems, such as airborne early warning radar, directed infrared countermeasures, a submarine warfare combat system and so on.[52] In other similar areas

50 §312.
51 *United States v. Lockheed Martin Corp. and Northrop Grumman Corp* (1998).
52 Complaint, point 2–6.

> where the parties were active, some (but very limited) outside competition existed. In the development and application of stealth technology, important for next generation warships and military aircrafts, the merger would reduce the number of actors from three to two. Likewise, the two firms were leaders in high-performance fixed-wing military aircraft. In fact the only remaining competitor would be Boeing. In addition, the two remaining post-merger competitors (Lockheed and Boeing) would be teamed on virtually all aircraft in current production. Such an increased interdependence could lead to reduced competition. In the markets where the newly formed company would obtain a monopoly, the FTC foresaw higher costs, higher prices and less innovation in the systems required by the US military. A further issue was the fact that both parties acted as prime contractors and subcontractors for various military systems. The merger would allow Lockheed to favour its in-house capabilities and to foreclose competitors' subsystems. It would also be in a position to have access to competitively sensitive information concerning its competitors. All in all, the merger was, according to the FTC, likely to lead to less price competition and reduced innovation in the various markets.
>
> Entry onto the markets was subject to very high barriers, requiring very high experience and expertise, time and enormous amounts of money.

One may ask why the DOJ bothered investigating and alleging a reduction in future innovation stemming from this merger. In some markets other competitors existed, although few. Moreover, the Department of Defense continued to place orders for the development of different systems, thus providing demand and resources for product development. Is it in these circumstances appropriate to conclude that the reduced level of competition would also lead to less innovation?

Comments from officials indicate that the need to preserve a number of R&D paths was important to the decision and stress the importance of firm diversity when the path of innovation is hard to predict. In those cases innovation is not just a question of the amount of resources being devoted to R&D. According to Rubinfeld and Hoven, who focus particularly on the market for fixed-wing aircraft, the question in Lockheed was not whether a consolidation from three to two would reduce the intensity of innovative effort.[53] Rather, the number of independent innovators would be reduced by one. Diversity may stem from both the number of independent innovators and the opportunity for entry. Path-breaking advances are more likely from other than the current market leaders. Rubinfeld and Hoven give the example of unmanned aircraft – a hot prospect in the particular market – less likely to be encouraged by leaders such as Lockheed and Boeing.

The case suggests that the DOJ will be ready to defend diversity in R&D

---

53 Rubinfeld, Daniel L. & Hoven, John, 'Innovation and Antitrust Enforcement', in Ellig, Jerry (ed.), *Dynamic Competition and Public Policy,* Cambridge: Cambridge University Press, 2001, p. 88.

although there is no clear evidence that the different R&D sources are substitutes, that is, developing competing future products.[54] Compared to the innovation market concept in the guidelines' world, this would be taking yet another step away from a static neoclassical market perception towards an evolutionary view of the market process. To maintain duplicate R&D sources for undefined future developments necessarily incurs costs. But it might be considered that such static inefficiencies are necessary to sustain requisite variety and dynamics in the market.[55]

Regarding the vertical aspects of the case, it has been noticed that the combination could have affected future development contracts. Often, complementary capabilities are brought together in this industry when firms, even direct competitors, supply technologies for various systems (such as stealth airplanes). When integrating vertically, the firm may stop supplying competitor bidders or supply at less attractive terms and favour in-house technology, refraining from contracting competitors' technologies. The most important reason for all this would be to remain the prime contractor for coming rounds of bids. In this particular case, Northrop and Lockheed would favour their complementary in-house technologies and the other actors on these duopolistic/oligopolistic submarkets would thereby also 'unwillingly' form vertical alliances in the bids for systems. The concern was thus reduced competition in general and that the best combinations of subsystems would not be available after the merger. Moreover, this static vertical order in the market where the same actors form teams from time to time would presumably be less conducive to mutual learning, cross-fertilization of ideas and thus breakthrough innovation.[56]

4.5.5 Concluding Observations

In this first category of cases, the authorities acknowledge the importance of innovation competition when reviewing transactions between firms that currently compete on the same product markets. When innovation is an important aspect of the competition in which the merging parties engage, and heavy barriers to entry protect incumbent firms, the result of increased concentration

[54] Gilbert, Richard J. & Tom, Willard K., 'Is Innovation King at the Antitrust Agencies? The Intellectual Property Guidelines Five Years Later', 69 *Antitrust Law Journal* 43, 59f. (2001).

[55] See e.g. Metcalfe, Stan, 'The Economic Foundations of Technology Policy: Equilibrium and Evolutionary Perspectives', in Stoneman, Paul (ed.), *Handbook of the Economics of Innovation and Technological Change,* Blackwell Publishers, Oxford, 1995, pp. 415f.

[56] Rubinfeld & Hoven, *supra*, note 53, pp. 89f.

may have effects on the innovative output, just as it may have an impact on other competition variables. Competition in the product market will induce firms to outperform each other by various means, not least through successful innovation. Similarly, authorities may intervene when a transaction reduces incentives to innovate as competitors will be able to control or appropriate the benefits of R&D as in *Digital/Intel* (FTC 1998) and *Optical Fibres* (EU 1986).

Where the authorities are careful to characterize the innovation process of the industry together with the parties' strategic positions in that process, the competitive relationship between underlying technologies, other specific assets controlled by the parties and so on, the analysis becomes both complete and possible to evaluate. Note that, since barriers to entry differ between development, production and distribution, it may be possible to consider innovation aspects from a worldwide perspective, although the product market may be geographically more limited.

Whether a merger can be fully assessed as relating to current product markets only, or whether it warrants specific innovation analysis, depends on the situation. Where innovation is taking place through changes or improvements in currently marketed goods, creating products that might replace existing products over time, current product market analysis may suffice. Nevertheless, a clear and structured innovation analysis, as a part of the product market analysis, increases the chances of a comprehensive assessment. This will also make decision making more transparent than would be the case where various market effects are merely inferred from current market statistics. Where R&D cycles are transparent and it is likely that new products render older products obsolete, the need and applicability of an innovation market analysis increases.[57] Pipeline products may then give a picture of future product market developments in the short to medium term. To such situations we now turn.

4.6 POTENTIAL R&D ENTRANTS

4.6.1 R&D Competition and Future Product Markets

This category deals with transactions between incumbent firms and a potential entrant that may enter the market with a new product. Often difficulties arise in competition law analysis in determining whether and to what extent a product

57 See e.g. EU 2001 Horizontal Cooperation Guidelines, §43; *Wright Medical Technology, Inc.*, C-3564 (Mar. 23, 1995), 60 Fed. Reg. 460 (Jan. 4, 1995) discussed in the next section.

competes with certain other products (that is, what is the correct product market definition). A particular problem with an analysis of a potential entrant is the possibility that the new product will, entirely or to some degree, create its own demand (its own market) or will become a next generation product that will render currently marketed products obsolete. The less well-matching the current product market is – in other words, the more radical innovation is – the more emphasis is put on an R&D analysis to assess the competitive effects of a transaction.

In the *Boston Scientific Corp.* case[58] (FTC 1995) the FTC reviewed Boston Scientific's proposed acquisition of Cardiovascular Imaging Systems (CVIS) and SCIMED Life Systems – a three-party transaction.

The FTC was concerned about the effects of the acquisitions in the research and development, manufacture and sale of intravascular ultrasound (IVUS) catheters (including imaging catheters, imaging cores and imaging guidewires). The geographical area for which the effects were to be analysed was the United States. The FTC noted that patents and requirements for regulatory approvals and so on constrained foreign firms from selling in the US.

Boston and CVIS were the leading market actors accounting for approximately 40 and 50 per cent, respectively, of the sales of IVUS catheters in the US. The acquisition of CVIS would result in an increase of the HHI by 3850 points to over 7900. The only competitor in the IVUS market, Endosonics, used another kind of technology and its market shares were declining. Boston Scientific and CVIS were competing vigorously and were also engaged in patent litigation in which CVIS asserted that Boston Scientific was infringing certain patents, while Boston asserted that certain CVIS patents were invalid and that CVIS infringed its patents.

After several years of work SCIMED had developed a new prototype imaging guidewire. The FTC alleged that SCIMED had the capacity, incentives and economic interests to enter the market and that, but for the acquisition, it was likely to do so within two to three years. No other firm had an entry advantage similar to SCIMED's.[59] Further entry onto the market was considered unlikely, requiring substantial expertise, several years of R&D and design, and established production facilities. The three parties' broad patent rights further impeded such entry.

The result would be increased concentration and unilateral market power on the IVUS catheter market, as it eliminated competition between the two major competitors (Boston and CVIS) in all dimensions: R&D, manufacture and sales. The acquisition of SCIMED would eliminate important R&D competition and the leading potential competitor. Taken together this would diminish product innovation and increase prices.[60]

The consent order, while permitting the parties to merge, was designed to create an independent competitor in R&D, production and sale of the IVUS catheters. It required Boston Scientific to provide, on a royalty-free basis, a non-exclusive

58 *Boston Scientific Corp.*, File No. 951-0002, 60 Fed. Reg. 12,948 (Mar. 9, 1995).

59 Complaint, §13.

60 Ibid., §§15, 16.

> licence for the merged companies' patent portfolio to Hewlett-Packard or any interested and qualified entrant. This third party would hence receive 'a broad package of patents and technology relating to IVUS catheters'.[61] If the licensee so requested, Boston would also provide information, technical assistance and advice, *inter alia,* to enable the licensee to obtain all necessary FDA approvals. The order furthermore provided a three-year supply agreement for IVUS catheters between Boston Scientific and the licensee. In retrospect, it should be noted that the result was not a success: Hewlett-Packard has left the scene and Boston Scientific today controls the market for IVUS catheters.[62]

It is hardly surprising that commentators have regarded Boston's acquisition of SCIMED as a potential competition case with an R&D angle. Boston was active in a market where entry depended on successful R&D and SCIMED was a potential entrant, although entry was two to three years away. If the merged entity would have less incentive to pursue R&D as speedily and effectively as before, this could follow just from its position on the current product market and the concentration in R&D. But the latter dimension called for an analysis of the state of art in all relevant R&D.

In Europe there did not exist a clearly defined innovation market concept, at least not until the 2001 Horizontal Collaboration Guidelines described in Chapter 3. In the absence of such a concept or methodology, case law has tended to treat these issues less explicitly. Consequently, relevant cases are more difficult to identify, compare and analyse. However, just as in the American situation, European cases in which R&D competition analysis has been performed are most frequently found in the pharmaceutical industry. Here the European Commission has developed some standards to be applied in its analysis, for example with regard to market definitions.

From the number of merger cases in the pharmaceutical industry it is clear

---

61 See Analysis to Aid Public Comment on the Provisionally Accepted Consent Order.

62 The FDA approved Hewlett-Packard (HP) as a licensee, and HP and Boston entered into a licence agreement, which also was approved by the FTC. At the time HP was in the console market, but not the catheter market. However, HP gave up its efforts to enter the catheter market and also exited the console market altogether in late 1998. In 1999, HP filed a private action against Boston, alleging breach of contract, monopolization and attempted monopolization. This case was settled between the parties and withdrawn from litigation. However, in October 2000, the Department of Justice, on behalf of the FTC, sued Boston for breach of the terms of the order. According to DOJ's complaint, Boston failed to provide HP with a licence to a Webler patent, relating to a device for IVUS catheters. Boston also refused to provide necessary information for several catheters and to supply a new kind of catheter. The DOJ asked the Court to decree that Boston violated the order and order an appropriate civil penalty. In March 2003 the case was decided and Boston was fined $7 million for eliminating competition.

that relevant markets in the pharmaceutical industry are often grouped into pharmaceutical specialities, active substances and future products.[63] The analysis of what is denoted 'future products' or, sometimes, 'future markets', typically examines the 'products which are not yet on the market but which are at an advanced stage of development'.[64] This does not necessarily mean that no product market exists.[65]

The Commission looks at R&D potential 'in terms of its importance for existing markets, but also for future market situations'.[66] It appears from the bulk of merger case law that the Commission analyses the competitive state of future markets, and thus analyses the competitive situation with regard to products that have reached such levels of development that their competitive impact on the near-future market can be assessed.[67] However, sometimes the 'near future' seems rather distant. Moreover, as much as the competitive state

---

63 Case No IV/M.072 – *Sanofi/Sterling Drug* (1991); Case No IV/M.323 – *Procordia/Erbamont,* OJ C 128 (1993); Case No IV/M.426 – *Rhône-Poulenc/Cooper,* OJ C 113 (1994); Case No IV/M.457 – *la Roche/Syntex,* OJ C 178 (1993); Case No IV/M.500 – *AHP/Cyanamid,* OJ C 278/3 (1994); Case No IV/M.555 – *Glaxo/Wellcome,* OJ C 65/3 (1995); Case No IV/M.495 – *Behringwerke AG/Armour Pharmaceutical Co.*, OJ C 134/4 (1995); Case No IV/M.587 – *Hoechst/Marion Merell Dow* (1995); Case No IV/M.631 – *Upjohn/Pharmacia,* OJ C 294/9 (1995); Case No IV/M.737 – *Ciba-Geigy/Sandoz* (1996) OJ L 201/1 (1997); Case No IV/M.950 – *Hoffman LaRoche/Boehringer Mannheim* (1997); Case No IV/M.1229 – *American Home Products/Monsanto* (1999); Case No IV/M. 1403 –*Astra/Zeneca* (1999); Case No IV/M.1397 – *Sanofi/Synthélabo* (1999); Case No IV/M.1378 – *Hoechst/Rhône-Poulenc* (1999); Case No COMP/M.1846 – *Glaxo Wellcome/SmithKline Beecham.*

64 *Hoechst/Rhône-Poulenc* (1999), §26 and *Ciba-Geigy/Sandoz* (1996), §42.

65 In *Glaxo Wellcome/SmithKline Beecham* (2000), the future market analysis investigated overlaps in areas where either one or both parties had existing products on the market and pipeline products in development and areas where neither party was currently active on the market but both parties had products in pipeline.

66 *Hoechst/Rhône-Poulenc* (1999), §26. The same locution has been used in a number of cases.

67 Pharmaceutical R&D projects undergo three different phases of clinical testing: Phase I marks the start of clinical testing on humans, some eight to ten years before the product is launched. It has been claimed that, statistically, projects in phase I generally have a 10 per cent chance of being successful. Phase II, some four to five years before market introduction, involves working out the proper dose for the patient and defining the areas of application. The success rate of phase II is recognized to be approximately 30 per cent. Phase III, starting three years before launch, involves establishing the product's effectiveness on larger groups of patients. Even in phase III, 50 per cent are reported to fail. *Ciba-Geigy/Sandoz* (1996), §58, *Glaxo Wellcome/SmithKline Beecham* (2000), §70. These figures correspond well to other observations, see Ben-Asher, Dror, 'In Need of Treatment? Merger Control, Pharmaceutical Innovation, and Consumer Welfare', 21 *Journal of Legal Medicine* 271, 346 (2000).

of future markets may interest the Commission, it has also defined competing R&D poles and analysed R&D conditions with a view to maintaining a sufficient level of R&D competition.

Based on the products' characteristics and intended therapeutic use, the potential for these products to enter into competition with other products, already marketed or in development, can be assessed. As research and development is normally global, the geographical consideration of future markets 'should therefore at least focus on the territory of the Community and, possibly, on world-wide markets'.[68] Differences in the patent situation, inside and outside the Community, may lead to different competitive situations, which is why the Commission sometimes chooses the Community alone as the relevant geographical delimitation.[69]

In most pharmaceutical cases the delineation of the parties' R&D and pipeline products that may be affected by the merger is rather straightforward. However the delineation of a relevant market for these pipeline products and the delimitation of products, either already marketed or being developed, that should be included in such a market is often less clear-cut than is the case for current markets. The analysis is usually based on the existing ATC classes, grouping pharmaceuticals according to their composition and therapeutic properties, but it can also be guided by the overall characteristics of future products as well as by the indications to which they are to be applied.[70]

These issues were developed in *Glaxo Wellcome/SmithKline Beecham* (EU 2000).[71]

> In this case, the European Commission, under a future market analysis, investigated overlaps in areas where either one or both parties had existing products on the market and pipeline products in development and areas where neither party was currently active on the market but both parties had products in pipeline. In doing so

---

[68] *Glaxo Wellcome/SmithKline Beecham*, §75.

[69] See e.g. *Ciba-Geigy/Sandoz*, §51.

[70] Medicines can be broken down into therapeutic classes according to the Anatomical Therapeutic Classification ('ATC'), which is recognized and used by the World Health Organisation. This classification enables medicines to be grouped according to their composition and therapeutic properties into four levels, the fourth level being the most detailed. The third-level classes of the ATC classification provide a grouping of medicines according to their therapeutic properties, that is, their intended use, and therefore may be accepted as an operational market definition. It may also be appropriate to combine products from different classes, when these may be regarded as substitutes and the products from different classes compete as possible treatments for a specific diagnosed medical condition. Correspondingly, a certain third-level class may have to be subdivided, when the products' indications differ.

[71] Case No COMP/M.1846 – *Glaxo Wellcome/SmithKline Beecham* (2000).

the Commission particularly analysed anti-migraine, oncology, asthma/COPD, therapeutic vaccines ('pharmaccines')[72] and diabetes.

In the anti-migraine area there were no pure R&D concerns. SB had a pipeline compound in phase II while GW had two leading products on current markets. The parties had already committed themselves to outlicense SB's pipeline compound so the Commission could conclude there was no overlap between GW's existing products and SB's pipeline product.

SB and GW each had two pipeline products for the treatment of colorectal cancer. SB's products were in phase II and I whereas GW had two products in phase III. However, given the parties' (presumably modest) position on current markets and that a number of important competitors were active in the field, the Commission concluded that the overlapping activities in oncology were not likely to lead to adverse effects.

In the asthma/COPD (Chronic Obstructive Pulmonary Disease) area the Commission first carefully analysed the current market situation and eventually concluded that GW, overall, enjoyed a far stronger market position than any of its competitors. Adding the different products in this field, GW represented 40–50 per cent of the overall (ATC level 2) market in the EU.[73] Although SB did not produce or market any anti-respiratory products, the Commission stated that it had to take into account SB's pipeline products. More particularly, the Commission had to assess 'the impact of the transaction on existing markets and on R&D markets'.[74]

SB had two different pipeline products for treatment of asthma in phase I and II, respectively. GW had a number of existing products but no products in pipeline. A number of other companies were engaged in R&D in the same area, some rather similar to the phase II compound. The Commission concluded that there was 'no risk of eliminating actual R&D competition between SB and GW', but nevertheless considered that the merger would lead to a reduction of potential competition on existing markets. However, taking into account the other sources of potential competition (at least one similar competing new product was likely to be launched before SB's phase II product and a number of competitors had other phase I–III pipeline products for asthma), the elimination of potential competition between the parties was not found to strengthen GW's already strong position in the treatment of asthma.[75]

The Commission thus did not expect the acquisition to reduce actual R&D

---

[72] The main difference between prophylactic vaccines and pharmaccines is that pharmaccines have a therapeutic purpose and will be administered after the disease has been established (§198).

[73] Decision, §§160, 171. The Commission noted that asthma and COPD involved different clinical presentations, risks and therapies. The parties maintained that asthma was well understood and well treated, whereas there was limited agreement as to diagnosis and treatment of COPD. The existing COPD treatments were considered ineffective and patients were therefore normally treated with several products. For both diseases, the treatments involved different ATC level-3 products (§§151–8). For further details see also Case No IV/M.1403– *Astra/Zeneca* (1999).

[74] §174.

[75] §177.

competition in the market, but it concluded that an acquisition of a research programme in phase II could constitute a restriction of potential competition. Considering GW's strong position on the existing market, the R&D programme was regarded as a potential competitor, apparently in spite of the risks and uncertainties associated with the remaining development. The existence of competing R&D saved the day.

> In the area for treatment of COPD, GW had existing products on the market. Both parties also had pipeline products. Most importantly, they each had one product in phase III.[76] Although there was no direct overlap between GW's existing products and SB's phase III pipeline product (probably different ATC 3 categories), the Commission had to assess how SB's new compound affected the merged company's overall market position in the respiratory field, and whether the 'overall R&D potential' was likely to be reduced.[77] SB's pipeline product also differed compared to GW's pipeline product in that it had a different mechanism for action, with differing effectiveness for certain common COPD conditions. The different molecules were indicated for both first and second line treatment of COPD.[78] The Commission found the overall market for COPD treatment was an attractive R&D market: the future market potential was great.[79] Existing products were relatively inefficient, none of the pipeline products would serve as an effective single treatment for COPD, and there was much unmet clinical need and a large number of pharmaceutical companies conducting research at different levels.[80] This attractiveness combined with the fact that GW and SB pursued different lines of R&D in COPD, led the Commission to consider an elimination of *R&D currently being conducted by the parties* to be unlikely. Moreover, while the parties possibly would streamline their future R&D efforts, the Commission, given the number of other pipeline products and resourceful competitors, did not consider that the merger would lead to a diminution of the *overall R&D potential* either.[81]

The Commission thus explicitly evaluated the incentives and abilities for the

---

[76] GW's product Seretide was an existing asthma product (a mix of two different drugs) currently in phase III development for COPD. SB's phase III product was named Ariflow. In addition SB had a phase I development, but the Commission considered only the phase III relevant in this part of its assessment.

[77] §179.

[78] The first line treatment is used as the first treatment generally suitable for most patients. As disease severity increases, a variety of agents are added to improve symptomatic control, these being the so-called 'second line' treatments. The Commission defined, for the purposes of the specific decision, second line treatment as 'treatments used in combination with other therapies' (§180).

[79] COPD was expected to become the third most common cause of death by 2020.

[80] The parties estimated that over 20 different companies had 30 different compounds for COPD in various stages of development, representing 13 different therapeutic categories (§§184–6).

[81] §188.

parties to reduce anti-competitively their R&D efforts (some streamlining being acceptable). Moreover, the analysis considered the effects for R&D on the market in general. This part of the decision was thus devoted to innovation competition by an analysis of the general conditions for R&D. R&D programmes at all levels in the process, with potentially different future overlaps, were included to show the presence of dynamic R&D competition.

The Commission then turned to the question of future effects on existing markets.

> When assessing the effects from eliminating SB as a potential competitor in the field, the Commission divided the COPD market into first and second line therapies, considering the currently strong position of GW (40–50 per cent) and the fact that both SB's and GW's pipeline products were targets for second line treatment.[82] For second line therapies the Commission found four other competing compounds in phase III development (only phase III products were regarded as competitors in this assessment).[83] Three of these were developed by resourceful competitors (AstraZeneca and Byk Gulden), in a good position to launch the products on the market. Nevertheless, the strong market position of GW for existing products[84] implied that the elimination of SB as a potential competitor could further strengthen the position of GW, particularly if the other phase III products failed. '[U]nder the very special circumstances', the Commission accepted the merger after the parties had agreed an undertaking to outlicense SB's future product on an exclusive basis, in the event that all the competing phase III pipeline compounds for second line treatment failed.[85]

In this part of the decision, when explicitly analysing future developments on a product market in which the merger would have foreseeable effects in the shorter term, the relevant competing R&D programmes were limited to those in phase III. This analysis is thus conducted separately from the previous assessment of possible effects for general R&D competition in the area. The Commission clears the merger from a general R&D competition perspective, but concludes that the merger may strengthen the future position on an already concentrated product market. Hence the remedy did not aim at restoring R&D

---

82 In first line treatment for COPD, GW was currently behind Boehringer Ingelheim, whereas in second line treatment they were twice as strong as the closest competitor, AstraZeneca (§§171, 194).

83 According to the Commission, phase III products were likely to be launched within three years whereas phase II products could take four to five years. The expected risk of failure was 50 per cent for phase III products compared to 70 per cent for phase II (§190).

84 In the particular diagnosis segment of second line treatment for which GW's and SB's products were likely to be indicated, GW represented 35–40 per cent and AstraZeneca 20–30 per cent.

85 §§195, 222. For further details see annex to the decision.

competition but rather at restoring future product market competition in the event that competitors fail.

One could question whether such a remedy is really an adequate way of dealing with uncertain future market developments. It seems awkward to have a principal remedy that is conditioned by hypothetical future events in the first place, for the sake both of certainty and of enforcement. Secondly, one may ask what effect it would have on incentives. In the event that SB is successful and its competitors are not, it will lose the product (in exchange for royalties) in order to create competition.

The Commission also investigated two further areas, pharmaccines and diabetes, rightfully belonging to category 3 (treated below under section 4.7) in this case law categorization: that is, areas where neither of the parties was active in current sales of similar products but where both were active in R&D. Here the Commission decided not to intervene, but only after having delineated and assessed competing R&D in each area.

> In pharmaccines there was a potential overlap in the treatment of some antivirals. Neither party had any pharmaccines on the market and the potential for pharmaccines could not readily be predicted at the time. GW had an existing hepatitis B product and a hepatitis B pharmaccine in phase I. SB had a hepatitis B pharmaccine in phase II. Both parties had existing drugs for the treatment of herpes simplex and GW also had a pharmaccine in pipeline that could represent a new generation in the area. However, there was a lot of uncertainty regarding pharmaccines, the pipeline products were more than five years from a potential commercialization and potential future markets and their competitiveness were unknown (testing on humans had not even substantially started).[86] Together with the fact that a large number of players were active in pharmaccine R&D (for example, Aventis, Bristol-Myers Squibb, Schering-Plough and Roche) the Commission did not consider the pipeline products further strengthened the parties' position. Interestingly, when the Commission had already considered current antiviral markets (under the 'pharmaceutical specialities' heading), it had found serious competition problems. Apart from creating dominance on the current markets, competitors alleged that the merger would 'discourage any tentative research and development attempts by third parties to develop antiviral drugs' and the Commission's investigation confirmed that the merger would significantly increase entry barriers for competitors with pipeline products under development. The Commission thus found serious doubts as to compatibility with the common market and required the parties to license out one of the existing products. This divestiture was sufficient.[87]
>
> In diabetes neither party had any drugs on European markets. However, SB had a product available in the US which was expected to be launched in Europe in the same year, and GW had two pipeline products, one in phase I and one in phase III. The Commission concluded that no competition concerns arose from the pipeline products as neither party was currently established on the European market, and

86 §§201, 205.
87 §§96, 204, 205.

given that a number of (large) competitors were active both with existing products and with pipeline products.

In 2002, the FTC faced the merger between *Amgen and Immunex*,[88] in which it was necessary to investigate the effects from overlaps between current market participation and product pipelines.

The merger affected three therapeutic areas, in two of which one party had some product already approved while the other had a potentially competing product in development.

In the area of TNF inhibitors, used primarily to treat arthritis but also other autoimmune diseases, Immunex and J&J were the only companies with products on the market. Three other companies had TNF inhibitors in clinical development. As one of these, Amgen was developing an inhibitor similar to that of Immunex, with an expected launch in 2005. Among the five firms active in this market, the merging firms were the only ones developing soluble TNF receptor products. The merger was therefore considered to lessen potential competition between the two companies' products, which would probably lead to higher prices and fewer alternatives for consumers. The consent agreement provided for the licensing of certain Amgen patents to a sixth company, Serono, which was developing a soluble TNF inhibitor in Europe, but which was otherwise unlikely to be sold in the US owing to blocking patents held by Amgen.[89]

It is interesting to note that the FTC intervened although there would remain four companies in the sales or development of competing products. But it was stressed that the merger would combine the closest potential substitutes. Moreover, it seems that an unusually satisfactory remedy was available, that would not spoil the chances of dynamic efficiency gains from the merger but would introduce a new actor on the market without causing any significant additional costs, time lags or other inefficiencies.

IL-1 Inhibitors essentially work similarly to TNF inhibitors, but restrain a different type of cytokine from causing inflammation, and are also used to treat rheumatoid arthritis. In this market Amgen sold the only product. Immunex and Regeneron were the only companies engaging in clinical trials in this area, where *de novo* entry was estimated to take six to ten years and cost over $200 million. Moreover, the Regeneron product, in phase II, was endangered by Immunex, which had indicated that it would seek to block it by patent litigation. According to Regeneron, such litigation could foreclose the ability to commercialize – regardless of the outcome in the case. The FTC therefore concluded that Immunex was likely to be successful in precluding Regeneron's successful commercialization. If merged, the companies were also likely to use their combined patents to stop Regeneron.

Although the Immunex IL-1 project was only in phase I clinical trials, the FTC

---

88 *Amgen Inc. and Immunex Corporation*, Docket no. C-4053 (2002).

89 Analysis of Agreement Containing Consent Order to Aid Public Comment.

therefore concluded that the merger was 'likely to lead to unilateral anti-competitive effects in the IL-1 inhibitor market by eliminating potential competition between Amgen and Immunex as well as the ongoing research and development competition between the companies'.

Furthermore, Immunex and Amgen were the only ones involved in the development of TNF/IL-1 combination therapies which could prove more efficacious than using either drug alone.

Immunex was required to license certain patents to Regeneron in order to give it operational freedom to enter the market and compete against Amgen.

In the merger between *Pfizer and Pharmacia*[90] (EU and FTC 2003) the American and European authorities collaborated closely, particularly on issues regarding pipeline products and remedies.[91]

Apart from competitive concerns regarding the two parties' currently marketed products, two product areas warranted closer R&D analysis: treatments for erectile dysfunction (ED) and incontinence (or overactive bladder).

At the time of the merger, Pfizer marketed its blockbuster drug Viagra for the treatment for ED. Viagra dominated the market with very high market shares throughout the EU (ranging from 70 to almost 100 per cent). Similarly, the product represented about 95 per cent of the US market. Although Pharmacia marketed an older product for ED (administered through injection), competition aspects particularly arose from Pharmacia's two pipeline products under development: one apomorphine product in the form of a nasal spray and a dopamine D2 receptor in oral tablet form.

A number of other competitors were developing products for the treatment of ED, particularly PDE-5 inhibitors – the same kind as Viagra. In Europe, both Bayer in cooperation with GlaxoSmithKline (the product Levitra) and Eli Lilly/ICOS (Cialis) were expected to launch a product in 2003. A large number of other firms were also engaged in the development of similar products.

In the US, where Pfizer had been granted a broad 'method of use' patent covering PDE-5 inhibitors, the company had commenced patent litigations against Bayer/GSK and Eli Lilly/ICOS. In Europe, the European Patent Office had held a field of use patent invalid in 2001 in an interim decision. Pfizer had appealed the decision and the final decision was pending.

In view of the patent situation and current litigation, the FTC concluded that, with the exception of Pharmacia's two products in development, entry into the ED market was unlikely. The European Commission stated that '[u]nder the worst case scenario, should the patent be held valid both in the US and in Europe, Viagra would be the only PDE-5 inhibitor on the market'.[92] In any event, if the US patent were to be upheld, this would have a negative spillover effect on the European market.

[90] Case No COMP/M.2922 – *Pfizer/Pharmacia* (2003); *Pfizer Inc. and Pharmacia Corporation*, File No. 021 0192, Docket no. C-4075 (2003).

[91] Loughran, Mary, Parplies, Kay & Schade, Roosmarijn, 'Merger Control: Main developments between 1st January 2003 and 30th April 2003', *Competition Policy Newsletter* 2:70, 73 (2003).

[92] Commission decision, §88.

> Losing more than 50 per cent of the ED market, the competitors' profitability would be reduced, forcing them to retrench their strategic plans for Europe and moreover discouraging or delaying further research and creating uncertainty among physicians as well as a negative presumption among customers.
>
> Apart from the Pharmacia pipeline products, a number of other firms were developing non-PDE-5 inhibitors, thus outside Pfizer's patent realm, but these were 'in relatively early phase of development' and the companies in question were relatively smaller and less experienced in the ED field.[93] The worldwide remedy to the problem was to order divestiture of the two Pharmacia products.

It could be noted here that the two competing products, Levitra and Cialis, were in fact introduced in the US in late 2003. Patent litigation is currently pending in the US, a conflict that both sides seem confident of winning. In Europe, Cialis had been approved by EMEA[94] already in November 2002, whereas Levitra was approved a few days after the merger decision.

In contrast to the decision in *Ciba-Geigy/Sandoz* (EU 1996),[95] which will be discussed later, the European Commission here interpreted uncertainties regarding the patent situation to the disadvantage of the firms.

> As for the area of incontinence, Pharmacia sold Detrusitol, a strong product with some 40–95 per cent of the national European markets. The US market was a duopoly, where Pharmacia and J&J were the only actors.
>
> Pfizer had a compound in phase III development, with the same indication and mechanism of action as Detrusitol, and the products were therefore considered to be substitutes.
>
> Entry onto the US market within two years was expected by two new products, one from Pfizer and the other from Yamanouchi.[96] Other pipeline products were considered well behind.
>
> The European Commission identified two pipeline products in phase II, one belonging to Schwarz Pharma and one to AstraZeneca[97] However, given that the Pfizer product was in phase III, it was considered unlikely that the competitors would be able to challenge the market position in the near future. Pfizer was required to divest its pipeline product to Novartis.

The reasoning of the two authorities is interesting. According to the complaint,

---

93 Ibid., §§82, 90.

94 The European Agency for the Evaluation of Medicinal Products (www.emea.eu.int).

95 Case No IV/M.737 – *Ciba-Geigy/Sandoz* (1996) OJ L 201/1 (1997), see section 4.8, below.

96 Analysis of Proposed Consent Order to Aid Public Comment.

97 The information about which phase of development any of the products is in is omitted from the Commission decision, but freely available at the relevant companies' websites, www.astrazeneca.com, www.schwartzpharma.com (last visited 11 October 2004); according to the latter 'The phase IIb clinical studies were successfully concluded beginning of 2003', moving the Schwartz Pharma product into phase III.

the FTC defines the markets as the 'research and development, and the manufacture and sale' of the two categories of products. Since the merger would eliminate 'actual, direct and substantial competition' in both these markets it would reduce innovation and eliminate potential competition in manufacture and sale, thereby (a) increasing the likelihood that the combined entity would delay or forgo the launch of the product under development, and (b) increasing the likelihood that the combined entity would delay or eliminate the additional price competition that would have resulted. In its 'Analysis to Aid Public Comment', the FTC stressed the importance of potential competition in the ED market. Instead of a price-reducing entry by Pharmacia, the merger would preserve Pfizer's monopoly. Also the reduction from four to three rivals in the incontinence market was considered likely to force the consumers to pay higher prices and reduce R&D competition.

The European Commission's conclusions are basically identical for each of the two product areas. The strong market position of the incumbent party would be reinforced by the acquisition of one or two potentially important substitutes.

However, the R&D situation differed substantially in the two areas. The two Pharmacia ED products had both merely entered phase II clinical trials.[98] Even though a product has successfully passed the first phase, the future remains very uncertain both in terms of chances of success and also as regards the final product characteristics. This was particularly so here, since the ED products had different action mechanisms. In fact, the firm acquiring one of the compounds expresses uncertainty regarding its potential.[99] The European Commission considered the pipeline products to be alternatives to Viagra since they both treat ED and, '[a]ccording to third parties, both products stand a good chance of eventually reaching the market'. Despite the early phase of development, the Commission considered that these products should be taken into account, given Pfizer's existing strong market position and the patent litigation. Nevertheless, it could be questioned whether the authorities really

[98] The acquiring firms' websites contain valuable information about the state of art of the divested pipeline products; see www.nastech.com and www.neurocrine.com (last visited 11 October 2004).

[99] Regarding the dopamine receptor '[t]he compound has demonstrated high intrinsic activity in animal models of sexual dysfunction. Neurocrine will conduct a Phase II proof of concept clinical study in the area of male erectile dysfunction (ED) early next year in order to determine its potential efficacy. ED affects nearly 77 million men in the world's seven major pharmaceutical markets, and PDE-5 inhibitors such as Viagra are the only effective oral treatment. NBI-69733 may offer a more selective mechanism of action and an improved product profile to this currently underserved market' (Neurocrine Biosciences Reports Second Quarter 2003 Results, www.neurocrine.com, last visited 11 October 2004).

proved that Pharmacia's two pipeline products would reinforce a dominant position, thereby reducing future product market competition. Moreover, the conclusions drawn from the pending patent case are not obvious. If it is plausible that the competing products, of the same kind as Pfizer's Viagra, will be put on the market (which they were a few months after the decision), to what extent is it an antitrust issue that the merged entity retains the possibility of regaining its currently dominant position in the future by successfully developing and introducing new kinds of products?

On the other hand, owing to dominance in the current product market and concentration in R&D, the risk of lessened incentives for future R&D ought to be a relevant concern, possibly resulting in limited product variety in the future and reduced innovation in the area. This aspect was addressed, but not stressed, by the FTC, but, in the light of present competitors in R&D, such a conclusion does not seem substantiated. Yet it is plausible that the product market concerns and R&D concerns taken together could support a finding that the merged entity would possess such a strong position in current products, pipeline products, IPR, know-how and experience that, in spite of some competition in the pipeline, future competition in the product market was likely to be hurt.

Regarding the incontinence products, things were different. Here the Pfizer product was close to launch. In fact a press release from Novartis reveals that an agreement by Novartis to pay Pfizer US$ 225 million for the Detrusitol product was conditional on certain marketing approvals being obtained in the US and EU.[100] The US drug application was filed in 2002 and the product was expected to reach the market in 2004 if approved. European approval was also expected in 2004. Consequently, a lessening of competition between substitutable products seems sufficiently likely. Nevertheless, besides reduced potential competition, the FTC also emphasized the likelihood of reduced R&D competition.

In another recent case, *Cytyc Corp. and Digene Corp.*[101] (FTC 2002), the FTC maintains that an innovation market analysis was used.[102] The FTC sought to block the proposed merger of two corporations that manufacture and

---

[100] 'Novartis to acquire Enablex® (darifenacin), Media Release, Basel, 18 March 2003, available at novartis.com (last visited 11 October 2004).

[101] *Cytyc Corp. and Digene Corp.*, FTC File No.0210098 (2002).

[102] That the case involves potential competition is clear, see Federal Trade Commission, *FTC Antitrust Actions In Pharmaceutical Services And Products*, October 2003, available at: http://www.ftc.gov/bc/0310rxupdate.pdf , but according to FTC Chairman Muris the innovation market concept was employed, see 'Statement of Chairman Timothy J. Muris in the matter of Genzyme Corporation/Novazyme Pharmaceuticals, Inc.', footnote 3, available at: http://www.ftc.gov/os/2004/01/murisgenzymestmt.pdf (last visited 11 October 2004).

sell tests used in screening for cervical cancer. Cytyc accounted for 93 per cent of the market, with only one competitor. Digene was the only FDA-approved supplier of a DNA-based test for a virus thought to be the cause of cervical cancer. This test was used as a back-up test, but was likely to become a primary screening test. The FTC maintained that the proposed merger would not only have eliminated future competition between Cytyc's and Digene's tests but also meant that Cytyc would be able to eliminate the only current competitor by limiting access to Digene's test and would also prevent further entry.

4.6.2 Next-generation Entrants

Some cases have concerned entrants with a new product clearly belonging to a new generation. When *Hoechst* and *Rhône-Poulenc* (FTC 2000)[103] merged into Aventis there were competition concerns in the market for direct thrombin inhibitors, used in the treatment of various blood clotting diseases.

> Although other products existed for this kind of treatment, the inhibitors in question were supposedly more effective and safer than any of the available alternatives.[104] According to the complaint, the two companies were leading in developing these products, and were years ahead of other companies in the highly concentrated market for such inhibitor development. Hoechst had already obtained FDA approval for a product designed to treat a certain blood-clotting disease and Rhône-Poulenc was in the final stage of development of an equivalent. In addition, both parties were in or near clinical development for the treatment of other blood-clotting diseases. The merger would eliminate the direct competition that would exist when RP obtained its FDA approval. Moreover, potential competition and innovation competition would be hurt by the elimination of one competitor, and by the raised barriers to entry ensuing when Hoechst and RP combined their patent and patent application portfolios.
>
> The consent agreement obliged the transfer of all RP's rights to its product to Novartis or another third party. Novartis was the original licensor of the technology used and developed by RP. The transfer was supplemented by service undertakings in order to ensure the continued development of the product.

In the very brief complaint and analysis, the FTC gives no precise information about other potential competitors or competing R&D programmes but does provide a rather comprehensive entry analysis. This could indicate a potential competition analysis, which is also how the case has been categorized by the FTC.

When a technology shift is expected within a foreseeable future, incumbent firms are presumably eager to defend their positions. In such cases the inno-

---

103 *Hoechst AG*, File No. 991-0071, Docket no. C-3919 (2000)

104 Analysis of proposed consent order.

vation process typically involves a high degree of competition *for* the future market, since the technology leader may expect to dominate the future product market.

Wright Medical Technology[105] (FTC 1995) concerned the acquisition by Wright of Orthomet, a firm engaged in R&D for an improved orthopaedic finger implant. Wright was the dominant actor on this market controlling some 95 per cent and the FTC alleged that the acquisition of Orthomet would have effects both on the market for the sale of these implants and on the market for the R&D on such implants. Orthomet's next-generation finger implants could compete with Wright's current products, but it was even more likely that they would render most current products obsolete.[106] Although Orthomet still had a long way to go, including going through the FDA approval process before market launch of the new product, they were still regarded as a potential entrant. Hence the acquisition would eliminate Orthomet's status as a potential competitor to Wright's implants. But the acquisition would also reduce actual competition in research and development of the next-generation implants. The FTC claimed it used both traditional potential competition theory for the product market and the more novel theory of actual competition in research and development markets.[107]

The information provided in the complaint is very limited; for example it simply asserts that the relevant markets were highly concentrated. The entry analysis is limited to stating that '[e]ntry into the relevant markets is difficult'.[108] Moreover, apart from the assertion that Wright and Orthomet were actual competitors in R&D, it does not offer any details about the R&D conducted at Wright. According to one FTC official, 'the merger would lead to a merger-to-monopoly in the research and development of next-generation implants'.[109] Considering Wright's position on the market for current generation implants, the FTC may have concluded that the merger would reduce incentives to pursue the R&D in question.

Orthomet's business was based on a licence from a third party[110] for development and clinical trials of the new generation implants. In order to reinstall R&D competition, the consent agreement focused on providing an additional licensee. In order for Orthomet's licensor to find a credible and approved licensee, Wright had to transfer to the licensor a complete copy of all of Orthomet's orthopaedic finger implant research information, and a licence to these assets with full right to sublicense in perpetuity. If after six months no such licensee had been found, Wright would have had to take whatever steps would be needed to terminate its licence and divest all its relevant Orthomet business.

---

105 *Wright Medical Technology, Inc.*, C-3564 (Mar. 23, 1995), 60 Fed. Reg. 460 (Jan. 4, 1995).

106 Varney, Christine A., 'Antitrust and the Drive to Innovate: Innovation Markets in Merger Review', 9 *Antitrust* 16, 19 (Summer 1995).

107 Azcuenaga, Mary L., *Antitrust and Intellectual Property: Recent Highlights and Uncertainties,* Remarks before the American Law Institute-American Bar Association Boston, Massachusetts April 24, 1997, available at www.ftc.gov.

108 Complaint, §§11, 12.

109 Varney, *supra*, note 106, p. 19.

110 The Mayo Foundation for Medical Education and Research.

When a technology shift is in sight, the natural point of departure for analysing the effects of a transaction would be to assess the level of competition from alternative sources of the future technology, rather than starting from current market positions. The current market structure is of secondary importance for evaluating the competitive pressure in current R&D and in the future product market but will be important when analysing post-merger incentive structures.

4.6.3 Acquisitions of IPRs and other R&D Assets

Regarding acquisitions of IPR, the US IP Guidelines assert that such a transaction (including exclusive licences that preclude all others, even the licensor, from using the IPR) will be analysed under the Merger Guidelines. This seems to be a sensible approach since the effect of the transaction will be consolidation rather than coordination between competitors. In Europe such a case will fall under Article 81 or 82.

In *Tetra Pak I*[111] the Court of First Instance (CFI 1990) affirmed the Commission's conclusion,[112] deciding that Tetra Pak abused its dominant market position when it obtained an exclusive licence for a new major technology under development by acquiring the licence-holder Liquipak. Both the Commission and the CFI thus attacked the acquisition of the licence, rather than the merger itself.

Tetra Pak dominated the market for cartons and machines for liquid food (especially milk) packaging, a market with high entry barriers. Through the acquisition of Liquipak it also acquired Liquipak's exclusive licence for a new technology for a new milk packaging process. This technology, licensed to Liquipak by BTG, potentially represented a major technological development in the market. Together with its exclusive distributor Elopak, Liquipak had invested in the development of a new packaging machine incorporating the new process. After the takeover of Liquipak, Elopak was unwilling to continue supporting the development/finalization of the new machine since it would benefit Tetra Pak. There was a disagreement regarding how much further development was necessary. Elopak maintained that the machine and technology was nearly operational. Tetra Pak argued that further research, and substantial investment, was necessary on the application of the BTG technology.

The Commission found that the transaction which allowed Tetra Pak to benefit exclusively from the technology prevented, or at least substantially delayed, Elopak from entering the aseptic packaging market, where very little if any competition was found. The combination of strengthening considerable dominance, weakening existing competition and raising barriers to entry of any competition constituted an abuse.[113]

The Court of First Instance agreed and stated that it is not a per se abuse for a

---

[111] T-51/89, *Tetra Pak Rausing SA v. Commission* (Tetra Pak I), ECR II-309 (1990).

[112] Case No IV/31.043 – *Tetra Pak I (BTG licence)*, OJ L 272/27 (1988).

[113] Commission Decision, §§27, 46, 60.

dominant company to acquire an exclusive licence, but found the specific circumstances indicative of abuse.[114]

Dominant firms' acquisitions of exclusive licences from other companies may consequently amount to an abuse under EU law. Richard Whish comments on the case by stating that 'the further issue is how far it could be applied to other ways in which a dominant undertaking acquires intellectual property rights, such as taking over a company with a strong R&D department'.[115] What he seems to address is mergers that fall outside the merger regulation, but also mere acquisition of IPR or other R&D assets. The Commission also analysed the Tetra Pak case under Article 81 and concluded that it would have revoked the automatic exemption provided under the block exemption applicable at the time, had Tetra Pak not renounced all claims to exclusivity before the Commission reached its decision. The Commission concluded that the exclusivity of the licence prevented the emergence of both inter- and intra-brand competition since both competitors and the licensor were prevented from using the technology. The exclusivity had the 'tendency in fact to eliminate competition'.[116] As a result, the Article 81(3) criteria did not provide for an individual exemption. According to the EU 2004 Technology Transfer Guidelines the acquisition of an exclusive licence to a competing technology by a dominant firm is likely to be caught by Article 81(1) and unlikely to be exempted under 81(3), if the technology constitutes a real source of competition and entry to the technology market is difficult.[117]

Under the EU Merger Regulation and under the US HSR act,[118] turnover thresholds determine which transactions must be notified to the authorities. But, at the same time, experiences from the US show the importance of technology, rather than turnover, in determining potentially anti-competitive effects from acquisitions. From a competition perspective, the acquisitions of a small research-based company may not differ from the acquisition of a particular R&D programme or an exclusive licence to some key patents.

In November 2000, the DOJ announced its intent to block the acquisition by *Varian Medical Systems Inc.* of IMPAC Medical Systems Inc.[119] The

[114] Judgment, §23.

[115] See Whish, Richard, *Competition Law,* 4th edn, Butterworths, London, 2001, p. 702.

[116] Commission Decision, §57.

[117] EU 2004 Technology Transfer Guidelines, §166.

[118] Hart-Scott-Rodino Antitrust Improvements Act of 1976, which includes Premerger Notification Requirements.

[119] Department of Justice, Press release, November 6, 2000, 'Justice Department announces its intent to block Varian Medical Systems' acquisition of IMPAC Medical Systems', available at http://www.usdoj.gov/atr/public/press_releases/2000/6908.pdf.

merger had attracted the authorities' attention although IMPAC's annual revenues were only $21 million. The department alleged that the merger would reduce innovation and price competition for software and equipment used in radiation therapy for cancer patients.

> The transaction affected markets for the medical devices – known as linear accelerators – as well as the software used to assist the operation of the accelerators. Linear accelerators are used to shrink or destroy cancerous tumours in the body.
>
> According to the DOJ, the parties 'competed directly in terms of innovation, quality and price for radiation oncology management systems software in the US'. IMPAC was an independent provider of software, unaffiliated to the linear accelerator manufacturers. IMPAC's software was used both in Varian's and its competitors' accelerators. Varian was the market leader in the sale of linear accelerators, with a market share of almost 60 per cent. At the time, they were providing software that worked only with their own accelerators. An element in the opposition by the DOJ was a decision by Varian, prior to the acquisition, to develop software also for competitors' accelerators. The transaction would therefore eliminate competition between the parties, leaving the market with one software provider.
>
> In addition, after the transaction, Varian's competitors in accelerators would have had to rely on software supplies from Varian both in terms of existing machines and of any future advances in treatment. Varian would thus be in a position to favour its own machines at the expense of competitors, reducing pressures for continued innovation and competitive pricing.

The day after DOJ announced its intentions, the parties abandoned their merger plans.[120]

4.6.4 Concluding Observations

For the cases in this second category – transactions with potential entrants – the potential competition doctrine often seems applicable. However, if the potential competition doctrine is limited to entry that is likely to be forthcoming fairly soon (for example, within two years), the innovation market approach may allow the authorities to focus on 'actual' R&D competition rather than potential product market competition. Not surprisingly, the application of innovation markets to cases like *Boston Scientific Corp.* (FTC 1995) has been viewed differently by commentators. Through this merger, the two dominant actors on the product market would be joined. In addition, the only potential entrant, with a new product in the late stages of development (two or three years to product launch) would be acquired. Some maintain that this kind

---

[120] Department of Justice, Press release, November 7, 2000, 'Varian Medical Systems and IMPAC Medical Systems abandon merger plans', available at http://www.usdoj.gov/atr/public/press_releases/2000/6915.pdf.

of case is in fact one of potential competition cases even if it is promoted as based on innovation markets, while others point to the limitations of the potential competition doctrine.[121] In Europe, that issue may be of less importance, as the limits of the potential competition doctrine, in terms of timing and likelihood of entry, are not handled as firmly. This is clearly apparent in *Glaxo Wellcome/SmithKline Beecham* (EU 2000) where GW enjoyed a strong position in the asthma area, but had no new drug in the pipeline. Since SB had a phase II product in the pipeline, the merger was considered as resulting in reduced potential competition on existing markets.[122] It should be noted that, in the same case, the Commission recognized a 70 per cent risk of failure for phase II products and a four or five year time lag before market launch.

The innovation market approach has most likely assisted the American agencies in extending the time span for likely entry by a potential competitor or product. In *Amgen/Immunex* (FTC 2002), the acquisition of what could be the only potential competitor, Immunex, was considered to eliminate potential and R&D competition, although Immunex's project was only in phase I clinical trials. The European Commission and the FTC also ordered the divestiture of two phase II products in *Pfizer/Pharmacia* (EU and FTC 2003).

The European decision in *Glaxo Wellcome/SmithKline Beecham* (EU 2000) shows that a deep analysis of the conditions for innovation may lead the European Commission to conclusions about incentives and abilities for continued R&D in an area, in that case the future of R&D in the COPD area. On account of GW's dominance in the field, a broadly defined innovation market was deployed in order to assess the competitive effects of the transaction. In the light of the general attractiveness of the area and the numerous products at various stages of development and so on, the Commission concluded that there was no reason to expect diminished R&D efforts from the parties or a reduced overall R&D potential for the market. An additional, more narrowly defined,

121 Richard T. Rapp maintains that Boston 'is an excellent example of a standard potential competition case promoted as innovation market analysis'. 'The Misapplication of the Innovation Market Approach to Merger Analysis', 64 *Antitrust Law Journal* 19, 42 (1995); Robert J. Hoerner, however, notes that, even if the FTC could not have proved at trial that SCIMED would have entered or that it was perceived to be a potential entrant, the allegation of existing direct horizontal competition in R&D would have been relied on to provide a basis under which the FTC might have obtained significant relief: 'Innovation Markets: New Wine in Old Bottles?', 64 *Antitrust Law Journal* 49, 57 (1995).

122 However, the fact that one competing pipeline product was likely to be marketed before SB's product and the presence of a large number of competitors with pipeline product in phase II led the Commission to conclude that the elimination of potential competition would not be likely to strengthen the merged company's strong position in existing markets (Decision, §177).

innovation market allowed for analysis of the more short-term effect on a particular product market.

A variant of this R&D entrant setting is more complex. This is when the product under development will constitute a new generation of products. In *Wright Medical* (FTC 1995), the FTC relied on both potential competition for the future product market (hand implants) and actual R&D competition. The next-generation implants were expected to replace those currently sold. Using current standards for defining relevant product markets (SSNIP tests and so on), the future generation implants could have constituted a separate product market. As a result, the acquired company would probably not have been a potential entrant to the current product market.[123] Framing the analysis merely in terms of the current market would most likely not lead to a correct assessment of current or future competitive restraints on market participants. The application of the innovation market focuses on the incentive for Wright, the dominant player (95 per cent) in the current market, to reduce R&D on the future product to the detriment of consumers. The new product could 'cannibalize' the profits derived in the current product market.[124] Note that R&D reductions relate to the pace of innovation and the quality or diversity of next-generation products.

As seen above, various cases on both sides of the Atlantic have involved incumbent firms' strategies towards innovation and new technologies. The *Tetra Pak I* decision (EU 1990) is on the verge of allowing for an innovation market, deeming the acquisition of a new technology abusive when acquired by a firm that is dominant in R&D and on product markets.[125]

4.7 COMPETITION FOR FUTURE PRODUCTS

The third category relates to instances where the conduct complained of relates to products under development but where neither of the parties has

---

[123] Chin, Andrew, 'Analyzing Mergers in Innovation Markets', 38 *Jurimetrics Journal* 119, 128f. (1998). See also Federal Trade Commission, *Anticipating the 21st Century, Competition Policy in the New High-Tech, Global Marketplace*, Staff Report, 1996, Volume 1, Chapter 7, pp. 12f.

[124] See US 2000 Competitor Collaboration Guidelines, §3.31(a).

[125] That limitations in innovation (e.g. from potential competitors) may be considered abusive has been considered in several cases. In this category falls *Microsoft III* (D.C. Cir. 2001), foreclosing a product market (internet browsers) for a competitor product (Netscape), thereby eliminating the likelihood that that product would be developed in a way that would increase interoperability and take over important functions in another, currently monopolized, market (operating systems). See section 4.9.2.

similar products on the market already. Under this category, the questions centre, *inter alia,* on what really constitutes a new product and a separate market. The authorities may use an R&D analysis, along the lines of the innovation market concept, to identify and address competition concerns in the R&D process, with a view both to the incentives for innovation and to considering future product market developments. Where the product is completely new, implying that neither of the parties, nor anyone else, currently has a competing product on the market, the R&D aspects alone frame the analysis. This also makes it harder for the authorities to show that a transaction is likely to lessen competition or even lead to dominance.

4.7.1 R&D for a Particular Future Product

Sensormatic[126] (FTC 1995) is an often cited case, involving a next-generation product with an uncertain future.

> Two manufacturers of current-generation products in the market for electronic article surveillance (EAS) systems for retail stores, Sensormatic and Knogo, had agreed to a partial merger. EAS systems are used to detect shoplifting. Disposable labels are attached to or embedded in the merchandise and trigger an alarm when leaving the shop unless they are neutralized by a store employee. According to the agreement, Sensormatic would acquire all of Knogo's assets outside North America, along with patents related to 'SuperStrip'. Knogo North America (the remainder of Knogo) would continue to compete in the current market and also be active in the development of the SuperStrip technology through a non-exclusive licence.[127] In addition, the agreement obligated Sensormatic and Knogo North America to grant royalty-free cross-licences to one another for any improvements to patents or trade secrets related to SuperStrip. The EAS systems on the market at the time required the retailers to attach or embed the electronic labels in the store, whereas the new generation would allow manufacturers, wholesalers and so on to apply them before distribution to retailers ('source labelling'). The relevant market was the research and development of disposable labels developed or used for source labelling and the research and development of processes to manufacture disposable labels. The relevant geographic area was the US and Canada.
>
> Both Sensormatic and Knogo were involved in R&D for new 'source labelling' systems. Entry into this market was not considered timely, likely and sufficient in view of the existing patent protection for important technology and the time lags involved in acquiring the necessary technical skill. The FTC feared that the acquisition and licence agreement would substantially lessen competition by reducing the incentive for Knogo North America to research and develop disposable labels for source labelling, decreasing the number of R&D tracks and increasing Sensormatic's ability to reduce R&D unilaterally. All of this would increase the

126 *Sensormatic Elec. Corp.,* FTC File No. 941-0126, 60 Fed. Reg. 5428 (Jan. 27, 1995).

127 Varney, *supra*, note 106, p. 20.

> likelihood that the output of R&D would be restricted both in the short and the long term.[128]
>
> The consent order prohibited Sensormatic from acquiring the patent rights to the SuperStrip technology in the US and Canada. The royalty-free cross-licence for improvements was also blocked. However, Sensormatic was allowed to obtain a non-exclusive licence of the SuperStrip technology in the US and Canada and furthermore to acquire the technology or other exclusive or non-exclusive rights outside the US and Canada.

If accepting the notion of source labelling constituting a new product market, the potential competition doctrine, as applied by some US courts, has perhaps been insufficient for enjoining the transaction. Both parties were active on current markets and in R&D for a new product generation. But neither of them was active on the market for next-generation labels and probably neither was 'on the edge' of entering that market. To focus on innovation may have been a way to deal with the incentives of Sensormatic and Knogo to develop the new generation product by competing so as to achieve the most attractive product, for example in terms of compatibility with other systems and product generations.[129] If a wider R&D analysis would be the means to detect whether the merger was likely to result in inferior EAS systems in future, the innovation market concept seems appropriate.

But was the innovation market analysis accurately applied? If the relevant element to be analysed is that of R&D for new surveillance systems, is it correct to define the market as R&D on disposable labels for source labelling? Other major market participants were active in the EAS market,[130] and the possibility that the R&D conducted by these actors could have restrained the firms' behaviour appears hard to dismiss. One Commissioner even pointed out that R&D of source labelling would be difficult or impossible to distinguish from other improvements in EAS systems.[131] Moreover, the relevant geographical area was limited to the US and Canada, which meant that

---

128 Complaint, §§16, 17.

129 See Dahdouh, Thomas N. & Mongoven, James F., 'The Shape of Things to Come: Innovation Market Analysis in Merger Cases', 64 *Antitrust Law Journal* 405, 424 (1996), suggesting that, with source labelling, buyers would increasingly demand compatible EAS standards or one commonly accepted standard, since manufacturers and wholesalers would deliver the labelled merchandise to numerous retailers. If Sensormatic acquired Knogo, the merged entity would lack incentives to make the new generation compatible, rather making its technology the de facto standard.

130 Sensormatic and its competitor Checkpoint together represented over 70 per cent of the current market: Baer, William J. and Balto, David A., 'New Myths and Old Realities: Recent Developments in Antitrust Enforcement', 2 *Columbia Business Law Review* 207 (1999).

131 See separate statement of Commissioner Azcuenaga, concurring in part and dissenting in part.

possibly competing technologies being developed in other parts of the world were not included. At least one European firm was active in potentially important research.[132]

Other cases also draw attention to the question of whether a future product will constitute a separate market, and what the primary aim of authority intervention would be. *Glaxo-Wellcome* (FTC 1995)[133] was one of the first major mergers in the pharmaceutical industry merger wave that started in the mid-1990s.

According to the very brief complaint, the FTC considered that the merger would have an effect on the market for the research and development of a non-injectable anti-migraine drug (5HT sub1D agonists). According to the FTC, the merger would eliminate actual R&D competition between the parties, decrease the number of relevant R&D tracks and increase the ability of Glaxo to reduce unilaterally the R&D on the drugs in question. Taken together, this would restrict output of R&D both in the near future and in the long run.[134]

> Glaxo already marketed a product for the treatment of migraine attacks, but this product was only approved in injectable form. Both parties had products in the FDA approval process that would use oral dosages.[135] No such product existed on the market. It has been maintained that the differences between injectable and non-injectable drugs were so important that the two forms were not considered substitutable but constituted separate markets.[136] While the FTC probably had in mind potential effects both for R&D and for future product markets, it was natural to outline the competing R&D for non-injectable forms.
>
> According to the complaint, the R&D market was highly concentrated with the heavy entry barriers that are common in the pharmaceutical industry. FTC officials have alleged that the parties were the ones that had come farthest by far in this kind of R&D. Moreover, it was claimed that after the merger Glaxo would have an incentive to reduce its R&D effort, since 'the remaining research effort would presumably produce a monopoly product until the third-best effort could complete the FDA approval process some years hence'.[137] The authority thus feared that one of the programmes would be shut down.
>
> The relevant geographical area in which to analyse the effects of the merger was limited to the US. While this in itself does not seem to preclude global R&D being taken into account, the FTC focused on products in the FDA approval process when analysing R&D effects.

---

132 Ibid.

133 *Glaxo plc.*, FTC File No. 951-0054, 60 Fed. Reg. 16,139 (Mar. 29, 1995).

134 Complaint, §§10, 11, see also Analysis of Proposed Consent Order To Aid Public Comment.

135 Dahdouh & Mongoven, *supra*, note 129, p. 424.

136 Baer, William J. & Balto, David A., 'Antitrust Enforcement and High-Technology Markets', 5 *Michigan Telecommunication Technology Law Review* 73, 80f. (2001).

137 Ibid.

> In the consent order, the FTC required Glaxo to divest Wellcome's worldwide non-physical R&D assets (patents, testing data, research materials and so on) for the non-injectable migraine drugs to an approved acquirer. Glaxo furthermore had to provide information, technical assistance and advice. These additional requirements were rather far-reaching in order to ensure that it was possible to continue current R&D at a competitive level and provided the acquiring firm, Zeneca, *inter alia*, with consultation and training from Glaxo employees knowledgeable about the project.

FTC officials consider the divestiture a success since Zeneca, with the required assistance from Glaxo, received complete FDA approval in only 15 months.[138] The primary achievement of public intervention probably related more to product market competition than to preventing anti-competitive lessening of R&D. In addition, improved R&D output by way of product diversity was accomplished.

Interestingly, the European Commission had already approved the merger after analysing the likely effects for the market for anti-migraine treatments, and not differentiating between the means of administration.[139] This was probably not a problem for the Commission, since orally administered versions of Glaxo's best-selling product was being approved over Europe from 1994 and onwards. Still both parties had new products under development. Wellcome's pipeline product was expected to enter the market in 1997 and to become a close substitute for Glaxo's existing product. In contrast to the FTC, the Commission found several pharmaceutical companies worldwide, including top multinational firms, engaged in R&D on anti-migraine products with the same mode of action or pharmacological profile as Glaxo's. Among these, two firms were in phase III, indicating product launches within five years. Glaxo was at the time presumably dominant in the European anti-migraine markets, and had already undertaken to grant an exclusive licence of either its or Wellcome's pipeline product. In view of this undertaking and the competing products under development, the Commission concluded that the acquisition of Wellcome would only have a limited effect on competition.[140]

---

138 Ibid., p. 81; Tom & Newberg, *supra*, note 5, p. 223.

139 Case No IV/M.555 – *Glaxo/Wellcome,* OJ C 65/3 (1995)

140 Decision, §31. See also Temple Lang, John, 'European Community Antitrust Law: Innovation Markets and High Technology Industries', 20 *Fordham International Law Journal* 717, 749 (1997). In this case the Commission also considered the treatment of HIV and AIDS. Wellcome marketed the leading product, Retrovir, and was developing a product which, if successful, could be a complementary product to Retrovir. The Commission found that the merger would 'combine the R&D resources and expertise of two leading firms in this area'. However, there were no definitive treatments for HIV/AIDS and the merger was not likely to inhibit significantly the research for effective compounds being undertaken by other pharmaceutical companies worldwide (§§17, 18, 32, 33).

The merger cases just reviewed naturally differ from proposed joint ventures where the parties join together in a particular R&D project. If cooperation is necessary in order to succeed in developing the new product or technology, competition in innovation is clearly not reduced by such collaboration.[141] Moreover, even if the parties are not considered potential R&D competitors, the analysis will include possible spillover effects on current markets as well as the terms of use and commercialization of the R&D results.

4.7.2 Competition for Completely New Products

Let us now consider the development of products which are indeed completely new. As mentioned under the previous category, it is difficult to establish a lessening of competition regarding R&D and in the future product markets. For several reasons, this is no easier when the product under development is completely new. Firstly, since the parties do not profit from current product markets, they normally have strong incentives to develop at least one variant of the new product.[142] These incentives may thus limit the competition concerns. Secondly, it is difficult to establish the competitive forces and constraints on potential exercise of market power in a given situation. The uncertainty regarding the boundaries of the future market might be substantial, making market delineation a complicated enterprise. Finally, to estimate the chances of success for products under development is seldom straightforward, particularly for entirely new technology.

Roche/Genentech[143] (FTC 1990) is an early case where the FTC defined and employed R&D markets, partly in such a setting. This is an interesting case of potential competition and very early innovation market analysis.

---

141 The standards for assessing whether the parties are actual or potential competitors with regard to the conducted R&D are not fully clear. See e.g. Case No IV/32.009 – *Elopak/Metal Box-Odin*, OJ L 209/15 (1990) where the parties, who were two manufacturers of food containers were not considered competitors for a new carton container, with a metal lid, since short-term entry would require technology which could not be developed without significant and time-consuming investment. In Case No IV/32.363 – *KSB/Goulds/Lowara/ITT*, OJ L 19/25 (1991), the parties were considered potential competitors with reference to the possibility of obtaining necessary technologies by way of licence and likewise of achieving the necessary scale in production of the resulting products by means of licensing out or producing for third parties.

142 'Other considerations being equal, R&D agreements are more likely to raise competitive concerns when the collaboration or its participants already possess a secure source of market power over an existing product and the new R&D efforts might cannibalize their supracompetitive earnings': US 2000 Competitor Collaboration Guidelines, §3.31(a).

143 *Roche Holdings Ltd.* 113 F.T.C. 1086 (1990).

> The FTC opposed the acquisition by Roche of control of Genentech, alleging that it would hurt competition in the research, development, production and marketing of (1) vitamin C, (2) therapeutics for treatment of human growth hormone deficiency, and (3) CD4-based therapeutics for the treatment of AIDS and HIV infection. The geographic market for vitamin C was considered worldwide. For the other products it was limited to the US.
>
> At the time, the vitamin C market, both in the United States and worldwide, was highly concentrated and dominated by Roche. Genentech had however developed a new, patented, process for producing vitamin C using recombinant DNA technology. Production and marketing of growth hormone in the US was also highly concentrated. In that market Genentech had a near-monopoly[144] and Roche conducted advanced clinical trials with a product (a human growth hormone-releasing factor) which would potentially compete with human growth hormone. Moreover, Genentech was the most advanced of a limited number of companies developing CD4-based therapeutics for the treatment of AIDS/HIV infection. Roche was also engaged in R&D of CD4-based therapeutics with pending patent applications.
>
> As usual in this kind of market, entry was difficult and time consuming, owing to FDA regulatory approvals, patents and so on.
>
> In the vitamin C market, the parties had to divest Genentech's technology under development. Likewise, in the treatment of human growth deficiency, the parties had to divest the potentially competing technology, Roche's human growth-releasing factor business, as an ongoing business, to an FTC-approved buyer. Innovation competition concerns were more apparent in the market for CD4-based AIDS/HIV therapeutics, a product market in which no firm at the time was present and no products yet existed. The order required Roche to grant non-exclusive licences under Roche's CD4-based US Patent Portfolio, at prescribed royalties, to anyone requesting such a licence within ten years.[145]

The setting allowed for the application of both potential competition theory and analysis of actual competition in innovation. According to FTC officials, the FTC concluded that the transaction would reduce potential competition in the supply of the new products and lessen actual competition in research and development directed at these classes of therapeutics.[146] Although no developed innovation market approach existed at the time, the case is often referred to as a mix of both theories.[147] The FTC did not, however, signal the adoption

[144] Furthermore, Genentech was protected by the Orphan Drug Act, and had sued its only human growth hormone competitor for patent infringement.

[145] Five years later, during the FTC Hearings, it was testified that neither party had developed a product in this area: Widnell, Nicholas A., 'The Crystal Ball of Innovation Market Analysis in Merger Review: An Appropriate Means of Predicting the Future?', 4 *George Mason Law Review* 369, 388 (1996).

[146] Gilbert, Richard J. & Sunshine, Steven C., 'Incorporating Dynamic Efficiency Concerns in Merger Analysis: The Use of Innovation Markets', 63 *Antitrust Law Journal* 569, 586 (1995).

[147] Dahdouh & Mongoven, *supra*, note 129, p. 430, footnote 101.

of a new theory and, interestingly, one Commissioner dissented on the ground that the analysis did not follow established theories of potential competition since it involved speculation about the prospective entry and the relatively distant market (see analysis in section 5.3.1. below).[148]

In *American Home Products*[149] (FTC 1995), the FTC examined the acquisition by AHP of American Cyanamid Company. Apart from claiming horizontal overlaps and negative effects in a number of existing vaccine markets and one drug market, the Commission also identified a market in the research and development of a vaccine.

> Rotavirus is a diarrhoea-type disease that causes death in children, for which there was no existing vaccine available. According to the FTC there were three existing research projects in, or near, clinical development, aimed at such a vaccine. Among these, AHP and Cyanamid were two. Again, entry was difficult and time-consuming, involving great and risky up-front expenditure. Moreover, Cyanamid conducted its research along a different path than the other two companies, and it was possible that it could develop a different or superior vaccine.[150] The FTC was anxious that AHP would have insufficient incentives to pursue the Cyanamid programme effectively. In addition, the FTC alleged that the likelihood of collusion between the two remaining competitors in R&D would increase. The consent agreement obliged AHP to license, on a non-exclusive basis, Cyanamid's research in Rotavirus vaccines and to provide technical support to an FTC-approved third party. The alleged basis for the action was not a reduced number of potential vaccines in the future market, but that R&D competition would be hurt if only two independent research programmes remained.[151]

From the wording it appears that the FTC cared about quality and speed aspects more than competition in the future product market.[152] But the FTC did not show why or to what extent the merged firm would really have an incentive to reduce its innovation efforts unilaterally, although there remained only one competitor in the relevant R&D market.[153] Such a conclusion does

---

[148] Dissenting Statement of Commissioner Owen. See also Azcuenaga, *supra* note 107.

[149] *American Home Prods. Corp.*, C-3557 (Feb. 14, 1995), 60 Fed. Reg. 60,807 (Nov. 29, 1994).

[150] Wolfram, Richard, *Entering European Innovation Markets: Antitrust Implications of Innovation Markets and Intellectual Property Licensing – A U.S. Perspective,* conference paper at 'Entering European Innovation Markets', February 3–4, 2000, Lund University, Sweden. p. 9; Varney, *supra*, note 106, p. 19.

[151] In one of the markets for existing products, the FTC alleged that, apart from reducing product market competition, the merger would also reduce R&D competition.

[152] Widnell, *supra*, note 145, p. 388; Dahdouh & Mongoven, *supra*, note 129, p. 425.

[153] Chin, *supra*, note 123, p. 128; Federal Trade Commission, *supra*, note 123, Volume 1, Chapter 7, pp.12f.

not seem self-evident, particularly if Cyanamid's product was likely to be superior (although probably at an earlier stage of development). At this time, early 1995, the FTC seems to have been taking steps towards a theory of pure markets for competing R&D, although it did not use an established innovation market method or terminology. According to Commissioner Azcuenaga, 'this was a transitional period and the Commission was still feeling its way along'.[154]

In *Upjohn/Pharmacia* (EU 1995)[155] the European Commission assessed, *inter alia*, the effects on competition in terms of R&D.[156]

> First the Commission identified the existence of overlaps in relevant R&D programmes. The inquiry showed that Upjohn was active in R&D in the stroke sector whereas Pharmacia already marketed a stroke drug and had no R&D activities in this field. As the two products represented different approaches to the stroke treatment, negative effects on the product market were considered very unlikely. Similarly, the two parties' AIDS research programmes belonged, according to the Commission, to 'different R&D markets' because the Upjohn product aimed at suppressing the virus whereas the Pharmacia compound was aimed at a secondary bacterial complication. In the end, only R&D for solid tumours and Parkinson's were affected.[157]
>
> In the sales of medicines, the Commission, largely referring to the arguments made earlier in this chapter, assumed the geographical markets to be national. However, in R&D, the firms were engaged in competition on a wider basis, using worldwide strategies.[158]
>
> In the field of solid tumours, the research related to the same class of compounds, although it was not clear whether the compounds, would eventually offer therapeutic alternatives.[159] Pharmacia's product launch was expected in 2001 (six years after the merger) and the product was presumed to meet competition from at least three and possibly four competing products currently being developed by large competitors. The Upjohn product, which could be launched within one to three years, originated from a Japanese company. It was licensed to Rhône-Poulenc for Europe, while the Upjohn licence covered the Americas, Australia and New Zealand.
>
> The Commission noted that it was not clear whether there would be any

---

154 Azcuenaga, *supra*, note 107.

155 Case No IV/M.631 – *Upjohn/Pharmacia,* OJ C 294/9 (1995).

156 The Commission also identified 14 affected national markets for current products. On two of these markets the parties' market shares exceeded 30 per cent, but the presence of important competitors made further analysis unnecessary. In the end only two markets, where market shares exceeded 50 per cent, required deeper analysis. However, mitigating factors (primarily therapeutic differences between the products and possibilities for generic entry) led the Commission to conclude that the merger would not cause dominance on these markets either.

157 Decision, §§7–11.

158 §15.

159 §§26, 28. The therapeutic profile of the Pharmacia product was not yet ascertained.

geographical overlap so far as Europe was concerned. In view of the doubts about product overlap, it was concluded that the operation did not 'create or increase a dominant position in R&D of solid tumours'.[160]

Likewise, the parties' phase III compounds for treatment of Parkinson's disease were both dopamine agonists with expected launch in two years, but the Commission found at least 12 competing drugs under development and five incumbent firms on the market.[161] These were mainly, but not only, dopamine agonists. As a result the merger would 'create or increase a dominant position neither on the R&D/compound market nor for future developments'.

In the area for Parkinson's disease, where the future market was in fact rather close in time, it seems the Commission primarily regarded potential competition. In the R&D for solid tumours, the reference to worldwide R&D competition and strategy making, combined with the fact that Rhône-Poulenc was the licensee for Europe, seems to imply the primary importance of innovation competition.

Interestingly, the Commission also referred to the fact that the parties were medium-sized and that their costs for R&D and for implementing successful products (regulatory approval) were becoming very heavy to bear. The Commission continued that '[t]herefore it is likely that the notified operation will actually create a joint critical mass allowing the merged entity via pooled skills and resources to be a competitive player on the worldwide R&D markets of developing and inventing active compounds and resulting pharmaceutical products'.[162] This seems very close to an efficiency parameter in an analysis along the Gilbert & Sunshine model. However, these comments on prospective efficiencies were not used to counterbalance anti-competitive effects.

When reviewing the same pharmaceutical merger, *Upjohn and Pharmacia*[163] (FTC 1996), the FTC was concerned about the effects on competition in research, development, manufacture and sale of drugs (topoisomerase I inhibitors) for the treatment of colorectal cancer. Yet the underlying overlapping R&D programmes were the same as the cancer treatment aspects of the European case.

No such drugs existed on the US market at the time but sales anticipated by 2002 would, according to the complaint, exceed $100 million. The US was considered the relevant geographic area.[164]

There were only a very small number of firms, worldwide, in advanced stages of

---

160 §§26–9.

161 §§30–2.

162 Decision, §25.

163 *The Upjohn Co. and Pharmacia Aktiebolag*, 121 F.T.C. 44, FTC File No. 951-0140, Docket no. C-3638, (Feb. 8, 1996).

164 Complaint, §§5–7.

development for these inhibitors, out of which Upjohn's product was expected to be the first to receive FDA approval and to reach the market. Pharmacia had a few years left before their product could reach the market. The complaint alleged that the merger would eliminate direct and substantial R&D competition. Furthermore, the number of R&D tracks could potentially decrease if the parties lacked incentives to continue the Pharmacia project. In addition, the merger would eliminate the potential for direct price competition between the two products in the future product market. Important to these conclusions were the large barriers to entry, especially lengthy clinical trial periods and FDA approvals, which made it impossible to reach advanced stages of development quickly.

In order to ensure that the relevant research and development would continue, the consent order required the parties to divest Pharmacia's topoisomerase inhibitor assets related to the treatment of colorectal cancer to a Commission-approved buyer.

The complaint claims not only reduced R&D competition but also a decreased number of R&D tracks and eliminated future price competition as likely anticompetitive effects.[165] Although very brief, the analysis is somewhat more specific compared to the previous decision in *Glaxo-Wellcome* (FTC 1995), and indicates the relevance of worldwide R&D and the consequences of the US patent situation. However, the Analysis of Proposed Consent Order to Aid Public Comment states that the information obtained during the investigation of the status of the R&D projects is highly confidential, which is why the FTC cannot disclose 'what, if any, other research projects are currently underway'.

Baxter's acquisition of Immuno International[166] (FTC 1997) raised competition concerns both on a current product market (Factor VIII Inhibitors) where the two companies were the only suppliers in the US and an innovation market (fibrin sealant) where no firm had yet been granted FDA approval but where the two companies were two of only a small number of firms seeking such approval.

More particularly, the complaint defined the two relevant markets as

- the research, development, manufacture and sale of Factor VIII Inhibitor Treatments approved by the FDA for sale in the United States, and
- the research, development, manufacture and sale of fibrin sealant to be approved by the FDA for sale in the United States.

From this market definition, the relevant geographical area was the United States.

According to the FTC, new entry into the fibrin sealant market would be difficult, time-consuming and expensive. Broad patent rights governing the formulations and manufacture made new entry unlikely. The consent agreement required Baxter to license Immuno's product in development to an approved licensee.

165 Ibid., §9.

166 *Baxter International Inc.*, File No. 971-0002, Docket no. C-3726, (1997).

This is an innovation market case, as categorized by the FTC officials.[167] Still it has the appearances of a normal potential competition case. The FTC was not interested in the international R&D situation, but focused on timing in the approval process. The fact that the products were already in use elsewhere in the world is highlighted in the Analysis of Proposed Consent Order to Aid Public Comment, where it is stated that fibrin sealant was used in Europe and Japan in a wide variety of surgical procedures and to treat burn and trauma victims. According to one study, fibrin sealants were used in 35–40 per cent of all internal surgical procedures in Europe and Asia. Moreover, many US surgeons mixed and applied their own fibrin sealants, but as yet no firm had obtained FDA approval, and Baxter and Immuno were the only firms that could enter the market in the short term, a market estimated at $400 million.[168] It does not seem that innovation was at the centre here, but rather the structure of the product market just around the corner.

Since no other competing product could be approved and launched before 1999, the FTC maintained future product market competition by the licence required. In retrospect, the FTC considers the remedy a success since the licensee was able to market its sealant shortly after Baxter's product was approved in May 1998.[169]

In the acquisition by *Pfizer* of *Warner-Lambert* (FTC 2000),[170] the FTC found that competition would be lessened in four different markets, in three of which the parties were actual competitors with current products.

> In the fourth market, that of EGFr-tk inhibitors used to treat solid tumour cancers, no products had yet received FDA approval. However, the two parties were the two most advanced among four identified developers. If they combined there would only be three independent programmes left and the FTC feared that this would lead to an increased likelihood that 'the merged entity would unilaterally delay, deter or eliminate competing programs to research and develop EGFr-tk inhibitors [. . .] potentially reducing the number of drugs reaching the market and thus resulting in higher prices for consumers'.[171]
>
> As a result the FTC ordered Pfizer to divest its EGFr-tk assets, including inhibitors, technology and know-how, to its partner, OSI. Pfizer should also provide OSI with any assistance and advice, reasonably necessary to obtain FDA approvals

---

167 Federal Trade Commission, *FTC Antitrust Actions in Pharmaceutical Services and Products,* May 2000, available at www.ftc.gov/bc/rxupdate.pdf (last visited, 11 October 2004).

168 Analysis of Proposed Consent Order to Aid Public Comment.

169 Federal Trade Commission, *supra*, note 167.

170 *Pfizer Inc., and Warner-Lambert Company*, File No. 001 0059, Docket no. C-3957 (2000).

171 Complaint §29 and Analysis of Proposed Consent Order to Aid Public Comment.

> to manufacture and sell EGFr-tk. Details of the divestiture were attached to the order in a non-public appendix, but FTC officials maintain that OSI *inter alia* was granted a worldwide irrevocable licence to rights and patents jointly owned with Pfizer, and that Pfizer had to pay OSI's costs for completing clinical trials on the drug.[172]

According to the FTC, this case involved both actual markets and innovation markets. Looking at *Hoechst/Rhône Poulenc* (FTC 2000), which was labelled a potential competition case, one sees there are some similarities. In both cases the FDA approval process is central, and the analysis of competitors and their future possibilities is kept rather brief. The key difference would seem to be that, in Hoechst, the products in question were a new generation of drugs for the disease – and older products already existed. Also, FDA-approval had already been granted for one party's new product whereas in Pfizer/Warner-Lambert, neither party was active on the market. No product market existed yet and there was a time lag, which may have made it more difficult to apply traditional potential competition doctrine.

Similarly in *Baxter* (FTC 1997), no firm had yet obtained FDA approval, although this was obtained the year after. In Baxter only 'a small number of firms' were seeking FDA approval and in Pfizer/Warner Lambert there were four firms seeking such approval. The FTC maintains that the other products were more than a year behind, and the order therefore allowed for two competing products to be introduced simultaneously. Without the intervention 'only one product likely would have prevailed'.[173] It is notable that the FTC, despite similar market definitions and innovation analyses, categorizes the cases differently. It seems that, by keeping up the number of R&D programmes, product variety and competition on the future product market was maintained. That this was the primary objective is further supported when considering the European version of the case.[174] In the European setting, Pfizer developed an EGFr-tk inhibitor whereas Warner Lambert's product was another kind of inhibitor, with an unknown mode of action, but which would attack cancer in different ways. The Commission did not consider the overlap in R&D to constitute a problem, in presence of vigorous competition in the oncology field and numerous pipeline products of which some were already in phase III.[175]

---

172 Feinstein, Richard A., Pender, David R. & Meier, Markus H., *FTC Antitrust Actions in Health Care Services and Products*, Health Care Services and Products Division, Bureau of Competition, Federal Trade Commission Washington, DC, June 29, 2001, available at http://www.ftc.gov/bc/hcindex/hcaindex.htm (last visited 11 October 2004).

173 Federal Trade Commission, *supra*, note 167.

174 Case No COMP/M.1878 – *Pfizer / Warner-Lambert* (2000).

175 Decision, §§78–80.

In a recent American case, *Genzyme/Novazyme Pharmaceuticals, Inc.* (FTC 2004),[176] innovation competition analysis was truly central and forced the FTC to take a stance on delicate issues. In particular, the case highlights the difficulties in establishing reductions in innovation, arguments apropos of working with presumptions in antitrust analysis and the significance of R&D efficiencies from firm combinations. A split among the five Commissioners in the FTC also gave rise to three separate statements, allowing for further insights regarding the underlying analysis and policy positions in the FTC.

> Following a 3–1–1 vote (one commissioner dissenting and one not participating in the vote), the FTC decided to close the investigation following Genzyme's acquisition of Novazyme in September 2001. At the time of the acquisition, Novazyme, a small research company founded in 1999, was conducting pre-clinical studies relating to enzyme-replacement treatment (ERT) for Pompe disease – a rare, often fatal, disease primarily affecting infants and children. Genzyme, one of the largest biotechnology companies in the world, was engaged in animal testing of ERTs. According to the FTC, 'the investigation focused on the transaction's potential impact on the pace and scope of research into the development of a treatment for Pompe disease'.[177]
>
> The majority, following Chairman Timothy J. Muris, found that the facts of the case did not support a finding of any anti-competitive harm.[178] According to Muris's written statement, the FTC has followed the policy indications of the 1996 'Staff Report on Competition Policy in the New High-Tech, Global Marketplace', and uses the innovation market approach with caution.[179] Muris based his opinion on the notion that 'neither economic theory nor empirical research supports an inference regarding the merger's likely effect on innovation (and hence patient welfare) based simply on observing how the merger changed the number of independent R&D programs. Rather, one must examine whether the merged firm was likely to have a reduced incentive to invest in R&D, and also whether it was likely to have the ability to conduct R&D more successfully'.[180]

---

[176] *Genzyme/Novazyme Pharmaceuticals, Inc*, File No. 021 0026, Closing letter, January 13, 2004; available at http://www.ftc.gov/os/2004/01/040113genzyme.pdf (2004–01–20).

[177] Press release, 'FTC Closes its Investigation of Genzyme Corporation's 2001 Acquisition of Novazyme Pharmaceuticals, Inc.' January 13, 2004, available at http://www.ftc.gov/opa/2004/01/genzyme.htm (last visited 11 October 2004).

[178] 'Statement of Chairman Timothy J. Muris in the matter of Genzyme Corporation/Novazyme Pharmaceuticals, Inc.', available at http://www.ftc.gov/os/2004/01/murisgenzymestmt.pdf (last visited 11 October 2004).

[179] Federal Trade Commission, *supra*, note 123, Volume 1, chapter 7 (1996). This Report, following extensive hearings at which economists and lawyers from academia and practice testified, concluded that a careful, intense factual investigation is necessary to distinguish between pro-competitive and anti-competitive combinations of innovation efforts.

[180] 'Statement of Chairman Timothy J. Muris in the matter of Genzyme Corporation / Novazyme Pharmaceuticals, Inc.', pp. 5f.

Pompe disease is rather rare and, owing to the relatively limited number of patients (approx. 10 000 worldwide), therapies for the disease fall under the Orphan Drug Act.[181] This implies that the first therapy to gain FDA approval will be granted a seven-year exclusivity on the US market. A second product could break this exclusivity, but only by showing superiority over the first product.

Prior to the acquisition of Novazyme, Genzyme had formed joint ventures with two other Pompe ERT R&D programmes, in 1998 and in 2000. One of these programmes had been abandoned prior to the Novazyme acquisition and the other was abandoned in 2002. As a consequence, the Genzyme (internal) programme and the Novazyme programme, both initiated in 1999, were the only still active R&D programmes in the world.

At the time of the acquisition, the Novazyme programme was at an early, preclinical stage, with promising results in mice, but also facing research obstacles that needed to be resolved before going into clinical trials. Compared to the Genzyme programme it was expected to result in a superior product, but it would take longer to develop.

According to Muris, one potential anti-competitive effect from this merger would be the elimination of a 'race to market'. But the investigation did not reveal any evidence that either of the firms believed that changed expenditures on R&D would significantly change the probability of beating the other firm. Therefore no race existed. Genzyme would have incentives to introduce a product (the Genzyme product) as soon as possible to earn profits and likewise an incentive to get a superior product to the market as soon as possible (the Novazyme product). Thus the two programmes did not affect each other at the time of the acquisition.[182]

Similarly, Muris found that, in the event that the Genzyme project was successful, the merged entity would not have less incentive to introduce a second, superior, product to the market or to delay such entry until the end of the seven years of market exclusivity in order to obtain a total of 14 years of exclusivity. To reach these conclusions Muris pointed to the fact that, without the merger, Novazyme would not have been able to market the product unless it was sufficiently superior (owing to the ODA). With the merger, such a superior product would increase total demand and might reduce variable costs of production and thereby give the merged company incentives to bring it to the market. Also, the company wished to develop the Novazyme technology for a range of other, similar, diseases.

Muris also pointed at internal evidence suggesting that Genzyme was not planning to delay the Novazyme programme. First, according to the terms of the merger agreement, Novazyme shareholders would receive two milestone payments (in total $87.5 million) if the Novazyme technology was granted FDA approval within certain time limits. Secondly, key shareholders were placed in the merged company's Pompe programme. Novazyme's CEO and chairman (who had two children suffering from Pompe disease) became the senior vice president of Genzyme Therapeutics and was to manage the programme. The chief scientist, on whose

[181] The Orphan Drug Act (P.L. 97–414) was signed into law on January 4, 1983. The Act is intended to provide incentives for pharmaceutical manufacturers to develop drugs, biotechnology products and medical devices for the treatment of rare diseases and conditions.

[182] 'Statement of Chairman Timothy J. Muris in the matter of Genzyme Corporation/Novazyme Pharmaceuticals, Inc.', pp. 11 *et seq.*

research the Novazyme programme was based, would continue to lead the team at the Novazyme site. Lastly, the majority found no evidence that the company had reduced any R&D spending or slowed progress along any of the R&D paths after the merger.

To the contrary, Muris underlined the efficiencies created by the merger. By enabling comparative experiments and sharing of information, the Novazyme programme had possibly been accelerated, its chances of success increased and synergies created that would help avoid delays. Such benefits were considered merger-specific, since they could not be compared to a hypothetical joint venture with another biotechnology company without a Pompe programme.

Dissenting Commissioner Thompson asserted that the basic facts of the case were clear and mostly uncontested. It was a merger to monopoly in the R&D of a highly specialized drug, and entry was not likely to replace the eliminated competition. The presumption of negative effects from a merger to monopoly had not been rebutted. This was sufficient to indicate that a Commission challenge was warranted.[183]

Thompson nevertheless went on, further analysing the case, for the sake of illuminating 'other issues important to innovation in America'. He pointed to the race between the companies that would have taken place in the absence of the merger. According to Thompson, the merger afforded Genzyme 'the power to decide unilaterally and at any time whether to postpone or terminate its own research efforts or Novazyme's R&D project'. In addition, without the merger, Genzyme would have had an incentive to get to market before Novazyme with as great a lead as possible, in order to gain a first-mover advantage in case the latter should break its exclusivity via a superior product.

Questioning Genzyme's motives and the effects of the merger, Thompson pointed to the willingness of Genzyme to pay $120 million for Novazyme, which was a considerable sum for an unproven company with research at a pre-clinical stage. Moreover, after the merger, the Novazyme project had been delayed by at least four years, compared to the original schedule. Thirdly, Novazyme chose to merge with its direct competitor, rather than forming a joint venture with Genzyme or some other well-capitalized partner with similar, or greater, biotech expertise.[184]

Although it was not possible to foretell with certainty what the market would have brought in the absence of the merger, Thompson was troubled by the possible harm to innovation competition. The merger extinguished any chance for competition to push innovation and bring products to the market sooner. Considering the potentially superior product possible in the Novazyme research path, such competition could be significant.

Regarding the arguments for the merger and Muris' claim that no post-merger evidence indicated anti-competitive effects, Thompson noted that the ultimate test

---

[183] 'Dissenting Statement of Commissioner Mozelle W. Thompson Genzyme Corporation's Acquisition of Novazyme Pharmaceuticals Inc.', p. 1, available at http://www.ftc.gov/os/2004/01/thompsongenzymestmt.pdf (last visited 11 October 2004).

[184] 'Dissenting Statement of Commissioner Mozelle W. Thompson Genzyme Corporation's Acquisition of Novazyme Pharmaceuticals Inc.', p. 6, available at http://www.ftc.gov/os/2004/01/thompsongenzymestmt.pdf (last visited 11 October 2004).

in merger analysis is 'whether the merger is likely to create or enhance market power or to facilitate its exercise'.[185] Any reduction or delay in innovation would be difficult to detect. The merger could thus be found to create or enhance market power without evidence that the market power was being exercised during the time of the merger investigation.

He also rejected the arguments that other market incentives and mechanisms would regulate the company's behaviour, *inter alia* questioning the incentives created by the contingent payment conditions and also questioning the ability of key Novazyme people to monitor Genzyme. As an illustration, Novazyme's CEO and chairman (with the children suffering from Pompe disease) had resigned from Genzyme in December 2002, following a conflict of interest. Citing the US Supreme Court, Thompson pointed out that 'good motives will not validate an otherwise anti-competitive practice'.

Finally, regarding the alleged efficiencies, Thompson did not find such evidence, although it was an examination of a consummated merger where post-merger efficiencies could be taken into account.

Commissioner Jones Harbour supported Thompson's claim of presumed anti-competitive effects created by the merger to monopoly on the worldwide market for the innovation of Pompe ERT. She found the decision to close the investigation under the circumstances 'puzzling'. Although she decided not to participate in the vote (owing to the fact that she joined the FTC at a late stage in the review) she issued a statement expressing her 'views on the relationship between competition and innovation'.[186]

Referring to renowned economists she stressed the importance of competition in the innovation process, pointing to the greater incentives to innovate in a competitive market in contrast to a monopolist facing no threat of immediate entry.[187] She also pointed to the importance of diversity of R&D efforts. She admitted that it could be questioned whether the point had been reached where a general presumption of anti-competitive effects in highly concentrated innovation markets was applicable. But she found such a presumption appropriate in the case of a merger to monopoly that eliminated all competition and diversity in the innovation market. This was particularly so in the pharmaceutical industry, where a monopoly would eliminate race-to-innovate competition, diminish diversity in research approaches and increase the likelihood and likely duration of product market monopoly following successful innovation. This was particularly the case where a firm has acquired

---

185 US 1992 Horizontal Merger Guidelines, §0.2.

186 'Statement of Commissioner Pamela Jones Harbour, Genzyme Corporation's Acquisition of Novazyme Pharmaceuticals Inc.', available at http://www.ftc.gov/os/2004/01/harbourgenzymestmt.pdf (last visited 11 October 2004). Jones Harbour declared that the reason for not participating in the vote was that, when she joined the FTC (August 2003), it was already in the final stages of considering the complex issues of the case.

187 Reference was made to Kenneth Arrow's and Daniel L. Rubinfeld's testimonies in Hearings on Competition and Intellectual Property in the Knowledge-Based Economy, Department of Justice and Federal Trade Commission, Feb. 25, 2002; Baumol, William J. & Ordover, Janusz A. 'Antitrust: Source of Dynamic and Static Inefficiencies?', in Jorde, Thomas M. & Teece, David J. (eds), *Antitrust, Innovation and Competitiveness,* Oxford University Press, New York, 1992.

all immediate rivals and is unencumbered by possible entrants. Such a presumption could, she considered, be rebutted by evidence of merger-specific efficiencies.

In her view, a presumption-free approach towards innovation market mergers would create difficulties, difficulties which would multiply in the common prospective merger cases where determination of effects is essentially forward-looking.

4.7.3 Concluding Observations

In this third category, the transactions considered affect the structure competing R&D; which is clearly the case if no current product exists at all. The analysis is, by nature, uncertain and often limited to a 'body count'. The bodies (competing R&D lines) must be credible and reasonably predictable, and must satisfy some qualitative test in order to be given competitive importance. In quite a few of the cases the authorities have investigated competitive effects in all dimensions: innovation incentives, product variety and potential competition on future markets.

Where the transaction takes place at a stage long before the R&D can possibly result in a marketable product, the authorities may take the stance that it is the pace and scope of the conducted research that is of primary interest. If a transaction will affect the portfolios and strategies of product development, an anti-competitive slowdown or tapering could result. Such analysis is evident in *Genzyme* (FTC 2004) but seems to have been part of *Roche/Genentech* (FTC 1990), *American Home Product* (FTC 1995) and *Upjohn/Pharmacia* (EU 1995).

However, as much as any anti-competitive reduction in R&D competition could lead to slower or less innovation, or inferior product quality,[188] the competitive impact may be a lessening in competition in a future product market. This would materialize through less diversity and higher prices. In this sense, product variety is an R&D output that actually creates a bridge between innovation and product market competition.

The European Commission concluded that the merger between Upjohn and Pharmacia (EU 1995) was unlikely 'to create or increase a dominant position in R&D of solid tumours', in view of uncertainty concerning the overlaps in the R&D[189] and the future products and considering the level of competition from equivalent research. Similarly, the AIDS research programmes were considered to belong to 'different R&D markets', as one focused on the suppression of the virus and the other on a secondary complication. As has

---

188 In this category *Sensormatic* (FTC 1995) may also be included.

189 The licence on which Upjohn was developing its product was limited to the Americas, Australia and New Zealand, for Europe the product was licensed to Rhône-Poulenc.

been seen, the relevant R&D is compared by way of the competitive relationship of the expected future products. Hence the R&D analysis could support conclusions regarding both competition in innovation and prospective product markets. In *Upjohn/Pharmacia* the analysis of R&D for the treatment of Parkinson's disease led the Commission to conclude that the merger would result in dominance 'neither on the R&D/compound market nor for future developments'. Similarly, in *Glaxo Wellcome/SmithKline Beecham* (EU 2000), regarding pharmaccines,[190] an R&D analysis was conducted to explore the competition effects resulting from the integration of the parties' R&D programmes (this separate from current market analysis). The purpose was nevertheless to conclude whether the parties' position would be strengthened, without defining more closely in what dimension such dominance would arise.

In the US too, future product market concerns are often part of the merger challenge. In *Pharmacia/Upjohn* (FTC 1996) the FTC relied on lessened incentives to pursue R&D for the Pharmacia product since that product was a few years behind Upjohn's. This would reduce not only actual competition and diversity in R&D but also future product market competition. Although the major likely anti-competitive effect would be fewer cancer inhibitors on the future market, the FTC relied on reduced innovation efforts to reach its conclusions. *Pfizer/Warner-Lambert* (FTC 2000) follows the same scheme, the number of independent developers being reduced from four to three.[191] Where the products are close to launch such concern is natural, as in *Baxter* (FTC 1997), but, where the future product market is more remote, this effect is often added to the list of potential negative effects.[192] In these cases, the FTC, apart from competition in R&D, adds future manufacture and sale to the relevant markets.

Even if the potential competition doctrine were applied to cases where no product market yet exists, it might be difficult to predict the exact effects on that market when it does arise. Owing to the time lags and uncertainties involved, it could be difficult to enjoin a merger under the potential competition doctrine, alleging that, as it would eliminate the likelihood of future competition between two products, currently under development, the situation amounts to a substantial lessening of potential competition in the product market. Moreover, the fact that the merger would give the parties the ability

---

190 Outlined under section 4.6. above.

191 The FTC neatly summarized the different aspects stating that 'the merged entity would unilaterally delay, deter or eliminate competing programs to research and develop EGFr-tk inhibitors [. . .] potentially reducing the number of drugs reaching the market and thus resulting in higher prices for consumers'.

192 See *Roche/Genentech* (FTC 1990).

and, perhaps, the incentive to close or delay one R&D project, thus decreasing the likelihood of two different future products, could arguably also be outside the realm of potential competition on a product market. More importantly, regardless of the possible limitations of the potential competition doctrine, these kinds of anti-competitive effects must be analysed with a view to the competitive situation in R&D.

In *American Home Products* (FTC 1995), the FTC based its action on the reduced number of independent R&D sources (from three to two) for a particular vaccine, considering the incentives and abilities to stall the development of a potentially superior vaccine and increased risk of collusion between the remaining developers. In *Glaxo Wellcome* (FTC 1995), Glaxo currently marketed a product and both parties competed in a new generation (non-injectable anti-migraine medicine) that could constitute its own product market. Again the FTC concluded that reduced competition in the R&D market would reduce the parties' R&D efforts, particularly by halting the development of one of the products. According to the FTC, the merger would result in less R&D output both in the short and the long term.

In addition, there is no major analytical difference if one of the parties already markets a product or not. If anything, the result in the former case would be increased likelihood of anti-competitive reductions in R&D, thus reinforcing the concern for negative effects on innovation. Both current product markets and innovation markets may accordingly have to be delineated. The boundaries of the particular market for the resulting future product can perhaps be defined more accurately when some product already exists, but it may still be difficult correctly to assess how products under development would fit into or affect those boundaries. Evidently, this category also covers concerns for both innovation competition as such and potential product market competition.[193]

When it comes to pure innovation effects, there seems to be a policy shift in the presumptions operating in American Home Products, intervening in the reduction from three to two early R&D sources, and in *Genzyme/Novazyme* (FTC 2004) allowing an R&D monopoly. Although the case involves some unusual facts, it is important, not only as it is the most recent, but it is also the Republican FTC administration's development of the innovation market

[193] Several variants can be applicable to one case. In *Hoechst/Rhône-Poulenc* (FTC 2000) the parties were developing a new generation of pharmaceuticals, safer and more effective than any other available alternatives. Based on this technology, Hoechst had already obtained FDA approval, whereas Rhône-Poulenc was in the late stages of development for the same market. In addition, both parties developed products for adjoining markets. The FTC found restrictions in direct product market competition, potential competition and innovation competition.

approach, perceived as the Clinton era's big antitrust invention.[194] While it acknowledges the applicability and use of the doctrine, it also narrows it down. It makes it clear that, when future markets are close, the concept is used as a means to safeguard competition in the future product market. But when the future market is indeed distant – and innovation is really at the centre – not even merger to monopoly will currently be per se contestable. Negative effects must be established. The outstanding question is then how negative incentives or consequences are to be established and how distant/certain the future market must be for future product market competition to matter.

4.8 GENERAL R&D COMPETITION

The fourth category leads to the problem of defining relevant markets for R&D itself. In the previous cases presented, the future product limited the R&D programmes to be looked at. Competing future products tomorrow implied competing R&D today. Sometimes such a narrow articulation of competition in innovation will be inappropriate. Fully to apprehend the competitive aspects of a transaction a wider delimitation may be required.

4.8.1 Technology Bases

In *Pasteur Mérieux and Merck*[195] (EU 1994) the parties planned to group their activities in human vaccines in a joint venture. Although the joint venture's activities comprised R&D, production and distribution, the Commission considered it was not sufficiently autonomous to qualify as a full-function joint venture and the transaction thus had to be analysed under Article 81 rather than under the Merger Regulation.

> Each vaccine, aimed at a specific disease, was found to form a different product market since there was no substitutability between the different vaccines. In addition, different technologies were used in the development and production of different vaccines, subject to regulatory requirements. The Commission also made a further distinction between multivalent and monovalent vaccines.[196] Although the

---

[194] See *The Economist*, 'The New Enforcers', article, October 7, 2000; Rai, Arti K., 'Fostering Cumulative Innovation in the Biopharmaceutical Industry: The Role of Patents and Antitrust', 16 *Berkeley Technology Law Journal* 813, 826 (2001); Hart, David, M., 'Antitrust and technological innovation', 15(2) *Issues in Science & Technology* 75 (1998/99).

[195] Case No IV/34.776 – *Pasteur Mérieux/Merck*, OJ L 309/1 (1994).

[196] A multivalent vaccine is a combination of several antigens, directed towards different diseases, into one vaccine. Consumers generally prefer multivalents for general immunization whereas monovalents are mainly used either for brush-up immunization or as a booster for non-protected persons. See §54 of the decision.

launch of a multivalent vaccine would have the effect of replacing some monovalent vaccines, that effect was not sufficient to consider both products as one market. Geographically, vaccine markets in Europe were still considered national, since different conditions prevailed in the various Member States. Thanks to epidemiology, legal frameworks and medical tradition, these differences were not expected to disappear in the near future.

The Commission found the joint venture likely to restrict appreciably *actual* competition only in two German vaccine markets. Regarding *potential* competition, things were more complicated. The JV was likely to restrict potential competition in one French vaccine market. For another kind of vaccine, all EEA countries were affected. In these markets, one of the parties was currently active and the other party was, absent the JV, expected to enter. Moreover, the Commission analysed potential competition in terms of future vaccines. The parties were active in R&D work for a series of vaccines, but overlaps between R&D *pipelines* in later stages of development at the time only existed with regard to Hepatitis A and varicella vaccines. The Commission thus found that the creation of the JV would result in an appreciable restriction of competition on the future Hepatitis A and varicella vaccine markets, as the JV would 'take over the post phase II clinical trials and [. . .] distribute the final products'.[197] Apart from these concerns, the parties' product portfolios would also have allowed them independently to combine existing vaccines in order to develop a new multivalent varicella vaccine. Merck already had a vaccine which could be combined with varicella, and Pasteur Mérieux, absent the JV, would have improved its vaccine in order to enter this market. For other kinds of multivalents, the parties' respective product portfolios did not allow them to prepare the vaccines alone. Although other actors could have offered some complementary products via licences and supplies, such arrangements were unavailable for important antigens and such contractual arrangements with several parties were considered unsuitable for R&D team cooperation. As a consequence, the Commission only considered the JV appreciably to restrict competition for the multivalent varicella vaccine and not for other multivalents.

However, under the *Potential Competition* heading the Commission also assessed competition for other new vaccines at earlier stages of R&D, in this case denoted 'future pipeline products'. The Commission here undertook a more general R&D competition analysis, while noting that such an assessment was far more difficult, 'in view of the extremely broad range of such future research and the lack of precise indications as to the chances of bringing successful products to the markets'.[198] The parties would remain autonomous in their basic R&D decisions and respective budgets, particularly regarding early phases of clinical work and fundamental basic research (or when such research was bought from specialized institutes). However, when new vaccine products were developed and entered post-clinical phase II, the parties would offer them on an exclusive licence to the JV, for continued development. If the JV turned down the offer, the offering party could transfer or license all rights to a third party. The JV would set up a Development Committee in which the R&D activities of the parents, including relevant discoveries, were going to be discussed. The Commission could not therefore exclude the possibility that basic R&D would be coordinated. Considering the parties' important position on the

197 Decision, §63.
198 Decision, §64.

vaccine markets (being two of four leading firms worldwide), their worldwide presence and large R&D budgets, such coordination was likely to have an appreciable effect on R&D for *future pipeline products* in the EEA, and thus fall foul of Article 81(1) also in this respect.

From the above it is apparent that the Commission's view of potential competition was broader than what is recognized in American case law. Not only did potential competition analysis include prospective markets where neither party was currently active (Hepatitis A and varicella), it also included R&D for undefined future products in general. Whether the primary aim for doing so was to protect competition in innovation or future product markets we are not told. It seems that the Commission did not consider that question decisive. R&D strategies and decisions affect innovation competition that, in turn, determines diversity and competition in future markets.

Observations from third parties (competitors) indicated that the creation of the JV might have detrimental effects on them. It was particularly noted that the competitive process in the European vaccines markets would be restricted, and access to technology would no longer be ensured. The Commission found that the JV resulted in an appreciable restriction of competition regarding other producers' opportunities to obtain supplies or licences of *existing* vaccines and vaccine technologies (including those in the pipeline). According to the Commission, such outside sourcing could become important for the development of multivalents, providing producers with necessary 'missing' antigens or vaccine technologies. However, as far as *future* antigens and vaccine technology were concerned, the number of potential competitors for the wide range of future vaccines and vaccine technology (including all kinds of firms and bodies involved in basic biotech research) led the Commission to conclude that the JV would not appreciably restrict competition by reducing the sourcing-out possibilities of third party producers.

Thus, considering the parties' strong position in the area, the Commission expected diminished R&D competition for undefined future pipeline products, in breach of Article 81(1). Foreclosure effects were likely to arise in the short term, but, in view of the technological opportunities, there were no clear indications that third parties would be foreclosed to an appreciable extent from distant future technologies.

In assessing whether the JV could be exempted under 81(3), the Commission noted that the arrangement would allow the parties to share R&D experiences, cooperate from post phase II clinical trials for 'European'-oriented vaccines, and by combining their antigen and vaccine technology portfolios allow the JV to develop new and better performing vaccines, adapted to the specific needs of each individual country. By avoiding R&D overlaps and benefiting from the parties' respective strengths, this would lead to a qualitative promotion of technical progress.[199]

The JV would, for example, be able to start a development programme for multivalents combining DTP, polio, HIB and Hepatitis B, being the first producer to possess all the necessary antigens. The Commission anticipated a great demand for

---

199 Decision, §§82 *et seq.*

such vaccines, tailored to meet specific national needs. In other respects too, the Commission pointed to the possibility of the parties being able to stimulate and speed up the development of new and better vaccines. No vaccine producer was able to realize many of these positive effects alone and the Commission believed that only a JV provided a mechanism flexible enough to achieve the required open-ended and far-reaching cooperation. As previously mentioned, alternative contractual arrangements would constitute too rigid a solution to attain the ambitions. Moreover, the JV did not eliminate competition in any respect, partly because it did not create an insurmountable entry barrier to future vaccine markets. The Commission consequently exempted the JV.[200]

This is an interesting and important case for innovation issues. It acknowledges that general conditions for competition in R&D are part of the analysis under 81(1). Likewise, dynamic considerations can save the day under 81(3). Taken as a whole, the decision indicates that safeguarding acceptable competitive conditions in the R&D environment while allowing cooperation promoting technological development is a balancing act that can be performed under EU competition law.

In this case competition was not eliminated. Third parties were not substantially foreclosed in the long run since no 'insurmountable' entry barrier was created, although the two parties combined two very potent complementary asset portfolios.

In the merger between *Ciba-Geigy* and *Sandoz* (FTC 1997), the FTC identified three markets of interest: gene therapy, corn herbicides, and flea control products.[201]

The overall market for gene therapy technology and R&D of gene therapy, in which innovation issues particularly arose, constituted a separate market. In addition to this overall market, gene therapy was divided into specific gene therapy product markets.[202] The analysis therefore included R&D, manufacture and sale of:

- herpes simplex virus-thymidine kinase ('HSV-tk') gene therapy for the treatment of cancer;
- HSV-tk gene therapy for the treatment of graft versus host disease;
- gene therapy for the treatment of hemophilia; and
- chemoresistance gene therapy.

The FDA had not yet approved any gene therapy product and the first products were not expected until the year 2000. But gene therapy had a great potential as treatment for a wide array of diseases and the sales of these products were projected to reach up to $45 billion by the year 2010.

Each of the markets was highly concentrated. Ciba (acting in this field through

200 The parties had during the process made some changes in the set of agreements surrounding the JV, especially regarding technology licences for Germany and France.

201 *Ciba-Geigy Ltd.*, 123 F.T.C. 842, Docket no. C-3725 (1997).

202 Complaint, §9.

46.5 per cent ownership in Chiron) and Sandoz were two of only a few entities having the necessary development capabilities. Although many firms were engaged in pioneering research in gene therapy, only these two controlled substantial proprietary rights (including patents, patent applications and know-how) and other capabilities allowing them to develop commercially a broad range of therapy products.[203] In the market for overall gene therapy, the Commission concluded that Ciba and Sandoz together would control an 'unmatchable' portfolio of key intellectual property rights necessary to commercialize gene therapy products.[204] The same conditions applied for the four specific therapy markets, which were also highly concentrated. In each of the markets, Ciba and Sandoz were in, or near, clinical development, being the two leading commercial developers, controlling key IPR and know-how. Only in chemoresistance gene therapy was a third company considered capable of conducting commercial product development.[205] Moreover, entry into each of the gene therapy markets was already very difficult, expensive and time-consuming, with entry times up to 10 to 12 years, or more. Entry was impeded by technical, regulatory, patent, clinical and production barriers.[206]

Ciba and Sandoz had virtually all the IPRs needed to develop gene therapy independently. This actual and substantial innovation competition would be lost if the parties merged. The incentives for development were likely to be further reduced when the R&D pipelines were combined and parallel development projects were likely to be eliminated or delayed. Also potential competition in future markets would be eliminated.

Moreover, the new entity would have a disincentive to license IPRs or otherwise to collaborate with others. Before the merger, the two parties acted as rival centres from which others could obtain needed licences, in return for marketing or other rights.[207] A substantial number of companies were able to conduct gene therapy R&D, but without licences to key IPR held by Ciba/Chiron and Sandoz they were unlikely to continue development.[208] Also, the two parties' extensive patent portfolios and pending patent applications were of uncertain breadth and validity, diminishing incentives and abilities for other gene therapy researchers to continue developing their products. Consequently, the merger would heighten barriers to entry.

The chosen remedies involved requirements for the new company, Novartis (and Chiron), to grant various licences. It was required to grant a non-exclusive licence (including necessary information, know-how and so on) to certain technologies essential for the general development and commercialization of gene therapy products. The FTC also called for licences for specific gene therapy products. For HSV-tk gene therapy for treatment of cancer and graft versus host disease, the consent

---

[203] Proprietary inputs necessary for the different applications included genes, vectors (delivery vehicle for gene therapy), cytokines (proteins) and manufacturing technology.

[204] Analysis to Aid Public Comment.

[205] Three companies were capable of developing chemoresistance gene therapy using the MDR-1 gene and only two of these (Chiron and Sandoz) could also develop products using the MRP gene. See complaint, §19.

[206] Complaint, §26.

[207] Analysis to Aid Public Comment.

[208] Complaint, §31; Analysis to Aid Public Comment.

agreement attempted to restore pre-merger incentives for R&D, manufacture and sale by requiring licensing of worldwide patent rights on a non-exclusive basis to Rhône-Poulenc Rorer or another pre-approved licensee. Also Factor VIII hemophilia genes were to be made available to other entities. In addition, the merged company was not allowed to acquire certain exclusive rights in IPRs and technology related to chemoresistance gene therapy.[209]

This seems to be a case where the innovation market approach very much lived up to its aim of identifying and remedying anti-competitive effects in innovation, yet it does not follow the standard method for innovation market analysis as described in the guidelines. It handled structural effects of the merger on innovation competition between the parties, foreclosure effects on third parties' innovation activities and product development, particularly via analysis of existing and potential technology markets, while providing for an enhanced likelihood of future product market competition, even with respect to as yet undefined products.[210]

It is informative to compare the FTC's handling in the Ciba case with that of the European Commission. When reviewing *Ciba-Geigy/Sandoz* (1996),[211] the European Commission also closely examined, *inter alia,* the parties' research activities in the field of HS-TK gene therapy (the term used in the case) for the treatment of various tumours.

According to the parties, HS-TK gene therapy did not involve healing a disease, but constituted a method of applying a therapeutic substance to the appropriate place. The parties consequently argued that HS-TK gene therapy was in direct competition with other gene therapies and with other processes such as chemotherapy, immunotherapy and radiation.

The Commission agreed, 'only in so far as there are other therapies being pursued for the treatment of tumours'.[212] Such therapies, however, clearly differed in their mode of action from HS-TK gene therapy and the Commission declared that reference could not be made to a common treatment objective without also taking into account the different active principles leading to different degrees of effectiveness and tolerance. Thus HS-TK gene therapy for the treatment of tumours could be regarded as a separate future product market. Nonetheless, for this decision, the Commission did not find it necessary to decide on the inclusion of other therapies. It simply continued to analyse HS-TK gene therapy.[213]

Sandoz's subsidiary GTI conducted gene therapy research at phase II/III with a

---

209 Analysis to Aid Public Comment.

210 See, e.g., Tom, Willard K., 'Licensing and Antitrust: Common Goals and Uncommon Problems', Address Before the American Conference Institute, 9th National Conference on Licensing Intellectual Property (1998), available at www.ftc.gov.

211 Case No IV/M.737 – *Ciba-Geigy/Sandoz* (1996) OJ L 201/1 (1997).

212 Decision, §45.

213 Ibid.

possible market entry within three to five years. GTI's future patent position was potentially strong, with pending patent applications covering different relevant retroviral constructs and treatment methods. Ciba's research efforts, through a 49.9 per cent stake in Chiron, were only at a pre-clinical (before phase I) stage. Chiron also had numerous patent applications pending which eventually could give them broad protection in the area. The parties could have exclusive access to a combination of broadly defined patents, which could largely exclude competitors from parts of research in gene therapy for tumours. Such foreclosure could block the development of gene therapies, according to the Commission's information. At the least, third parties would have a worse position when bargaining for licences from GTI or Chiron. However, concerning Chiron's patent applications, there was substantial uncertainty about what would be the scope of the patents, if finally granted. In addition, Ciba did not have exclusive access to the Chiron patents.

The Commission stated that the analysis had to include the likelihood that gene therapy would prove successful, the likely future patent situation and the probabilities of competitors finding ways to circumvent the patent situation. The Commission was especially interested in the likelihood, as alleged by other market participants, of Chiron's patents blocking competitors of GTI. The future patent situation, and the extent and effect of foreclosure, depended on the specification of the patents finally granted. These conditions were not yet known. However, it was realized that the pending applications could have a disruptive effect on the decisions of other firms interested in investing in this area. According to the Commission, this alone was not enough to conclude dominance. Since there was not enough information to rule out the possibility that ways (however costly) of circumventing the patent problem could be found, the Commission concluded that it could not ultimately say 'with sufficient probability' that the merger would create or strengthen a dominant position on any future market.

As previously noted, the FTC had ordered (through Chiron) the issuance of non-exclusive licences for some of Ciba's gene therapy technology. During the proceedings before the European Commission, the parties agreed to issue non-exclusive licences, on customary terms and conditions, to interested firms for each European patent and for national patents based on two international patent applications.[214] This was 'noted' by the Commission after its assessment and conclusion. In the absence of any assessment in the decision, it is hard to say to what extent the Commission's conclusion was affected by this fact.

At the outset of the analysis, the Commission stated that the undertakings' R&D potential could not be ignored 'since their future competitive strength is based precisely on such potential'. Contrary to the FTC, the European Commission focused its assessment on dominance in future markets for gene therapy in treatment of tumours, not gene therapy R&D as such. Nevertheless, since the competitive status of the future markets were directly related to the possibility of patents blocking the development of gene therapies or other treatment methods, particularly by preventing competing products from being marketed, the

214 Decision, §107.

Commission also considered the conditions for R&D competition. But, in the light of the uncertainties in the validity and scope of patents, future dominance could not be established.

Pasteur Mérieux/Merck and *Ciba-Geigy/Sandoz* raise important and difficult questions regarding lessened competition in innovation, foreclosure effects for third parties, and efficiencies from the combination of unique R&D capabilities and asset portfolios. A particular complexity lies in the unification of patent-protected technologies that may affect the development and commercialization of a variety of potential products. Rather than unifying competing R&D projects towards a *particular* future product, the combination of such assets may create an IPR bottleneck with broader effects, possibly affecting the development (not least by restricting third party access) in a whole area of technology. The same problems may arise in another kind of arrangement – patent pools.

4.8.2 Industry Standards and Patent Pools

Case law is also sparse when it comes to patent pools. However, both US and EU authorities have recently dealt with a couple of important high-technology patent pools for industry standards, where, among other things, competition in innovation has been discussed.

In 1997, the US DOJ cleared the *MPEG-2* patent pool by way of a business review letter.[215] DOJ stressed the pro-competitive effects of integrating complementary technologies and making them available through a blanket licence, reducing transaction costs, holdout problems and patent infringements, while increasing availability of licences and disseminating the licensed technology. Yet potential adverse effects were also investigated. The European Commission also investigated the pool along the same lines, and seemingly accepted it on the same grounds.[216]

In 1994, the Moving Picture Experts Group (MPEG), a working group of

---

[215] MPEG Pool Letter. Business Review Letter from Joel I. Klein, Acting Assistant Attorney General, Antitrust Division, Department of Justice, to Garrard R. Beeney, Esq. (June 26, 1997). A business review letter serves, very much like the administrative 'comfort' letters previously issued by the European Commission, as a declaration that the Department is not 'presently inclined to initiate antitrust enforcement action against the conduct . . . described'. The DOJ reserves the right to bring action if the actual operation proves to be anti-competitive in purpose or effect.

[216] The Commission issued a comfort letter under 81(3). See Case No IV/C-3/36.849 – *MPEG-2 Licensing Programme*, OJ C 229/19 (1998), and press release IP/98/1155, 'Commission approves a patent licensing programme to implement the MPEG-2 standard', December 18, 1998.

ISO/IEC,[217] adopted the MPEG-2 Video and Systems standard for video compression technology. Subsequently, an IP Working Group (formed by a number of firms that participated in the development of the standard) issued a public call for submission of patents that could be infringed by compliance with the standard. An independent patent expert evaluated the submitted patents. Approximately 8000 US patent abstracts were reviewed and about 800 US patents belonging to over 100 patentees were studied.

A patent pool was established to assure interoperability and implementation of digital video, providing access to patents deemed essential for the MPEG-2 standard. At the outset it comprised 27 patents from nine patent holders.[218] These patents constituted most, but not all, essential patents, that is, patented technology necessarily used in order to comply with the standard. The holders licensed their patents to a common licence agent (MPEG LA) on a non-exclusive basis. The agent was given the task to license out the pooled technology as a package, on non-discriminatory terms, to anyone requesting a licence in order to make products according to the standard.

The independent expert continues to examine patents submitted for inclusion in the pool as well as reviewing claims of non-essentiality of already included patents. By April 2004, the pool had grown to include 23 patent holders worldwide, licensing more than 640 patents (128 patent families plus their worldwide counterparts).[219]

The DOJ pointed to both the potential efficiencies and anti-competitive effects that may result from patent pools. The starting point for the analysis is the relationship among the patents. Apart from invalid or expired patents, the inclusion of which would be anti-competitive, serious competitive concerns may arise if competing technologies are pooled and priced together. For complementary patents, pools are often an efficient and pro-competitive method of dissemination, particularly if the patents otherwise block the application for which they are jointly licensed.

In this case the patents were 'essential', meaning that there was no technical alternative for any of the patents and moreover a pooled patent was only useful in conjunction with the others. This implies that the pool does not foreclose competing implementations of the standard (by bundling non-essential patents).

But competition effects could still arise and the FTC considered whether the pool would be a vehicle to disadvantage competitors, allow collusion on prices or impair technology or innovation competition.

In this regard, some aspects should be highlighted. First of all, it was stressed that the blanket licence was made available on non-discriminatory terms and conditions to all potential licensees. Although they were only offered as a package, this did not constitute a tying since there were no technological alternatives to any of the patents. Besides, the patents were also made available individually by the single licensors, outside the pool.

Moreover, there were no expected negative effects from the development of rival

[217] International Standards Organisation and the International Electrotechnical Commission.

[218] Columbia University, Fujitsu, General Instrument, Lucent, Matsushita, Mitsubishi, Philips, Scientific-Atlanta and Sony.

[219] www.mpegla.com.

technologies. The licensees remained free to develop or support rival standards. Royalties were only paid for products that used at least one pooled patent. Since the pool consisted of patents essential to the MPEG-2 standard, this implied that, if the standard was used, by necessity all patents were used.

Grantback obligations are particularly suspect from an innovation perspective. The licensees were subject to a grantback provision that required them to grant the licensors, and any other licensee, a non-exclusive worldwide licence to any essential patents. For this the licensee would receive a 'fair and reasonable' royalty based on the licensor's per-patent share. Alternatively the licensee could become a member of the pool. Failure to comply with this provision constituted a material breach of the licence which in turn gave a right to termination.

The DOJ concluded that these provisions did not extend to mere implementations or even to improvements on the essential patents. They only obliged essential patents to be available to all and eased a potential holdout problem (that a producer with a new essential patent would control the standard) and would not create a disincentive to innovation (particularly since little innovation was expected in the core of the standard).

More interestingly, the licensees also agreed to a partial termination right for the licensors (that is, the members of the pool). If a licensee brought proceedings against a licensor for patent infringement of an essential patent *or an MPEG-2 related patent* and refused to grant the licensor a licence on fair and reasonable terms, the licensor could direct the MPEG LA to withdraw that licensor's patents from the particular licensee's portfolio. The DOJ stated that, 'in different circumstances', this termination right could raise difficult competition issues.

Since related patents are not essential, there could be alternatives to choose from even if the licensee chooses not to license its patent. If a pool member was denied a licence to a related patent and decided to infringe the related patent, the licensee's decision to sue could render it unable to comply with the MPEG-2 standard. Now, other commitments (to the international standard setting bodies, such as ISO and ITU-T) obliged the licensors to license their MPEG-2 essential patents. But the DOJ still considered a risk of lower royalty levels for the licensees (probably the intentional consequence of providing extra bargaining power to the pool members) and the consequential dampening of the incentives to invest in the MPEG-2 standard. Such effects would limit some of the benefits of the openness of the standard and the prospect for improvements on the essential patents.

According to the DOJ, the potential negative effects would have been worse if the termination right would benefit all licensees to the pool. That would have amounted to a compulsory grantback of related patents, depriving the licensees of the opportunity to choose among and negotiate freely with potential users. Here only the licensors of the essential patents were benefited. These pool members also had an interest in supporting related innovation, boosting the value of the standard, and would probably be cautious in applying the partial termination right. Moreover, there could be positive effects from this kind of non-exclusive grantback since licensors would capture some of the value they had added to the related patents by creating the pool, thereby enabling the parties to share risk and rewards in supporting and improving the standard.

The DOJ consequently accepted the pooling arrangement.[220]

220 See note 215 regarding the legal status of this kind of written opinion.

More recently DVD technology pools have been cleared by the DOJ and the European Commission. DVD technology was developed by a consortium of ten firms. After lengthy negotiations for a common licensing scheme had failed, three firms decided to create a first pool.

> This pool was set up by Philips, Sony and Pioneer, comprising essential patents for the manufacturing of DVDs and players in compliance with the DVD-ROM and DVD-Video formats. The pool was structured by two pairs of licences. Sony and Pioneer licensed their patents, on a non-exclusive basis, to Philips. Philips subsequently disseminated the technology through two different standard licences: one for DVD makers ('the Disc License' – 95 patents) and one for player manufacturers ('the Player License' – 115 patents). The essentiality of the patents would continuously and independently be supervised by a patent expert. Licensees were requested to license back any essential patents under their control. The pool was cleared by the DOJ in 1998.[221]
>
> A second, complementary pool was approved by DOJ in 1999 and the EU Commission in 2000.[222] Six companies[223] entered a multilateral agreement regarding their essential patents for the same formats, whereby Toshiba would receive a licence to the patents of each licensor and grant sublicences to makers of discs, players and decoders. At the start, the pool comprised 29 disc patents and 22 player patents. Patent expert review and grantback provisions were similar to the previous DVD pool.

From an antitrust perspective, these pools seem to be role models. All licensors grant non-exclusive licences to a pool, which comprises only essential (non-competing) patents (for which there are no available alternatives) and are evaluated by an independent expert. The patents are licensed to any interested third party on a non-discriminatory basis for a reasonable royalty. Grantbacks are limited to licensees' essential patents (although the MPEG-2 pool got away with a more extensive grantback/partial termination clause).[224]

---

221 DVD Pool Letter. Business Review Letter from Joel I. Klein, Acting Assistant Attorney General, Antitrust Division, Department of Justice, to Garrard R. Beeney, Esq. (Dec. 16, 1998).

222 Case No IV/C-3/37.506 – *DVD Patent Licensing Programme*, OJ C 242/5 (1999); Press release IP/00/1135 'Commission approves a patent licensing programme to implement the DVD standard', October 9, 2000.

223 Hitachi, Matsushita, Mitsubishi, Time Warner, Toshiba and Victor.

224 For further comments regarding these pools see, e.g., Charles River Associates, *Report on Multiparty Licensing*, Report to the European Commission, (2003); available at http://europa.eu.int/comm/competition/antitrust/legislation/multiparty_licensing.pdf (last visited 3 March 2005); Newberg, Joshua A, 'Antitrust, Patent Pools, and the Management of Uncertainty', 3 *Atlantic Law Journal* 1 (2000); Beeney, Garrard R., 'Pro-Competitive Aspects of Intellectual Property Pools: A Proposal for Safe Harbor Provisions', Submission to the DOJ and FTC Hearings on Competition and Intellectual Property Law and Policy in the Knowledge-Based Economy (2002);

It is clear that this kind of pool, covering industry standards, generally carries great benefit to consumers by allowing industry to settle important technological aspects so as to provide attractive products. Interoperability may be achieved and a cost-effective way is provided for prospective product manufacturers to navigate through the patent thicket.[225] At the same time innovation competition issues, both at the architectural level, between different competing standards, and at the module level, between different applications, may arise in pooling situations. As for incentives for innovation at the implementing level, it is clear that the authorities take an interest in the competitive nature of the patents involved, accessibility to the pool and, above all, the effects of grantback provisions.[226]

Regarding the first dimension, competition between standards, the antitrust authorities may have to decide whether to allow the industry to choose a

---

available at www.ftc.gov/opp/intellect/020417garrardrbeeney.pdf (last visited 3 March 2005). See also EU 2004 Technology Transfer Guidelines, §§210–35. Richard J. Gilbert neatly summarizes the DOJ position, recently approving pools based upon the following safeguards:

1. Limitation of the portfolio to technically essential patents which, by definition, are not competitive with each other.
2. Portfolio patents are clearly identified and can be licensed individually as well as in a package.
3. Issue of worldwide non-exclusive licences.
4. Licensee liability for royalties conditioned on actual use of the patents.
5. Freedom of licensees to develop and use alternative technologies.
6. Requirement that licensees grant back non-exclusive, non-discriminatory licences to use patents that are essential to comply with the technology.

'Antitrust for Patent Pools: A Century of Policy Evolution', 2004 *Stanford Technology Law Review* 3, 2 (2004). See also the approved patent pool concerning 3G telecom technologies. 3G Patent Platform Partnership. Business Review Letter from Charles A. James, Assistant Attorney General, Antitrust Division, Department of Justice, to Ky P. Ewing, Esq. (November 12, 2002) available at http://www.usdoj.gov/atr/public/busreview/200455.pdf (last visited 11 October 2004) and COMP/37.920 – '3G Patent Platform', Press release IP/02/1651, 'Antitrust clearance for licensing of patents for third generation mobile services'; Choumelova, Dessy 'Competition Law Analysis of Patent Licensing Arrangements – The Particular Case of 3G3P', 1 *Competition Policy Newsletter* 41 (2003).

225 Merges summarizes the DVD pools as 'the continuation of the tradition of industry-wide institution formation as a response to patent bottlenecks'. Their characteristics are 'all earmarks of an ongoing, functioning institution designed to overcome the inherent problems of valuing complementary patents' (Merges, Robert P., *Institutions for Intellectual Property Transactions*, University of California at Berkeley, 1999, p. 36); available at www.law.berkeley.edu/institutes/bclt/pubs/merges/pools.pdf (last visited 11 October 2004).

226 Regarding access see, e.g., IGR Stereo Television, European Commission, *Eleventh Report on Competition Policy,* 1981, p. 63.

winning standard. Clearly, variety is not a genuine good that can be maximized, particularly where network effects are present. At some point consumers would benefit if a general standard was adopted. As far as possible such a standard should be singled out on its merits, possibly by letting the market decide or at least by using a legitimate standard-setting process.[227] Moreover, a patent pool must not be allowed to fend off alternative standards by adopting strategies for extinguishing the opportunities for upcoming superior technologies.

In a case from the 1970s Philips and a number of German firms,[228] all 'interested in the developing market for video cassettes and video cassette recorders', notified to the European Commission of an 'agreement on uniform application of technical standards for the VCR system'.[229]

> At the time, only Philips and Sony (U-MATIC) had developed marketable videotape systems for sales in Europe, while Sanyo was trying to gain a foothold and Telefunken was preparing to introduce a videodisc system. Philips had a 'preeminent' position on the market and, together with the smaller Sony, accounted for over 70 per cent of sales.
>
> The agreement provided the parties with the complete Philips system for the production and marketing of equipment. The uniform application of this technical standard, the parties alleged, was necessary to ensure compatibility between as many manufacturers as possible, to the benefit of consumers. Moreover, the parties granted each other royalty-free, non-exclusive licences to their patents, where this was needed to ensure compatibility.
>
> The agreement also provided for the exclusive use of the VCR standard, both in production and in distribution. This would turn out to be decisive. Philips asserted that the non-compete clause was justified as a quid pro quo for the royalty-free licences and necessary to assure a firm foothold on the market. The same applied, according to Philips, to the termination clause according to which the terminating party forfeited all its licences while the remaining parties retained their licences to the terminating party's patents. The Commission considered both these limitations in violation of Article 81(1).

---

[227] The topic of antitrust policy for standard setting will not be expanded upon here, but for recent contributions see, e.g., Dolmans, Maurits, 'Standards for standards', Joint DOJ/FTC hearings on Competition and Intellectual Property Law and Policy in the Knowledge-Based Economy, May 22, 2002, http://www.ftc.gov/opp/intellect/020522dolmans.pdf (last visited 3 March 2005); Balto, David A., 'Standard Setting in a Network Economy', Address at Cutting Edge Antitrust Law Seminars International, February 17, 2000; available at http://www.ftc.gov/speeches/other/standardsetting.htm (last visited 3 March 2005); Shapiro, Carl, *Navigating the Patent Thicket: Cross Licenses, Patent Pools, and Standard-Setting*, University of California at Berkeley, 2001; available at http://faculty.haas.berkeley.edu/shapiro/thicket.pdf (last visited 3 March 2005). See also US 1995 IP Guidelines, particularly 5.5., 5.6.; EU 2001 Horizontal Cooperation Guidelines, §§159–78.

[228] Blaupunkt, Bosch-Siemens, Grundig, Loewe, Nordmende and SABA Werke and their associated companies outside Germany.

[229] Case No IV/29.151 – *Video cassette recorders*, OJ L 47/42 (1978).

As for the applicability of Article 81(3) the Commission found the uniform application of the VCR standard to have achieved its purpose, disseminating the system to other manufacturers. On the other hand, the Commission did not acknowledge an improvement in production or distribution to the benefit of consumers, since compliance with the VCR standard 'led to the exclusion of other, perhaps better, systems'. This was particularly serious bearing in mind Philips' strong market position.

It was noted that Philips had licensed other European firms without an obligation on the licensee not to manufacture competing systems. The Commission did not consider this restraint indispensable for the attainment of spreading the VCR standard. Further analysis under 81(3) was therefore superfluous, but it was nevertheless asserted that the conditions for termination would not be considered indispensable to the attainment of the agreement's legitimate objectives.

4.8.3 Concluding Observations

In *Ciba-Geigy/Sandoz* (FTC 1997) the FTC concluded that the transaction would eliminate important competition in the overall R&D market for gene technology. No product was about to be introduced for several years and when introduced a new product would not compete in existing product markets. Hence a traditional approach to potential competition would not have been appropriate fully to capture all the competition aspects in this case. But neither would an innovation market concept (along the guidelines) strictly limited to competing R&D for a particular future product.

Although the FTC was able to identify four kinds of resulting products (future product markets), gene therapy research was also conducted outside their areas of application.[230] This research ultimately aimed at a variety of applications, not yet reasonably identifiable nor even predictable enough to allow the depiction of a future market. For this broad category of R&D, the relevant market was delimited by the key technology at its centre. The analysis (and remedy) thus aimed at assessing and restoring competition in the most genuine form of innovation market (as something different from a product market).[231]

The European Commission in *Ciba-Geigy/Sandoz* (EU 1996) touched upon the same R&D problems as the American counterpart. But the analysis aimed at future gene therapy products and was therefore concerned with the future gene therapy treatment of tumours (thereby putting the matter in category three). Heightened entry barriers and diminished incentives and abilities for

---

[230] In the identified four specific future product markets, where the research programmes of Ciba and Sandoz were completely superior, the complaint alleged elimination of actual, direct and substantial competition as well as potential and perceived potential competition, see complaint, §31.

[231] Kattan, *supra*, note 12, p. 27.

third parties to acquire licences and pursue research, alone, were not enough to establish dominance on this future market, particularly in view of the still uncertain patent situation.

In Europe, the analysis may yet encompass settings that are comparable to the US *Ciba-Geigy/Sandoz* decision. In *Pasteur Mérieux/Merck* (EU 1994) general aspects of R&D for unidentified 'future pipeline products' were assessed, *and found restricted.* Although the analysis was made under a potential competition heading, that competition would be for an innovation market and not a product market. But compared to the innovation market as outlined in both the US and EU guidelines, it has in fact more the character of the US Ciba-Geigy/Sandoz analysis, that is, a much more widely defined innovation market where end products are not identified. The analysis aimed, among other things, at detecting possible restrictions of future competition in the vaccine area, following the combination of exceptional R&D capabilities and powerful technology portfolios. Here both the dimension of less competition between the parties and the availability of technologies for third parties in this area were highlighted. The case is, furthermore, important as the transaction-specific efficiencies, of a purely dynamic nature, nevertheless allowed for an exemption of the transaction.

Although this situation represents the most extreme form of R&D competition analysis, it is certainly not the typical situation. As expressed in the US and EU guidelines, the innovation market approach was designed to treat product-oriented R&D, not general basic research. The further we move from a potential product market, the less predictable becomes the impact of a transaction on some particular output.[232] This does not mean that it is impossible to analyse consequences from transactions relatively distant from product markets. In the cases mentioned, the action did not aim at restoring competition in basic research. The objective was to ensure continuous competition and development in a certain area, in which a variety of as yet unidentified products were expected to result.

When safeguarding incentives and abilities for market participants to continue innovating in an area – and particularly when reviewing the merits and dangers of intellectual property combinations – the link to patent pool assessments is evident. In fact, Ciba-Geigy can be seen as a pool of upstream patents for the commercialization of gene therapy research. In Pasteur Mérieux/Merck the pooled IPRs were more product-oriented (particularly when relating to the different antigens needed to create new multivalent

---

[232] Kattan, Joseph, 'Antitrust Considerations in Innovation-Driven Markets', 21 *Canada–United States Law Journal* 115, 117 (1995).

vaccine variants).[233] In both cases the combined IPRs were not strict complementarities, that is, not in a blocking relationship, and were thus valuable to the owners without being pooled. Moreover, some technologies were probably competing. But efficiencies in R&D and superior products were enabled if the assets were joined together.

Patent pools in general, like mergers and JV, often display a number of pro-competitive and efficiency-enhancing features, such as the integration of complementary technologies, reduction of transaction costs and clearing of blocking positions, thus avoiding infringement litigation. For such arrangements, a rule of reason analysis is applied. However, both competition in current product markets and the incentives and abilities for the parties and third parties to engage in R&D in the area may be affected by the arrangements. This is similar to the other category four cases: the relevant market may not best be described by defining the resulting applications rather than the technology at the centre. Moreover, it is not necessarily the combination of competing patents that creates harm to innovation; combination of complementary patents could also create bottlenecks that diminish competition in innovation.

4.9 UNILATERAL CONDUCT

4.9.1 Multiple Markets Analysed

The question of market definition is crucial for many competition analyses, not only for analysing mergers and joint ventures. It is critical in abuse cases, where the existence of dominance or monopoly power is a central legal requisite. But, here too, there are recent examples where the analysis of the upstream markets for technology and innovation may be essential to investigate the competitive effect of conduct by a dominant party on a downstream market.

In 1998, the FTC took action against Intel, alleging that the company, on several separate occasions, had acted to monopolize the market for general-purpose microprocessors.[234]

233 This is not to deny that the upstream anti-competitive effects from the JV were more far-reaching than the mere pooling of IPRs. The likely lessening of competition for future pipeline products was the result of joining these more product-oriented current technologies, general vaccine technologies and the coordination of the R&D conducted by two parties with particular capabilities in vaccine R&D.

234 *Intel Corporation*, Docket no. 9288 (complaint 1998, consent order 1999).

The complaint defined this market ('line of commerce') in broad terms, to include current-generation microprocessors as well as 'future-generation microprocessors and technologies for current-generation and future-generation microprocessors'.[235] It also suggested that narrower markets could be contained within the market for general-purpose microprocessors.

According to the complaint, Intel's allegedly abusive conduct had the effect of entrenching Intel's monopoly power in the market, where the company accounted for approximately 80 per cent of the worldwide sales in the previous five years. More particularly, Intel had ceased to provide technical information and prototype products in advance at a pre-lease stage to three of its customers, Digital Equipment Corporation, Intergraph Corporation and Compaq Computers Corporation. These were computer manufacturers (original equipment manufacturers – OEMs) purchasing microprocessors from Intel. The withheld information and prototypes were essential for the firms, enabling them to develop and introduce new computer products incorporating the latest microprocessor technology as early and efficiently as possible.[236] Lacking access to such information and samples put these OEMs at a serious competitive disadvantage towards their competitors, and provided Intel with strong coercive means of persuasion. The FTC considered denial of advance product information virtually tantamount to a denial of actual parts.

Intel's action was a response to patent infringement litigation initiated by the firms and their refusals to grant Intel royalty-free patent licences to their IPRs in the field. Digital and Intergraph sought injunctive relief to prevent Intel from selling its flagship microprocessor products, while Compaq sought to prevent the sales of motherboards.[237]

The FTC regarded Intel's conduct as a way of preventing the companies from enforcing their patents. By coercing them into royalty-free licensing, Intel expropriated the innovation results. In fact, Digital and Compaq quickly surrendered and agreed to license their technology to Intel, while Intergraph resisted by obtaining a preliminary injunction against Intel, requiring the company to continue to supply Intergraph until the case was decided.[238]

Again according to the FTC, such conduct would reinforce Intel's domination and give Intel preferential access to a range of innovative technologies developed by other firms in the industry. To the extent that other firms wished to compete with Intel, they were put at a serious disadvantage. Moreover, coercion to license away patent rights would have a chilling effect on the patentees' incentives to innovate, affecting various ancillary markets. Lastly, the conduct would make it more difficult for OEMs to differentiate against each other, in order to gain a competitive technological edge. It also made it harder for a manufacturer actively to support an alternative microprocessor producer, since the licences to Intel would create a chan-

---

[235] Complaint, §4. Considering this very broad market definition, the case should also be considered in relation to section 4.8.1. on technology base competition.

[236] Analysis of Proposed Consent Order to Aid Public Comment.

[237] Intel Corporation's Pretrial Brief, February 25, 1999, p. 8; available at http://www.ftc.gov/alj/D9288/intelbrief.pdf (last visited 11 October 2004).

[238] See Analysis of Proposed Consent Order to Aid Public Comment; *Intergraph Corp. v. Intel Corp.*, 3 F.Supp.2d 1255 (N.D. Ala. 1998).

nel for technology flow between competing OEMs. Competing microprocessor manufacturers were thus also indirectly affected.[239]

It was thus considered that these three firms, which both manufactured computers based on Intel processors and developed their own technologies, would have less incentive to innovate in microprocessors and related technologies, and that Intel consequently would lose incentives to compete against such innovations.[240] A cementing of Intel's dominance through unjustified means was expected, tilting the playing field against new entrants and fringe competitors.[241]

The relevant information concerned ways to make Intel processors work in the manufactured computers, and did not involve anything that would help the firms in their own competing product development. The FTC therefore considered the conduct 'not reasonably necessary to serve any legitimate, procompetitive purpose'.[242]

The case was on the verge of being tried in court. Among other things, Intel pointed to the fact that Intergraph and Compaq were not current competitors in the microprocessor market (Intergraph had previously left the market). Moreover, it was argued that its conduct would not have any impact on R&D competition, in a market where innovation and competition were thriving. Not a single R&D project could be identified, neither at the three firms nor any other firm in the industry, which had been adversely affected, in light of the cross-licence agreements concluded with various firms.[243] Since Advanced Micro Devices, IBM, Motorola, Sun and Hewlett-Packard were all active in microprocessor R&D, Intel maintained that the innovation market safe harbour of the IP Guidelines was more than fulfilled. The FTC dismissed this argument since (a) cross-licence arrangements between microprocessor manufacturers implied that Intel could copy any innovation of the other competitors and (b) the arrangement did not immunize the firms from being cut off from essential trade secrets or physical products.[244]

The FTC claimed that Intel had an incentive to deny certain manufacturers the ability to differentiate their products. If these manufacturers were allowed single control over some important features, they would capture a larger share of the joint product: the microprocessor and the rest of the computer.[245] Intel maintained that, according to economic theory, it was, on the contrary, benefiting from innovations and improvements in complementary products, since it wanted to sell as many microprocessors as possible. Also, the sales of competing microprocessors were at an all-time high, and being sold by an increasing number of OEMs, which indicated that there was no correlation between the OEMs' innovation efforts and their propensity to supply competing microprocessors.[246]

---

239 Complaint Counsel's Pretrial Brief, February 25, 1999, pp. 40 *et seq*; available at http://www.ftc.gov/alj/D9288/990225ccpb.pdf (last visited 11 October 2004). See also Baer & Balto, *supra*, note 136, p. 86.

240 Complaint, §§13, 14, 39. Gilbert & Tom, *supra*, note 54, pp. 66f.

241 Analysis to Aid Public Comment.

242 Complaint, §§20, 30, 36.

243 Intel Corporation's Pretrial Brief, February 25, 1999, pp. 12–20, 26f; available at http://www.ftc.gov/alj/D9288/intelbrief.pdf (last visited 11 October 2004).

244 Gilbert & Tom, *supra*, note 350, p. 68.

245 Ibid.

246 Intel Corporation's Pretrial Brief, February 25, 1999, pp. 30 *et seq.*

> Moreover, according to Intel, cross-licences were an absolute necessity since it would be impossible to manufacture microprocessors without cross-licence arrangements netting out many royalty claims and providing 'value for value'. The alternative would be hundreds of individual licences, implying prohibitive costs at the already very low royalty rates. Intel's conduct was a legitimate response to the threat to microprocessor innovation posed by the minefield of patents and the risk of Intel being 'held up' by extortionate licensing demands from the OEMs.[247]
>
> The resulting settlement prevented Intel from denying customers access to such information and products as were routinely given to customers, unless these customers tried to obtain an injunction preventing Intel from selling its products. The FTC hoped that a sensible compromise had been struck between the pro-competitive cross-licensing arrangement and protection of Intel's legitimate IPRs, on the one hand, and the possibility for smaller firms to be rewarded for innovation on the other (these would still be able to sue for damages in the case of infringements).[248]

There is an interesting twist worth mentioning. As pointed out, Intergraph sought, and obtained, an injunction against Intel's conduct in a federal district court.[249] The Court of Appeals for the Federal Circuit did not share the view of the district court.[250] Intel did not have any monopoly power and did not acquire or maintain such market power in Intergraph's downstream market. Moreover, Intel had monopoly power in markets for microprocessors, but since Intergraph had left the microprocessor product market and had no intention of re-entering, the court concluded that the harms to Intergraph's business would not weaken competition or extend Intel's monopoly power. While acknowledging that Intergraph had patents on microprocessor technology, the court maintained, 'the patent grant is a legal right to exclude, not a commercial product in a competitive market'.[251] It was held that firms are competitors in the same market if their products are interchangeable enough to be able significantly to take business away from each other. According to a former FTC official, the difference between the FTC's consent order and the appeals court judgment is that the FTC also considered upstream markets. Although Intergraph did not have any intention of entering the market for microprocessors, it might be a source of competition, being active in a current technology market and an innovation market in which future microprocessor technology and ancillary technology were being developed.[252] Intel did not have

---

247 Ibid. pp. 41f.

248 Gilbert & Tom, *supra* note 350, p. 73.

249 *Intergraph Corp. v. Intel Corp.*, 3 F.Supp.2d 1255 (N.D.Ala.1998).

250 *Intergraph Corp. v. Intel Corp.*, 195 F.3d 1346 (Fed. Cir.1999).

251 Ibid. p. 1355.

252 Valentine, Debra A., 'Abuse of Dominance in Relation to Intellectual Property: U.S. Perspectives and the Intel Cases', Address before the Israel International Antitrust Conference, November 1999; available at www.ftc.org.

the right to leverage its market power in the existing product market so as to harm the ability and incentives for rivals in the microprocessor R&D.

The FTC action has been criticized, particularly on the ground that the authorities could not show that Intel's practice actually led the injured firms to cancel any R&D projects or in other ways reduce R&D spending. Nor had any other actual or potential competitor's R&D been adversely affected.[253] Thus it had not been shown that the industry suffered from any lessening in R&D competition.

The FTC brought the case under Section 5 Federal Trade Commission Act (15 U.S.C. §45),[254] recognizing that under this stipulation the FTC has power 'to arrest trade restraints in their incipiency without proof that they amount to an outright violation of . . . other provisions of the antitrust laws'.[255] Nevertheless, the case was prepared according to the standards of monopolization in §2 Sherman Act (15 U.S.C.§2),[256] acknowledged as the logical starting point of unfair conduct.[257] In this regard FTC argued that '[t]he anti-trust laws are as much violated by the prevention of competition as by its destruction'.[258]

---

253 See Lopatka, John E. & Page, William H., 'Monopolization, Innovation, and Consumer Welfare', 69 *George Washington Law Review* 367, 415 *et seq.* (2001); Kattan, Joseph & Arp, D. Jarret, 'Trends in Intellectual Property Antitrust Enforcement', 566 *Practising Law Institute – Patents, Copyrights, Trademarks, and Literary Property Course Handbook Series* 401, 432f. (1999). It should be noted that the latter authors represented Intel in the particular case. See also Intel Corporation's Pretrial Brief, February 25, 1999, pp. 12–20, 26; available at http://www.ftc.gov/alj/D9288/intelbrief.pdf (last visited 11 October 2004).

254 Sec. 45: Unfair methods of competition unlawful; prevention by Commission *(a) Declaration of unlawfulness; power to prohibit unfair practices; inapplicability to foreign trade; (1) Unfair methods of competition in or affecting commerce, and unfair or deceptive acts or practices in or affecting commerce, are hereby declared unlawful.*

255 Complaint Counsel's Pretrial Brief, p. 4 with reference, e.g., to *FTC v. Brown Shoe Co., Inc.*, 384 U.S. 316, 322 (1966).

256 Sec. 2: Monopolizing trade a felony; penalty: *Every person who shall monopolize, or attempt to monopolize, or combine or conspire with any other person or persons, to monopolize any part of the trade or commerce among the several States, or with foreign nations, shall be deemed guilty of a felony, and, on conviction thereof, shall be punished by fine not exceeding $10,000,000 if a corporation, or, if any other person, $350,000, or by imprisonment not exceeding three years, or by both said punishments, in the discretion of the court.*

257 The FTC has the power to enforce the Clayton Act directly and may, under Section 5 of the FTC Act, also condemn conduct that offends the Sherman Act or the 'spirit' of the Sherman and Clayton Acts. See Areeda, Philip & Kaplow, Louis, *Antitrust Analysis: Problems, Texts, Cases*, 5th edn, Aspen Law & Business, New York, 1997, pp. 68f. Violations of §2 Sherman Act are also violations of Section 5 FTC Act, but the scope of the latter is wider.

258 Complaint Counsel's Pretrial Brief, p. 4 with reference to *Lorain Journal Co. v. United States,* 342 U.S. 143, 154 n.7 (1951).

4.9.2 Prevention and Restriction of Innovation

Determining whether unilateral conduct prevents or destroys innovation competition highlights a number of challenging issues. In particular it requires a dominant actor's strategies for outcompeting its competitors being distinguished from conduct that rather tends to exclude competition. Antitrust law enforcement would have undesired consequences if major actors were penalized merely for successful innovation and superior efficiency. For legal instruments to benefit consumers in the long run, they must get the balance right between the competition that is created by limiting dominant firms' behaviour and the discouragement of competition that such a limitation will also produce. For the purpose of highlighting innovation issues and the balance between them, this section will cover a dominant firm's duty not to diminish incentives and abilities for innovation in the light of the Microsoft cases.

The prevention and restriction of innovation competition has been at centre stage in the Microsoft saga.[259] In *Microsoft III* (D.C. Cir. 2001),[260] it was

---

[259] In 1994 the DOJ filed suit against Microsoft based on, among other things, unlawful maintenance of a monopoly in the operating system market, through anti-competitive terms in licensing and software developer agreements. A consent agreement was reached, *United States v. Microsoft Corp.*, 56 F.3d 1448 (D.C. Cir. 1995) ('Microsoft I'). Later, the DOJ filed action against Microsoft for violating the decree provisions. Awaiting the appeal judgement from a grant of preliminary injunction, *United States v. Microsoft Corp.*, 147 F.3d 935 (D.C. Cir. 1998) ('Microsoft II'), the DOJ and a number of State plaintiffs filed new complaints against Microsoft, primarily for its strategies against Netscape Navigator. In April 2000, the US District Court for the District of Columbia found Microsoft liable under §1 for tying of Windows and Internet Explorer, and §2 for violation of monopoly maintenance in the market for Intel-compatible PC operating systems and attempted monopolization in the market for internet browsers, but found there not sufficient evidence of a §1 exclusive dealing violation: *United States v. Microsoft Corp.*, 87 F. Supp. 2d 30 (D.D.C. 2000) ('Conclusions of Law'). In June 2000, the Court approved the proposed remedies, imposing an interim restriction on Microsoft's commercial behaviour, and requiring Microsoft to submit a plan for the way the company was to be broken up into one operating systems business and one applications business. *United States v. Microsoft Corp.*, 97 F. Supp. 2d 59 (D.D.C. 2000) ('Final Judgment'). After the Court of Appeals judgement in Microsoft III, in June 2001 (summarized below), the United States and Microsoft agreed a settlement which was adopted by the district court in November 2002, *United States v. Microsoft*, Civil Action No. 98-1232 (CKK); *New York et. al. v. Microsoft*, CA No. 98-1233 (CKK). Two industry groups (*CCIA and SIIA v. United States & Microsoft*, No. 03-5030) and one State, Massachusetts, (*Commonwealth of Massachusetts v. Microsoft* No. 02-7155) appealed against the settled remedies. In June 2004 the Court of Appeals affirmed the district court's decision to approve the settlement: *Commonwealth of Massachusetts v. Microsoft Corp.*, No. 02-7155 and No. 03-5030, (D.C. Cir. June 30, 2004).

[260] *United States v. Microsoft*, 253 F.3d 34 (D.C. Cir. 2001).

considered whether Microsoft monopolized the market for Intel-compatible PC operating systems in violation of §2 of the Sherman Act.

Microsoft enjoyed a very strong position in this market, with a market share exceeding 95 per cent. This near-monopoly was associated with an 'applications barrier to entry' which created a catch-22 for any potential contestant. Put simply, in order to attract customers in the market for operating systems, there would have to be an array of software applications compatible with the operating system. At the same time, to encourage software developers to develop compatible applications, the operating system would have to have many users.

The basis for the government's allegation of abusive conduct was that Microsoft, anticipating that this entry barrier could otherwise be lost in the future, sought to eliminate the threat of 'middleware' applications, primarily Netscape's Internet browser and Sun's Java technologies. These had the potential of getting in between the operating system and software application, taking over many of the functions of current operating systems. If middleware was compatible with multiple operating systems and software developers wrote programs based on middleware rather than operating systems, Microsoft's position could be considerably weakened.

Through both technological and transactional arrangements, Microsoft sought to prevent this from happening. This was achieved primarily by the following means.

1. Various restrictions in the licence agreements with computer manufacturers (OEMs) to reduce usage of Netscape. The OEMs were prohibited from removing desktop icons, folders and Start menu entries and thus could not remove Microsoft's Internet Explorer (IE). They were also prevented from modifying the initial boot sequence, which prevented Internet Access Providers (who commonly preferred Netscape in their Internet access software) from using this sequence to promote their services. Lastly, the OEMs could not alter the desktop, adding icons or folders and using 'Active Desktop' to feature third-party brands.

Microsoft's primary business justification for these licence restrictions was that it simply exercised its rights as holder of valid copyrights, denying that the exercise of lawfully acquired IPRs can give rise to antitrust liability. According to the Court this argument 'borders upon the frivolous'. 'That is no more correct than the proposition that use of one's personal property, such as a baseball bat, cannot give rise to tort liability.'[261] Microsoft was, however, justified when restricting manufacturers from automatically replacing the Windows desktop in such a way that this original desktop was never even seen. The Court agreed that such a replacement was a drastic alteration of Microsoft's copyrighted work that outweighed the marginal anticompetitive effect incurred by preventing the alteration. But the rest of the licence restrictions were considered violations of §2 Sherman Act.

2. By excluding IE from the 'Add/Remove Programs' utility in Windows and by placing Web browsing code in the same file as code for operating system functions, IE was integrated with Windows, thereby deterring the use of other Internet browsers.

Microsoft denied, as a matter of fact, that code had been commingled. Although testimonies were contradictory on the issue, the Court stated that, in light of the evidence supporting the District Court's finding that Microsoft commingled code, that finding could not be held 'clearly erroneous'. Since such commingling deterred

261 *Microsoft III* (D.C. Cir. 2001), 253 F.3d 34, 63.

manufacturers from installing rival browsers, it had an anti-competitive effect. Moreover, although Microsoft made general claims regarding the benefits from the technical integration of browser and operating systems, they had not proffered any justification for commingling and thus failed to meet the burden of proof that the conduct served a purpose other than protecting its monopoly. Such proof would have been necessary to rebut the prima facie finding of an anti-competitive effect.

It should be underlined that the District Court's finding of a per se illegal tying under §1 Sherman Act was remanded. The Court of Appeals rejected the notion of a per se prohibition of the contractual and technological bundling of IE to Windows. The per se tying doctrine involves a test as to whether the practice indeed involves two separate products being tied together, basically asking whether there is a separate demand for the two products.[262] This only involves proxies for, but not any direct analysis of, efficiencies that might result from the combination. The Court considered this a bad proxy for the net efficiencies arising from recently integrated products. Credit was given to Microsoft's argument that the per se test would 'chill innovation to the detriment of consumers by preventing firms from integrating into their products new functionality previously provided by standalone products'.[263] Apart from Microsoft's general claim of innovative integration, there were some indications that efficiencies would possibly result (*inter alia,* the fact that other operating systems were bundled with browsers). Moreover, the Supreme Court had not previously encountered, and thus not factored into the per se doctrine, the efficiencies potentially created by tying in innovative software markets. Since the case involved integration of a software platform with software of a complementary nature, a claim that the tie would bring consumer benefits applied with 'distinct force'.[264] Accordingly, such a tying allegation should be analysed under the rule of reason.[265]

The fact that Windows 98 was designed to override the user's choice of anything other than IE as the default browser (only when accessing the Internet through certain means and features in Windows) also contributed to exclude rival browsers. In this respect Microsoft referred to technical reasons such as that Navigator would not enable the use of all the purposes of Window's features. Since the plaintiff had not rebutted this proffered justification and had not demonstrated that the anti-competitive effect outweighed it, Microsoft was not held liable on this issue.

3. Regarding Java, Microsoft had created its own software, a so called Java Virtual Machine (JVM), which translates code into instructions to the operating system, which allowed Java applications to run faster on Windows than did Sun Microsystem's JVM for Windows. The Court of Appeals maintained that a monop-

---

262 According to the Court there are four elements to a per se tying violation: (1) The tying and the tied goods are two separate products; (2) the defendant has monopoly power in the tying product market; (3) the defendant affords consumers no choice but to purchase the tied product from it; and (4) the tying forecloses a substantial volume of commerce. See Microsoft 2001, p. 85 with reference to *Eastman Kodak Co. v. Image Tech. Servs., Inc.,* 504 U.S. 451, 461f. (1992).

263 *Microsoft III* (D.C. Cir. 2001), 253 F.3d 34, 89.

264 253 F.3d 34, 95.

265 The other conducts by Microsoft found to violate §2 included exclusive contracts with Internet Access Providers as well as exclusivities in dealings with Internet Software Vendors and with Apple.

olist does not violate the antitrust laws merely by developing a product that is incompatible with its rivals'. The anti-competitive effects must outweigh any pro-competitive justification. Since Microsoft's JVM was not merely incompatible, but allowed applications to run faster, it did not in itself have any anti-competitive effect. The court overruled the District Court in this part. But it nevertheless condemned Microsoft for entering into agreements with Internet Software Vendors with mechanisms that entailed exclusive use of Microsoft's JVM, for having deceived developers into believing that applications written with the help of software provided by Microsoft would be able to run on different platforms when they would in fact run only on Windows, and for coercing Intel to stop assisting Sun in improving its Java technologies.

Microsoft's actions could be described as the entrenchment of current market dominance, by preventing an ancillary, potentially overlapping, market from developing. It is not the typical leverage situation where a monopolist would like to extend its domain to include a second market and make more profits there. Rather it is the protection of the primary market that is at stake. Interestingly, Microsoft argued that the court could not exclude Navigator and Java from the relevant market when considering Microsoft's strength in operating systems, and still base an action on Microsoft's attempts to suppress the competitive threats that these firms gave rise to. According to the court, the middleware threat was 'nascent'. In order to be included in the relevant market, products must be substitutes acting as constraints, currently or 'in the reasonably foreseeable future'.[266] But §2 of the Sherman Act may be applied to actions taken against threats that are not that well developed. After the Court of Appeals judgment, the parties agreed to a settlement, via a consent decree which was approved by the District Court.[267]

Tetra/Sidel (CFI 2002) and *Microsoft III* (D.C. Cir. 2001) are similar in that a position of world dominance is allegedly threatened by technological developments in a neighbouring market. The cases differ, *inter alia*, in the ability of Microsoft to take effective action against this technological threat (of middleware marginalizing a current dominance in the operating system (OS) market). Microsoft was able to use its market power to determine the identity of the leading middleware – to decide the winner. The dominant company was able to prevent the innovative path in this market, and secure its dominance in the 'threatened market'. In Tetra Sidel, the CFI rejected the claim that the merged entity would be able to lever Tetra's dominance into dominance in PET. It could not effectively hinder the technological development in the PET packaging market. The court in Tetra/Sidel in any event went the extra step in investigating whether a smaller lessening of potential competition from the

266 *Microsoft III* (D.C. Cir. 2001), 253 F.3d 34, 54.
267 See note 259 above.

neighbouring market would diminish innovation incentives in the 'threatened market' and concluded that such effects must be substantiated, taking the full economic context into account.

The European Commission's *Microsoft* decision (EU 2004)[268] does not relate to the same conduct as the American case. This decision holds Microsoft liable for a leveraging strategy that comprises two separate abuses. First, by refusing to supply essential interface information for interoperability with Microsoft's client PC operating system products to competitors in the market for group server operating systems, it was able to extend its dominance on the latter market to the former. Secondly, by tying Windows Media Player (WMP) to the Windows operating systems, Microsoft foreclosed competitors and harmed competition in the market for streaming media players.

The case originated from a complaint to the Commission, filed by Sun Microsystems who had requested information that was required in order to make Sun's Solaris fully compatible with Windows work group networks. The request encompassed specifications for the protocols used by Windows work group servers in order to provide services (limited to file, print, and group and user administration) for Windows work group networks.[269] The failure to meet Sun's request as regards interface information for core group server tasks, essential to compete in the group server market, constituted, according to the Commission, an abuse of dominance. This despite the fact that the requested information involved both client-to-server and server-to-server interoperability, thus also comprising features of Windows server products. The Commission maintained that all interconnections and interactions were related to the client PC and that Microsoft's abuse derived from their dominance on the client PC operating system market (enjoying a market share over 90 per cent).[270] Moreover, while the withheld information may have been copyrighted, the case did not involve a refusal to license source code, but specifications describing what must be achieved (by Sun) to achieve interoperability.

Apart from Sun, other actors in the group server market confirmed that they received too little interoperability information and that thereby they were put at a strong competitive disadvantage vis-à-vis Microsoft. Prior to the development of Windows 2000, such information was more viably available, *inter alia,* via licence arrangements with AT&T. According to the Commission, by the discontinuing of the supply of essential information, competitors were put at such a disadvantage that there was a risk of elimination of competition in the group server operating system market (defined to be servers for file, print, and group & user administration services).[271] To prove this point the Commission pointed to Microsoft's market shares rapidly rising from 20–25 per cent to at least 60 per cent between 1996 and

---

268 Case COMP/C-3/37.792 – *Microsoft* (2004).

269 Computers are often operated in conjunction with other computers and PC users use both the computing capability of their 'client PC' and of more powerful, multi-user 'servers', which they access indirectly through their client PC. Decision §47.

270 §§567, 434.

271 §589.

2002, whereas shares of the three main competitors had declined. Taken together with market information suggesting that new features (particularly network administration) in Microsoft's newer versions were expected to result in even more migration from alternative products, the Commission concluded there was a risk of competition being eliminated.

The Commission did not claim that competition *was* eliminated or that it was impossible to achieve *some* interoperability without the withheld information, but that Microsoft's disclosure was insufficient to enable competitors to stay in the market.[272] Moreover, *immediate* elimination was not considered a requirement, particularly in a market where network effects tend to make elimination of competition irreversible.[273]

Microsoft contested the link between refusal to supply and progressive elimination of competition. The Commission, however, found Microsoft's arguments (such as attributing rivals' falling market shares to inferior products) contradictory and failing to rebut the Commission's analysis. Moreover, despite Microsoft's arguments to the contrary, the Commission found no substitutes (such as open industry standards, reverse-engineering and existing licensing programme) for Microsoft's interoperability information.

Since the lack of interoperability would lock consumers into one solution and prevent innovative features being brought to market and new products developed, the refusal was considered to limit technological development to the detriment of consumers, and was thus prohibited under Article 82(b). In view of Microsoft's control over the PC operating system market, the company was able to impose the Windows domain as a de facto standard. Although Microsoft contended that, if it had to disclose its interface specifications, beneficial interspecification competition would be hindered, the Commission found ample scope for innovation beyond the specifications, through variation and feature enhancement in the implementations.[274]

Rejecting Microsoft's claim that evidence of harm to consumers was lacking, the Commission pointed at case law suggesting that an abuse does not have to prejudice consumers directly, but that by impairing the effective competitive structure consumers may be indirectly harmed.[275] The Commission also cited official Microsoft sources stating that the disclosures made under the US settlement would bring new ways to achieve interoperability between licensees' servers and Windows desktops and that this would create more consumer choice in the marketplace. Moreover, the refusal had already enabled Microsoft to achieve a dominant position, impairing the effective structure of competition.[276]

Microsoft also provided justifications for its refusal, the foremost of which was that its incentives to innovate would be diminished if forced to disclose information protected by intellectual property rights: the outcome of 'billions of dollars of R&D investments in software features, functions and technologies'.[277] The Commission

272 §589, note 712.

273 §622.

274 §§697f.

275 §704, Reference to Case 85/76, *Hoffmann-La Roche & Co. AG v Commission*, ECR 461 (1979), §125.

276 §§702–8.

277 §709.

did not deny that some of the requested information might be protected by intellectual property rights, but argued that the central function of such rights is to protect moral rights and ensure reward for creative effort, with the essential objective being that creativity should be stimulated for the general public good. Under exceptional circumstances a refusal to license may have harmful effects on innovation and on consumers.[278] Since Microsoft's refusal to supply concerned an indispensable input, and the refusal risked eliminating competition and would have a negative impact on technical development, the Commission maintained that exceptional circumstances were at hand. A refusal could not be justified merely by reference to IPR protection. Therefore the Commission could go on to assess whether Microsoft's incentives to innovate arguments outweighed the exceptional circumstances.[279]

It is thus clear that the Commission allowed the circumstances of the case to qualify as 'exceptional' so that it could break the fundamental right of an intellectual property owner to exclude others, particularly rivals, from using its assets. Thus the supply (or licence) of an indispensable input cannot automatically be refused, if it risks eliminating competition in the relevant market and has a negative impact on technical development to the prejudice of consumers. But it is clear that a refusal might still be justified, and the Commission therefore went on to consider whether Microsoft's innovation incentives would be diminished in a way that overweighed the found anti-competitive effect. In essence, finding such a justification would invalidate the last criterion in the IPR-breaking test – the consumer impact – since technological development and consumer welfare would then be hurt rather than promoted by the granting of a compulsory licence.

When doing this latter weighing the Commission investigated a number of arguments made by Microsoft, on how its incentives would be reduced if forced to meet the Commission's standards. First, Microsoft contended that features in the Window's operating systems family would be easier to 'clone'. Even if the information did not include source code, the specifications were, according to Microsoft, blueprints telling competitors how to replicate the product's functionality. The Commission, however, rejected the ease of such replication.[280] Since Microsoft would have control over the specifications, competitors would still be disadvantaged as regards the quality of implementation, compared to Microsoft, and forced to provide additional value beyond interoperability in order to compete. The cloning argument therefore failed.[281]

As regards incentives to innovate with respect to the specifications, the Commission emphasized that the question is about incentives to innovate in the products as a whole, not in interface design. Moreover, the situation should be

278 §711.
279 §712.
280 §720.
281 §§721f.

compared to doing nothing, a situation in which Microsoft could succeed in eliminating competition. That would have serious negative effects on the incentives to innovate, even for Microsoft, since competitors' innovative steps spur innovation.

The Commission rejected Microsoft's argument that the company would not, had it anticipated a Commission decision along these lines, have tried years ago to offer Windows' client software that worked as well as possible with Windows' server software. The simple reason being that these products need to interoperate, and greater availability of complementary interoperable work group server operating systems means greater value of (willingness to pay for) Microsoft's client PC operating systems. At the oral hearing a Microsoft official had also acknowledged he had not noticed any negative impact on the incentives to innovate, as a result of the Communications Protocols Licensing Program that was instituted in the aftermath of the US judgment.

The Commission also pointed at industry practice being interoperability-oriented, meaning that non-dominant market actors generally provide information in order for complementary products to be compatible, since this enhances the value of the products.[282] It was pointed out that Microsoft also did this at the time it was not dominant on the group server operating system market – even disclosing source code.[283] Moreover, it was shown that Microsoft would have incentives to leverage its market power from client PC operating systems into the group server operating systems market, both to increase profits in the latter market and to reinforce entry barriers to the former.

The remedy decided on was thus that Microsoft should supply, on reasonable and non-discriminatory terms, what had been refused, that is, complete and accurate specifications for the protocols used by Windows work group servers for the file, print and administration services to work group networks. The specifications must not be reproduced, adapted, arranged or altered by the receivers but only used to write their specification-compliant interfaces.

It is apparent that the European Commission wants to take on the task of monitoring this industry, and the dominant Microsoft in particular, and to do so develops existing case law on the duty to deal and intellectual property rights.[284] Moreover, the decision takes on the explicit evaluation of innovation incentives and designs remedies for its protection, where 'the possible negative impact . . . on Microsoft's incentives to innovate is outweighed by its positive impact on the level of innovation of the whole industry (including Microsoft)'.[285]

Regarding the second abuse, the tying of Windows Media Player (WMP) with Windows the Commission started off by the requirements for finding a

---

[282] §§732f.

[283] §734.

[284] See particularly Joined Cases 6 and 7-73, *Commercial Solvents and Others v. Commission,* ECR 223 (1974), Case 311/84; *Télémarketing v. CLT and IPB,* ECR 3261 (1985); Joined Cases C-241/91 P and C-242/91 P, *RTE & ITP v. Commission* (Magill); Case C-7/97, *Oscar Bronner GmbH & Co. KG v Mediaprint,* ECR I-7791 (1998).

[285] §783. See also §712.

tying abuse under Article 82: (i) the tying and tied goods are products; (ii) the undertaking concerned is dominant in the tying product market; (iii) the undertaking concerned does not give customers a choice to obtain the tying product without the tied product; and (iv) tying forecloses competition.[286] Besides showing that Microsoft's conduct fulfilled these elements, the Commission also claimed that the asserted justifications for the tie did not prevail over the anti-competitive effects.[287] Thus, whereas the first part of the decision corresponds well to the American doctrine of a per se prohibition, the latter engages in rule of reason arguments.

Regarding the first prerequisite, the separate products, the Commission pointed to the existence of a separate consumer demand for media players, simply because the market indeed provided such.[288] Commenting on the US Court of Appeals judgment and the notion of the consumer demand test being inappropriate for newly integrated products, the Commission pointed to a direct consumer demand for alternative streaming media players four years after the tying commenced.[289] Nor could Microsoft defend its practice by showing that it had already bundled media players in 1992 or that several other software vendors also bundled operating systems and media players. The Commission concluded that the anti-competitive tying did not start until 1999, when Microsoft developed a competitive player capable of media streaming that matched the rival products on the (separate) market. The argument that other vendors bundled was dismissed (a) since their media players were also sold separately, (b) since they did not bundle their own media players but third party players and (c) since none of these bundled players were made unremoveable.

As to the third prerequisite for a tying offence – consumers' lack of choice – this primarily hit the computer manufacturers (OEMs), normally the ones that license Windows, and to a lesser extent users that buy Windows in a retail store. Yet, in both ways, consumers would end up having WMP installed. Microsoft emphasized that it did not charge anything for the media player and that the consumer could very well use another player if they so wished – and that many in fact did. The Commission noted that there were no technical means to un-install WMP, which, according to Microsoft, was due to the fact that other parts of the operating system and third-party products relying on WMP then would not function properly. The Commission dismissed the argument that the consumers did not pay for WMP, stating that Microsoft 'conflates the coercion and foreclosure of competition elements of tying'.[290] Consumers need not be forced to use the product, the relevant question is rather whether competition is foreclosed 'because customers and suppliers of complementary software and content are *likely to use* the bundled product at the expense of non-bundled products'.[291]

---

286 §794.

287 §795.

288 These included RealNetworks' RealPlayer, Apple's QuickTime and Microsoft's own versions of WMP for Apple's Mac and for Sun's Solaris client operating systems, §804.

289 §808.

290 §831.

291 §832.

Such a treatment of the third prerequisite is naturally linked to the last, foreclosure of competition. Here the Commission relied on the judgment of the ECJ in *Hoffman-La Roche*,[292] stating that a tie by a dominant undertaking is abusive since it deprives the consumer of the possibility to choose freely his source of supply and denies other producers access to the market. More recent case law from the CFI also confirmed that the foreclosure must not be insignificant, but did not have to be complete,[293] and that a concrete foreclosing effect did not have to be shown as long as the conduct was liable to have such effect.[294]

Microsoft, on the other hand, argued that the Commission must do more than show that the company distributes Windows only together with WMP. Considering that other media players were also given away, and that there were different ways to reach the customers, and given the pro-competitive effects of this tie, Microsoft saw no negative effect on competition.

Giving some merit to these arguments, the Commission considered there were good reasons, despite earlier case law from the Commission and the Courts to the contrary, *not* to assume that the tie was liable to foreclose competition without further analysis. Yet, after going through these arguments, the Commission found that the tying gave Microsoft an unmatched ubiquity on client PCs worldwide, which could not be offset by competitors entering installation agreements with OEMs, by using downloading as a distribution channel or any other means of distribution. Even if home users may put value on having *a* media player pre-installed, computer manufacturers should provide the bundling of hardware and software demanded by consumers, not decided by Microsoft. Moreover, since WMP was going to be the platform of choice for complementary content providers and developers of applications software, competition in the media player market was likely to be foreclosed and expected to result in spillover effects into other markets such as media encoding and client PC operating systems were.

Microsoft also put forward justifications: efficiencies of distribution and of the integration as such. The Commission rejected both these justifications.

Alleged transaction cost savings for consumers (with an integrated media player integrated there is no need to set default options), was dismissed since it does not take into account the role of the OEMs. Rather, the Commission's intention was to allow these to make a variety of packages corresponding to consumer demand. As for possibly reduced transaction costs from one distribution system (selecting, purchasing and installing only one product rather than two), the Commission pointed out the insignificant distribution costs in software licensing, and concluded that such savings could not possibly outweigh the distortion of competition. The argument that Microsoft must be able, like other operating system vendors, to provide a media player was dismissed on two grounds. First, Microsoft could instruct the manufacturers to pre-install *a* media player of their choice. Secondly, the impact on competition is vastly different since only Microsoft will foreclose the market with its tying practise. Therefore the competitors' conduct may be legal whereas Microsoft's is abusive.

Microsoft also claimed efficiencies from integrating the operating system and the

292 Case 85/76, *Hoffmann-La Roche & Co. AG v Commission*, ECR 461 (1979).
293 Case T-65/98, *Van den Bergh Foods v. Commission* (2003).
294 Case T-219/99, *British Airways* (2003).

> media player code. In particular, integration would facilitate for software developers since the operating system making will make the media player's application programming interface (API) available, and developers building applications for Windows do not have to 'reinvent the wheel' every time they wish to implement a functionality. This amounts to claiming that the WMP and Windows should be considered as one product. The Commission found these efficiencies unsubstantiated. Moreover, Microsoft had not supplied any evidence that the tie is indispensable in order to create such benefits to software developers, since the media players can exhibit APIs themselves.
>
> The Commission therefore decided that Microsoft should unbundle, and thus offer, both to OEMs and to end users, a version of Windows for client PCs that does not include WMP.

Interestingly, the current DOJ administration repudiates the per se tying claim made by the government in *Microsoft III*. Assistant Attorney General Hewitt Pate moreover notes that the DOJ did not allege, in the alternative, a 'rule of reason' case with regard to the product design. That would have required, *inter alia*, 'evidence of harm to consumers, which is harder reliably to develop than information about effects on competitors'.[295] He also points to the 'unintended consequences' potentially resulting from the European remedy in terms of chilling innovation and competition by dominant companies.[296]

4.9.3 Further Duties versus Competitors

Regarding the duties for Microsoft to provide interface information, it should be noted that the settlement between the DOJ and Microsoft in 2002 requires Microsoft to hold protocols for an array of server operating system products available to third parties, in order to ensure interoperation and communication.[297] While there thus is less practical divergence between the American and European handling of Microsoft in this regard, the question is whether a similar case, based solely on a refusal to supply interface information, would

295 Pate, Hewitt R., *Antitrust in a Transatlantic Context – From the Cicada's Perspective*, Address at 'Antitrust in a Transatlantic Context' Conference, Brussels, Belgium, June 7, 2004; available at http://www.usdoj.gov/atr/public/speeches/203973.pdf (last visited 3 March 2005).

296 Assistant Attorney General for Antitrust, R. Hewitt Pate, Issues statement on the EC's decision in its Microsoft Investigation, Press release March 24, 2004, available at http://www.usdoj.gov/atr/public/press_releases/2004/202976.pdf (last visited 3 March 2005).

297 An important difference pointed out by the European Commission is that Microsoft's licensing program, which is based on these settlement obligations, is limited to client-to-server communication and does not cover server-to-server protocols that are functionally related to the client PC. (§§276 *et seq.*)

be tenable under the US system.[298] Obligations to deal were an important part of the *Trinko* case, recently decided by the US Supreme Court.[299]

This case originated in a consent decree in 2000 between the Federal Communications Commission (FCC) and Verizon, following the latter's non-compliance with the 1996 Telecommunications Act. The purpose of the 1996 Act was to install competition in the local telephone loop by ending the monopolies (exclusive franchises) held by incumbent Local Exchange Carriers (LECs), by requiring the LECs to share their networks with competitors. Competitive LECs complained that Verizon – former exclusive franchisor – was violating its obligations under the 1996 Act and subsequently specified access mechanisms, to certain support systems. The public investigations ended with financial penalties and performance remedies imposed on Verizon.

Trinko, a customer of Verizon's competitor AT&T, then filed a class action alleging that Verizon's behaviour was part of an anti-competitive scheme to discourage customers from becoming or remaining competing LECs in violation of §2 of the Sherman Act. After the District Court dismissed the complaint and the Second Circuit reinstated the antitrust claim, the Supreme Court granted *certiorari*.

The DOJ and the FTC jointly filed amicus briefs in support of Verizon, arguing that the Second Circuit's decision would expand antitrust liability for failure to assist competitors when, relying on the essential facilities doctrine, it established a duty for monopolists to provide reasonable access to its facilities without which one cannot compete, regardless of whether the monopolist could earn more by selling such services at a monopoly price.[300] A firm is 'under no obligation to sacrifice its own profits for the public weal'. Rather 'the harm to competition must be disproportionate to consumer benefits (in terms of providing a superior product, for example) and to the economic benefits to the defendant (aside from benefits that accrue from diminished competition)'.[301] The Agencies thus argued that the essential facility doctrine cannot be used as an independent basis for §2 liability, since some exclusionary or predatory conduct is required.[302] A duty to assist a competitor

298 Pate, *supra*, note 295.

299 *Verizon Communications, Inc. v. Law Offices of Curtis Trinko, LLP*, 540 U.S. 398 (2004).

300 Brief for the United States and Federal Trade Commission as Amici Curiae, *Verizon Communications, Inc. v. Law Offices of Curtis V. Trinko*, No. 02-682 (May 23, 2003), pp. 13, 20 *et seq*; available at http://www.usdoj.gov/atr/cases/f201000/201048.pdf (last visited 11 October 2004); Pate, R. Hewitt, 'The Common Law Approach and Improving Standards for Analysing Single Firm Conduct', in Hawk, Barry E. (ed.), *International Antitrust Law & Policy*, 30 Fordham Corporate Law Institute 2003, New York, 2004, p. 206.

301 Brief for the United States and Federal Trade Commission as Amici Curiae, *Verizon Communications, Inc. v. Law Offices of Curtis V. Trinko*, No. 02-682 (May 23, 2003), p. 14; available at http://www.usdoj.gov/atr/cases/f201000/201048.pdf (last visited 11 October 2004).

302 The essential facility doctrine as applied by some appellate courts has required a monopolist to share a facility if otherwise it can 'extend monopoly power from one stage of production to another' and the following prerequisites are fulfilled:

would then not arise '*unless* it would make no economic sense for the defendant but for its tendency to eliminate or lessen competition'.[303] If a refusal involves a sacrifice of short-run profits or business advantage in order to recoup in the long run, that criterion could be fulfilled.

The Supreme Court had an opportunity to decide the future of the much-debated essential facility doctrine. The Court in this respect found 'no need either to recognize or repudiate' the doctrine, since, in light of the rights and duties under the 1996 Act and the powers of the monitoring agencies, one of the indispensable requirements – the unavailability of access to the essential facility – was not at hand.[304]

The Court's subsequent handling of the case may have important repercussions for future cases of an essential facility character. It emphasized that the mere possession of monopoly power and the charging of monopoly prices is 'an important element of the free-market system' and thus not unlawful. The opportunity to charge such prices attracts 'business acumen' and induces risk taking that produces innovation and economic growth. 'To safeguard the incentive to innovate, the possession of monopoly power will not be found unlawful unless it is accompanied by an element of anti-competitive *conduct*.'[305] To protect market actors' incentives to invest and bearing in mind that enforced sharing requires the antitrust courts to act as central planners (determining price, quantity and other business terms), the Court affirmed monopolists' general right to decide with whom to deal. While recognizing that this right is not absolute, the Court said it would be cautious in recognizing exceptions. *Aspen Skiing,* on which Trinko had relied heavily, the Court asserted to be 'at or near the outer boundary of §2 liability'.[306] The Court underlined that in *Aspen*, in which the Supreme Court found a party's refusal to cooperate a violation of §2, the party terminated a voluntary ('and thus presumably profitable') course of dealing, showing a willingness to forsake short-term profits for an anti-competitive end. Since Verizon had not engaged in any voluntary course of dealing with its competitors, there was no prior conduct to shed light upon the motivation for refusal

(1) control of the essential facility by a monopolist; (2) a competitor's inability practically or reasonably to duplicate the essential facility; (3) the denial of the use of the facility to a competitor; and (4) the feasibility of providing the facility. Brief for the United States and Federal Trade Commission as Amici Curiae, *Verizon Communications, Inc. v. Law Offices of Curtis V. Trinko*, No. 02-682 (May 23, 2003), pp. 20f. Reference was made to *MCI Communications Corp. v. AT&T*, 708 F.2d 1081, 1132-1133 (7th Cir.), cert. denied, 464 U.S. 891 (1983).

303 Brief for the United States and Federal Trade Commission as Amici Curiae, *Verizon Communications, Inc. v. Law Offices of Curtis V. Trinko*, No. 02-682 (May 23, 2003), p. 15.

304 124 S.Ct. 872, 880f. Moreover, the Court found that just as the 1996 Act explicitly applied without prejudice to existing antitrust laws, 'it [did] not create new claims that go beyond existing antitrust standards'.

305 124 S.Ct. 872, 879.

306 124 S.Ct. 872, 879f. *Aspen Skiing Co. v. Aspen High-lands Skiing Corp.*, 472 U.S. 585 (1985). The case involved the Aspen ski area, consisting of four mountain areas, of which the defendant owned three and the plaintiff the fourth. The parties had previously cooperated in selling an all-area ski ticket. After the defendant cancelled the cooperation, the plaintiff desperately tried to recreate the all-area ticket, even offering to buy the defendant's tickets at retail price.

to deal. Moreover, in *Aspen*, the defendant refused to supply the competitor even at the resale price it offered to its other customers. Here, the withheld services are not available to the public, but 'exist only deep within the bowels of Verizon', brought out only on compulsion by the 1996 Act – to its competitors and not to its consumers – at considerable cost.[307]

Trinko's allegations thus did not fly under existing precedents and the Court saw no reason to add to those exceptions from the rule that there is no duty to aid competitors. The Court added that an antitrust analysis 'must always be attuned to the particular structure and circumstances of the industry at issue', noting in this context the 'significance of regulation' and went on to discuss the limited benefits of antitrust in industries where regulation exists which were designed to deter anti-competitive conduct, and, at the same time, the considerable disadvantages and costs of antitrust enforcement.[308] Allegations of violations of the duties under the 1996 Act were found 'difficult for antitrust courts to evaluate, not only because they are highly technical, but also because they are likely to be extremely numerous, given the incessant, complex, and constantly changing interaction of competitive and incumbent LECs implementing the sharing and interconnection obligations'. Rounding up, the Court quoted Professor Areeda saying: 'No court should impose a duty to deal that it cannot explain or adequately and reasonably supervise.'[309]

It should also be mentioned that the Court, in a footnote, dismissed the Court of Appeals' finding that the respondent's complaint might state a claim under a 'monopoly leveraging' theory, stating that '[t]o the extent the Court of Appeals dispensed with a requirement that there be a 'dangerous probability of success' in monopolizing a second market, it erred'.[310] This would thus be the end of the more permissive standard for monopoly leveraging operated by the Second Circuit, which has relaxed the 'dangerous probability' requirement – only requiring that a monopolist uses its market power to gain a competitive advantage in a second market. Other Courts of Appeal have now, like the Supreme Court, insisted that the conduct must threaten to monopolize the adjacent market, making reference to *Spectrum Sports*.[311]

The Trinko case is interesting, not least considering that this field may be one exception to the general convergence between American and European standards. Recently, the European Court of Justice decided the *IMS* case,[312] further developing its case law under Article 82 in the field of 'duty to deal' and 'compulsory licensing'. The Court considered the balance between the property owner's rights and the potential benefits of a duty to license.

---

307 124 S.Ct. 872, 880.

308 124 S.Ct. 872, 881.

309 124 S.Ct. 872, 882.

310 Footnote 4 of the opinion.

311 *Spectrum Sports, Inc. v. McQuillan*, 506 U.S. 447 (1993).

312 Case C-418/01, *IMS Health GmbH & Co. OHG v. NDC Health GmbH & Co. KG*, (2004).

IMS is a company engaged in providing regional sales data of pharmaceutical products in Germany. For the collection and processing of data, it had, several years prior to the judgment, developed a 'brick structure', a geographical division of Germany into 1860 areas (and a derived structure of 2847 bricks) based on certain criteria such as the boundaries of municipalities, postcodes, population density and so on. This structure was developed and optimized in cooperation with its customers in the pharmaceutical industry, for example through a joint working group.

When a former IMS manager in 1998 started a competing business (later NDC), which first offered services based on another system but later used a structure very similar to that of IMS, the latter was able to obtain an interlocutory order prohibiting the company from using a brick structure derived from the IMS 1860 system. The injunction was confirmed on appeal, considering the brick system a database, which may be protected by copyright.

NDC complained to the European Commission in December 2000, claiming that the refusal to grant a licence was a violation of Article 82. The Commission adopted interim measures in July 2001, ordering IMS to grant a licence, and declaring that the brick system had become an industry standard, the refusal to licence which would likely eliminate all competition on the market. Taken together this amounted to 'exceptional circumstances'.[313] On appeal, the President of the CFI in October 2001 suspended these interim measures,[314] a decision later upheld by the President of the ECJ.[315]

Meanwhile, the main proceedings continued in Germany where IMS persisted in its objective of prohibiting NDC from using its brick structure. A German court found that IMS could not obtain an injunction against NDC if the company acted abusively within the meaning of Article 82, by refusing to grant a licence on reasonable terms. To clarify whether an abuse was committed, the German court stayed the proceedings and referred to the ECJ three questions relating to (a) whether it is abusive to refuse to grant a licence to the use of a copyright-protected databank to a potential rival in the same geographical and actual market, where the customers in the market would reject any product not using the said databank; (b) whether it is relevant whether the customers in the market have been involved in the development of the databank; and (c) whether the switching costs that a customer would incur if switching to a product not using the copyrighted databank is relevant to the question of abuse.

Answering the second and third question in the affirmative, the Court, with reference to *Bronner*,[316] noted that the question of indispensability depends on the availability of alternative solutions (even if these are less attractive) or whether economic technical, legal or economic obstacles make it 'impossible or at least unreasonably difficult' to create alternative products or services.[317] When considering the evidence, the national court should therefore take into account whether the

---

313 Case COMP D3/38.044 – *NDC Health v. IMS Health*: interim measures, OJ L 59/18 (2002).

314 Case T-184/01, *IMS Health v. Commission,* ECR II-3193 (2001).

315 Case C-481/01 P(R), *NDC Health v. IMS Health and Commission,* ECR I-3401 (2002).

316 Case C-7/97, *Oscar Bronner GmbH & Co. KG v Mediaprint,* ECR I-7791 (1998).

317 §28.

customers participated at a high level in the development of the brick structure, which created a dependency, particularly at a technical level, to that structure. If so, it is likely that a switch to acquire studies based on another structure would only come with 'exceptional organisational and financial efforts'.[318]

Answering the first question, the Court noted that the question assumed the 1860 brick structure was indispensable for a potential competitor entering the market.

The parties read *Magill*,[319] a natural precedent in the field, differently. IMS argued that the Magill facts allowing a refusal to constitute an abuse included the prevention of a new product on a secondary market.[320] Since NDC was not trying to introduce a new product onto a secondary market, IMS continued, these criteria were not fulfilled. NDC, on the other hand, contended that it wished to supply a new product, and did not accept the notion that a separate second market was necessary, arguing that it was sufficient that the infrastructure was 'at a stage of upstream production'.[321]

The Court set out by stressing that a refusal to grant a licence cannot in itself be abusive, since the exclusive right of reproduction is part of an owner's rights, irrespective of dominance. Only in exceptional circumstances may an exercise of an exclusive right be abusive. Referring to the summary of Magill made by the Court in *Bronner*, a refusal to license an indispensable product or service will be abusive if three cumulative conditions are satisfied: (a) the refusal prevents the emergence of a new product for which there is a potential consumer demand; (b) the refusal is not objectively justified; and (c) it is likely to exclude all competition in the secondary market.[322]

As for the dispute concerning the 'secondary market', the Court made it clear that, while it is relevant to distinguish an 'upstream market', it is sufficient that a potential market, or even a hypothetical market, can be identified. Moreover, such a market can be identified when there is an actual demand for a product or service that is indispensable for the requesting firm in order to carry on a particular business.[323] Therefore 'it is determinative that two different stages of production may be identified and that they are interconnected; the upstream product is indispensable in as much as for supply of the downstream product'.[324] In other words, the German court should decide whether the 1860 brick structure constitutes an upstream factor that is indispensable for the downstream supply of sales data. If so, it should be examined whether the refusal to grant licence eliminates all competition on the downstream sales.

Regarding the requirement of a new product, the Court considered this a balance between, on the one hand, the interest in protection of copyright and the economic freedom of its owner and, on the other hand, the protection of free competition. This

318 §29.

319 Joined Cases C-241/91 P and C-242/91 P, *RTE and ITP v. Commission* ('Magill'), ECR I-743 (1995).

320 These conditions would be, in brief, (a) the refusal prevents the emergence of a new product; (b) it is unjustified; and (c) it reserves a secondary market for the dominant company.

321 §33.

322 §§37, 38.

323 §44.

324 §45.

> balance can only tip in favour of the latter if a refusal 'prevents the development of the secondary market to the detriment of consumers'.[325] Consequently, a refusal to license can only be abusive if the potential licensee 'does not intend to limit itself essentially to duplicating the goods or services already offered on the secondary market by the owner of the copyright, but intends to produce new goods or services not offered by the owner of the right and for which there is a potential consumer demand'.

Considering the language in *Trinko* (US Supreme Court 2004), it is clear that the ECJ is more favourable to a duty to deal for dominant firms. Like the Supreme Court, it affirmed that a mere refusal to license is not abusive, but that there needs to be an additional element. But the ECJ considers the prevention of a *new* product for which there is a *potential* demand to be such an additional (foreclosing) element, although the new product will compete in the same market as the licensor's product.

The IMS judgment is a balancing act between the interests of the property owner and the benefits of competition and follow-on innovation. Still, there are some elements that would limit wide application of the EU standard. Although 'internal' inputs at an upstream level in the production may be considered for mandatory supplies it is not certain what may constitute 'different' but 'interconnected' stages. In addition, the refusal must deny a 'new product' being introduced on the market. The ECJ is silent on how to evaluate this criterion. Moreover, the dominant firm may be objectively justified in denying access. Since the judgment does not require any further anti-competitive act than the refusal to supply, the justification criterion is potentially of great importance in preventing successful product development from being penalized by compulsory delivery of vital product inputs to rivals.

4.9.4 Concluding Observations

Dominant firms' strategies may be considered abusive if they allow the firm to control developments in the relevant area – and thereby maintain its dominance – by means other than 'competition on the merits'. If their conduct diminishes other firms' abilities and incentives to innovate, such strategies may be hard to justify objectively. Nevertheless, dominant firms are supposed to compete vigorously and the underlying technological, economic and legal conditions must be carefully addressed.

Intel (FTC 1999) highlights the potential importance of working with multiple market concepts. Upstream markets may shed new light on parties' competitive relationships, shifting the focus from merely vertical settings to

---

325 §48.

horizontal competition in certain technology or innovation markets. Questions nevertheless remain regarding the standards for proving anti-competitive effects on the upstream market and how the showing of efficiencies can rebut such effects.

It is clear that *Microsoft III* (D.C. Cir. 2001) has important ramifications for the application of antitrust law to innovative sectors of the economy. Microsoft's overriding defence in various antitrust actions has been that they must be free to use their innovative abilities to serve their customers through continuous product development – no matter how difficult that makes the lives of their competitors. The Court of Appeals, on the other hand, ran every allegation through a work order in order to find out whether the particular acts constituted a monopolization under §2. According to the Court, to be condemned as an unlawful exclusionary exercise, the act must have an anti-competitive effect. Hence harm to the competitive process, and thereby to consumers, must be proved. Harm to competitors will not suffice. And it is for the plaintiff to show that the monopolist's conduct indeed has the requisite anti-competitive effect. The case is thus not about Microsoft being punished for achieving a near-monopoly through innovation, but for the actions taken to preserve that situation.[326] If the plaintiff succeeds in doing this, the defendant may proffer a 'pro-competitive justification'. Should the defendant be able to explain how its conduct constitutes competition on the merits, for example by increasing efficiency or enhancing consumer appeal, the burden shifts back to the plaintiff, either to rebut the justification or to show that the anti-competitive harm outweighs the pro-competitive benefit. This is a similar exercise to that conducted under a §1 rule of reason approach. The court also stated that intent matters, but only to help understand the likely effect of the conduct, hence not as a weight in the balancing act itself.

As for the European *Microsoft* decision (EU 2004), the Commission's work order is in principle the same as that of the American court. It found that ceasing to provide information with regard to the interface between PC OS and group server OS will exclude competition on the latter market in a way that lacks justification. With a compulsory supply of such information, the competitive landscape would liven up and competitive pressure would drive innovation incentives. The major difference in the Commission's stance with regard to Microsoft compared to its American colleagues (at least the current FTC administration) is the willingness of the former to assess and remedy the effects of the adding of new features, in this case WMP, to Windows.

Finally, comparing Trinko (US Supreme Court 2004) and IMS (ECJ 2004)

---

326 See, e.g., Fisher, Franklin M. & Rubinfeld, Daniel L., 'United States v. Microsoft – An Economic Analysis', 46 *Antitrust Bulletin* 1, 4f. (2001).

it is clear that the American standard for abuse liability is more limited than the European. A test in which an exclusionary conduct must lack any legitimate purpose or be unprofitable and undertaken solely to weaken competitors (a sacrifice test), which may apply in the US, is not the rule in Europe.[327] In Europe, a duty may arise even if the refusal is clearly profitable for the dominant company. The ECJ thus recognizes a wider scope for exclusionary abuses, seemingly on account of its ambition of maintaining a dynamic market process.

327 Such a limiting standard was argued by the FTC, but not explicitly adopted by the Supreme Court

5. The framework for innovation analysis

This chapter aims to provide a deeper understanding of the analysis of competition in innovation. Key questions relate to the framework for the analysis that was developed after the introduction of the innovation market concept and the relationship with other kinds of market definitions and analysis doctrines. The assessment of innovation competition in the defined markets, the role of efficiencies in the appraisal of a transaction and possible remedies to alleviate anti-competitive effects will be handled in the next chapter.

In this chapter it will be shown that the analysis of competition in the innovation process may be conducted for the purpose of detecting a variety of competitive effects. Although competition is a broad notion that affects various parameters such as the pace of innovation, variety, quality and price of products, it is for the antitrust authorities to establish the effects of a particular market practice. To identify the innovating firms and products under development, and to assess the terms of innovation in the area, may be the key to drawing any prospective conclusions – whether the primary effect relates to product innovation, variety or price.

Second, it will be shown that innovation analysis is applied at different market levels. When analysing actual and potential competition in existing markets, it is generally acknowledged that innovation may be an important dimension. Innovation aspects may be integrated when analysing the competitive conditions prevalent in the product market. But the R&D dimension of the market may also be analysed through the framework of the innovation market concept. An innovation market may thus be delineated as a supplement to the product or technology market.

When existing markets do not provide a sensible point of departure, typically where the transaction relates to R&D which is expected to result in radical innovation, the innovation market concept itself delimits the relevant market. Rather than starting from existing products or trying to depict the boundaries of future product markets, a delineation of competing R&D is used to identify the competitive restraints on market participants. This could be called an 'orthodox' innovation market, since it neatly fits the policy of the guidelines' world.

A variation of the innovation market concept provides the relevant market in another category of cases, in situations where the market practice may affect innovation in a broader sense, not confined to particular future products or technologies. Although these cases do not precisely follow the methodology as expressed in the guidelines, the notion of an upstream market for innovation is decisive in these instances, and consequently also controversial.

Third, since the innovation market concept, in one way or another, can be applied in all these settings, the overlaps and related functions of innovation, product and technology markets deserve a thorough examination. The comparative problems and merits of the use of the innovation market concept will be highlighted.

Fourth, the delimitation of innovation markets in various situations is examined. Since, for antitrust purposes, a defined market should reflect the relevant competitive restraints that discipline market participants, an innovation market analysis must also closely track the particular circumstances to which it is applied.

Finally, the chapter ends with some observations regarding the limits and particularities of delineating and conducting an innovation market analysis.

5.1 MULTIPLE PURPOSES OF INNOVATION ANALYSIS

Ultimately, antitrust policy is concerned with the exercise of market power. Such exercise could manifest itself in several ways. It could entail the ability to raise prices beyond a competitive level or to reduce product quality or the level of services provided to customers. Market power can also be exercised with respect to innovation parameters such as pace and variety in the development of products and technologies.[1] But in order to show the effects of a market practice that involves some restriction of competition, the analysis must be more precise, particularly if it could also produce pro-competitive results. Generally, a causal link between the practice and its (likely) effect must be established. Since the conditions for improving or introducing new products and technologies take effect at different levels, innovation analysis may be warranted in various settings. Such analysis may identify and establish, but also serve to alleviate, suspected anti-competitive effects.

Regarding analysis under the innovation market concept, the US IP Guidelines provide reduced R&D investment as an example of exercise of market power in such a market. This can thus take other forms.[2] In an illustrative example, the guidelines provide an assessment of an R&D joint

---

[1] According to the European Commission the agreements should be scrutinized for adverse effect on 'parameters of competition on the market, such as price, output, product quality, product variety and innovation': Guidelines on the application of Article 81(3) of the Treaty, OJ C 101/97 (2004) §§16, 25.

[2] US 1995 IP Guidelines, §3.2.3.

venture, where it is considered whether the parties would have 'an incentive and ability collectively to reduce investment in, or otherwise retard the pace or scope of, research and development efforts'.[3] Although the innovation market approach seems designed to detect innovation-related competitive effects, the American rule of reason analysis necessitates a flexible inquiry dependent on the nature of the transaction and the market circumstances, in order to assess the overall competitive effect (on price, output, quality, service and innovation) of a transaction.[4] The authorities will assess parameters of market power and firms' abilities and incentives to compete, and evaluate whether entry or other market circumstances may counteract anti-competitive harms.[5]

According to the EU Horizontal Cooperation Guidelines the innovation market approach seems intended for analysing the incentives to reduce R&D efforts, rather than as a method to assess future product market effects. It is asserted that, at the beginning of an R&D cooperation, 'its success and factors such as the parties' future market position as well as the development of future product or technology markets are often not known'.[6] The analysis is therefore confined to innovation markets (and possible spillovers on existing products and technology markets), focusing on possible restrictions of innovation, not only the speed of innovation, but also the quality and variety of future products and technologies.[7]

Consequently, there is no pronounced difference in approach between the US and EU. Since the examination is sensitive to the stage in the R&D process at which a transaction is formed, it seems reasonable to assume that, the closer the products are to being launched on the market, the more will (future) product market competition matter. Close to product launch, the centre of gravity of the transaction is not so much innovation, as production and marketing,[8] so the centre of gravity for analysing competition effects will also shift – a sort of sliding scale of primary effects.

---

3 Ibid., example 4.

4 The FTC states that '[a] transaction that combines an existing innovation effort with a competing innovation effort or with a competing good may substantially lessen innovation competition and thereby harm consumers in two basic ways. First, a next-generation product might not reach consumers as quickly or with the same quality or diversity as would be the case absent the transaction. Second, consumers may be deprived of likely potential price and quality competition in current or future goods markets' (*Anticipating the 21st Century – Competition Policy in the New High-Tech, Global Marketplace*, Staff Report, 1996, Executive Summary and Principal Conclusions, pp. 4f.).

5 US 2000 Competitor Collaboration Guidelines, see, e.g., §§1.2, 2.2, 3.3.

6 EU 2001 Horizontal Cooperation Guidelines, §73.

7 Ibid., §65.

8 Ibid., §64.

Landman even asserts that neither the American nor the European authorities prove that innovation competition will be diminished. Rather they show that the number of credible and predictable R&D programmes aimed at the relevant product will be reduced below a critical point.[9] Moreover, he maintains that the true reason for maintaining multiple independent R&D programmes is to preserve competition in the future goods market.[10]

There could nevertheless be several reasons for maintaining independent R&D programmes. One reason could be that competition is supposed to have positive effects on performance in R&D. Hence, if too few independent R&D programmes exist, firms might have less pressure to perform efficiently. Although the links between market structure and dynamic efficiency are indistinct, it may be assumed that monopolists 'are not superior engines of technological progress'.[11] Thus the pace of development could suffer if incumbent firms are unthreatened by entry.[12] Firms may also have incentives anti-competitively to reduce their R&D efforts.[13] For example, a new product may merely erode profits currently obtained in a product market where little competition exists, which would create an incentive to delay its development. Moreover, some diversity of products constitutes a value in itself. If parties will, after a transaction, combine two development efforts into one, or have incentives to end or delay the development of a certain product, this will deprive consumers of a benefit which would otherwise come from innovation and competition, namely, choice between different (although more or less substitutable) products. Reduced variety would persist even if the parties marketed the resulting product in competition with each other, for example following an R&D joint venture or licensing arrangement. In addition, to maintain a reasonable number of competing R&D programmes could enhance the chances of there being any future products at all. R&D is often risky and projects frequently fail. More independent projects could enhance the possibility of some success.

The reasons for safeguarding variety are closely connected to the last reason

---

9 Landman, Lawrence B., 'The Economics of Future Goods Markets', 21 *World Competition – Law and Economics Review* 63, 84 (1998).

10 Landman, Lawrence B., 'Innovation and the Structure of Competition', 81 *Journal of the Patent and Trademark Office Society* 728 (1999); 'Innovation Markets in Europe', 19 *European Competition Law Review* 21 (1998); 'Competing in the Global Pharmaceutical Industry: Innovation and Future Potential Competition', 2 *The Journal of Biolaw & Business* 29 (1998).

11 Scherer, Frederic M., 'Antitrust, Efficiency, and Progress', 62 *New York University Law Review* 998, 1019 (1987).

12 Scherer, Frederic M. & Ross, David, *Industrial Market Structure and Economic Performance,* Houghton Mifflin, Boston, 1990, pp. 634 *et seq.*

13 Gilbert, Richard J. & Sunshine, Steven C., 'Incorporating Dynamic Efficiency Concerns in Merger Analysis: The Use of Innovation Markets', 63 *Antitrust Law Journal* 569, 592f. (1995).

for seeking to maintain some minimum number of R&D sources: this enhances the chances of a competitive future product market. Any policy for maintaining competition in R&D for future products is also a policy for safeguarding potential competition in the future product market. Besides bringing more products to the market, sold at lower prices and with better services, maintaining a competitive product market will also increase the incentives for market actors to keep on innovating. Innovation is a repeated game, particularly in markets where the incumbent is under pressure from actual or potential competitors.

Looking at the case law dealt with in Chapter 4 in this light, it seems that the authorities in reality pursue multiple goals. In some cases the authorities maintain that a transaction will reduce competition, resulting in lessened incentives to maintain R&D efforts.[14] Particularly when a party has a dominant position on the current market, that concern may be appropriate as any new product could cannibalize current profits.[15] In other settings, a reduced number of independent R&D actors has been expected rather to diminish innovation speed and variety.[16] Negative effects for other firms' research, such as in obtaining licences to key technology have also been highlighted.[17] The possibility of a firm being able to limit others' innovation potential by obstructing crucial feedback into R&D has also been challenged, as are practices that limit innovation incentives by exploiting market dominance to 'expropriate' innovation results from other firms.[18] Similarly, continued incentives and abilities for innovation by members and non-members have been central to the assessment of patent pools for industry standards.[19] At times, the authorities have been confronted by a merger of R&D programmes, of which one has been relatively behind in the R&D process, and the elimination of which would decrease variety and quality in the future product market.[20] Frequently, the authorities also highlight the possible effects of fewer competitors and less competition on the future product market, supposedly leading to higher prices. Often effects on innovation, variety and price are all expected to occur.[21]

---

14 See generally *Montedison* and *Montecatini* cases (FTC 1995 and EU 1994), *Crown Cork* (EU 1995).

15 *Wright Medical* (FTC 1995), *Pfizer/Pharmacia* (FTC and EU 2003).

16 *Lockheed Martin* (DOJ 1998). See also dissenting opinions in *Genzyme/Novazyme* (US 2004).

17 *Ciba/Geigy* (FTC 1997), *Ciba/Geigy* (EU 1996), *Hoechst/Rhône-Poulenc* (FTC 2000), *Pasteur Mérieux/Merck* (EU 1994)

18 *Digital/Intel* (FTC 1998), *Intel* (FTC 1999).

19 *MPEG-2* (DOJ 1997 and EU 1998), *DVD* (DOJ 1998, 1999 and EU 2000).

20 *American Home Products* (FTC 1995).

21 *Wright Medical* (FTC 1995), *Boston Scientific Corp.* (FTC 1995), *Amgen/Immunex* (FTC 2002), *Upjohn/Pharmacia* (FTC 1996), *Pfizer/Pharmacia* (FTC and EU 2003).

Consequently, where the R&D process is rather lengthy and transparent and entry is difficult, a decrease in the number of independent actors and R&D projects may constitute a lessening in innovation competition. This may happen where the concentration entails some incentive and ability to reduce or retard the development of other new products and technologies in a way that would not have arisen, had further R&D sources existed. Substantial foreclosure of third parties from acting in the area may lead to the same result. The analysis may also foresee a lessening in competition in existing or future product markets if the parties are reasonably near product launch or the R&D involves low risks of failure. Competition aspects in the R&D process and current and future product and technology markets all come together and lead to an overall assessment. For all these dimensions current R&D conditions are central.[22]

5.2 MULTIPLE LEVELS OF INNOVATION ANALYSIS

In order to assess the impact of a market practice and to prescribe a rational remedy for potential problems, it is important to understand the general conditions under which innovation takes place, not least to identify and assess the impact of relevant sources of innovation, potential entrants, potential new products under development, and so on. The execution of appropriate innovation analysis varies according to the situation in which it is applied. Three general categories may be identified.

5.2.1 Innovation in Current Markets

Analysing actual and potential competition in relation to existing markets may still warrant closer assessment of the conditions for innovation. The analysis focuses on existing products and technologies and the boundaries and conditions for innovation in relation to these. It is often adequate to identify important innovators in the market (both current and potential), the conditions under which R&D is undertaken and the effects of a market practice on innovation.

---

[22] As outlined in the EU 2001 Horizontal Cooperation Guidelines §43, the relevant market to base the analysis may be a goods markets (when the R&D aims at improvements to marketed goods), technology markets (when IPRs are marketed separately from the resulting goods) and R&D efforts (when R&D aims at a new products/technology that will create a separate market). However, since it is realized that most of the cases probably concern situations in which innovation efforts may create products or technologies which, over time, replace existing ones, careful analysis may have to cover all three aspects.

Where current products constitute the point of departure, the analysis is more likely to look at the conditions for incremental innovation: improvements on current products and production processes. While drastic innovation, altering current market conditions altogether, is often spectacular and attracts more attention, incremental innovation is the dominating form of technological progress in many industries and constitutes the lion's share of progress in science and technology. It clearly has a tremendous economic importance for society.

It may nonetheless still be appropriate to conduct an innovation analysis that goes outside the realm of current actors and products, not least in order to assess potential technology shifts or other important developments. It is possible that competition in relevant R&D is broader than competition in current products. Also, when R&D is important, but at the same time is long-term and transparent, a delineation of viable actors and projects in that dimension is more likely to capture the pressure on market participants to introduce new products and to constitute a workable basis for a prospective assessment of product market competition, than merely defining the competitive restraints in terms of currently marketed products.

In transactions between an incumbent firm and a potential entrant, it is even clearer that competitive effects depend on more than the level of competition between current market participants. The competitive importance of the entrant in terms of its potential technologies and products, as well as the existence and viability of other potential entrants, must be assessed. This will often include a structured analysis of R&D competition.

Although current products determine the main relevant market, an analysis of the innovation market can serve as a good supplement for addressing the R&D dimension. Moreover, since there may be advantages in executing the innovation analysis separately from the analysis of current products, it may be useful to make explicit use of an innovation market. This concept may thus provide an additional relevant market or the innovation analysis may be conducted within the existing product market (possibly structured along the same lines anyway).

5.2.2 Potential Future Markets

Where a transaction relates to the development of a new product, which may create a new market or has the potential to change current markets (for example, by rendering current products obsolete), current markets clearly do not provide an accurate basis for competition analysis. Rather, the product under development and any other similar products under development together constitute the relevant competitive restraints. They themselves constitute a relevant market. In consequence, the analysis will focus on R&D for future product(s). This kind of analysis is appropriate where innovation is likely to be drastic rather than incremental. This is also the realm of the innovation market approach as formulated in the American and European Guidelines.[23]

The analysis may still be supplemented by an assessment of current markets. Cooperation in R&D may have spillover effects on competition here and current market positions may affect parties' R&D incentives.

Where the transaction takes place at an early stage in the R&D process, where substantial uncertainty prevails regarding chances of success and future product market characteristics, questions about future product market dominance is of less interest. In these cases, which could be denoted competition for *distant* future markets, the analysis will aim at discovering whether incentives and abilities for continued performance in the innovation market are negatively affected. This involves a case-by-case assessment of competing R&D sources.

In practice, merged or otherwise combined R&D assets and projects are often at more advanced levels of development and the primary question for the authorities is whether the transaction will impede competition in the future product market. Otherwise put, the question is whether it will lead to an anti-competitive narrowing of the range of products and lessening of consumer choice. The more *imminent* the future market, the clearer the overlap with potential competition doctrines. The relevant market could plausibly be defined as the future product market and the assessment would be one of potential competition on that market. Still, this would not change the conditions for the underlying analysis. Also, since the border between early and late stages is imprecise and case-specific (as is the border between innovation concerns and product market concerns), it is appropriate to call this innovation market analysis.

5.2.3 Technology Bases

Competition in the innovation process may be affected by transactions in R&D which are not directed at specific future products: this brings us to a broader class of research. Here the analysis aims to detect the creation of a powerful technology base which may constitute a bottleneck. Such a bottleneck can be created by transactions that combine key inputs to research or into marketable products deriving from research. For example, when upstream activities are protected by intellectual property rights, such as research tools in biotechnology, transactions by which such assets are combined may have effects on the development of various potential future

---

23 See section 3.3.

products. The unification of such inputs can affect the parties' innovation incentives and may impede and foreclose third parties' possibilities of conducting R&D in the area.

Where competitive impact is not tied directly to R&D of more or less specific competing future products, the delineation of an innovation market as in previous cases is not the adequate basis for analysis. The focus must rather be on the importance of the technology base and the foreseen effects on innovation due to its creation and management. Since upstream bottlenecks may affect the development of a variety of future products and technologies, some kind of innovation market concept is even more essential here.

5.3 OVERLAPPING MARKET DEFINITIONS AND IMAGINARY MARKETS

If innovation analysis is conducted in relation to both existing markets and future markets and in more general terms, the question arises how the innovation market concept relates to more traditional market concepts. The relationship between actual and potential competition on product, technology and innovation markets deserves closer scrutiny.

From both the guidelines and case law it seems to follow that any market definition chosen will be based on the underlying facts in each case. This could be both flexible and rational, since the market definition does not have an independent purpose, apart from identifying relevant competitive constraints. The merit of elaborating different market definitions is that they may shed new light both on possible anti-competitive effects and on sources of competition that limit such concerns. It bears repeating that a full analysis – particularly in borderline cases – may require delineation of product, technology and innovation markets. But even though different markets can be distinguished there are considerable overlaps between them.

The key to the problem of overlaps is that the innovation market concept defines an upstream market for inputs. Analysis of this input market can be used to identify problems relating both to the R&D activity itself and to potential future problems on downstream markets for products and technologies. Consequently, it may both provide an alternative market definition (to existing product and technology markets) and supplement the potential competition doctrine. The fact that innovation market analysis offers not only a relevant market distinguishable from others, but also a methodology for assessing impacts on relevant downstream markets, means it can be used instead of, or in relation to, other market definitions.

5.3.1 Actual and Potential Competition in Innovation and Product Markets

According to Gilbert & Sunshine, analysis of innovation markets differs from that of potential competition in that it deals with the effects of changes in *actual* competition in innovation markets, rather than *potential* competition in product markets.[24] They maintain that the FTC in *Roche-Genentech* (FTC 1990) in part focused on the 'consequences of structural change in innovation for the state of future competition'.[25] But is that something plainly different from analysing effects on potential competition from a merger between two prospective market entrants?[26] This case was decided before the introduction of the innovation market concept, but still provides some important insights into the discussion.

Innovation issues arose above all in the area of AIDS/HIV therapeutics, where no product had received FDA approval. Since the parties were among 'a limited number' pursuing research, they had to license out Roche's patent portfolio. Interestingly, Commissioner Owen, in a dissenting separate statement, highlighted the potential relationship and conflict between innovation markets and potential competition doctrines. She asserted that the FTC had accepted the consent agreement and proposed order based on a doctrine of actual potential competition. By doing so, the FTC departed from past precedent in potential competition cases, as well as from the Merger Guidelines. This was the basis for her dissent. Under the theory of actual potential competition, she maintained, the prospective entrant 'must be willing and able imminently to enter a market which is not now performing competitively'.[27] Moreover, in FTC practice and under the guidelines, new entry should generally be expected within two years and the entry should be supported by more than mere hypothesis.[28] Here, however, the FTC took relief in markets where there was substantial doubt about willingness and only speculation about abil-

---

[24] What is here discussed regarding the relationship between innovation markets and product markets is also applicable to the relationship between innovation markets and technology markets.

[25] Gilbert & Sunshine, *supra*, note 13, pp. 570f.

[26] Howard M. Morse asserts that this situation at the time was dubbed a 'double potential competition' case. 'The Limits of Innovation Markets', 2(1) *Antitrust & Intellectual Property* 22f. (2001) (The Intellectual Property Committee Newsletter, The Section of Antitrust Law of the American Bar Association).

[27] Regarding the potential competition doctrine and the separation of an actual potential competition theory and a perceived potential competition theory, see section 3.2.2.

[28] *B.A.T. Industries, Ltd.*, 104 F.T.C. 916 (1984) and U.S. Department of Justice Merger Guidelines.

ity to enter. It was certain that entry was not imminent. Lastly, as no firms or products were on the market, Commissioner Owen regarded conclusions about competitive performance in the relatively distant future as at best speculative.

This raises some interesting issues, in particular the narrow boundaries of the potential competition doctrine as applied in the US. To focus on the competitive state of R&D, rather than the potential future product market, would be a way to widen the scope of the antitrust analysis, both regarding factual and time dimensions and the types of competitive restraints considered.

In Europe, the differences between the potential competition doctrine and the innovation market concept are less pronounced. Compared to US standards, the Commission's application of potential competition doctrine to R&D transactions does not seem so limited regarding timing, likelihood of entry or the markets to which it applies. It has performed different types of prospective analyses of R&D and future products, denoting them all as analyses of 'potential competition'. This is obvious in *Pasteur Mérieux/Merck* (EU 1994) where the potential competition analysis included unidentified future pipeline products.

But the American practice is, in fact, far from clear-cut. Potential competition does not only play a role when one party is active on the market and the other party is an entrant. In *United States v. Penn-Olin Chemical Co.*, the US Supreme Court endorsed potential competition theory regarding two joint venture participants neither of whom was currently active in the particular product market.[29] Irrespective of the trial court's finding that both parties would not have entered the market absent the joint venture, it was, according to the Supreme Court, to be considered whether one party could have entered and the other remained as a significant potential competitor.[30] Both parties could consequently have had some effect on the market, although they did not both plan to enter.

In any event, the traditional perspective of the potential competition doctrine is to depart from an existing market and analyse the effect of a transaction with regard to entry onto that market. In order to claim reduced potential competition, American courts at least tend to demand strong evidence that the merger precluded entry.[31] Entry must thus be probable and imminent. In general, that is also the European position.[32]

29 *United States v. Penn-Olin Chemical Co.*, 378 U.S. 158 (1964).

30 See Areeda, Philip & Kaplow, Louis, *Antitrust Analysis: Problems, Texts, Cases*, 5th edn, Aspen Law & Business, New York, 1997, p. 868. This can thus be taken as an acceptance of the perceived potential competition theory: Dahdouh, Thomas N. & Mongoven, James F., 'The Shape of Things to Come: Innovation Market Analysis in Merger Cases', 64 *Antitrust Law Journal* 405, 432f. (1996).

31 See *BOC International Ltd. (British Oxygen) v. FTC*, 557 F.2d 24 (2d Cir. 1977).

32 Cook, C.J. & Kerse, C.S., *E.C. Merger Control,* 3rd edn, Sweet & Maxwell,

If the relevant R&D is directed at a completely new product for which no current market exists at all, the application of the potential competition doctrine could be dubious. In fact, in describing the differences between innovation market and potential competition analysis, the latter doctrine allegedly involves the effects of transactions on a product market in which revenues are already being derived.[33] The innovation market analysis, on the other hand, involves analysing competition between companies which as yet produces no direct revenues.

While that distinction may provide some indication of two typical situations suitable for grouping under the two concepts, it does not put the finger on the focal point. This is not firmly anchored in case law either.[34] As seen in the FTC and DOJ case law discussed in the previous chapter, lessening of potential competition has also been claimed where parties were active in the development of new product generations or even completely new products. In other cases, where products existed, focusing on the effect on an innovation market has been a means of justifying the claim of anti-competitive effects where the parties were better characterized as competitors in innovation than in the resulting products. That is apparent in cases such as *GM/ZF* (DOJ 1993) and the *Intel* (FTC 1999).

The innovation market approach was designed to remedy gaps in traditional doctrines and develop existing analyses that would allow the appreciation of competition aspects that could have been disregarded or analysed inappropriately under a pure product market analysis.

In the late 1990s, the European Commission commented on its practice as compared to the US innovation market concept, stating that, in the light of the

London, 2000, p. 154. The EU 2004 Horizontal Merger Guidelines, §74, and the EU 2000 Guidelines on Vertical Restraints, §126, indicate a policy for potential competition based on a high likelihood of entry within a time frame that is dependent on the characteristics and dynamics of the market, but which normally would be two years.

33 Widnell, Nicholas A., 'The Crystal Ball of Innovation Market Analysis in Merger Review: An Appropriate Means of Predicting the Future?', 4 *George Mason Law Review* 369, 380f. (1996).

34 I do not intend to imply that the authorities have been clear on the use and overlaps of different market definitions and doctrines. In the mid-90s, during the early, most active, application of the innovation market approach, Joseph Kattan noted: 'The cases in which innovation concerns had formed an independent basis for challenging a transaction have been few and far between. In virtually every case in which the government attacked a transaction based on its effects on innovation competition, the parties were also head-on competitors in the sale of existing products, and concerns about price competition with respect to such products had been the key aspect of the challenge. Having said that, there is a sense in which the Federal Trade Commission has made innovation competition its theory du jour . . .', 'Antitrust Considerations in Innovation-Driven Markets', 21 *Canada-United States Law Journal* 115, 119 (1995).

uncertainties surrounding concentration and innovation, it did not apply competition policy to innovation markets *directly*. However, it used the innovation market concept to base its decision on likely effects on the market of the future products involved.[35] What this means is that, even under a policy which focuses on future product market effects, the analysis conducted may benefit from a concept that takes competing R&D as the point of departure.

In addition, the underlying analysis does not necessarily change because some product is already on the market. First of all, it may be uncertain whether, and to what extent, a new product will create its own demand or render current products obsolete, and thereby not fit neatly into existing markets. Secondly, even if a relevant product exists, an inventory and assessment of R&D actors and products under development may be essential in order to investigate the competitive effects of a transaction. However, the existence of current products, together with the features of the products under development, may affect the outcome of the subsequent analysis; it could have an impact on whether the parties will have incentives to reduce their R&D and the extent to which future product market competition will be affected.

The overlaps between potential product market competition and innovation market competition will be further reviewed below. To complete the picture, technology markets will be commented upon.

5.3.2 Antitrust going Upstream

According to both EU and US guidelines a technology market exists when a technology is actively being licensed. In the US, the technology market comprises all goods and technologies (whether licensed or not) working as substitutes for the particular technology, and hence constraining the exercise of market power from that technology.[36] According to the EU Technology Transfer Guidelines a technology market consists of the licensed technology and the technologies which the licensee considers to be substitutes. Analogous to the definition of product markets, the technology market includes the technologies to which a licensee could switch in response to an increase in relative

---

35 OECD, 'Application of Competition Policy to High Tech Markets', *OECD Working Papers*, Series Roundtables on Competition Policy no. 9, Paris, 1997, p. 90. As described in Chapter 1, nowadays the EU 2001 Horizontal Cooperation Guidelines refer to competition in innovation and R&D efforts and also uses the term 'innovation markets'. The EU 2004 Technology Transfer Guidelines distinguish between product, technology and innovation markets. Among the European guidelines for horizontal transactions, only the merger guidelines lack innovation markets. This corresponds to the American situation.

36 US 2000 Competitor Collaboration Guidelines, §3.32(b); US 1995 IP Guidelines, §3.2.2.

royalties.[37] The European approach therefore differs slightly from the US guidelines. Nevertheless, the European Commission also acknowledges that a holder of technology currently not being licensed may choose to license as a response to higher relative prices (royalties) and thus become a technology market competitor. And it is also recognized that the power of a licensor to raise royalties may be restrained by a competitive downstream product market (limiting the licensee's willingness to pay).

Similar to an innovation market, technology markets therefore include (or are at least affected by) both traded and captive technologies. When competing technologies have been identified, an assessment must be made whether the transaction may influence the terms upon which the relevant technologies are licensed. Particularly if the parties are competitors in the technology market, classical horizontal effects – royalty increases and output decreases – may appear. But even when the transaction involves parties or technologies in a vertical relationship (non-substitutes), competition may still be restricted, particularly through foreclosure of third parties.

Another similarity between innovation and technology markets lies in the fact that licensing transactions are often concluded in ways that cannot be quantified in monetary terms,[38] which is why the technology market analysis must take a pragmatic attitude in the identification and assessment of rival alternatives. This is confirmed in *Montedison* (US 1995) and *Shell/Montecatini* (EU 1994). Moreover, the demand for a licence to a particular technology is based on the potential productivity or competitive advantages the technology may provide in future goods – hence a 'derived demand' for an input.[39]

Neither of the guidelines emphasizes the importance of entry into the technology market from technologies currently in the R&D process. Particularly when the parties' R&D aims at new but substitutable technology, this ought to be most relevant. Whether one talks of innovation market or potential technology market competition is not of primary importance.

Innovation markets appear to take the last step in an upstream recourse starting from product markets, passing through technology markets (in the case where such a market exists) and ending at innovation markets. When reviewing allegations of unlawful monopolization from patent pooling, fraudulent procurement of patents and so on. US courts have traditionally been analysing the effects on product markets stemming from the technological

[37] EU 2004 Technology Transfer Guidelines, §22.

[38] US 1995 IP Guidelines, §3.2.2, note 21. Licences may be royalty free cross-licences or form part of broader licence packages.

[39] Newberg, Joshua A., 'Antitrust for the Economy of Ideas: The Logic of Technology Markets', 14 *Harvard Journal of Law and Technology* 83, 104f. (2000).

situation.[40] In other words, to assess the effects on product markets, an analysis of the exclusionary power of the patented technology or technologies has been required. Such an analysis must necessarily investigate possible substitutes, that is, alternative technologies, that would limit the parties' market power. Subsequently, the antitrust authorities have, through guidelines, lifted technology markets 'from the realm of the implied and ancillary to that of the express and primary'.[41] This holds both in the US and in the EU.

While the structure of the market influences firms' strategies and affects the competitive impact of various types of conduct, various strategies and behaviours may affect that market structure. In order to understand and analyse the competitive effects of various agreements and practices, the economic context to which the transactions apply is essential. 'Firms do not merely react to given external conditions, but try to strategically shape their economic environment by modifying, in a credible manner, market structure and market conducts of competitors. Then, unidirectional causality, from structure through conduct, breaks.'[42] The same rationality applies for the use of technology markets as well as for innovation markets. Conduct may affect the structure of competition on a level that is appropriately analysed upstream from the finalized products.

5.3.3 Imaginary Markets as an Analysis Tool

Compared to product markets and technology markets, innovation markets have their peculiarities. They are not ordinary markets where some product is bought and sold and market power typically results in anti-competitive effects to the detriment of buyers. Although R&D is being traded to an increasing extent (for example, through outsourcing), such activity most often leads to commercialization on a downstream market. This may be a technology market, where licences for patented technologies compete with other licensed or non-licensed (in-house) technologies. Still, more often R&D aims at the internal (captive) production of products and services.

The innovation market approach formulated by Gilbert and Sunshine treats innovation as a product.[43] As the research activity produces an input – knowledge

[40] Ibid., pp. 93 *et seq.* Newberg refers, e.g., to *Hartford-Empire Co. v. United States*, 323 U.S. 386 (1945) and *Walker Process Equip., Inc. v. Food Mach. & Chem. Corp.*, 382 U.S. 172 (1965).

[41] Ibid., p. 98. See US 1988 Antitrust Enforcement Guidelines for International Operations and the US 1995 IP Guidelines.

[42] Jacquemin, Alexis, 'Theories of Industrial Organisation and Competition Policy: What are the Links?', working paper, European Commission, Forward Studies Unit, 2000, p. 11.

[43] Gilbert & Sunshine, *supra*, note 13, p. 581.

– which, combined with more tangible inputs such as labour, capital and raw materials produces final goods and services, it could constitute an upstream research market, as opposed to the downstream market for goods and services that are produced using the technologies developed by the research activity.[44] However, according to their model, only R&D that can have a significant impact on one or more downstream markets may be included in an innovation market. Moreover, they also require that the innovation market analysis evaluate actual and potential competition from downstream products (if such products exist). They even maintain that strong competition from downstream products may offset the negative effects of monopolization in R&D since the monopolist may not have incentives to reduce the level of R&D.[45] Clearly this is not an independent market in the traditional sense. Particularly in light of *Genzyme/Novazyme* (FTC 2004), where an innovation market monopoly was allowed,[46] it is evident that the innovation market approach in American policy is a methodology allowing the authorities to analyse various consequences of structural changes in R&D. Despite the fact that the direct purpose of an intervention may be to hinder anti-competitive reductions in the speed of development or the variety of R&D, the lack of independence of the innovation market implies that the beneficial effect will be realized downstream, on a product market.[47] The mere fact that competing R&D is usually defined in terms of some future product implies that keeping independent R&D sources ultimately protects the establishment, or at least the performance, of a future product market. As a consequence, irrespective of whether such an intervention takes place at a stage rather distant from a potential future product market or at a stage where the potential competition doctrine could apply, the authorities ultimately protect a (more or less well-defined) future product market.[48]

This does not detract from the merits of an innovation market approach.[49]

---

44 Grossman, Gene M. & Shapiro, Carl, 'Research Joint Ventures: An Antitrust Analysis', 2 *Journal of Law, Economics and Organization* 315, 319 (1986).

45 Gilbert & Sunshine, *supra*, note 13, p. 596.

46 The FTC did not find any proof that the resulting R&D monopolist had incentives to reduce the level of R&D, although there were no competing downstream products.

47 See Gilbert, Richard J. & Tom, Willard K., 'Is Innovation King at the Antitrust Agencies? The Intellectual Property Guidelines Five Years Later', 69 *Antitrust Law Journal* 43, 49f. (2001).

48 Similarly, when the concept is used in relation to technology bases, the authorities consequently protect a possible array of applications markets, although the closer identity of these may be largely unknown.

49 The use of the 'market' terminology when it comes to paying special attention to innovation 'is awkward and potentially confusing, but does little harm so long as we all know what we are talking about': Davis, Ronald W., 'Innovation Markets and Merger Enforcement: Current Practice in Perspective', 71 *Antitrust Law Journal* 677, 680 (2003).

While noting that the European Commission did not then define innovation markets, an official asserted that the Commission would investigate whether a merger or agreement was likely to 'restrict substantially competition in R&D' between firms that are leading research in the field, and the R&D 'is directed specifically towards producing or improving the same product or process, and is associated with specialized R&D programmes'.[50] The Commission seemed 'more likely to use this approach than a potential competition approach, implicitly considering the R&D approach more convincing, practical, and immediate.'[51]

A particular feature of the innovation market concept is that it starts from the situation in R&D and may be used to draw inferences from factual and competitive features of the innovation process and to assess various consequences of strategic behaviour in that process.

The value of a structured R&D analysis along the lines of the innovation market concept is apparent in *Glaxo Wellcome/SmithKline Beecham* (EU 2000). The Commission investigated overlaps in areas where one of the parties had existing products on the market and pipeline products in development in addition to areas where neither party was currently active on the market but both parties had products in pipeline. When analysing the COPD[52] area where GW was dominant on current markets and both parties were active in R&D, the analysis consisted of two parts, differing both in terms of the R&D projects taken into consideration and of the conclusions derived and remedies prescribed. The Commission was thus able to distinguish between relatively short-term effects on existing markets and more long-term effects on the R&D incentives and potentials; that is, there was one analysis of potential competition in the classical sense and one more novel R&D competition analysis. But both analyses followed from an approach departing from looking at competing R&D for future products.

In *Genzyme/Novazyme* (FTC 2004) the whole investigation was aimed at analysing whether the merged company had incentives to reduce the scope or speed of the relevant R&D. Analysing innovation competition is thus something more than assessing entry to an existing concentrated market. Apart from imminent future product market effects, a transaction's consequences which more closely relate to R&D, in terms of incentives and abilities for different market participants, can also be addressed.

50 Temple Lang, John, 'European Community Antitrust Law: Innovation Markets and High Technology Industries', 20 *Fordham International Law Journal* 717, 760f. (1997).

51 Ibid., p. 761.

52 Chronic Obstructive Pulmonary Disease.

As noted in Chapter 2, it is maintained that analysis of dynamic competition requires, *inter alia,* an investigation into investment patterns in the development of new products, the control of critical assets, and qualified assessments of the nature and pace of innovation as well as whether a transaction is likely to slow down innovation or significantly reduce incentives to innovate.[53]

At the same time such analysis increases the stakes of intervention, both in terms of the benefits of correct assessments and the negative consequences of errors. This may be an additional reason for developing and refining a separate innovation market doctrine.[54] It could also allow increased transparency in policy and decision making. Apart from contributing to predictable legal standards, continued evaluation of the difficult concept of innovation competition, and its implementation by authorities and courts, can be facilitated. In fact, the debate surrounding the innovation market concept, in which both economists and lawyers have taken part, has affected the development of legal standards in the area.

In European merger practice, the exact delineation of future product markets has at times been relatively relaxed, allowing the Commission to focus on maintaining competing R&D sources. But the European Commission has occasionally had difficulties establishing impact on the future market structure. A regime that requires the authority to show that a dominant position will be achieved on a future product market, as did the former European merger regulation, is unlikely to grasp all anti-competitive effects relating to innovation. This is not least apparent where the negative effects asserted relate to R&D assets used for a variety of as yet undefined products (the setting of *Ciba-Geigy/Sandoz* FTC 1997, EU 1996).[55] In addition, it should be noted that, unless the parties are powerful in current markets, the Commission only tends to consider overlaps from R&D projects at advanced stages of develop-

---

[53] Evans, David S. & Schmalensee, Richard, 'Some Economic Aspects of Antitrust Analysis in Dynamically Competitive Industries', *NBER Working Paper*, no. 8268, 2001, p. 47; OFT, *Innovation and Competition policy*, Economic Discussion Paper 3, Report prepared for the Office of Fair Trading by Charles River Associates, 2002, p. 7.

[54] For example, to prove anti-competitive effects in the innovation market context it should not suffice to show a 'concentrated' market. Various other parameters (uncertainty, incentive mechanisms etc.) must be evaluated in order to predict competitive effects where also the potentially large efficiencies, foremost in innovation, must be factored in. See sections 6.1. and 6.2.

[55] The potential use of the innovation market approach in these circumstances has also been acknowledged in economic policy reviews. See, e.g., OFT, *supra*, note 53, pp. 130 *et seq.*

ment.[56] This is probably due to the fact that future dominance would otherwise be hard to establish.

The potential need to consider combinations in terms of R&D structure and long-term strategies, as well as the inherent difficulties involved in such an assessment, has been acknowledged by the Commission. In a submission to an OECD best practice roundtable it stated:[57]

> In relation to the long term strategies parties may have when agreeing on a merger, an analysis, only taking into account a snapshot of today's market situation (or when assessing pipeline products perhaps a future period of three years) may be considered as unsatisfactory. On the other hand it appears difficult if not impossible to predict the economic success of future products, especially if they are in early stages of development. Market shares may change quickly in [the pharmaceutical] sector as long as enough companies have the capacity to develop new products and to bring them successfully onto the market.

If a transaction might affect the conditions and capacities for developing new products, this should be relevant for antitrust analysis. Apart from offering an apt method for forecasting competition in future product markets, the innovation market approach could then be used to analyse the competitive effects of a transaction in broader R&D terms (such as speed, scope and variety), allowing the impact on future product markets to become a secondary, sometimes even implicit, effect. Realizing the inherent difficulties in such an analysis, not least the lack of general indicators for anti-competitive market power, the authorities must use this power with prudence. But economics by no means invalidate the analysis per se.[58] Such a use of the innovation market concept would fit well into the antitrust law system at large and finds support in recent case law from the US and EU authorities. It also corresponds strikingly well

---

56 Reviewing mergers in the pharmaceutical industry, the Commission typically focuses on phase III products unless the parties are dominant on current markets. But for example in *Glaxo Wellcome/SmithKline Beecham* (EU 2000) the Commission analysed pipeline products in phases I and II for a market where GW had a strong market position.

57 OECD, *Competition and Regulation Issues in the Pharmaceutical Industry*, Roundtable in June 2000, Paris, 2001, p. 345.

58 For example, where competition takes place *for* a market rather than *on* a market (e.g. owing to economies of scale and network effects) it is argued that competition analysis should focus on whether the practice can 'harm competition in the innovative activity related to a future product market, rather than whether competition in the market will be restricted': Europe Economics, *The Development of Analytical Tools for Assessing Market Dynamics in the Knowledge Based Economy*, Report to the European Commission, (2003), p. 77; available at http://europa.eu.int/comm/enterprise/library/lib-competition/doc/analytical_tools_final_report.pdf (last visited 3 March 2005).

to a model presented in a recent study of competition policy in dynamic markets. Although the report, written for the European Commission by an independent economics consultancy, is rather negative regarding the innovation market approach,[59] their suggested model for merger analysis (Figure 5.1) incorporates the very same elements as does the innovation market deployed in practice.[60]

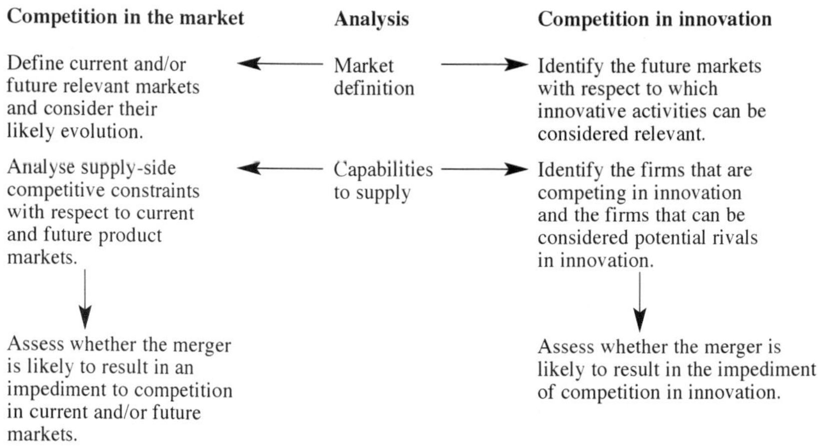

Figure 5.1 Merger analysis in dynamic markets

5.4 DEFINING INNOVATION MARKETS

> In theory, market definition involves identifying the nontrivial constraints on the ability of firms to exercise market power and evaluating whether these constraints are sufficient to prevent consumer harm from a particular business practice or combination. In practice, market definition involves determining whether particular firms are in or out of the market and therefore involves determining a bright line that defines the boundaries of the market.[61]

---

[59] See section 3.4. The report does not contain any analysis of the innovation market approach as deployed in practice.

[60] The figure is recreated from Europe Economics, *supra*, note 58, p. 85. Here it is further stated that '[a]lthough the two dimensions of the merger assessment can conceptually be considered separately, in practice they are the joint outcome of the same process of analysis of the available evidence'.

[61] Lutz, Alyssa A. & Stiroh, Lauren J., 'The Relevant Market in Intellectual Property/Antitrust Litigation', 658 *Practising Law Institute – Patents, Copyrights, Trademarks, and Literary Property Course Handbook Series* 75, 86 (2001).

Gilbert and Sunshine allege that '[t]he boundaries of an innovation market are typically broad, usually encompassing the world and often including products that, if defined at the goods level, would bc in multiple product markets. Goods markets are often more local because of the need for local distribution assets, regulatory barriers, etc'.[62] They exemplify this with the *GM/ZF* case (DOJ 1993) where the innovation market was determined to be worldwide and included all improvements for heavy-duty truck and bus automatic transmissions. The goods markets were application-specific national (US) markets, such as automatic transmissions for intra-city buses. GM and ZF were found to be actual competitors in only two application-specific markets in the US, and ZF was not a potential entrant into any other market. By the use of the innovation market approach, analysing the worldwide market for technical innovation of such transmissions, it was possible to detect anti-competitive effects that would have been missed by focusing on product markets alone.[63]

5.4.1 Reference to Future Products

The case law exposition suggests that the definition of innovation markets usually is not that broad. Since the competitive restraints that affect firms' behaviour and decision making depend on the particular economic context, the market delineation should follow industry characteristics and market conditions in the particular case. When a transaction affects R&D directed at a specific new product, the analysis also tends to be directed at this. Competing R&D is then identified on the basis of the particular products that may be the future outflow.

Generally, when parties assess the value (price, costs and turnover) of potential future products, this is affected by the degree of substitution between such products. Consequently, for strategic activities in the R&D process, these variables are also important motivators: for example, when deciding to merge or combine certain R&D projects. As the likelihood and level of such substitution is part of corporate decision making and is the key variable for future product market competition, it should be reflected in the relevant market for competing R&D.

This more narrow approach also corresponds to the definition of innovation

---

62 Gilbert, Richard J. & Sunshine, Steven C., 'The Use of Innovation Markets: A Reply to Hay, Rapp, and Hoerner', 64 *Antitrust Law Journal* 75, 81 (1995).

63 Gilbert and Sunshine also maintained that the innovation market analysis thus 'may find anticompetitive effects in markets where the merging firms are neither actual nor potential competitors'. Often, however, one of the claimed merits of the innovation market approach is that it focuses on actual R&D competition rather than potential product market competition.

markets in both the US guidelines and the EU guidelines for horizontal cooperation. It is natural to examine an R&D joint venture with regard to the product or technology to be developed and the competing actors or R&D projects. Yet, following this reasoning, the question of which R&D projects to include in the market (constituting competitive restraints) must depend on how precisely the future products may be characterised. The market definition depends on the stage the R&D has reached at the time the transaction takes place. Where the future product market is reasonably close, the likelihood of R&D success and product launch is promising and the future product characteristics are already fairly well determined, a narrow approach seems warranted.

In some cases the market has been very narrowly defined. In the *Sensormatic* decision (FTC 1995), Commissioner Azcuenaga agreed with the majority that the relevant market involved competition in R&D, but dissented against too narrow a market definition, both with regard to the technologies included and the geographical delimitation. In this case the market included R&D directed towards 'disposable labels developed or used for source labelling' and processes to make them. Commissioner Azcuenaga reminded her colleagues about the FTC's burden of proof regarding the relevant product market and maintained that 'distinguishing research and development of source labelling from other improvements in EAS [electronic article surveillance] systems may be difficult or impossible'. The relevant market, in her view, should not have been limited to R&D in source labelling but should have comprised R&D in EAS systems and components. The chosen definition may indicate that the primary concern was the particular future product market, yet, even if that was the case, Azcuenaga's arguments could be valid, particularly since there are indications that the FTC was also concerned about future product quality. Without further assessment, source labelling cannot be treated as separate from other improvements in EAS. Only if the differences in the resulting products are such that the EAS market is split into distinct submarkets could the R&D analysis also track this. Even if the R&D under scrutiny is limited to specific projects and future products, it is crucial for markets where technology is central that competition is seen in a broad and dynamic sense. This may best be achieved by using a broad definition of competition rather than a narrow market definition.[64]

In pharmaceutical cases the market usually consists of competing R&D for particular products. That holds both for cases where the resulting products will compete with existing products such as in *GW/SB* (EU 2000) *Amgen/Immunex*

---

[64] Charles River Associates, *Report on Multiparty Licensing*, Report to the European Commission, (2003), pp. 46f; available at http://europa.eu.int/comm/competition/ antitrust/legislation/multiparty_licensing.pdf (last visited 11 October 2004).

(FTC 2002) *Pfizer/Pharmacia* (FTC and EU 2003) *Boston Scientific Corp.* (FTC 1995) and *Wright Medical* (FTC 1995), and where the R&D is directed towards completely new products as in *Roche/Genentech* (FTC 1990), *Upjohn/Pharmacia* (EU 1995), *Pfizer/Warner-Lambert* (FTC 2000) and *Genzyme/Novazyme* (FTC 2004). This is quite natural since pipeline products then provide a picture of current R&D and future product market developments in the short to medium term. The relevant R&D is sometimes very narrowly defined since different products, although potentially treating the same disease, may have different characteristics and use.[65]

In European merger decisions where the typical R&D analysis expressly aims at future product markets, the third-level ATC classification has become something of a standard for the Commission's market definitions. In view of the uncertainty involved in this kind of R&D, the Commission has mostly focused on overlaps in product development that have reached phase III clinical trials. However, if the parties are already strong in existing markets, pipeline products in earlier stages of development will also be analysed and possibly subject to remedies.[66] In US merger control, the authorities have been more willing to go further back in the R&D process even without current product market dominance.[67]

When considering combinations at an early stage of development, there is generally substantial uncertainty regarding the characteristics of the resulting products, the likelihood of success and the properties of future markets. When assessing the possible anti-competitive effects of a market practice, a broader perspective ought to be taken, which takes into account the restraints on corporate decision making (and therefore the competitive effects that could result). Thus, in deciding whether to stop or delay the development of a second product

65 To correctly define markets pharmaceuticals is particularly difficult, since a market (defined by the level of substitution) based on the therapeutic indication could be modified by mechanisms of action, therapeutic profiles, side effects, administration methods etc: Morse, Howard M., 'Product Market Definition in the Pharmaceutical Industry', 71 *Antitrust Law Journal* 633, 643f., 676 (2003).

66 In *Glaxo Wellcome/SmithKline Beecham* (EU 2000) the Commission assessed R&D effects in the area of asthma, in two dimensions. The Commission considered the combination of existing GW products and SB pipeline products in phase I and phase II development. The Commission concluded that there was 'no risk of eliminating actual R&D competition between SB and GW', but still considered that the merger would lead to a reduction of potential competition on existing markets. Owing to the credibility and timing of competing pipeline products, the Commission nevertheless concluded that the elimination of potential competition would not be likely further to strengthen GW's position. In *Amgen/Immunex* (FTC 2002), the FTC intervened in the acquisition by a current dominant entity of a potentially competing product in phase I (although 'only' mandating a licence).

67 *American Home Products* (FTC 1995) and *Genzyme/Novazyme* (FTC 2004).

– or, perhaps less dramatically, when downsizing the priority and budget of that development – a broader category of competing projects could constitute restraining factors.[68] For example, it may not be known until the last stages of development what the relevant future product market for a potential drug will be. This implies that different R&D programmes directed at treating a certain disease could, at an early level of development, be ideal competitors in the sense that they exert competitive pressure on each other in the R&D process, even though it later may turn out that the resulting drugs appeal differently to different segments.

Thus, if an analysis aims at assessing whether the parties may have an incentive anti-competitively to decrease R&D or affect overall R&D conditions, it may not be optimal to identify competing R&D programmes by reference to narrowly defined future product markets. Although the authorities have indeed often identified and assessed competing R&D as that directed towards specific future products, in some cases substantially broader markets have been defined, this both in US case law and in European practice.

In the European *Ciba-Geigy/Sandoz* assessment (EU 1996), the Commission maintained that '[i]nsofar as research and development must be assessed in terms of importance for future markets, the relevant product market must, . . . be defined in a less clear-cut manner than in the case of existing markets'. This indicates a partial shift. While being dependent on some identification of a future product market, the particular market definition requirements are lessened when emphasis is put on the conditions in R&D, in a broad sense, rather than the resulting future product market directly.

In *Glaxo Wellcome/SmithKline Beecham* (EU 2000), the Commission analysed the area of treatment for COPD in two dimensions. They first looked at the effects on the innovation market in a broad sense, including the incentives and abilities for the parties to reduce current R&D efforts, as well as the overall R&D potential of this area. This was followed by a more narrow analysis of the future effects on an existing product market. Such a practice could be a way of scrutinizing the effects of combined R&D efforts more closely since it allows for the separation of genuine innovation conditions from near-future product market conditions. This is not a merely semantic exercise. When analysing general conditions on the COPD innovation market, the Commission included a variety of COPD R&D programmes at different stages

---

68 See Kattan, Joseph, 'Antitrust Analysis of Technology Joint Ventures: Allocative Efficiency and the Rewards of Innovation', 61 *Antitrust Law Journal* 937, 954 (1993), maintaining that '[i]ntermediate research may also involve a broader group of competitors than advanced product development, particularly in markets in which technological change is reasonably foreseeable'.

in the R&D process,[69] that is, a long-term general assessment of the innovation potential in a therapeutic area. In comparison, when analysing potential product market effects, only phase III compounds aimed at second-line therapies were considered. Thus a potential competition analysis was conducted as well, even if it was carried out by assessing competing R&D efforts along the lines of the innovation market concept. As a consequence, although the remaining R&D programmes would constitute important constraints of market power in both the general innovation market and the product market, the former was considered competitive whereas the latter required precautionary remedies.

According to this line of argument, is it appropriate, in a case like *Genzyme/Novazyme* (FTC 2004), to limit the market to equivalent research projects for enzyme-replacement treatment for Pompe disease? The legal assessment was aimed at discovering incentives for reduced scope or pace of product development, including that of a second, plausibly superior, product. Alternative therapies, albeit with different mechanisms of action, would plausibly constrain the parties in such a case. While other relevant R&D in the particular case seems to have been at an even earlier, conceptual, stage, and not likely to exert any particular constraining force even at the R&D level, the relevant market in this kind of situation should be able to include such projects and their possible impact.[70]

To sum up, in the guidelines, the innovation market concept is expressed in terms of competing R&D for particular new or improved products or technologies. The expected outcome sets the boundaries of the relevant market. Yet what R&D to include in the relevant innovation market is dependent on how well the characteristics of the future products or technologies can be determined. This uncertainty will most often relate to the stage in the R&D process at which the analysis is conducted. With greater uncertainty regarding future overlaps, a broader category of R&D will discipline the actors, thus qualifying for inclusion in the relevant innovation market.

---

[69] Different compounds acting through different mechanisms aimed at both first and second line treatment and at substantially different phases of development (I–III).

[70] According to Genzyme's website for Pompe disease (www.pompe.com) there is gene therapy research being conducted at 'early stages of investigation'. This approach would correct Pompe disease by introducing a working copy of the relevant gene into the body 'so that, theoretically, the body can begin to generate sufficient quantities of functioning [enzyme] on its own'. In addition, attempts with bone marrow transplantation had not been successful, but limited data suggest next-generation techniques could be more effective. (Website last visited 11 October 2004.)

5.4.2 Reference to Firm Capabilities or Technologies

Gilbert and Sunshine's conclusion about broad innovation markets may find support in cases like *GM/ZF* (DOJ 1993) where both parties are active in current product or technology markets and the analysis relates to innovation in these markets. It applies also in the *Montedison* and *Montecatini* cases (FTC 1995, EU 1994), *Lockheed Martin* (DOJ 1998) *Halliburton* (DOJ 1999) and the EU decisions in *Optical Fibres* (EU 1986), *Crown Cork & Seal* (EU 1995). The common link is that the parties are currently active in a concentrated product market where innovation is an important competition aspect, and where the incumbent firms are protected by heavy barriers to entry. The parties are vertically integrated, which is why the product market actors are also the providers of innovation in various inputs to the finalized products or services (otherwise potentially provided by upstream suppliers). The conditions for competition in innovation may then be analysed in a broader perspective, relating to different segments or aspects of the market, as part of, or as a supplement to, the product market analysis. Even so, the innovation market is seldom broader than the product market.

Also when the relevant R&D relates to existing product markets, it is sometimes the continued development of particular products or technologies that is in focus. Nevertheless, the analysis does not necessarily relate to particular R&D projects, but to innovation competition in a more general sense, as in *Digital* (FTC 1998) (Alpha microprocessors and technology), *Intel* (FTC 1999) (certain microprocessor technologies), *Microsoft III* (D.C. Cir. 2001) (web browsers and java technology), *Microsoft* (EU 2004) (group server operating systems and media players).

As seen in the merger context, R&D analysis may supplement a current product market analysis, investigating whether the parties control specific assets and characteristics that, if combined, would diminish the role of innovation as a competitive force in the market in question. Similar results could occur if a joint venture is set up to carry out substantial R&D that previously has been, or could have been, conducted by the parents individually. Whether competition at any level may be threatened depends on the parents' market position with regard both to current products and to R&D. Firms often cooperate through joint ventures in the development of particular new products or processes and the analysis may then explicitly address R&D regarding this specific purpose (5.4.1).

But there is another important development of the innovation market concept. Where innovation markets are confined to the continued development of existing products or competing R&D for particular future products, there is still an R&D analysis with static characteristics. This implies that the future products must be identifiable. When a market practice affects inputs that can be deemed necessary for the development or introduction of a range of potential future products, that bottleneck in itself is of the utmost relevance for a dynamic competition analysis. It could ultimately entail the creation of a technology base (through merger, joint venture, licensing agreement and so on), access to which could be essential in order to develop products and compete on various downstream markets. Typically, this relates to the unified control over key inputs in the form of research assets, in the form of intellectual property rights and know-how, without access to which firms would not be able to (fully) develop the area and provide competition.

In *Ciba-Geigy/Sandoz* (FTC 1997), the FTC defined and analysed several R&D markets for future products. However, the FTC also defined a broader market for overall gene therapy R&D and technology. Apart from the merging parties, there were a number of firms conducting pioneering research on various applications in the area. The area was very attractive for R&D, considering the vast technological and commercial opportunities. However, the merging parties controlled unmatchable IPR portfolios, the combination of which would allow them to command the transformation of basic gene therapy research into marketed products. Since product development by third parties would require a licence to this key technology, the merger would create a bottleneck that would seriously diminish the incentives and abilities of third parties to conduct gene therapy R&D. The innovation potential for gene therapy would thus be threatened.

To some extent the defined market appears to be a technology market, where the two parties were rival firms, offering licences to key technology. The FTC considered that the parties, prior to the merger, had incentives to licence their technologies and collaborate with other companies. Since it was not fully known what future applications to expect, it seems likely that different technology licensing arrangements were still to be defined.[71] Also, the parties' patent portfolios consisted of a variety of patents and patent applications of uncertain breadth and validity, covering alternative technologies and approaches to R&D. According to the wording in the US IP Guidelines and EU Technology Transfer Guidelines, a technology market consists of the intellectual property *that is* licensed and the close substitutes hereto.[72] Hence some

71 'Before the merger, if developers of potential gene therapies were unable to reach agreement with Sandoz [. . .], in many instances they could have worked with Ciba and used other technologies [. . .].' Separate Statement of Chairman Robert Pitofsky, and Commissioners Janet D. Steiger, Roscoe B. Starek and Christine A. Varney.

72 The US 1995 IP Guidelines, §3.2.2; US 2000 Competitor Collaboration Guidelines, §3.32b; EU 2001 Horizontal Cooperation Guidelines, §48; and EU 2004 Technology Transfer Guidelines, §22.

current licensing transactions seem to be required.[73] In addition, the parties constituted rival centres for other kinds of arrangement, particularly various joint ventures which allowed third parties to develop their research in collaboration with either Ciba-Geigy or Sandoz. Such more far-reaching collaboration could satisfy needs that a mere technology licence could not fulfil. A pure technology market approach would plausibly not have captured such a variety of future licence requirements and the additional collaboration forms. Moreover, such a market would not have captured the lessened competition in innovation between the parties, such as the likely elimination or slowdown of development projects.

Just as with a technology market, however, it must be assessed to what extent the control of this bottleneck forecloses third parties and protect its holders from competition, that is, any possibilities for supply or demand substitution, when determining the relevant market. In *Ciba-Geigy/Sandoz*, gene therapy technology was a large, unexplored area, and one expected to provide a range of applications that would involve products very different from those derived from current technologies. Since the whole area could be controlled by the merged entity, third parties would have nowhere else to turn.

In *Pasteur Mérieux/Merck* (EU 1994), the far-reaching cooperation between two leading firms, pooling their current vaccine antigens and technologies and teaming up regarding future R&D in the field, would limit competition between the parties for an 'extremely broad range' of research for potential future vaccines. For such future vaccines and technologies, third parties would not be able to obtain key inputs from the joined entity. Nevertheless, the important difference from Ciba-Geigy is that the investigation revealed a number of other entities that could serve this need: a variety of firms, research centres and academic institutions all qualified as potential providers of future technologies. Thus, without identifying the potential future products, it was possible to assess both a lessening of competition between the parties in a technology area, and the likely emergence of other providers for critical inputs in that same area.

In these cases the competitive capabilities of the firms are not tied to specific products under development. The analysis is limited rather to assets controlled by the firms, which may provide them with unique potentials to develop a technology base and to bar third parties from the same area.[74]

The relevant innovation market for a patent pool would be analysed in much the same way. If the pool consisted of essential patents for an industry

---

[73] See also Newberg, *supra*, note 39, p. 127: 'If there are current market transactions in intellectual property used in R&D efforts, those current transactions may justify defining a technology market as well as, or instead of, an innovation market.'

[74] Similar consideration is found in *Lockheed Martin* (DOJ 1998).

standard, it would effectively foreclose all outside competition for products derived from the standard, since by definition essential patents do not have competing alternatives. Other licensing terms, such as grantbacks, would affect licensees in various downstream markets, but all would be analysed with regard to the standard. Analysing the availability or future potential of competing industry standards can be straightforward, since these are normally the result of a rather transparent process.

A closer evaluation would be necessary for less substantial pools, perhaps including some blocking and otherwise complementary patents, access to which the pooling parties wish to restrict. The relevant competitive restraints, which would discipline the pooling parties and constitute an alternative source for third parties, would be competing patents. Even though the substitutability of the inputs investigated relate to their use, the relevant markets would not consist of the downstream applications. This is particularly true for areas under development, where a multitude of applications and future developments may be foreseen.[75]

To sum up, where the market practice does not relate to a particular R&D project, but a broader structural change in a market for existing products or technologies (such as a merger or a far-reaching joint venture), innovation analysis can be performed in broader terms. Scrutinizing the innovation process of the particular industry, the parties' strategic positions in that process and the specific assets and capabilities they control are an important element in the analysis of a transaction. Another category here relates to transactions that bring together assets access to which is critical for future R&D in a broader area. Rather than defining the relevant market in terms of the array of potential future applications, the relevant market is defined with reference to the technology base.

5.4.3 Geographical Delimitation

> For innovation markets, the logical presumption is that the relevant geographical market is the world (assuming that no trade or regulatory barriers would prevent R&D at particular locations).[76]

Both the FTC and the European Commission in the *Montedison* and

[75] 'In fact, in many cases analysis of potential exclusionary behaviour can be made more robust and transparent by identifying formally the access service that pertains to this potential exclusion and then defining the market for this service and analysing the competitive effects explicitly. This may be appropriate even if the access service is not seen as a traditional product in which there is trade' (Europe Economics, *supra*, note 58, p. 70).

[76] Gilbert & Sunshine, *supra*, note 13, pp. 594f.

Montecatini cases (FTC 1995, EU 1994) considered a global polypropylene technology market but more limited geographical markets for the production and sale of the products. This naturally also implies global competition in innovation for relevant technology.

In Europe, the Commission frequently maintains that R&D may be global and, at the least, EU-wide. But although innovation ought to be global, the Commission recognizes that other factors, such as intellectual property issues, may preclude such a global market. Frequently the FTC defines an area in which to analyse *the effects*, plainly the US. That does not mean that the geographical market with respect to R&D is necessarily the US, but it makes more obscure the authorities' analysis.

When the FTC has been explicit in its analysis, it has been surprisingly unwilling to include other parts of the world in the geographical dimension of its innovation markets. In *Sensormatic* (FTC 1995), Commissioner Azcuenaga disagreed with the geographical limitation, confining the market to the US and Canada. As intellectual property moves freely across international boundaries and foreign firms can license intellectual property without being established in the area, such geographical limitation seems erroneous. In the specific case, this narrow market excluded 'potentially important research activity of at least one European firm'. Such a narrow geographical limitation is also found in a number of pharmaceutical cases.[77] Most often R&D sources in the pharmaceutical sector are equated with those in the FDA approval process. This may however be correct if R&D projects that have not even entered the FDA approval process involve too much uncertainty or, because of the time-lags involved, do not constitute a sufficient constraint on the behaviour of incumbents in relevant innovation and product markets. The European process for the approval of pharmaceuticals is speedier than the US process, which may be why the Commission does not limit the analysis as strictly as the US authorities tend to do.[78]

In *Lockheed Martin* (DOJ 1998) the buyers – the Department of Defense and US military prime contractors performing on US military programmes – had not previously turned to any foreign producers in the face of a small but

---

[77] *Glaxo Wellcome* (FTC 1995), *Baxter* (FTC 1997). 'The FTC's enforcement actions in this industry reflect the view that the U.S. is the relevant geographic market for the sale of drugs, based upon the need for FDA approval to sell drugs in this country. The relevant geographic market for pharmaceutical R&D may be worldwide, but, in the later phases of development, the FTC considers the relevant market to be the territory covered by the regulatory authority that will approve a new drug' (Starek, Roscoe B., 'International Cooperation in Antitrust Enforcement and other International Antitrust Developments'), Prepared Remarks before 'Antitrust 1997' Conference, 1996; available at www.ftc.gov (last visited 30 September 2004).

[78] See Temple Lang, *supra*, note 50, p. 762.

significant, and non-transitory, price increase by domestic suppliers, and were unlikely to do so in the future. Thus the US was considered the relevant geographical market. The price test was also used for innovation, although the question ought to be whether the parties would go outside the US in face of superior future innovation by foreign suppliers. Similarly, in *GenCorp* (FTC 2004), US export regulations and national security issues made it less attractive to buy foreign suppliers and led the authority to limit the geographical market to the US.

To this may be added the recent dispute on the geographical limitation in *Oracle* (N.D. Cal. 2004). The DOJ argued that, although the relevant business software systems were developed by global firms, and could presumably be offered worldwide, other aspects of the complete product, most importantly the highly specialized services provided, on site, along with the technological systems, made entry into new geographical areas difficult. The relevant geographical area should thus be the US.

Without making too much of this particular case, the question remains what such entry barriers would do to an innovation analysis. Even if services and other support relationships between vendors and customers are part of the 'overall' product, technology can still travel. In *Oracle*, the district court held that this high-technology market should be considered worldwide, similar to the markets for computers or copy machines, even if other services such as installation and maintenance are combined with sales of the products.

5.5 GENERAL CONDITIONS FOR INNOVATION ANALYSIS

5.5.1 Preconditions for Intervention

In the US, both the IP Guidelines and the Competitor Collaboration Guidelines declare that '[t]he Agencies will delineate an innovation market only when the capabilities to engage in the relevant research and development can be associated with specialized assets or characteristics of specific firms'. The EU Horizontal Cooperation Guidelines state that, in order to assess effects on innovation competition, R&D should be structured in such a way that the number of alternative R&D poles can be identified at an early stage. This is also in line with the Gilbert & Sunshine model for merger enforcement.

Much of the early debate on the innovation market concept concerned these issues. It was feared that the agencies would, in practice, ignore the prerequisite of specialized assets or characteristics, and apply the innovation market approach in all kinds of cases. This was especially feared as, in early innovation market cases, the FTC did not identify what assets had triggered the innovation market challenge.[79] Suspicions were also reinforced by the fact that the Department of Justice in the *GM/ZF* case (DOJ 1993)[80] approximated market shares in the innovation market 'by the number of units produced worldwide by each manufacturer of medium and heavy automatic transmissions for commercial and military vehicles'. However, GM/ZF is an early case, and the US Agencies have developed their approaches, taking some of the early criticism into account.

In recent case law, market shares have not been attributed in innovation markets. The analysis is rather an assessment of concentration in other terms. An inventory of relevant R&D actors and projects is made and their competitive significance is assessed. In order to do this, information concerning the attractiveness and uniqueness of different technologies, access to financial and human resources, stage of development, regulatory approvals already obtained and known problems and delays, and so on, provide an overall picture.[81]

How the authorities evaluate these more qualitative aspects, which affect the competitive advantages of different R&D sources, is rather hard to tell from decisions, complaints and other public documents. But, generally, references are made to resourceful competitors, scope of patent portfolios, timing and attractiveness of technologies under development, all implying that these aspects are given weight, at least for the identification of relevant competitors.

Access to critical assets is also highlighted in the literature, since the risk of suppression of innovation is greatest when the merging or collaborating parties account for a large share of these inputs.[82] Moreover, timing has been emphasized since first-mover advantages in R&D may lead to strong competition with a view to getting an early lead, as when cost advantages are achieved through learning by doing. The presence of network effects and industry standards has also been acknowledged as an indicator of market power in R&D.[83]

The bulk of the case law suggests that transactions may be faced with a challenge based on the innovation market concept when R&D is essential for the ability to compete in a market (existing or potentially existing), when that R&D is very concentrated, and when there are substantial barriers to entry into

---

79 Rapp, Richard T., 'The Misapplication of the Innovation Market Approach to Merger Analysis', 64 *Antitrust Law Journal* 19, 37 (1995).

80 *United States v. General Motors Corp.*, Civ. No. 93-530 (D. Del. filed Nov. 16, 1993).

81 According to both US and EU Guidelines, the credibility of the R&D sources is assessed in terms of nature, scope, size, timing, and access to know-how/patents or other specialized assets: EU 2001 Horizontal Cooperation Guidelines, §51; US 2000 Competitor Collaboration Guidelines, §4.3.

82 See, e.g., Kattan, *supra*, note 68, p. 954.

83 OECD, *supra*, note 35, pp. 19f.

the R&D and/or the product market. To this should be added the (potentially fewer) instances where the innovation market analysis may apply to technology bases, when the authorities evaluate the possibility that a transaction or practice would create control over a powerful bottleneck. Any investigation would focus on the identification of key assets, access to which could turn out to be essential to further innovation in the industry, and would evaluate the incentives for competition between and within such technology bases. If R&D assets are spread, innovation incentives are maintained and foreclosure of third-party R&D is unlikely.

Innovation market analysis is not confined to biotech products, pharmaceuticals and the like where R&D cycles are very lengthy and transparent. In markets where entry barriers such as network effects, switching costs and scale economies in production protect the position of incumbent firms, the maintenance of a minimum level of independent R&D may be vital. When applied to this kind of context, innovation analysis usually supplements a more traditional product market analysis. Intervention based on innovation analysis could be relevant in markets for next-generation telecom systems, computer electronics and even some software, whereas it is unlikely in other markets for telecom applications and software where comparable entry barriers do not exist.[84]

In markets where innovation is taking fast and unpredictable turns, providing opportunities for newcomers with new and enhanced technology, the authorities are not likely to raise any obstacles based on this kind of R&D analysis. If opportunities are rich and entry barriers low, not only will prospective competition analysis be largely uncertain, but this uncertainty will also keep actors innovating as long as there are profits to make. This kind of industry has been described as a market where the suppliers compete with their own

---

[84] In *United States v. Compuware, Corp. and Viasoft, Inc* (D.D.C filed Oct. 29, 1999) the DOJ claimed that 'less innovation in product development' would result from an acquisition in two software markets (test/debug and fault management software). The dominant firm, accounting for more than 60 and 80 per cent in the markets, respectively, would acquire the closest and potentially most threatening competitor (one of only two rivals). It was noted that the transaction was the latest in a series, where Compuware had acquired competitors 'only to cease sales and upgrades for those products after the acquisitions'. The market was described as mature with 'relatively static demand', making entry unattractive. In *Aspen Technology, Inc.*, Docket No. 9310 (2004), the FTC blocked an acquisition in 'process engineering simulation software' that would eliminate the closest competitor and leave post-merger market shares in the range of 68–80 per cent worldwide. The acquisition was likely to result in price increases and reduced levels of innovation. Innovation market analysis may also be potentially important in the control of standard setting and patent pools. See, e.g., Case No. IV/M042 – *Alcatel/Telettra*, OJ L 122/48 (1991) regarding the role of the ETSI in limiting barriers to entry in telecommunication systems.

installed base of durable products. That is, when the physical lifetime of the products is significantly longer than the technological life, continued improvements in functionality and performance are needed to convince the buyers not to be satisfied with their current product, but rather to desire new generations of goods.[85] This keeps the R&D incentives up and often leads to healthy R&D competition.

5.5.2 Entry

According to the US IP Guidelines, potential competitors on an innovation market should be those firms that, within two years, could acquire the assets necessary for the particular R&D, in response to a small but significant non-transitory reduction in R&D. This definition is analogous to the mainstream entry analysis conducted in product market analysis (with 'reduction in R&D' replacing 'increase in price'). Such identification and assessment would generally be very hard to conduct, particularly where no product currently exists.[86] R&D competition, in contrast to competition on ordinary product markets, is not typically an outward-oriented activity, but is rather a more or less secret business where substantial resources are even spent just to impede information from reaching the public domain. The FTC has also asserted that entry analysis will be conducted in a pragmatic manner, stating that the timeliness of entry should be considered in all the circumstances of the particular case, so as to identify entrants who would counteract anti-competitive conduct. Similarly, the sufficiency of entry might depend on whether entry would involve the same or a different research track and whether the potential entry would involve resource commitments sufficient to make the effort likely to succeed.[87]

Still, the nature of R&D competition makes the identification of innovation market participants difficult – particularly future entrants.[88] And case law suggest that the approach is largely confined to markets where participants are reasonably well known and the (un)likelihood of timely and sufficient entry into relevant R&D can, to a large extent, be determined even without such a precise identification.

Since innovation market intervention is possible where the relevant R&D

---

[85] Kattan, Joseph, 'After the IP Guidelines: Trends in Intellectual Property Antitrust Enforcement', 11 *Antitrust* 26, 27. (Summer, 1997).

[86] See Landman, Lawrence B., 'Innovation and the Structure of Competition', 81 *Journal of the Patent and Trademark Office Society* 728, 738f. (1999).

[87] Federal Trade Commission, *Anticipating the 21st Century, Competition Policy in the New High-Tech, Global Marketplace*, 1996, Volume 1, Chapter 7, p. 39.

[88] Kattan, *supra*, note 85, pp. 26f.

is associated with some specialized assets or characteristics of specific firms, it also follows that entry into relevant R&D is limited. Intellectual property rights, along with substantial know-how and experience, often constitute specialized assets and relevant R&D is consequently a characteristic of specific firms only. In industries such as information technology and telecommunications, network effects may limit entry. Moreover, entry into these markets may be contingent on regulatory notifications and approvals in several steps (such as FDA and EMEA approvals for pharmaceuticals), making the process even more lengthy, expensive and transparent. Even if the authorities cannot have full knowledge about all potentially relevant R&D that is being, or will be, conducted in a particular case, they can assume that the parties' competitive behaviour is constrained by R&D sources that can be identified.[89]

89 Federal Trade Commission, *supra*, note 87, Volume 1, Chapter 7, pp. 38f. The R&D could have reached such a level of development that public authorities are involved (such as pharmaceuticals) but there are other industries where patents and even scientific publication may provide sufficient ground for an entry analysis (biotechnology).

6. The competition assessment

This chapter deals with the conclusions regarding competition that might be drawn from analysing markets, actors, assets, technologies and conduct. It thereby touches the centre of the debate on the proper application of antitrust policy in innovative markets.

In *Microsoft III* (D.C. Cir 2001), the company maintained that, regardless of the market structure, it did not behave like a monopolist since software competition is uniquely dynamic. Therefore the company suggested a new rule for this industry: that monopoly power should be proved *directly* by examining the company's behaviour and not by structural evidence. But the Court of Appeals rejected Microsoft's argument, stating that, even if the market happens to be uniquely dynamic in the long term, it is still correct to apply a structural approach in order to determine whether the company faces competition in the short term.[1]

The antitrust laws presumably mandate intervention to preserve competition in the short term, even if technological development and market forces in the long run would probably have reinstated competition. Nevertheless, caution is warranted in the application of static tools for protecting dynamic processes.

In this chapter, the scope for anti-competitive effects of lessened competition in the innovation process will be investigated. Section 6.1 covers the assessment of different kinds of transactions at the various market levels outlined in section 5.2.[2] Moreover, since transactions that relate to R&D are often associated with efficiencies, section 6.2 examines the role of efficiencies in relation to the innovation market concept. Efficiency considerations may not only outweigh anti-competitive effects and make a transaction allowable, they also play an important role in designing adequate remedies where there are anti-competitive effects. This section also covers another aspect of antitrust analysis, the time perspective. Particularly since transactions often involve both large upfront expenditure and uncertainty regarding future developments, the appraisal of a particular agreement will depend upon whether it

1 *Microsoft III* (D.C. Cir. 2001), 253 F.3d 34, 57.

2 What was labelled Potential Future Markets in section 5.2 is here divided into 'Distant Future Markets' and 'Imminent Future Markets'.

is conducted before the formation or later in time. Finally, the application of innovation analysis to unilateral conduct in the light of some recent case law is commented on in section 6.3.

6.1 ANTI-COMPETITIVE EFFECT

6.1.1 Introduction

Given that competition, particularly in innovation, is difficult to measure whether by way of exact concentration rates or in terms of other, more qualitative, structural variables, a central question surrounding the innovation market concept has been how many competing sources of innovation, that is, R&D projects or entities in control of similar resources and capabilities, are required for an innovation market to be competitive. When delineating such a market, the US Competitor Collaboration Guidelines establish a safety zone if, after the transaction, four or more independent R&D entities remain.[3] Such an innovation market is thus considered competitive. At the same time the Guidelines underline that the innovation market safety zone does not apply to mergers. The European Horizontal Cooperation Guidelines suggest a similar approach, by maintaining that the analysis of innovation competition aims to assess whether there are a 'sufficient number of R&D poles left'.[4]

Based on the merger control experience, it has been concluded that antitrust intervention based on innovation competition typically involves transactions that reduce the number of independent research efforts from three to two or two to one.[5] As seen, for example, in *American Home Products* (FTC 1995) a reduction from three to two independent R&D tracks was found to diminish R&D competition. In *Upjohn/Pharmacia* (FTC 1996) the FTC found only 'a very small number' of firms in advanced stages of development. The FTC therefore concluded that the merger would eliminate direct and substantial R&D competition and that the number of R&D tracks could decrease if the parties did not have the incentive to continue the Pharmacia project. However, in *Pfizer/Warner-Lambert* (FTC 2000), *Halliburton* (DOJ 1999) and possibly *Baxter* (FTC 1997), the authorities found a lessening in R&D competition when moving from four to three independent R&D centres.

---

3 US 2000 Competitor Collaboration Guidelines, §4.3. This safety zone is thus more generous than that in the US 1995 IP Guidelines, §4.3, requiring five remaining innovation market participants.

4 EU 2001 Horizontal Cooperation Guidelines, §51.

5 Kattan, Joseph, 'Antitrust Considerations in Innovation-Driven Markets', 21 *Canada–United States Law Journal* 115, 118 (1995).

This practice has been taken to reflect a more aggressive attitude in the US, compared to European practices where the Commission has been considered less eager to find anti-competitive effects from fewer comparable R&D lines.[6]

The suggested American policy would broadly follow the lines proposed by the (then) Chairman of the FTC, William F. Baxter, in 1985.[7] When defining and evaluating R&D markets he suggested that the creation of an entity which does not control more than 33 per cent of the 'R&D-oriented assets in the field that is under consideration', should probably be allowed, at least if there were substantial economies of scale in R&D. Once down at 15 to 20 per cent of all R&D assets the transaction would be deemed benign. According to Baxter, this would boil down to a break point at 20–25 per cent, that is four or five (at least potentially) competing R&D sources in the field. This also finds support in one of the hypothetical 'case examples' provided in the US IP Guidelines.[8]

Still, both the seemingly stricter American innovation market policy and the European standards deserve further elaboration and analysis. As previously shown, the factual circumstances in which innovation analysis is applied are heterogeneous. Therefore any conclusions and evaluations regarding the state of law must be sensitive to the background of the cases. Based on the categorization in section 5.2, the case law presented in Chapter 4 will be further analysed to provide guidance as to when anti-competitive effects in innovation can be expected. These conclusions, based primarily on merger case law, are followed by observations regarding other kinds of transactions, these being mainly based on the antitrust authorities' guidelines.

6.1.2 Innovation in Current Product and Technology Markets

General observations and merger case law

When merging parties are active in a market where innovation is an important means of competition and where heavy barriers to entry protect the incumbent firms, the result of increased concentration may have effects on the innovative output, as it may on other competition variables. Competition in the product market will induce firms to outperform each other by various means, not least

---

[6] Landman, Lawrence B., 'Competing in the Global Pharmaceutical Industry: Innovation and Future Potential Competition', 2 *The Journal of Biolaw & Business* 29, 37 (1998); Temple Lang, John, 'European Community Antitrust Law: Innovation Markets and High Technology Industries', 20 *Fordham International Law Journal* 717, 761 (1997).

[7] Baxter, William F., 'The Definition and Measurement of Market Power in Industries Characterised by Rapidly Developing and Changing Technologies', 53 *Antitrust Law Journal* 717, 722 ff. (1985).

[8] US 1995 IP Guidelines, §3.2.3, example 4.

through successful development of products and services. In these instances innovation analysis may shed light on competitive conditions in the market, but will seldom be the decisive basis for intervention.[9] Conclusions about restricted competition in innovation typically follow from the same overall analysis as in other dimensions of competition. In other words, where mergers have been blocked, this would typically have been warranted from a price competition perspective too.[10]

As usual, there are no magic market share thresholds above which a merger in an oligopolistic market will substantially reduce competition.[11] In *Halliburton* (DOJ 1999), where four independent market participants/R&D sources would become three, the merged firm's share of the LWD oil drilling equipment market would be 45 per cent and the HHI index would have increased by almost 1000, to 3600. As seen in the cases in Chapter 4, where innovation market analysis has been used in conjunction to existing product markets, even higher post-merger market shares and concentration ratios have been indicated in the relevant product market.[12]

---

9 The differences between innovation and other means of competition, such as likelihood of collusion between oligopolists, may still be important. See, generally, the oligopoly discussions in Chapter 2 and Baumol, William J., *The Free-Market Innovation Machine: Analyzing the Growth Miracle of Capitalism,* Princeton University Press, Princeton, 2002.

10 In a survey of American merger cases between 1995 and 1999, it is concluded that, out of 47 cases in which innovation was mentioned as a competitive effect, such effects probably were central and necessary to the enforcement decision, in whole or in part, only in eight. According to the survey innovation probably was an important concern also in the other cases, but they could have been challenged for effects in existing product and services based on price effects in existing product market or by using the potential competition doctrine. In some additional cases innovation considerations resulted in broader remedies: Gilbert, Richard J. & Tom, Willard K., 'Is Innovation King at the Antitrust Agencies? The Intellectual Property Guidelines Five Years Later', 69 *Antitrust Law Journal* 43, 44, 51 (2001).

11 According to both EU and US horizontal merger guidelines, market shares and concentration indexes may be used to single out cases where anti-competitive effects are unlikely, possible or likely. Even if an anti-competitive effect can thus be expected, the analysis will cover other mitigating factors, such as entry and efficiencies.

12 In *Flow International* (DOJ 1994) the parties' joint market shares would exceed 90 per cent; in *Crown Cork* (EU 1995) the merged firm would control 60–70 per cent of the market; similarly in the *Montecatini* and *Montedison* cases (EU 1994, FTC 1995) post-merger market shares in the relevant technology market were calculated at 60–80 per cent and a rise in HHI by 2300 to 5100; in *GenCorp* (FTC 2004) the two viable competitors would merge; in *Digital* (FTC 1998) Intel had over 90 per cent of the market and would gain vertical control in respect of a small (1 per cent) but important competitor; and in *Lockheed Martin* (DOJ 1998) the number of R&D sources in the different markets would be reduced from 3 to 2 or from 2 to 1.

It is not surprising that antitrust authorities may challenge mergers between strong actors in an established, highly concentrated, oligopolistic market, alleging that reduced competition among the remaining actors would negatively affect market performance in more than the price dimension. The innovation market concept may here constitute a method of analysing the innovation dimension, rather than being an independent relevant market.

Sometimes, the effects of a merger in existing markets would be insufficiently assessed if innovation was not explicitly considered. In *Lockheed Martin* (DOJ 1998), the parties' unique capabilities to develop military aircrafts were at the heart of the government's intervention. It was maintained that losing the third source of development (Northrop) and leaving just the two firms that had dominated the previous public procurements in the market (Lockheed and Boeing) would reduce innovation competition. This was not dependent on any immediate new tenders for which the parties were competitors. It appears that the DOJ wanted to safeguard long-term innovation potential by maintaining diversity.[13]

Similarly, in the vertical setting between *Digital* and Intel (FTC 1998), analysis revealed that strategic control at the level of production (and thereby the feedback mechanism between manufacture and design), could have negative effects upstream in the innovation market where the parties were competitors. More generally, explicit innovation analyses add an important perspective. An investigation of R&D conditions may be central to correctly apprehending the particular market in terms of current competition and likely future technological developments. The importance of historical market shares may thus be more accurately evaluated. In this regard, innovation analysis is naturally linked to an entry analysis. The likelihood and timeliness of entry onto a dynamic market will often require identification and assessment of R&D actors and projects. When innovation takes place in long and transparent R&D cycles, the innovation market approach can cope with an entry analysis extending beyond a two-year horizon.

An elaborate innovation analysis also increases the authorities' possibilities of assessing specific effects of a transaction, for example where the parties are leading innovators and when they are particularly strong in certain R&D segments. Incumbent firms may be in a unique position to undertake R&D to

---

[13] Similar notions regarding the particular competitive force of a smaller market actor, although innovation aspects were not so highlighted, appear in the European decision in Case IV/M.877 – *Boeing/McDonnell Douglas*, OJ L 336/16 (1997), where McDonnell Douglas in spite of continuously decreasing market shares was considered to pressure prices and influence purchase conditions in the market for new large commercial aircraft.

improve the performance of their specialized products.[14] This is crucial for a full appreciation of the competitive effects of a merger, as well as for the question of adequate remedies.

It should also be remembered that an innovation market analysis can alleviate concerns that the long-term R&D potential (and thus long-term general competitiveness) of a market would be diminished. In *Glaxo Wellcome/SmithKline Beecham* (EU 2000) the analysis of COPD showed strong R&D competition and an attractive field for future R&D investment, which precluded the need for any R&D divestitures, although the merged firm both dominated the current market and was active in relevant R&D. Similarly, in *Tetra/Sidel* (CFI 2002) an investigation of the particular conditions for innovation led the court to conclude that the Commission's conclusions about lessened innovation incentives were not substantiated once the full economic context was taken into account.

To this category of cases can be added acquisitions by an incumbent firm of a potential entrant with a product or technology in the pipeline, which is expected to compete on the current market. If the merger involves an incumbent and a potential entrant with promising pipeline products, the competitive impact of the transaction may largely depend on innovation conditions, both on the current market and for potential entrants. Acquiring an entrant may reduce variety if the merged entity has incentives to stall the development or close the pipeline project, and may in any event restrict competition on the product market.

The authorities have intervened where an incumbent with high market shares has acquired an entrant with an important lead over other entrants in highly concentrated R&D.[15] In industries where the innovation market concept is typically applied, the authorities have extended the traditional standards for potential competition. While it is rational that these standards depend on the characteristics of the particular industry, the authorities sometimes seem to have extended the scope for intervention to such a degree that it can be doubted whether any anti-competitive effect was substantiated, in terms either

---

14 Kattan, Joseph, 'After the IP Guidelines: Trends in Intellectual Property Antitrust Enforcement', 11 *Antitrust* 26, 27 (Summer, 1997).

15 See *Boston Scientific* (FTC 1995) which, merged with *CVIS*, would have 90 per cent of current sales and also proposed to acquire the only entrant to the market, *SCIMED*. *Wright Medical* represented 95 per cent of current sales and acquired the new generation entrant in finger implants. *Pfizer* controlled 70–100 per cent of current sales of ED products and acquired two Pharmacia products in phase II and with pending patent infringement lawsuits threatening other potential entrants. *Cytyc* (FTC 2002) accounted for 93 per cent of the relevant market and acquired a strategic entrant with competing/complementary product.

of lessened incentives for continued innovation or of strengthened future market power.[16]

R&D joint ventures

Where parties to an R&D joint venture were already active in the relevant R&D, or if they could have been, there is cause to investigate further how this arrangement will affect competition. If the parties would not have been able to carry out the R&D independently, the joint R&D should not restrict competition.[17]

Analysis similar to that performed in the merger cases should take place if a joint venture is set up to take over its parents' R&D activities, as in *Pasteur Mérieux/Merck* (EU 1994). The parties' market positions in current product markets and relative strengths in R&D are relevant when assessing the likelihood of anti-competitive effects. Innovation market analysis may thus supplement current product market analysis, allowing an investigation of whether the parties control specific assets and characteristics which, if combined, would diminish the role of innovation as an important means of competition in the particular market.

While joint ventures may include such far-reaching arrangements, they usually constitute more limited exchanges or organizational collaborations. The cooperation is often directed at the development of particular products or processes only and the analysis should address relevant R&D for this purpose. When incumbent firms cooperate for non-drastic improvements in current products or technologies, current markets are the natural point of departure

---

[16] Both the insufficiency of competition from other potential entrants and the likelihood that the acquired product will reach the market can sometimes be questioned. See *Glaxo Wellcome/SmithKline Beecham* (EU 2000) where the acquisition of asthma products in phase I and II were considered to lessen potential competition (although alleviated by a large number of other potential entrants). Moreover, since GW was particularly strong in a COPD segment, the fact that both parties had a phase III product could, according to the Commission, strengthen the position of GW, although four other phase III products existed. In *Amgen/Immunex* (FTC 2002), the FTC intervened (with a licensing remedy) although the potential entrant's product was merely in phase I and two other firms were involved in R&D for similar (but not identical) products. In *Pfizer/Pharmacia* (FTC and EU 2003) the company dominated the ED market and had to divest two Pharmacia products in phase II, although two competitors (threatened with patent litigation) were about to launch competing products.

[17] EU 2001 Horizontal Cooperation Guidelines, §56; *Elopak/Metal Box-Odin*, OJ L 209/15 (1990). The European Commission has sometimes, however, gone rather far in treating resourceful companies as competitors for particular R&D. See Case No IV/32.363 – *KSB/Goulds/Lowara/ITT*, OJ L 19/25 (1991). Moreover, other conditions, particularly those relating to the exploitation of results, may still be considered restrictive of competition even if the parties' collaboration does not reduce competition in innovation.

also for innovation aspects. As in merger cases, a structured R&D analysis may nevertheless shed light on the innovation process and be vital for any assessment of incentives and competition effects.

According to the American guidelines, the analysis will include the parties' abilities and incentives to compete independently, which is largely determined by the degree of exclusivity and the duration of the collaboration. Also important to the market power assessment will be the timeliness, likelihood and sufficiency of entry by others as well as other market circumstances that may counteract anti-competitive harm.[18] R&D agreements may raise competitive concerns particularly 'when R&D competition is confined to firms with specialized characteristics or assets, such as intellectual property, or when a regulatory approval process limits the ability of late-comers to catch up with competitors already engaged in the R&D'. For example, if the parties have market power both in current markets and in R&D, they might consider the new R&D could 'cannibalize their supracompetitive earnings'.[19] Such anti-competitive effects lead to a reduced level of innovation: fewer products, delayed product launch and lower quality.

Similarly, the European Horizontal Cooperation Guidelines assert that anti-competitive innovation effects in existing markets are likely only if the parties are strong, entry is difficult and few alternative innovation activities exist. It would seem that such cooperation may restrict innovation by allowing the parties to control development and reduce the risk that they will be overtaken by a partner acting alone. The cooperation may not only reduce competition for the improved goods, and the assessment can also include the possibilities of spillover effects and collusion in the production and distribution of current products.

The scope of the joint venture is also an important factor. In practice, pure R&D cooperation is treated more leniently than collaborations extended into the post-innovation stages of production and marketing. The European authorities have developed a 'hierarchy of acceptability' depending on the extension of the R&D joint venture.[20] Although pure R&D collaboration will usually be allowed, both sets of guidelines make clear that competition in innovation and incentives to reduce R&D efforts will be investigated. Such agreements are only problematic if effective innovation competition is significantly

[18] US 2000 Competitor Collaboration Guidelines, §3.3.

[19] Ibid., §3.31(a).

[20] Bellamy, Christopher W. & Child, Graham D., *Common Market Law of Competition*, Sweet & Maxwell, London, 1993, §5-094; and Gutterman, Alan S., *Innovation and Competition Policy: A Comparative Study of the Regulation of Patent Licensing and Collaborative Research & Development in the United States and the European Community*, Kluwer Law International, London, 1997, p. 344.

reduced.[21] The relative importance of the R&D also matters: slight improvements of existing products are less susceptible to anti-competitive coordination in innovation compared to the development of new vital components. Where the cooperation extends into production or even distribution, the scope for anti-competitive effects is naturally also extended. Not only can such an arrangement protect the parties from the risk of being distanced by a competitor, but production and pricing also become part of the coordinated area.

Under both sets of guidelines, the extension of joint R&D for improvements in current products or technologies into joint production and distribution of the resulting goods can be efficient and pro-competitive, but the effects must be analysed more closely in context.[22] Even if the concerns from an innovation perspective are less, the slighter the expected improvements to products are, the more will potential product market effects matter if the joint venture is extended to include the commercialization of the R&D results. At some point the arrangement will be assessed as a production joint venture rather than an R&D joint venture.[23]

An important feature in the European setting is the previously described block exemption for R&D agreements.[24] This Regulation provides R&D collaborators with an automatic exemption provided they fulfil certain criteria. If the parties are actual or potential competitors in a market which will be affected by the R&D (for which the R&D may create substitutes), their combined market share must not exceed 25 per cent. Since R&D partners are frequently, at least potentially, active in a market where products may be improved or replaced by a product resulting from the specific R&D programme, this market cap may be effective.

The American equivalent is two safe harbours in the Competitor Collaboration Guidelines. Accordingly, the agencies will normally (failing extraordinary circumstances) not challenge a collaboration when the parties (and the JV) together account for no more than 20 per cent of each relevant market. The corresponding innovation market threshold requires three or more independent research efforts in addition to those of the collaboration.[25]

Licensing agreements

The innovation aspects of licensing transactions are often similar to those of R&D joint ventures and mergers, especially if the actual or potential competi-

---

21 EU 2001 Horizontal Cooperation Guidelines, §58.

22 US 2000 Competitor Collaboration Guidelines §3.31(a), EU 2001 Horizontal Cooperation Guidelines, §64.

23 EU 2001 Horizontal Cooperation Guidelines, §64.

24 See section 3.3.5.

25 US 2000 Competitor Collaboration Guidelines, §§4.2, 4.3.

tors are exclusively licensing technology or dividing fields of application among themselves. However, some particular innovation concerns regarding licensing agreements deserve further comment.

According to the US IP Guidelines the owner of intellectual property will not be required to create competition in its own technology. If, however, a licensing arrangement reduces competition among entities that would have been actual or potential competitors absent the licence, antitrust concerns may arise. Also foreclosure effects from vertical arrangements will be investigated.[26] Similarly, according to the EU 2004 Technology Transfer Guidelines, the first relevant question is, 'Does the licence agreement restrict actual or potential competition that would have existed without the contemplated agreement?'[27] In this context, the US guidelines stress the potential application of innovation market analysis to cross-licences and pooling arrangements, and to grantback provisions.

Through cross-licensing and pooling, IPR owners may integrate complementary technologies, reduce transaction costs, clear blocking positions and avoid costly infringement litigation. If cross-licences and patent pools reduce obstacles to innovation by removing the blocking effects of patents, for example, and thereby facilitate a dynamic market (where innovators will be compensated through licence fees from the pool members), the innovation market approach will not be an obstacle.[28] But where influential market actors get together to solve their IPR issues – even if this leads to a patent pool or cross-licences to loosen up the blocking situation or bring together essential patents – this means that the firms cannot invoke their patents against each other. If third parties are not allowed access to the patent package or participation in the pool, the foreclosure effect may be substantial.[29] Both sets of

---

26 US 1995 IP Guidelines, §§3.1, 4.1.1, 4.1.2, 5.4.

27 EU 2004 Technology Transfer Guidelines, §12. Nevertheless, the question of a baseline with which to compare effects is more delicate than this. Particularly in Europe, the state of competition after the agreement is compared not only to the situation without any agreement, but also to other, less restrictive, agreements. In this respect the European standards probably go further than the American approach.

28 See Rai, Arti K., 'Fostering Cumulative Innovation in the Biopharmaceutical Industry: The Role of Patents and Antitrust', 16 *Berkeley Technology Law Journal* 813, 848f. (2001).

29 For a recent example see the European Commission's clearance, in 2003, of a worldwide licensing programme by Philips and Sony regarding CD standards (Commission Press release, *Commission clears Philips/Sony CD Licensing program*, 07/08/2003). This marked the end of an investigation that had been sparked by complaints from CD manufacturers, alleging that the two patent holders had entered into anti-competitive agreements and abused their position through the various licensing arrangements they jointly offered. After modifications had been made, the bilateral agreements between Sony or Philips establishing their licensing programme and the implementation of that programme, the 2003 SLA were cleared. This creates a

guidelines indicate that such effects may arise when the parties possess market power and access to the licensed technology is essential in order to compete effectively in the product market.[30] The pool may then allow its members collectively to control the industry and divide the overall oligopoly rent.[31] This may affect the innovation incentives of both the involved parties and third parties. If entry of competing technologies is effectively impeded and the parties have agreed to license their future technologies and improvements, the incumbents cannot take a technological lead against each other and they lose the risk of being outperformed in innovation; innovation incentives are thus reduced. Such effects could occur if the arrangement includes 'a large fraction of the potential research and development in an innovation market'.[32]

In bilateral licence agreements too, innovation issues are central to the analysis of grantback obligations, which provide the licensor with rights to the licensee's improvements to the licensed technology. The licensor may have a justified interest in obtaining such improvements in order not to be harmed by developments of its own technology. But when such a grantback is exclusive, the licensee, who thus cannot license the improvement to others, may have limited incentives to invest in such developments at all. As noted in both doctrine and case law, antitrust concerns about the effects of exclusive grantbacks should not arise if competitive alternatives to the licensor's technology exist.[33] According to the US IP Guidelines, an important factor in judging the potential effects of a grantback provision will be whether the licensor has market power in a relevant technology or innovation market. If the provision is likely to reduce the licensee's innovation incentives, the analysis will have to consider offsetting benefits.[34] The EU Technology Transfer Guidelines do

---

programme, combining the parties' essential patents for the manufacturing of CDs and allowing licence options for the different kinds of possible discs.

30 EU 2004 Technology Transfer Guidelines, §§167, 207; US 1995 IP Guidelines, §5.5.

31 EU 2004 Technology Transfer Guidelines, §207; Barton, John H., 'Patents and Antitrust: A Rethinking in Light of Patent Breadth and Sequential Innovation', 65 *Antitrust Law Journal* 449, 463 *et seq.* (1997).

32 US 1995 IP Guidelines, §5.5. See also EU 2004 Technology Transfer Guidelines, §228.

33 See, e.g., Kattan, Joseph & Arp, D. Jarret, 'Trends in Intellectual Property Antitrust Enforcement', 566 *Practising Law Institute – Patents, Copyrights, Trademarks, and Literary Property Course Handbook Series* 401, 426f. (1999) referring to *Santa Fe-Pomeroy Inc. v. P & Z Co.*, 569 F.2d 1084, 1101-02 (9th Cir. 1978).

34 US 1995 IP Guidelines, §5.6. For example, the provision may nevertheless encourage the licensor to innovate and license out in the first place, for example by reducing risk of being outperformed in his own technology. It may also improve dissemination of both parties' improvements and thereby increase competition in relevant technology and innovation markets.

not discuss innovation markets in this context, but refer to innovation competition in the technology market.[35] Where competing or blocking technology is licensed and a grantback obligation eliminates or substantially reduces the possibility of gaining a competitive advantage from innovation, an essential part of the competitive process is adversely affected. Such an agreement will not only be caught by Article 81(1), but it will also be unlikely to satisfy the requirements of Article 81(3).[36] As seen in *Optical Fibres* (EU 1986) non-exclusive grantbacks can also restrict competition and incentives for innovation if the licensees lose the ability to gain a competitive advantage against each other. Thus a key element of competition in the market was lost and all actors in the market would follow the same technological development, reducing variety in R&D. However, the agreement was exempted under Article 81(3).

Apart from a number of rules on the content of licence agreements, the application of the new European block exemption for technology transfer (TTBER)[37] is limited by thresholds for the parties' combined market shares: 20 per cent for agreements between competitors and 30 per cent for agreements between non-competitors. These market caps must be satisfied vis-à-vis both relevant product markets and relevant technology markets. Regarding product markets, both actual and potential competitors fall under the criterion of 'competing undertakings', whereas only actual competitors are considered to be this when dealing with technology markets.[38]

The safety zone provided by the US IP Guidelines is equivalent to the one provided in the US Competitor Collaboration Guidelines, except for innovation or technology markets where, if adequate market share data are unavailable, four *additional* independent technologies or comparable R&D entities are required.[39]

Acquisitions of IPRs and small firms

A further question is how the authorities will assess IPR acquisitions. The competitive effects of purchasing competing technology are very much the same as acquiring a competitor with some product under development. According to the US IP Guidelines these IPR acquisitions, including an exclusive licence that

35 EU 2004 Technology Transfer Guidelines, §110.

36 Ibid., §§142, 208.

37 Commission Regulation (EC) No 772/2004 of 27 April 2004 on the application of Article 81(3) of the Treaty to categories of technology transfer agreements.

38 TTBER, Article 1.1.h. See also section 3.3.8.

39 US 1995 IP Guidelines, §4.3. As mentioned, in the US 2000 Competitor Collaboration guidelines, the innovation market will normally not be contested if *in total* four R&D entities exist.

precludes all others, even the licensor, from using the IPR, will be analysed under the Merger Guidelines. In Europe, however, such a case may fall under Article 81 or 82.

In *Tetra Pak I*[40] the Court of First Instance (CFI 1990) affirmed the Commission's conclusion[41] that Tetra Pak was abusing its dominant market position under Article 82 when it obtained an exclusive licence for a new major technology under development, by acquiring the licence-holder Liquipak. Both the Commission and the CFI thus attacked the acquisition of the licence, rather than the merger itself. Interestingly, the Commission stated that '[i]n this case the acquisition of the exclusive licence is the tangible effect . . . of the take-over. Furthermore, it can be considered as equivalent in effect . . . to a take-over'.[42] It should be borne in mind that, at the time of the Tetra Pak decision, no separate merger regulation existed in European competition law and mergers were occasionally dealt with under Article 81 or 82.

The Commission also analysed Tetra Pak's acquisition under Article 81 and stated that the exemption on which Tetra Pak relied, provided by a block exemption regulation, would have been revoked if Tetra Pak had not renounced all exclusivity claims.

It is natural to analyse licensing practices under Article 81. And there is no reason why full acquisitions of IPRs or R&D assets should be treated differently from exclusive IPR licences precluding the licensor from using the technology, since the practical consequences for competition will be the same. The American approach of analysing such transactions under the standards for merger analysis seems to have some advantages. Whether the transaction involves taking over control of a company or acquiring significant R&D assets (including IPRs) seems irrelevant to the standards for analysis. In the end, these cases involve consolidation rather than coordination. In Europe, however, a regular licence agreement would fall outside the formal scope of the merger regulation. At the same time, the substantive tests under Article 81 and the merger regulation, as well as the European Commission's analytical frameworks for their implementation, have become increasingly similar.

However, in *Tetra Pak I*, the Commission considered the exclusive licence equivalent to a 'take-over' and found an infringement under Article 81 and 82. Richard Whish comments on the case by stating that 'the further issue is how far it could be applied to other ways in which a dominant undertaking acquires intellectual property rights, such as taking over a company with a strong R&D

40 T-51/89, *Tetra Pak Rausing SA v. Commission* (Tetra Pak I), ECR II-309 (1990).

41 Case No IV/31.043 – *Tetra Pak I (BTG licence)*, OJ L 272/27 (1988).

42 Commission Decision, §47.

department'.[43] A potential need to investigate acquisitions of small high-tech innovation market players (falling outside pre-notification requirements), has been highlighted in the wake of ex officio challenges by the American authorities, for example in *Varian Medical Systems* (DOJ 2000).

Concluding observations

Innovation analysis of some kind is often part of the assessment of transactions between firms that currently or potentially compete in product or technology markets. The foreclosure effects from vertical arrangements may require particular attention being paid to the innovation dimension too. A careful assessment of the innovation process in the particular case, various actors' strategic positions in that process and the competitive relationship between technologies and other specific assets increases understanding of the industry and provides a basis for forecasting future market developments and entry. Potential negative effects on innovation, and on other variables of competition, can be discovered and alleviated. The innovation market concept may provide a structured basis for the analysis of this dimension. To be able to draw inferences of anti-competitive effects from the conditions of the innovation market, the innovation process must be associated with identifiable assets or competencies of a limited range of firms. And for the full assessment of incentives and abilities to compete, current market conditions remain the core of the analysis in this category of cases.

6.1.3 Distant Future Markets

Introduction

The need for and appropriateness of delineating an innovation market depends on the character of the R&D and the nature of the industry involved. If a transaction relates to innovation that is radical and protected by substantial barriers to entry, it is necessary to outline competing R&D in order to assess the competitive effects. In such a case, current products do not describe competition as accurately as do similar products or technologies under development. An innovation market is thus the natural point of departure when a transaction relates to R&D for new products or technologies, which are likely to create new markets or change existing ones. As previously explained (section 5.2, Potential Future Markets), this is also the realm of genuine innovation market

43 Whish, Richard, *Competition Law,* 4th edn, Butterworths, London, 2001, p. 702. What he seems to indicate is mergers that fall outside the merger regulation, but also mere acquisition of IPR or other R&D assets. There seems to be no reason why other kinds of acquisitions, having similar effects, should fall outside the scope of Article 82.

analysis according to the guidelines. Case law is sparser regarding combinations of R&D at an early stage in the development of new products, where the chances of future success and market developments are largely uncertain and possible effects on competition in innovation are at the centre of the analysis. Still, this is an increasingly common type of transaction, not least among research-based companies, and one for which the relevant legal standards deserve illumination.

Although competition policy is concerned about the exercise of market power and aims to maintain competition so as to discipline firms' behaviour, it is not desirable to apply any traditional standard with respect to innovation markets, especially not presumption rules based on market concentration ratios. If, as suggested, the innovation market concept were employed systematically to uphold four independent competing R&D lines, this would be hard to defend on the basis of general findings in economic theory or results from empirical studies regarding innovation. There is no principled way of saying that, if there are less than four of them, firms would not have sufficient incentives to bring a new product to the market. Nor would a reduction in R&D expenditures generally constitute, or result in, an anti-competitive decrease of innovation, rather than an efficient saving of resources. As will be shown, where innovation is really at stake, such a presumption is not supported by case law, at least not the most recent.

For this category, a few American cases dominate the analysis. Since the US guidelines remain silent on how to assess anti-competitive effects in these circumstances, the standard set by the cases will first be analysed and commented upon and thereafter considered with a view to European conditions.

American standards

The early and controversial *Roche/Genentech* case (FTC 1990), involved questions of both variety and innovation.[44] Genentech was the most advanced of a 'limited number' of companies developing CD4-based therapeutics for the treatment of AIDS/HIV infection. Roche was also engaged in R&D for CD4-based therapeutics with patent applications pending. The research conducted was far from any marketable product. Without any further evidence or reasoning regarding the anti-competitive effect, intervention in such a case seems to be the result of a summary application of the innovation market concept. The remedy did not prescribe full divestiture, 'only' a non-exclusive licensing obligation regarding Roche's technology. It therefore seems plausible that the FTC sought to prevent the creation of a gatekeeper in command of a great

---

44 See Commissioner Azcuenaga's dissenting opinion.

patent portfolio for the development of this kind of AIDS/HIV therapeutics. Still, the inference that such anti-competitive effects would arise would need further vindication.

In *American Home Products* (FTC 1995), AHP and Cyanamid were two of three firms with research projects in, or near, clinical development of a Rotavirus vaccine: that is, with still far to go to reach the potential market. Cyanamid conducted its research along a different path from the other two companies, and it was possible that it could develop a different or superior vaccine.[45] The FTC was anxious that AHP would have insufficient incentives effectively to pursue the Cyanamid programme and also anticipated an increased likelihood of collusion between the two remaining competitors in R&D. AHP was forced to license out, on a non-exclusive basis, Cyanamid's research in Rotavirus vaccines.[46]

These rulings should be compared to *Genzyme/Novazyme* (FTC 2004), where the FTC decided to end a long investigation regarding the firm's acquisition of Novazyme in September 2001. The small research company Novazyme was conducting pre-clinical studies relating to enzyme-replacement treatment (ERT) for Pompe disease, showing promising results in mice. Genzyme, one of the largest biotechnology companies in the world, was also engaged in animal testing of ERTs. Important aspects of the Genzyme case have been outlined in Chapter 4, but it should be mentioned that Novazyme's product was potentially superior, though it would require a longer time to develop. No other firms were engaged in similar developments.

According to the FTC, 'the investigation focused on the transaction's potential impact on the pace and scope of research into the development of a treatment for Pompe disease'.[47] Three out of the five FTC commissioners

---

[45] Wolfram, Richard, *Entering European Innovation Markets: Antitrust Implications of Innovation Markets and Intellectual Property Licensing – A U.S. Perspective,* conference paper at 'Entering European Innovation Markets', February 3–4, 2000, Lund University, Sweden. p. 9; Varney, Christine A., 'Antitrust and the Drive to Innovate: Innovation Markets in Merger Review', 9 *Antitrust* 16, 19 (Summer 1995).

[46] However, to fulfil the 1995 consent order, a divestiture took place in 1995, when a Korean firm acquired rotavirus vaccine assets.

[47] Press release, 'FTC Closes its Investigation of Genzyme Corporation's 2001 Acquisition of Novazyme Pharmaceuticals, Inc.' January 13, 2004, available at http://www.ftc.gov/opa/2004/01/genzyme.htm (last visited 11 October 2004). FTC Chairman Timothy Muris noted that 'because there is currently no treatment for Pompe disease, the most important goal for patients is to get one effective treatment for Pompe disease on the market as soon as possible, in quantities sufficient to treat the patient population. Accelerating the first effective treatment by even a few months would greatly benefit patients. Patient welfare would also be increased by having a second effective Pompe treatment arrive on the market sooner . . . Some patients who do not

found in the end that the facts of the case did not lead to a finding of any anti-competitive harm. They therefore decided to close the investigation.

The opinion of the FTC chairman, who was the only one among the Republican majority who issued a statement, was based on the notion that 'neither economic theory nor empirical research supports an inference regarding the merger's likely effect on innovation (and hence patient welfare) based simply on observing how the merger changed the number of independent R&D programmes. Rather, one must examine whether the merged firm was likely to have a reduced incentive to invest in R&D, and also whether it was likely to have the ability to conduct R&D more successfully'.[48]

According to dissenting Commissioner Thompson, the ultimate test in merger analysis is 'whether the merger is likely to create or enhance market power or to facilitate its exercise'.[49] Any reduction or delay in innovation would be difficult to detect. The merger could thus be found to create or enhance market power without any evidence that the market power was being exercised during the time of the merger investigation. This was a merger to monopoly in the development of a highly specialized drug, and entry was not likely to replace the competition thus eliminated. The presumption of negative effects from a merger to monopoly had not been rebutted. To Thompson this was sufficient to indicate that an FTC challenge was warranted.

Thompson's claim of a presumption regarding the stifling effects of a merger to monopoly on the worldwide market for the innovation of Pompe ERT was supported by Commissioner Jones Harbour who found the decision to close the investigation in the circumstances 'puzzling'.[50] She admitted that it could be questioned whether there was an applicable general presumption of anti-competitive effects in highly concentrated innovation markets, but she found such a presumption appropriate in the case of a merger to monopoly that eliminated all competition and diversity in the innovation market.

---

respond to the first therapy may respond to the second, while others may simply respond better to the second than to the first. Further, entry of a second therapy would likely cause a reduction in prices. These are significant considerations. Nevertheless, for a fatal disease without any effective therapy, acceleration of the first effective treatment remains of paramount importance' (Statement of Chairman Timothy J. Muris, p. 18); available at www.ftc.gov/os/2004/01/murisgenzymestmt.pdf (last visited 11 October 2004).

48 Statement of Chairman Timothy J. Muris, pp. 5f.

49 'Dissenting Statement of Commissioner Mozelle W. Thompson Genzyme Corporation's Acquisition of Novazyme Pharmaceuticals Inc.', p. 7, citing the US 1992 Horizontal Merger Guidelines, §0.1. Statement available at http://www.ftc.gov/os/2004/01/thompsongenzymestmt.pdf (last visited 11 October 2004).

50 'Statement of Commissioner Pamela Jones Harbour, Genzyme Corporation's Acquisition of Novazyme Pharmaceuticals Inc.', p. 5, available at http://www.ftc.gov/os/2004/01/harbourgenzymestmt.pdf (last visited 11 October 2004).

Genzyme analysed

The question whether a presumption based policy is justified and appropriate in this category of cases is important. It could be decisive for the investigation of transactions that leave little competition in R&D for a particular product or technology.

The difficulties in determining not only the effects on innovation but also the facts regarding the conditions for innovation are apparent in the Genzyme case. In the separate statements there is disagreement on most issues: whether, without the merger, there would be a 'race to market', whether Genzyme would have sufficient incentives to introduce the second, probably superior, Novazyme product into the market as soon as possible, whether merger specific efficiencies were created, and so on.[51]

On the one hand, Chairman Muris requires the facts of the specific case to support the showing of an anti-competitive effect. This could be changes in post-merger investments in product development, indicating a called off race to market. It could also be showing that the merged firm would profit from discontinuing the development of the second product. On the other hand, the minority emphasizes the general importance of competition in innovation, pointing at the significance of races-to-innovate, stressing greater incentives to innovate in a competitive market compared to the situation of a monopolist facing no significant threat of entry and insisting on the importance of diversity of R&D efforts. Where a firm has acquired its immediate rivals, is unencumbered by entry and thus post-merger has nobody to defeat, it could decide to postpone or terminate projects as it wished.

The principal standpoints of both the majority and the minority seem sustainable, at least at a general level. Even 'an R&D-monopolist' has incentives to develop a new product efficiently and to put it on the market as soon as possible. A factual analysis at some level, covering all parties' incentives, abilities and efficiencies, seems inevitable for the assessment of anti-competitive effects.

It also seems reasonable to assume that the force of competition remains important even when it relates to the development of new products. There is reason to believe that firm priorities, management incentives, staff motivation and so on will not be unaffected by the presence of a rival.[52] Empirical studies

---

51 The Genzyme decision is also analysed in Balto, David A & Sher, Scott A., 'Refining the Innovation Focus: The FTC's *Genzyme* Decision', 18(2) *Antitrust* 28 (2004).

52 Although no one can fully anticipate all potentially relevant R&D that is being, or will be, conducted in a particular case, the parties are likely to make their decisions and priorities based on existing information. As a result, a firm may therefore *act* like a monopolist although some future entry will occur.

point to the importance of such outside challenge.[53] X-inefficiencies (or slacks) are well-recognized effects of monopolies, although hard to measure exactly. This is even suggested to be the largest potential inefficiency resulting from a product market monopoly, although such inefficiencies not only hurt consumers but may also adversely affect the monopolist's profits. The literature has highlighted that such inefficiencies or other similar limitations of innovative behaviour may be induced by absence of rivalry in the innovation process.[54] Also, the negative influences of eliminated rivalry may not only affect the first-round R&D race to market, it may also impede incentives for subsequent rounds of product improvements and further applications.

Moreover, in such an R&D monopoly there will not be room for variety in research strategies in the short to medium term. Even if the cases considered typically concern the development of a particular product, the unification of the two remaining R&D projects might streamline the development undertaken (for example in terms of clinical trials for pharmaceuticals) and there may be spin-offs in an evolutionary sense from maintaining more than one R&D frontier.

It seems both justified and apt to assume that a transaction to unthreatened R&D monopoly has some incentive-chilling and competition-restrictive effect. However, when some viable R&D competitor exists, that is, a transaction in-between monopoly and the safe harbour, a careful investigation must determine the likelihood of any potential negative effect. It should be investigated, for example, whether the novel products under development are likely to have repercussions for current product generations in which the parties have strong interests.

A policy that merely transplants concentrations assumptions from product market analysis onto the innovation markets for completely new products (as advocated, it seems, by Commissioner Thompson) neglects important differences between the two situations and lacks firm theoretical underpinning. Furthermore, even a presumption of unwanted effects in a transaction to

---

[53] Carlin, Wendy, Schaffer, Mark E., & Seabright, Paul, 'A Minimum of Rivalry: Evidence from Transition Economies on the Importance of Competition for Innovation and Growth', *CEPR Discussion Paper,* No. 4343. London, Centre for Economic Policy Research, 2004; available at http://www.cepr.org/pubs/dps/DP4343.asp (last visited 11 October 2004).

[54] See, e.g., Cohen, Seth A., 'To Innovate or Not to Innovate, That is the Question: The Functions, Failures, and Foibles of the Reward Function Theory of Patent Law in Relation to Computer Software Platforms', 5 *Michigan Telecommunication Technology Law Review* 1 (1998); Gerla, Harry S., 'Restoring Rivalry as a Central Concept in Antitrust Law', 75 *Nebraska Law Review* 209 (1996); Merges, Robert P. & Nelson, Richard R. 'On The Complex Economics Of Patent Scope', 90 *Columbia Law Review* 839, 872, 877 *et seq.* (1990).

monopoly should mean that such a case still warrants in-depth investigation for case-specific conditions that may refute the assumed consequences. Most importantly, if there is reason to believe that both parties would not succeed in conducting the relevant R&D and producing a marketable product of equivalent quality without the transaction, there is no harm done to competition. But other circumstances may also have to be factored in. In *Genzyme*, both minority and majority positions addressed the incentive effects of the Orphan Drug Act. Such circumstances may reinforce or alleviate any suspicion of inferior innovation incentives. In addition, the nature of the technology to be developed can shed light on the scope for alternative development paths and thus whether concerns for variety in R&D are really at stake.

A primary benefit of a presumption-based approach would be to induce firms to give a motivation for their transaction and convince the authority, or court, of the transaction's legitimacy and benefits. Information regarding the economic and technological context of a transaction is not readily available to the authorities but should be rather straightforward for the parties to amass. It is often stressed that dynamic efficiencies are difficult, if not impossible, to evaluate and verify, even ex post. But when combining the only two sources of possible competition regarding a future product, the advantages for the continued product development and the relative unattractiveness of less restrictive arrangements (such as teaming up with another partner) would reasonably have been part of the corporate decision making.[55]

The main caveat against any negative antitrust presumptions of R&D monopolies appears to be a possible lessening of smaller high-tech firms' freedom and corporate value. The stimulus to innovation and competition from research-based start-up companies is an important source of consumer welfare which is well worth protecting. For example, a company like Novazyme is often built on a strategy of developing a particular technology up to a level where it is best taken care of by a larger company.[56] If the smaller company is centred on a certain technology, a simple acquisition of a firm involved in similar research can be an efficient solution, enabling undistorted development of marketable products, while allowing the entrepreneur to sell at high value. Legal standards that impede the possibilities for smaller high-tech companies to team up with the leading firm in the field could possibly have a chilling effect on incentives for investment and on risk – both for physical and for human capital.

Still, most such aspects would be included in the case-specific analysis and may rebut the negative presumption. And if there are no case-specific reasons

---

55 See also section 6.2 on efficiencies.

56 See Chapter 2 regarding small and large firms acting both in cooperation and in competition with each other, exploiting different relative advantages.

to expect anti-competitive effects, apart from the creation of an R&D monopoly, the standard for rebuttal should not be very high. For example, the merging parties may show a likelihood of enhanced quality or innovation speed if the technology is acquired by the leading firm.[57]

Even if the FTC rejected a policy based on rebuttable presumptions in Genzyme, the standard for judging this kind of case still seems fairly open, for a number of reasons. First, no Commissioner rejected the use of innovation market analysis to investigate whether a transaction is likely to affect pace and scope of innovation. A rather extensive investigation was conducted in this case, featuring unique facts, and the Commissioners interpreted these differently. Although the majority found no anti-competitive effect, the question remains under which circumstances it would do so. In addition, it is worth noting that two majority Commissioners did not join Chairman Muris in his statement. Moreover, the Chairman described why an appropriate remedy in this case would be problematic, which could indicate that, if a suitable remedy could be found, the outcome could have been different. Finally, the decision mirrors the political balance among the Commissioners, which in the end makes it vulnerable to changes in the constellation of Commissioners.

European standards

How would these questions be handled in European competition law? As observed in Chapter 5, European merger control has typically aimed at establishing whether the merged firm will be dominant in the relevant future product market. Innovation market analysis has therefore played a limited role in situations like this where R&D is directed at new kinds of products and the prospects for success and future product market overlaps are uncertain. The new European merger regulation features a new substantive test, asking whether competition will be significantly impeded.[58] The future will tell whether this change, in combination with an increased acknowledgment of the innovation market concept in the control of joint ventures and licensing arrangements, will result in increased analysis of competition in innovation.

The recently issued Merger Guidelines do not go deeply into innovation issues (and do not define innovation markets). Reference is made, however, to mergers that eliminate an 'important competitive force', such as the merger between two important innovators with pipeline products related to 'a specific

---

57 This standard would thus be materially different from the creation of a product market monopoly. According to both guidelines, this generally cannot be saved even if substantial efficiencies are created.

58 Council Regulation (EC) No 139/2004 of 20 January 2004 on the control of concentrations between undertakings, OJ L 24/1 (2004).

product market'.[59] Similarly, according to the guidelines, a firm with a small market share can be considered an important competitive force thanks to its promising pipeline products. It is not clear in what dimension this competitive force would apply, but since any reduction in the R&D performance will eventually affect a product market, it seems theoretically justifiable to include potential effects on the scope and pace of R&D. However, no direct changes in the Commission's policy in this area can be detected from the language of the guidelines.

Extending beyond the realm of mergers to R&D joint ventures for new products, the EU Horizontal Cooperation Guidelines do allow the innovation market approach for assessing competition in innovation.[60] According to the guidelines, the analysis of R&D collaboration for new products at early stages of development, where prospects for success and future product market developments are unknown, aims to detect any reduction in effective innovation competition. The analysis is thus less concerned about joint exploitation of the R&D results. Anti-competitive effects in innovation typically include the quality and variety of future products and the speed of innovation and the Commission's analysis aims to tell whether there will be 'a sufficient number of R&D poles left'.[61]

Since it is likely that performance in R&D at an early stage of development will be disciplined if some credible competitor is present, even if the parties are generally strong in R&D, a lenient approach can therefore be expected, at least as long as R&D competition is not eliminated. According to the guidelines, cooperation for an entirely new product is usually pro-competitive. Still, the closer the parties are to market launch when the cooperation starts, the more likely are there to be restrictive effects on product quality and variety or the speed of innovation. It thus appears that the less risk involved in R&D, and the likelier the parties are to succeed individually in the innovation process, the more probable it is that there will be some anti-competitive effect from the cooperation and that more competing R&D sources will be required to maintain competition.[62] Alternatively, the parties would have to rely on offsetting efficiencies to fulfil the criteria for an individual exemption under Article 81(3).

It is also important to remember the previously described block exemption, according to which an R&D agreement directed towards completely new

59 EU 2004 Horizontal Merger Guidelines, §38.

60 The same applies to the EU 2004 Technology Transfer Guidelines (§25) where the term 'innovation market' is used while making reference to the 2001 Horizontal Cooperation Guidelines.

61 EU 2001 Horizontal Cooperation Guidelines, §§50f., 65, 73.

62 Ibid., §75, example 1.

products was automatically exempted. The Commission or a national competition authority would then have to rely on withdrawing the exemption for a specific agreement. Such a measure is provided for only in the case where the R&D agreement 'would eliminate effective competition in research and development on a particular market'.[63] It should also be noted that, even if products under development are radically new, they often replace an older category of products. If the parties are competitors for such products the 25 per cent market share cap in the block exemption applies.

An individual assessment following the guidelines will, besides the innovation analysis, consider possible repercussions for existing markets in which the parties are active. That may reveal both spillover effects in the sales of current products and incentives to slow down innovation.

That enhanced likelihood of success, speed of innovation and product quality may still offset strong dominance in R&D is apparent in the Commission decision in *Pasteur Mérieux/Merck* (EU 1994). On the other hand, in line with the wording of Article 81(3), the EU guidelines prescribe that 'no exemption will be possible, if the parties are afforded the possibility of eliminating competition in respect of a substantial part of the products (or technologies) in question. Where as a consequence of a R&D agreement an undertaking is dominant or becoming dominant either on an existing markets or with respect to innovation, such an agreement which produces anti-competitive effects in the meaning of Article 81 can in principle not be exempted. For innovation this is the case, for example, if the agreement combines the only two existing poles of research.'[64]

This brings us back to the central question, the standards for assessing whether any anti-competitive effect in innovation will be produced in the first place. If, for example, it is unlikely that parties independently (or through a less restrictive alternative) would have been able to carry out the necessary R&D, cooperation will not result in any 'anticompetitive effects in the meaning of Article 81'. Accordingly, if the likelihood of success in R&D, and thereby the likelihood of products reaching the market, is radically enhanced by the transaction, no anti-competitive effect would occur in the first place. In the same vein, under a qualitative 81(1) test, important improvements in prod-

---

63 Block Exemption Regulation, Article 7(e). For the powers of national authorities, see Council Regulation (EC) No 1/2003 of 16 December 2002 on the implementation of the rules on competition laid down in Articles 81 and 82 of the Treaty, Articles 5, 11(4) and Preamble 10.

64 EU 2001 Horizontal Cooperation Guidelines, §71. It is clear from Article 81 (3)(b) that an agreement which affords the parties 'the possibility of eliminating competition in respect of a substantial part of the products in question' cannot be exempted.

uct quality that are enabled by the cooperation would arguably be sufficient to outweigh reduced product variety and speed of innovation, if it would permit the launch of a superior product.[65]

On the other hand, as a matter of law, it appears difficult to obtain an exemption for an R&D monopoly based on efficiencies such as increased speed or decreased costs of development alone, if some anti-competitive effect (such as lessened variety) is considered a likely result.

A further question is whether a 'rebuttable presumption approach' is compatible with the European system where the party alleging that an agreement infringes Article 81 has the burden of proof for anti-competitive effects under Article 81(1). The language of the Horizontal Cooperation Guidelines does not suggest such a presumption-based policy. It is asserted that agreements which do not have an anti-competitive object must be further analysed. Moreover, it is not enough that the agreement limits competition between the parties, it is rather a question whether any anti-competitive effect is likely.[66] In addition, if a transaction to R&D monopoly would be assumed to have such an effect, it could not then be exempted under Article 81(3).

But the suggested presumption was based on a general assumption of the negative effects of an unencumbered R&D monopoly. Since the economic context, including the parties' market power and other structural factors, are to be included in the Article 81(1) assessment, it might be enough to establish a lack of effective competition in R&D to make a prima facie case. Even if there were a prima facie case on the creation of an R&D monopoly, the defendant could bring such case-specific evidence as would counteract any presumed anti-competitive effect. There would thus be a rebuttable presumption within Article 81(1).

Concluding observations

Where a market transaction concerns R&D for products or technologies with a distant and uncertain market introduction, an innovation market constitutes

---

[65] The EU 2001 Horizontal Cooperation Guidelines acknowledge that, if the parties are not able to carry out the necessary R&D independently, there is no competition to restrict. No doubt, what is 'necessary R&D' must include some quality parameter. A view that parties would be considered competitors because independently they would have been able to carry out R&D for substantially inferior products does not correspond to the elsewhere expressed positive view of R&D collaboration and dynamic competition (§§40, 56).

[66] Ibid., §§17–20. Unless an agreement contains 'obvious restrictions of competition such as price-fixing, market sharing or the control of outlets', an assessment under 81(1) should take into account the 'actual conditions in which it functions, in particular the economic context in which the undertakings operate . . . and the actual structure of the market concerned': Joined Cases T-374/94, T-375/94, T-384/94 and T-388/94, *European Night Services v. Commission,* ECR II-3141 (1998), §136.

the relevant market. In both *Roche/Genentech* and *American Home Products* the intervention took place early in the development process, although some competition remained. Still, in both cases, the proposed remedy was to offer licences to important patents and know-how, not to divest one of the R&D projects entirely. Thus the dynamic efficiencies of the proposed acquisition could still be achieved. (see section 6.1.5 below). The reasoning in *Genzyme* is important not least because it acknowledges the applicability of the innovation market concept, while mandating proofs of anti-competitive effects even for mergers to R&D monopoly. At the same time the case was unique in its underlying facts. Further, it highlights the difficulties in collecting and interpreting evidence and establishing the competitive outcome. In order to provide efficient allocation of the burden of proof, hence production of information, a rebuttable presumption of anti-competitive effects from transactions to R&D monopoly is proposed here. Between such a monopoly and the 'safe harbour' provisions, any anti-competitive effect would have to be supported by case-specific evidence. Such a policy could reasonably be accepted under the European legal standards as well.

6.1.4 Imminent Future Markets

Introduction

The further along in the R&D process a transaction occurs, at a point where the likelihood of R&D success is not so unsure and the characteristics of the resulting products not so uncertain, the more will antitrust analysis focus on preserving product variety and competition in the future product market. Under these conditions, there will also be less significant static or dynamic efficiencies from combining R&D efforts (since the bulk of R&D is completed and investments are made).

In fact, the US merger case law suggesting that the safe harbour is really a minimum requirement (that is, it maintains up to four independent R&D sources) typically concerns transactions where the products under development are not so far from market launch, in contrast to the cases in the previous category. This does not imply that innovation aspects are unimportant. The concern for product variety on the future market will warrant an investigation into whether the transaction can be expected to result in fewer alternative products on the future market, or whether product introductions are likely to be delayed.

General observations and merger case law

In *Baxter* (FTC 1997), the two parties were 'among few' seeking FDA approval for fibrin sealants. Although no product was approved on the American market, many US surgeons mixed and applied their own fibrin sealants, and some 35–40 per cent of all internal surgical procedures in Europe and Asia were believed to use this kind of product. Rather than a need to protect speed and efforts in innovation, the real concern appears to have been that Baxter and Immuno were the only firms that could enter the market in the short term. The intervention consequently related to competition in a future market that was just around the corner.

Similarly, in the merger between Upjohn and Pharmacia (FTC 1996) the FTC required a certain cancer treatment developed by Pharmacia to be licensed out. The parties were among a 'very small number' in advanced stages in development of such medicines. Upjohn was expected to be the first to launch its product whereas Pharmacia still had a few years to market introduction. The FTC foresaw elimination of direct and substantial R&D competition, and also that the number of R&D tracks could decrease if the parties had no incentives to continue the Pharmacia project; so the merger would eliminate the potential for direct price competition between the two products in the future product market.

Interestingly, when analysing the same merger and overlapping R&D, the European Commission (1995) had doubts as to whether the compounds would eventually offer therapeutical alternatives. Other reasons contributed to the Commission's conclusion that the merger would not 'create or increase a dominant position in R&D of solid tumours'. First, launch of Upjohn's product was expected within one or two years, whereas Pharmacia's product was not anticipated until 2001. At the later time, competition was expected from at least three products being developed by large competitors. Secondly, Rhône-Poulenc was the European licensee for the compound which Upjohn developed for other parts of the world (originating from a Japanese licensor). The geographical overlaps were therefore also uncertain.[67]

Pfizer and Warner-Lambert (FTC 2000) were the two most advanced of four companies in the development of EGFr-tk inhibitors. Because of their lead over competitors, the FTC feared that the merged entity might 'delay, deter or eliminate competing programs' which would potentially reduce the number of drugs reaching the market, thus resulting in higher prices for consumers. Although exact information was lacking about the level of development of these products, it is clear that the case was not based on the mere

[67] An FTC official commented that '[i]n light of differences between the European and U.S. markets, it should not be surprising that the EC and the FTC came to different conclusions about the colorectal cancer drugs in development. Nor is it startling that thinking about "innovation markets" is in flux on both sides of the Atlantic': Starek, Roscoe B., 'International Cooperation in Antitrust Enforcement and other International Antitrust Developments', Prepared Remarks before 'Antitrust 1997' Conference, 1996; available at www.ftc.gov (last visited 11 October 2004).

notion that concentration in R&D will automatically lead to reduced R&D output.

Transactions falling under this category have some common aspects worth consideration. In order to predict future product market effects, the uncertainty regarding the potentially resulting products must not be too significant. Likewise, the boundaries of the future markets must be sufficiently definable that the competitive effects can be determined. The parties are assumed to be willing to enter the potential future market and reasonably likely to do so within a predictable time frame (although not restricted to the usual two-year limit for entry analysis). Still, the factual basis on which the authorities rely in finding an anti-competitive effect, particularly in terms of the likelihood of entry in the potential future market, is seldom revealed. The American authorities' complaints and analyses to aid public comment are very short and sketchy. European decisions also lack information that would have been important to evaluating and verifying the adequacy of the authority's assessment. Presumably this is in part for reasons of confidentiality.[68]

In industries, such as the pharmaceutical industry, where product development is highly risky, in the sense that the failure rate for pipeline products is high right up to the last stages of development, analysis is usually limited to products at advanced stages. In Europe this typically means phase III clinical testing. It is possible that the American focus on the level of competition in R&D has triggered more intervention and at earlier stages in contrast to the European focus on future product market dominance. In *Pharmacia/Upjohn* it is obvious that the European Commission was unsure of the future substitutability of the resulting products.[69] Such concerns were absent in the US complaint.

If it appears likely that the parties would have completed product development individually and competed in the future market, a lessening of competition can result when the number of potential competitors is reduced. In the considered merger case law, there are no signs in the public documents that the parties made any efficiency claims.

As seen in section 6.1.2, when current products exist, and a party is strong in the relevant market, both US and EU authorities take greater account of earlier stage R&D. This is probably due to better knowledge of the product market in question in combination with greater risk of future market dominance and greater likelihood of anti-competitive reductions in the scope and pace of R&D. Similarly, when the parties' products are at different stages of development, it can be considered likely that the lagging product will be further delayed or cancelled.

---

68 Landman, *supra*, note 6, p. 37.

69 Similar ambiguity regarding future therapeutic overlaps was expressed regarding pharmaccines in *Glaxo Wellcome/SmithKline Beecham* (EU 2000).

Product variety: a bridge between innovation and price concerns?

The question of product variety may bridge innovation concerns and the assessment of future market conditions. An anti-competitive reduction of product variety could stem from a situation where a viable independent R&D project is acquired by a firm that already controls a competing project. In some industries, competing products under development tend to be acquired primarily as a follow-up option in case the first line project fails. If the first product makes it successfully to the market, the second product is less likely to be finalized and introduced to the market. Alternatively, it may be postponed in order to be launched at a later, strategic, point in time. To discontinue the development of a second product could be efficient, saving large resources in the development of a substitute with little added value for consumers. But it could also prevent the launch of a valuable (perhaps less perfect, but maybe even superior) substitute, the introduction of which there is a willingness to pay for. In the event that the firm faces competition from existing products or products under development, the firm's decision whether to launch the second product will be based on the merits of that product. But if competition (on the product market and in R&D) is weak, the question whether the second product should be finalized would not be based so much on the merits of the product. The less competition from other products, the more will the new product 'steal' revenues from the producer's other product(s), rather than from competitors' substitutes. Perhaps the decision is even taken from the profit-maximizing monopolist's point of view. Plausibly, as compared to a competitive market, the second product will be introduced less frequently or with a delay.

Since the risk of an anti-competitive reduction in consumer choice in this scenario depends on product and innovation market competition, intervention will be confined to instances where the product market is reasonably predictable. In other words, if no products exist yet, competition law is likely to safeguard product variety largely through the procedures that protect price competition. It is nevertheless conceivable that a risk of lessened product variety (in terms of a lost or delayed product introduction for which there is a willingness to pay), is easier to establish ex ante than the future level of price competition. Insufficient incentives of the acquirer to develop the additional product could then be established at a relatively earlier stage.[70] As seen above, such concerns were expressed in *American Home Products* (FTC 1995) (section 6.1.3). Considering that there must be a sliding scale between what have here been denoted as distant future markets and imminent future markets,

---

[70] See *Pfizer/Warner-Lambert* (EU and FTC 2000); *Upjohn and Pharmacia* (FTC 1996); *Glaxo-Wellcome* (FTC 1995).

product variety could then constitute a bridge between innovation concerns and concerns for product market competition.

A variant would be the combination of R&D programmes that will actually merge into one line of product development. Here the reduction of potential alternative products will be immediate. One example would be an R&D joint venture formed by two out of four competing developers of a new product, where the independent R&D programmes have shown positive results and are likely to succeed in reaching the market, but where the level of substitution between the future products cannot be established and the effects on price competition are therefore hard to determine. If such a reduction is considered an anti-competitive effect, it would be for the parties to show countervailing efficiencies.

Even so, the role of product variety raises a difficult question regarding the weighing of different consumer values. To challenge a merger between parties on the grounds that each would soon have launched a new product, and competition now is thus considerably lessened for a significant period of time, seems rather uncontroversial. But to uphold competing R&D projects further from the market to maintain diversity in relatively distant future products is more problematic. What would be the yardstick for an anti-competitive reduction?

Under both EU and US policy, product variety is a consumer value, and its diminution could be considered an anti-competitive effect. But competition law cannot act simply to maximize the number of products on the market or prohibit all transactions that would result in a reduction thereof.[71] Such combinations will often allow firms to economize and speed up development and production processes, by realizing economies of scale and coordination of complementary assets and knowledge, leading to better products introduced to the market sooner and sold at lower prices. But, at some point, consumer choice will constitute a value, plausibly accepted at a price (for example, of some forgone efficiency gain). An essential problem is that nobody ex ante can tell what the willingness to pay for this choice is.[72] The market's trial and error process will decide the value of a certain product, including whether it was worthwhile developing at all. This implies that antitrust authorities should be

---

[71] Lande, Robert H., 'Consumer Choice as the Ultimate Goal of Antitrust', 62 *University of Pittsburgh Law Review* 503f. (2001).

[72] This is analogical to R&D and technological progress in general. See Bork, Robert H., *The Antitrust Paradox – a policy at war with itself*, The Free Press, New York, 1978/1993, p. 132. Bork argues that since technological progress requires the use of resources and we do not know the willingness to pay for progress (the price), we do not know the 'proper' rate of progress and we should not give the matter any weight in antitrust analysis. See also Landman, Lawrence B., 'The Economics of Future Goods Markets', 21 *World Competition – Law and Economics Review* 63 (1998).

cautious and focus their attention on cases where the parties, with the prospect of market power, could have incentives to delay or stall the introduction of some new product.

R&D joint ventures

The US and EU guidelines for horizontal cooperation seem to reflect the same considerations as the merger case law. It appears that innovation competition may be important in several dimensions, both spurring fast and efficient R&D and ensuring competitive product markets in the future. From the wording of the two sets of guidelines, the innovation market analysis should detect reductions in R&D efforts, which could indicate that efficient R&D is the objective. However, it is also made clear that the anti-competitive effects of the exercise of market power in R&D include quality, diversity, speed of development and output and prices of future products.[73]

As mentioned, the European guidelines regard cooperation for entirely new products as generally pro-competitive. Restrictions in innovation would be most likely when cooperation is commenced at a level where each party is rather close to the launch of the product. In such a case innovation may even be restricted by a pure R&D agreement. A more likely restriction in such a case relates to product variety, since the arrangement could still allow for price competition between the parties (although similar or identical cost structures naturally facilitate price coordination).

According to the European guidelines, the general pro-competitiveness of cooperation for new products does not change significantly when joint exploitation (including marketing) is involved.[74] At the same time it is stated that joint exploitation is 'only relevant where foreclosure from key technologies plays a role' – a problem that could be offset by licences to third parties.[75] Since most R&D programmes, particularly those aiming at entirely new products, generally generate substantial intellectual property, foreclosure seems likely, the more successful the R&D is. Still, the scope for a licensing requirement ought to depend on when the cooperation was formed and how predictable the future market was at that time. It is asserted that, if the cooperation commenced at a stage where the chances of success and future market conditions were unknown, then joint exploitation will also generally be exempted, since high market shares in the future market will be regarded as a sign of success in innovation rather than a sign of anti-competitive collusion.[76]

73 US 2000 Competitor Collaboration Guidelines, §3.31(a), EU 2001 Horizontal Cooperation Guidelines, §42.

74 EU 2001 Horizontal Cooperation Guidelines, §65.

75 Ibid.

76 Ibid., §73.

Moreover, if the block exemption applies, the parties can jointly exploit the R&D results for seven years. The block exemption limits the terms of joint exploitation and also provides a blacklist of conditions that may not be included. After the seven years the parties may continue joint exploitation if their combined market share does not exceed 25 per cent. The same initial seven-year time frame applies as a standard for individual exemptions. If parties wish to exploit their results more than seven years after market launch, they must show that such period is 'necessary to guarantee an adequate return to the investment involved'.[77] In addition, for such exploitation not to fall foul of Article 81, restrictions that are not indispensable will not be accepted. The blacklisted clauses in the block exemption will generally be a good indication for individual exemptions as well. As a consequence, even if an R&D agreement is cleared after an innovation competition analysis, restrictions on joint exploitation are built into the system.

Licensing agreements

Anti-competitive effects on future markets, in terms of both variety and price, may naturally arise from various licensing arrangements. According to both the US and EU Guidelines, the analysis of licensing arrangements is dependent on the competitive relationship between the parties and the technologies involved. Considering the frequent uncertainty regarding the breadth and validity of patent claims and the fact that patents can be both vertical and horizontal (thus having both complementary and competitive attributes), this analysis is often very difficult to make. The line between what would presumably be anti-competitive arrangements between competitors and what could be pro-competitive vertical integration is narrow. An illuminating example is the FTC challenge in *Summit Technology and VISX*[78] of a cross-licensing agreement between two patent holders in photorefractive keratecomy (PRK) – a laser eye surgery technology. Summit was the first to receive FDA approval for its excimer laser in 1995, followed by VISX in 1996.[79] When FTC brought its action in 1998, no other firm had obtained such approval. In 1992, the two companies entered into an exclusive licence agreement, pooling at least 25 patents, containing more than 500 method and apparatus claims. The pool licensed all the patents back to the parties, with a right to sublicense to physicians performing PRK and related

---

[77] Ibid., §73. It is possible that Article 81(3) is applicable at the end of the seven years, depending on the existing market situation then: §74.

[78] *Summit Technology, Inc. and VISX, Inc.*, Docket no. 9286 (1998).

[79] Newberg, Joshua A, 'Antitrust, Patent Pools, and the Management of Uncertainty', 3 *Atlantic Law Journal* 1, 26 (2000).

procedures. VISX and Summit agreed to charge the users a $250 per procedure fee.[80]

The FTC maintained that the parties had pooled both competing and complementary patents, while the parties claimed that two of Summit's patents and six of VISX patents were blocking and the rest were complementary.[81] According to the FTC the parties could have competed with one another in the sale or lease of PRK equipment by exploiting their respective patents directly, licensing them, or both. In addition, they could have competed in the licensing of PRK technology.[82] While admitting that the pool reduced patent uncertainty and risk of litigation, the FTC maintained that this could have been achieved through a number of less restrictive means, such as a simple cross-licence.[83] The pool was regarded as a horizontal price-fixing scheme which eliminated competition in the product and technology markets while foreclosing potential third-party licensees.[84]

Nevertheless, the lesson here depends on the classification and assessment of the competitive nature of the pooled IPRs and the uncertainty connected to doing such an evaluation. Newberg provides two alternative interpretations of the evidence at hand.[85] First of all, the patents may have been mutually blocking. The FTC claimed that the broadest of the patents, a VISX method patent, was invalid and the complaint in this regard involved an additional allegation of fraud upon the patent office. It should be noted that the latter allegation was dismissed in administrative proceedings and, following a re-examination by the patent office, the FTC also later dismissed this part of the complaint.[86]

---

80 Complaint, §§8–13. The machines were designed to work when a key card was inserted – a card that was sold for $250. Moreover, the parties could veto the licensing of the pooled patents to third parties. In practice, such licences had not been concluded.

81 Newberg, *supra,* note 79, p. 27, note 86.

82 See Analysis of Proposed Consent Order to Aid Public Comment; available at http://www.ftc.gov/os/1998/08/d09286ana.htm (last visited 11 October 2004) and Complaint §13. The FTC estimated the resulting price overcharge for procedures performed in 1996 to have exceeded $10.5 million and in 1997 to have exceeded $30 million.

83 See Analysis of Proposed Consent Order to Aid Public Comment; available at http://www.ftc.gov/os/1998/08/d09286ana.htm (last visited 11 October 2004).

84 The FTC entered into consent agreements with the parties, mandating a royalty-free and non-exclusive licence for the patents; available at http://www.ftc.gov/os/1998/08/d09286suagr.htm and http://www.ftc.gov/os/1998/08/ d09286viagr.htm (last visited 11 October 2004).

85 Newberg, *supra*, note 79, p. 27.

86 See FTC Order Reopening the Record and Dismissing the Complaint; available at http://www.ftc.gov/os/2001/02/summitvisxorder.htm and news releases, available at http://www.ftc.gov/opa/1999/06/visx.htm (last visited 11 October 2004).

Secondly, VISX is known to have had the broadest and strongest patent portfolio, which also comprised a range of apparatus patents apart from the very broad method patent. It is possible that, even without a licence agreement, VISX would have been a lawful monopolist, and the agreement with Summit could be regarded as a vertical relationship.

When considering anti-competitive effects, less restrictive means and efficiencies, it should be kept in mind that the two companies were small start-ups in an area where the development of the technology had been plagued by patent conflicts and litigation. They were caught in a game with incomplete information and very high stakes. The future of the two firms was dependent on the scope and validity of their patents, and the need for extensive product development, clinical trials and the FDA approval processes. Not only an adverse patent ruling, but even the perception of vulnerability to such a ruling, could deprive the companies of access to capital and put them out of business.[87] In these circumstances, the companies agreed to pool their IPRs while continuing to compete on the sales of the machines. They set a joint royalty on the use of the machines; the $250 represented 10–15 per cent of the cost of a procedure.

Interesting, but very difficult, questions remain as to how parties should go about reducing genuine uncertainty regarding their property rights. For example, how far should they go in examining the scope and validity of each other's patents in a situation where the stakes are as high as in this case? Is mere cross-licensing of the contentious patents the only alternative? Could an otherwise legal pool of blocking patents also include some uncertain but potentially competing patents?[88] Where substantial and uncertain R&D work remains before market introduction it seems, as previously, reasonable to apply a more flexible antitrust approach. If, on the other hand, the development is at a late stage, there is less reason for extensive pooling of various IPRs as compared to cross-licences limited to plausibly blocking patents.

Concluding observations

In the case law that upholds several competing R&D projects aimed at future markets, there are some important points to consider. First of all, it is considered that, without the merger, the parties would have developed the relevant products independently. This precludes all necessity arguments in favour of the combination. As will be highlighted in section 6.3, in the public record there are no signs of efficiency arguments either. Probably, the merger case law also provides workable indications for the analysis of R&D joint ventures.

---

[87] Newberg, *supra*, note 79, p. 28.

[88] Shapiro, Carl, 'Competition Policy and Innovation,' *STI Working Papers* 2002/11, OECD, Paris, 2002, pp. 33f.

If parties are likely to succeed in completing the relevant R&D independently, some anti-competitive effects can arise when the transaction reduces the number of innovation market participants below the safe harbour limit. The test of whether some anti-competitive effect is likely looks at the level of uncertainty regarding R&D success and product substitutability, the number of competing R&D efforts, the proximity of market launch and the extension of the cooperation into production and commercialization. If some anti-competitive effect is considered likely, the likelihood and magnitude of counterbalancing efficiencies will be decisive.

Just as mergers and joint ventures should be permitted if they are necessary for R&D success and do not eliminate innovation competition that otherwise would have occurred, the same should apply to licensing arrangements. Such arrangements are often part of, and analysed with, R&D joint ventures. Firms may also decide to pool or cross-licence IPRs to solve problems of blocking patents and to combine complementary assets. Particularly where these arrangements are concluded at the innovation stage, difficult questions arise as to how far the firms must be able to assess the validity, scope and competitive relationship between the shared technologies and bear the risk of errors in that process.

6.1.5 Technology Bases

Introduction

When reviewing transactions that relate to the innovation process but where the potential effects are not primarily related to specific future products or technologies, a broader innovation analysis may be called for. This category typically includes transactions for inputs that are necessary to conduct research in an area or to develop marketable products from such research. If this kind of inputs to a large extent are merged or otherwise combined, competition between the parties in their quest to develop and commercialize products in the area could be diminished and the anti-competitive foreclosure could result.

Under such conditions it may not be possible, or appropriate, to frame the analysis on a potential future product. The various potential applications that may result from R&D based on the technologies at the centre may be difficult to identify and may not provide a workable point of departure. But it might still be possible to assess the more immediate effects on R&D conditions, by putting the technology base at the centre of the analysis. That is not an entirely new concept in antitrust analysis. When reviewing the setting of industry standards and the management of standard-related patent pools, the analysis is typically not fragmented along the various applications for which the standard may be applied. Rather, by focusing on the upstream standard, the incentives for continued innovation and the foreclosure of third parties regarding a whole range of applications may be assessed. Conducting a similar analysis outside the standard-setting realm in a case where parties are combining other kinds of upstream R&D assets for which the potential applications (resulting products) are largely unknown is a less conventional concept.

Nonetheless, there is some merger and joint venture case law suggesting the appropriate framework. Moreover, patent pools for R&D tools may become more frequent outside the context of industry standards, which would highlight the need for some kind of analysis. The technology base approach could also be appropriate in relation to other kinds of less wide-ranging licensing arrangements.

Mergers and joint ventures

In *Ciba-Geigy/Sandoz* (FTC 1997) the parties joined competing and complementary assets. The parties possessed the proprietary assets needed to perform independent gene therapy development and, according to the FTC, the combination of 'alternative technologies' in the merger would reduce innovation competition between the firms in the development of gene therapy, 'including reduction in, delay of or redirection of research and development tracks'.[89] Apart from four identifiable potential future products, the FTC considered the effect on competition in the overall market for gene therapy technology and R&D of gene therapy.

The parties controlled genes, vectors (delivery vehicles for gene therapy), cytokines (proteins) and manufacturing technology. The combination of unmatchable patent portfolios, including patents, patent applications and know-how, necessary for the commercialization of gene therapy, would create a bottleneck. Barriers to entry would be heightened, 'requiring potential entrants to invent around or declare invalid a greater array of patents' of uncertain breadth and validity.[90] The merged firm would also have less incentive to license out to or collaborate with other companies in the field. Absent the merger, they would have been rival centres for such services. Research at early stages was being conducted by a wide spectrum of entities along various paths. The merger was considered to create a massive bottleneck and there was a fear that the third parties would leave the field of gene therapy altogether.

According to the FTC the transaction would leave 'a post-merger picture of potentially life-saving therapies whose competitive development could be hindered by the merged firm's control of substantially all of the proprietary rights necessary to commercialize gene therapy products. Preserving long-run

---

89 Complaint, §31.
90 Ibid.

innovation in these circumstances is critical'.[91] The remedy was not to block the merger. Since the combination would also enable the parties to realize considerable efficiencies, the parties were instead required 'to provide to all gene therapy researchers and developers non-exclusive licenses or sublicenses to certain proprietary and patented technologies essential for the competitive development and commercialization of gene therapy products'.[92]

In *Pasteur Mérieux/Merck* (EU 1994), a joint venture coordinating two of four major market actors' basic research, the development of future products from phase II onwards, and the combination of current vaccines and vaccine technologies, led the Commission to find a foreclosure of third parties with regard to *existing* vaccines and technologies (including those in pipeline) and an appreciable restriction of competition between the parties for unidentified *future* products. However, competition for future vaccines and vaccine technologies would not be eliminated, as the merger did not create insurmountable entry barriers. There were a number of research entities (broadly defined) that could develop into competitors and provide third parties with future vaccines and vaccine technology.

According to the language of the decision, the combination did not so much have an impact on research tools critical for future vaccine R&D (although vaccine technology was pooled). Lessened competition for an undefined range of future products was expected because of the combination and coordination of two powerful, global and experienced actors, presumably with some unique R&D assets and capabilities. But these limitations did not substantially restrict the R&D conducted by third parties. The joint venture could be approved thanks to its significant dynamic efficiencies.

Reasonably, the inputs controlled by the parties in the US *Ciba-Geigy/Sandoz* were broader than in *Pasteur Mérieux/Merck*, with emphasis being put on the transformation from basic research into marketable products, essential for the commercial development of gene therapy. In that way they seriously affected all rival gene therapy research. Moreover, since the FTC concluded that alternative technologies were being combined, and the parties would have been able to develop gene therapy products individually, some of the assets appear to have been substitutes.

The merger decision in *Glaxo/Wellcome* (EU 1995) features less dramatic conditions but suggests a similar approach as far as HIV/AIDS therapy was concerned. The transaction would 'combine the R&D resources and expertise

---

91 Separate Statement of Chairman Robert Pitofsky, and Commissioners Janet D. Steiger, Roscoe B. Starek, and Christine A. Varney; available at http://www.ftc.gov/os/1997/04/others.htm (last visited 11 October 2004).

92 Analysis to aid public comment; available at http://www.ftc.gov/os/1996/12/ciba.pdf (last visited 11 October 2004). Discussed further in section 6.2.2.

of two leading firms' in the area.[93] But since there were no definitive treatments for HIV/AIDS and the merger was not likely significantly to inhibit the research for effective compounds being undertaken by other pharmaceutical companies worldwide, the integration was cleared.

From these cases it seems that the conditions for innovation mandate the delineation of an upstream market. While potential applications cannot readily be identified, it is possible to identify potential competitive effects on research that is taking place in a broader innovation market (such as gene therapy research). Defining the relevant market with reference to those assets and capabilities that are critical to the research, development and introduction of products in the area would then be appropriate.

Patent pools

As regards the market definition, technology base analysis resembles the analysis of patent pools resulting from industry standards. On account of the foreclosure effects of pooling complementary inputs, a patent pool linked to an industry standard, such as the MPEG and DVD pools, requires openness and non-discriminatory terms towards potential third-party licensees: this because the pool otherwise constitutes a closed entity in charge of the essential patents needed to develop and produce the full range of products based on the standard. It is also important in these cases that the patents are essential: that is, not only are the pooled patents complements to each other, but there are no substitutes outside the pool. If the pool included some patents for which there were substitutes available on the market, the outsider patent would be effectively foreclosed from this market, since the licensees would not care for an 'extra' licence. As a consequence, the scope for follow-on technological development by these competing technology providers would be diminished.

Likewise, in order to provide opportunities for superior technologies to emerge, and thus for continued innovation at the architectural level, licensees must be free to develop, support or commercialize competing standards. Similar principles could apply to slightly different forms of patent pools. As noted in Chapter 2, such arrangements may resolve 'anti-commons' problems in industries where narrow and fragmented upstream patents lead to patent blocks and stacking licences. Opinions differ regarding the attractiveness of patent pools in biomedicine as a means of solving the problems of upstream patent rights. Some maintain that pooling arrangements are less likely to materialize in biopharmaceutical industries, pointing to the heterogeneity of actors in these industries: a range of academic institutions, biotechnology companies and pharmaceutical

93 *Glaxo/Wellcome* (EU 1995), §§32, 33.

firms with different values and interests and diverging attitudes towards patents. At the same time, as this heterogeneity is diminishing, not least through vertical integration, the scope for pooling may increase.[94]

Others maintain that the general advantages of wide pooling arrangements apply to biotechnology too, even comparing genetic information to industry standards in electronics and telecommunications.[95] It is assumed that allowing increased patent protection of genetic materials, initially significant as research tools, could lead to a vast number of patents, the value of which would be uncertain without cooperation with other firms.[96] This is expected to render firms more willing to enter into pooling arrangements. Apart from the accessibility of technology, it is also maintained that the additional benefits of pooling normally resulting from standard-based pools also apply here. Reduced transaction costs, distribution of risks through joint collection and sharing of royalties among holders of essential patents, and exchange of information, should be attractive to the industry.[97]

An innovation market approach applied in this kind of context would favour aggregation by means of pooling rather than consolidation among competitors. Competition policy should not hinder transactions that aim to overcome upstream patent hurdles, whether in the form of numerous fragmented patent rights or of fewer but broader patents. But at the same time rivalry and accessibility at the upstream innovation level should be factored in.[98] Upstream transactions should not allow parties severely to limit the opportunities for rival R&D. It may be recalled that the Schumpeterian notions of competition and creative destruction, while favouring product market

---

94 Rai, *supra*, note 28, p. 847.

95 Sung, Lawrence M., 'Greater Predictability May Result in Patent Pools', p. 5. Submission at US DOJ and FTC hearings 'Competition and Intellectual Property Law and Policy in the Knowledge-Based Economy'; available at http://www.ftc.gov/opp/intellect/020417lawrencemsung1.pdf (last visited 3 March 2005).

96 Some important patents, often held by academic institutions, have been made available through extensive licensing programmes. One prominent example is the Cohen-Boyer patents, held by Stanford University and the University of California, covering the method of inserting a specific gene into a host cell. This technology has been widely disseminated through successful licensing at a reasonably low royalty (although estimated to bring in $200 million). It has been improved and applied to innumerable applications: Rai, *supra* note 28, p. 836; Eisenberg, Rebecca, 'Public Research and Private Development: Patents and Technology Transfer in Government-Sponsored Research', 82 *Virginia Law Review* 1662, 1710 (1996).

97 Clark, Jeanne *et al.*, *Patent Pools: A Solution to the Problem of Access in Biotechnology Patents*, United States Patent and Trademark Office, 2000, pp. 8 *et seq.*; available at www.uspto.gov/web/offices/pac/dapp/opla/patentpool.pdf (last visited 3 March 2005).

98 Rai, *supra*, note 28, pp. 848f.

monopolies as incentives for extensive innovation activities, do not consider monopolization of the process by which innovations are created.

Licensing agreements

As indicated by the merger and joint venture case law, the application of innovation market analysis to technology bases is not confined to wide-ranging patent pools. Consider for example a licence agreement involving blocking or complementary patents between two firms engaged in R&D in a particular area, where the firms' protected technologies constitute the core of their respective activities.[99] Complex questions arise when trying to define the borderline between, on the one hand, solving deadlocks and creating efficiencies between lawful holders of exclusive rights and, on the other hand, anti-competitive combinations that extend beyond the scope of the granted patents.

In a situation where two firms are leading in the R&D in a field and decide to cross-license complementary assets without offering them to third parties, the possibility of third parties obtaining necessary technology could be restricted. Moreover, if the complementary assets constitute inputs to R&D, the foreclosing effect may restrain the development of a whole range of (more or less defined) future product markets. Where the input can be used to develop different future products, the parties would be more likely to offer licences to third parties absent the licensing agreement. After the agreement, the parties may be bound by exclusivity restrictions, leaving no room for such licensing. In addition, the parties may be less interested in contributing to third-party R&D that could potentially result in competing products, and would prefer to maintain control of major developments in the industry.[100] If the parties together control the complementary inputs to a substantial degree, a licence arrangement may lead to foreclosure in an area although the agreement does not necessarily eliminate competition between the parties.

Where a transaction solves a problem of blocking patents and the agreement is unlikely to limit competition that otherwise would have occurred between the parties, the parties' willingness to deal with third parties may still be reduced while making it harder for third parties to 'invent around' the patents. Prior to the transaction a third party could invent around one party's

---

[99] In comparison, the members of the MPEG and DVD pools do not compete and get revenues as much from the licensing of its IPR as in the production of the downstream applications manufactured in accordance with the set standard, a standard they wish to maximize use of, and thereby also access to.

[100] Barton, *supra*, note 31, pp. 463 *et seq.*

patent and obtain a licence to the other. If these are so linked, the only alternative may be to invent around or, if possible, license both.[101]

If the legality of these kinds of transactions depends on the effects on the parties' innovation incentives and third party foreclosure effects, some principles are needed to set limits to the antitrust hurdles. Otherwise the problems envisaged in VISX recur and are magnified. Again, it may be useful to compare *Ciba-Geigy/Sandoz* and *Pasteur Mérieux/Merck*. If the pooled technologies are directed to the production of some downstream products, the combination should be analysed under a current market or a potential future market approach. But the more the technologies relate to R&D in a broader area, the fewer the competitive alternatives that are available, and the more apparent the need for accessibility among the entities conducting research in the area, the more weight should be given to potential foreclosure effects in the rule of reason analysis. A technology base approach may then be appropriate for investigating anti-competitive effects on innovation and the availability of less restrictive means.

For a further illustration of a situation where a technology base analysis *could* have been useful, consider the following example relating to breast cancer. In this field numerous patents covering the two identified genes that indicate susceptibility for breast cancer,[102] BRCA 1 and 2, are in the sole control of one company, Myriad Genetics. This is partly the result of the company's win in the race to sequence BRCA I in 1994, which subsequently lead to the filing of five patent applications in 1995. These patents were granted in 1997 and 1998.[103] About the same time, another firm, OncorMed, also filed applications and was subsequently issued a patent for very similar manipulations. Patent infringement claims and counterclaims arose. Meanwhile the race to sequence the second gene, BRCA 2, resulted in patent applications from both Myriad and another entity. OncorMed was subsequently granted a worldwide exclusive licence to the other entity's patent. The conflict between Myriad and OncorMed was thus extended to include BRCA 2. In the face of the legal disputes and the resulting delays in commercialization of cancer tests, OncorMed fell into financial distress. The disputes with Myriad were settled by an arrangement which, *inter alia*, included the acquisition by Myriad of the exclusive licence for BRCA 2 for an undisclosed

101 Gilbert, Richard J., 'Antitrust for Patent Pools: A Century of Policy Evolution', 2004 *Stanford Technology Law Review* 3, 65 (2004).

102 In the sense that mutations in these genes dramatically increase the risk for developing breast cancer.

103 For a thorough report on the developments in this genetic research area see Dalpé, Robert *et al.*, 'Watching the Race to Find the Breast Cancer Genes', 28 *Science, Technology, & Human Values* 187 (2003).

amount of money. In 2001, the European Patent Office granted Myriad Genetics three patents relating to BRCA 1.[104] Considering the massive research efforts dedicated worldwide to this area of research, it has been maintained that Myriad's monopoly has had serious repercussions for the development of a wide range of diagnostics, remedies and treatments.[105]

A technology base analysis seems appropriate for analysing the acquisition of OncorMed's exclusive rights. Plausibly, Myriad's and OncorMed's patents were partially blocking and partially complementary. If so, some form of combination would be efficient, such as allowing for complete screening and analysis to be conducted (similar to *Pasteur Mérieux/Merck*). But, based on an assessment of the patents involved, it could also be argued that Myriad gained control over a bottleneck through an acquisition which allowed the company to exclude rivals in a wide area of applications. Possibly, the same procompetitive effects could have been achieved through substantially less restrictive means. For example, it should be considered whether a crosslicence of blocking patents and/or non-exclusive licences to complementary patents would have sufficed. Such a solution would leave the firms in a position vis-à-vis third parties that is justified by their own patents, rather than by the unified control of an essential bottleneck. A greater scope for continued third party research in the field could then be expected.

In fact, in *Roche/Genentech* (FTC 1990) a non-exclusive licensing obligation for any interested third party was provided for following the parties' combination at early stages in HIV/AIDS research. Even if it is not explicitly stated in the decision, it is plausible that the control of certain critical HIV R&D tools was otherwise expected to result in third party foreclosure.

---

104 EP 699 754 covering any methods of diagnosing a predisposition for breast and/or ovarian cancer using the normal sequence of the BRCA 1, EP 705 903 relating to 34 mutations of the BRCA 1 gene and to diagnosis methods to detect such mutations, and EP 705 902 relating to the BRCA 1 gene itself and the corresponding protein with claims relating to any therapeutic application of the gene such as diagnosis kits, gene therapy, screening of drugs, production of protein and so on. The first of these patents has, upon opposition, been revoked by a first-instance division of the European Patent Office. This division has been challenged, and will go to second-instance proceedings. See the EPO press release, 'Myriad/breast cancer patent revoked after public hearing', available at http://www.european-patent-office.org/news/pressrel/2004_05_18_e.htm (last visited 11 October 2004).

105 See, e.g., Benowitz, Steve, 'French Challenge to BRCA1 Patent Underlies European Discontent', 94(2) *Journal of the National Cancer Institute* 80 (2002); Andrews, Lori B., 'Genes and patent policy: rethinking intellectual property rights', 3 *Nature Reviews Genetics* 803 (2002). It should be noted that Myriad's claims, not least its insistence on having the relevant blood samples sent to Myriad's laboratories for test and diagnosis, have triggered the disputes, compliance refusals and opposition procedures before patent authorities.

Policy discussion

Admittedly this kind of approach, delineating an innovation market for unidentified future products, is not explicitly endorsed by any American or European policy guideline. Markets are supposedly determined by investigating the degree of substitutability between products and technologies or, in the innovation market context, by identification of alternative R&D efforts directed to specific products or technologies. Rather, it is limited case law in combination with doctrinal discussions that supports such an application.

In the literature the potential need and advantages of considering innovation and competition in a broader context has been highlighted. Plausibly similar to the analysis framework previously advocated, Barton suggests that the impacts on follow-on innovators may necessitate 'technology lines' being considered. Transactions that concentrate control over a specific product line or combine complementary patents for a specific product are often addressed by technology or innovation markets in accordance with the guidelines. But concentration of basic patent rights or broad patents could also have repercussions for a variety of follow-on products. Barton does not further develop the technology line model, but suggests that, while one must be very careful in extending the technology and innovation market concepts, the threat to future technological development should be considered when basic or broad patents are brought together.[106] In more recent work, Barton endorses the development of the innovation market concept by FTC in Ciba-Geigy so as to include the impact on future unknown products in the merger analysis.[107]

Even innovation market sceptics have acknowledged a role for the concept in settings like Ciba-Geigy.[108] It has been stressed that, when firms' abilities to compete in innovative activity are dependent on key inputs that they need to obtain from other firms and organizations, such 'access services' and potential exclusionary behaviour relating to these can best be addressed precisely by defining a market for this service.[109]

---

106 Barton, *supra*, note 31, p. 465.

107 Barton, John H., 'Antitrust Treatment of Oligopolies with Mutually Blocking Patent Portfolios', 69 *Antitrust Law Journal* 851, 873 *et seq.* (2002). Another example is Rai, *supra* note 8.

108 OFT, *Innovation and Competition policy*, Economic Discussion Paper 3, Report prepared for the Office of Fair Trading by Charles River Associates, 2002, pp. 132 *et seq.*

109 Europe Economics, *The Development of Analytical Tools for Assessing Market Dynamics in the Knowledge Based Economy*, Report to the European Commission, (2003), pp. 70 *et seq.* A non-exhaustive list of potential access services is presented: physical assets which could represent bottlenecks to related markets; IP rights that are held, whether or not these are used in an innovation or held by a firm to protect itself from innovation and rivalry; and information that facilitates compatibility

Similarly, it has been asserted that, if the impact of patents on upstream invention is kept narrow, regulators will infrequently have to use innovation market analysis despite the difficulty of defining the relevant market. But where market transactions threaten to give a single entity control of what appears to be a fundamental platform, it is argued that this challenge will have to be faced.[110]

This is intrinsically linked to policy discussions regarding patent scope. Just like the infamous Selden patent from the late 19th century, covering the whole idea of a gasoline-powered internal-combustion car,[111] the problem of broad scope exclusivities is not so much the deadweight loss from monopoly pricing 'but rather that they foreclose avenues of future improvement and innovation'.[112] Langlois develops the issue of technological standards as essential facilities, precisely on account of the scope issue. Regarding essentiality he maintains that it is 'always an issue that speaks to *intra*system competition. As a result, the analysis of an essential facility will depend crucially on the degree of *inter*system competition in the industry'.[113]

Concluding observations

The role of the innovation market concept is to maintain innovation incentives and abilities. The concept will favour the integration of both blocking or essential patents, and other forms of complementary inputs which should thus be eligible for unification, through mergers, pooling or other mechanisms. Combinations of complementary resources allow efficiencies in research and production; further, patents often defy a strict categorization into competitive or complementary, blocking or non-blocking relationships.[114] These transactions should nonetheless be subject to a rule of reason antitrust analysis. The

between related products and therefore third-party supply; available at http://europa.eu.int/comm/enterprise/library/lib-competition/doc/analytical_tools_final_report.pdf (last visited 3 March 2005).

110 Rai, *supra*, note 28, p. 853. It has also been suggested that for the important issue of determining the essentiality of patents, in cases where the relevant area is not determined by an industry standard, a 'technology field' should be determined in order to classify valuable technology in an appropriate manner. Kulbaski, James J., 'Comments On Patent Pools and Standards For Federal Trade Commission Hearings Regarding Competition & Intellectual Property', available at http://www.ftc.gov/opp/intellect/020417jamesjkulbaski.pdf (last visited 11 October 2004).

111 U.S. Patent No. 549,160, issued November 5, 1895, covering the carriage, the drive mechanism and the engine.

112 Langlois, Richard N., 'Technological Standards, Innovation, and Essential Facilities', in Ellig, Jerry (ed.), *Dynamic Competition and Public Policy*, Cambridge University Press, Cambridge, 2001, p. 207.

113 Ibid., p. 214.

114 Newberg, *supra*, note 79, pp. 5f.

extent to which such arrangements will be allowed to limit competition should depend on whether the transaction is likely to have repercussions on parties' innovation incentives or on the R&D conditions of third parties in relation to various technology or product markets. In terms of the array of potential product developments that may be affected, the potentially foreclosing effects are greater, the further upstream they are from the final products they relate to. When combining research tools or other research-related assets, the impact and governance of such a potential bottleneck should therefore be carefully analysed.

A technology base analysis is similar to technology market analysis but it may include slightly different considerations. First of all, it is possible that the technologies have not previously been licensed and, after the transaction, the parties may have no incentives to license them. Rather than allowing the establishment of a technology market they will prefer to unite their assets in order to achieve possible efficiencies and be strategically well-positioned in the area.

Combining upstream technologies, or other assets needed at the R&D level, may affect R&D conditions in various contexts. Rather than creating market power in the commercialization of technologies for some specific downstream purposes, a bottleneck may thus allow the parties effective control of development in a broader area of research. In addition, the combined R&D assets which together create a bottleneck do not necessarily have to be limited to IPRs but may be reinforced by other forms of human or physical capacities, capabilities and resources.[115]

But it is a technology market in the sense that market power is restricted by the prospect of alternative assets, whether licensed or not. Regarding the definition of the relevant market, the case law suggests it be defined with regard to the bottleneck, rather than the resulting downstream applications. In the same way that a standard, around which various patents are pooled, may constitute the relevant area of investigation, the common denominator of other combined technologies can constitute a relevant technology base. As in the gene therapy case, broad patents on sequenced genes which are vital for R&D in an area could qualify. In other technological areas it is plausible that other bottlenecks may be defined. These could involve leading software developers in related markets exclusively exchanging interfaces to accomplish internal compatibility. In the latter case a contestant would have to develop, and offer to the market, all the interconnected software simultaneously and moreover persuade a critical mass of users to shift systems.

---

115 See, e.g., *Pasteur Mérieux/Merck* (EU 1994) and *Lockheed Martin* (DOJ 1998).

It should be noted that '[i]t is usually very difficult to undo the effects of a scheme to monopolize after it has occurred'.[116] This is an experience familiar to both American and European authorities, particularly when the resulting monopoly relies on intellectual property rights. Rather than entering into ex post discussions regarding limitations of dominant firms' freedom to enjoy their property rights, thereby risking expropriation of the legitimate rights of these holders, the authorities ought to focus on prevention of anticompetitive strategies which might enable them to achieve such a position in the first place. The primary role of public policy in innovative markets is to ensure that market positions are acquired through competition and without unnecessary limitations on future innovation. With a more developed ex ante analysis, there will be less pressure for ex post intervention. The case law relating to essential facilities shows the difficulties and potential dangers of such ex post regulation.

6.2 EFFICIENCIES, REMEDIES AND TIMING

6.2.1 Efficiency Analysis and Defence

Reference to technological progress is usually an important aspect of competition policy both in the US and in the EU. In both jurisdictions competition analysis aims at assessing whether consumers will ultimately suffer from the market practice being investigated. Nevertheless, there are differences in the ways in which the authorities handle claims that a market practice will encourage investment and speed up or enhance the quality of innovation, or otherwise benefit consumers to offset the effects of increased concentration or contractual restraints on counterparties.

At a general level, the likelihood that a certain type of agreement or conduct may create efficiencies will, under American law, be crucial to the question if it will be per se prohibited or analysed under the rule of reason. Once it has been established that analysis will consistently condemn a certain type of restraint, authorities and courts may find it unnecessary to go into detail regarding market effects in each case. Yet, the per se prohibitions are not fixed once and for all. In order to sort out the anti-competitive aspects of innovation-related conduct, further inquiry is regularly needed.[117] Although the same

---

116 Baer, William J. & Balto, David A., 'Antitrust Enforcement and High-Technology Markets', 5 *Michigan Telecommunication Technology Law Review* 73, 82 f. (2001).

117 See, e.g., *Microsoft III* (D.C. Cir. 2001) remanding the District Court's finding of a per se illegal tying under §1 of the Sherman Act, due to the potential efficiencies created by bundling the Internet Explorer with Windows.

categorization is not applied in Europe, some agreements belong to a category which always is considered restrictive of competition, that is, per se falling under Article 81(1). A difference from the US system is that these can (at least in theory) be exempted under Article 81(3).[118] As explained in Chapter 3, in both systems transactions that involve R&D are typically analysed with a view to the benefits that may result.

Apart from more easily recognized static efficiencies in terms of lowered costs of production and distribution, and so on, the authorities acknowledge the merits of the dynamic efficiencies that may stem from mergers, joint ventures and other transactions between competitors.[119] It is thus recognized that various transactions may 'result in benefits in the form of new or improved products, and efficiencies may result in benefits even when price is not immediately and directly affected',[120] may 'enhance the ability and incentive of the collaboration and its participants to compete, which may result in lower prices, improved quality, enhanced service, or new products',[121] and 'enable firms to offer goods or services at lower prices, better quality or to launch innovation more quickly'.[122] But even if consumers may benefit 'from efficiency gains in the sphere of R&D and innovation', the efficiencies must be quantifiable, verifiable and potentially pro-competitive, which limits their scope, particularly for dynamic efficiencies.[123]

American efficiency standards

In the US, the current standards for analysing efficiencies are the result of a series of policy amendments, a process that has been the subject of much discussion.[124] Although the Chicago School is famous for its efficiency orientation, its most prominent scholars have persistently held that no authority or court possesses the abilities to measure and quantify efficiencies and even less

---

118 Whish, *supra*, note 755, p. 95.

119 For an overview of economic benefits of joint R&D see section 2.3.2. See also Camesasca, Peter D., *European Merger Control: Getting the Efficiencies Right*, Intersentia-Hart, Antwerpen, 2000, pp. 148 *et seq*.

120 US 1992 Horizontal Merger Guidelines (revised 1997), section 4. See also EU 2004 Horizontal Merger Guidelines §81.

121 US 2000 Competitor Collaboration Guidelines, §3.36.

122 EU 2001 Horizontal Cooperation Guidelines, §32, in which it is also stated that 'these benefits relate to static or dynamic efficiencies'.

123 See EU 2004 Horizontal Merger Guidelines, §§81, 86; US 1992 Horizontal Merger Guidelines (revised 1997), section 4.

124 See e.g. Kolasky, William J. and Dick, Andrew R., *The Merger Guidelines and the Integration of Efficiencies into Antitrust Review of Horizontal Mergers*, 2002; available at http://www.usdoj.gov/atr/hmerger/11254.pdf (last visited 3 March 2005); OECD, *Competition Policy and Efficiency Claims in Horizontal Agreements*, Roundtable in November 1995, Paris, 1996, pp. 41 *et seq*.

to balance them against increased market power, so as to determine the likely net effect. That is simply regarded as 'beyond the capacities of the law'.[125] The 1982 DOJ Merger Guidelines reflected this scepticism and raised market share and concentration thresholds (and thus more willingly limited the scope for intervention in the first place) and provided efficiencies to be taken into consideration only in 'extraordinary circumstances', the requisites for which were handled in a footnote.[126] In 1984, the efficiency section was revised and a shift from a Chicago School towards more of an (Areeda-Turner) Harvard School approach could be detected as efficiencies were moved from 'defences' to the 'competitive effects' section.[127] Efficiencies were to be considered in the overall assessment of whether the merger was likely to restrict competition. When the DOJ and FTC jointly revised the guidelines in 1992, the efficiency section was largely untouched,[128] but it was again revised in 1997 (primarily to explain current practices rather than to reflect a change), following the 1995 hearings and subsequent Staff Report.[129]

According to the revised Merger Guidelines as well as the IP Guidelines and the Competitor Collaboration Guidelines, the Agencies may thus, in order to assess the overall competitive effect of a transaction, evaluate pro-competitive efficiencies that counteract potential negative effects. Such an analysis is also required by the Gilbert and Sunshine model (step 5).[130] Efficiencies must be 'cognizable', that is, verifiable and specific to the transaction, thus unlikely to be realized in some other practical, but substantially less restrictive, way.[131] An agreement may however be 'reasonably necessary' without being essential and less restrictive alternatives must be realistic ones in the light of existing business realities (including conditions for entrants, free riding or other opportunistic conduct). Since efficiencies must be substantiated and verifiable, the less proximate and predictable they are, the less weight they are given. Moreover cognizable efficiencies must be potentially pro-competitive and cannot result from mere reductions in output or services.

---

125 Bork, *supra*, note 72, pp. 126f. See also Posner, Richard A., *Antitrust Law,* University of Chicago Press, Chicago, 2001, pp. 133 *et seq.*

126 US Department of Justice 1982 Merger Guidelines, §10A. This was largely consistent with the 1968 Guidelines, but possibly somewhat more restrictive.

127 Kolasky & Dick, *supra*, note 124, pp. 18, 22.

128 However, a previous requirement that efficiencies would not be considered unless 'established by clear and convincing evidence' was taken out, which consequently opened for further efficiency considerations.

129 Federal Trade Commission, *Anticipating the 21st Century – Competition Policy in the New High-Tech, Global Marketplace*, Staff Report, 1996. See section 3.3.4.

130 See section 3.3.3.

131 US 2000 Competitor Collaboration Guidelines, §3.36 (a) and (b).

These considerations will almost never justify a transaction creating a monopoly or near-monopoly. Efficiencies are consequently most likely to make a difference when the potential anti-competitive effects are limited.[132] In practice, efficiency assessments are very rarely included in the competition analysis of mergers analysed under the innovation market approach, but do seem part of the evaluation of transactions falling short of mergers as well as in suspected abuse situations.[133] There are different reasons for this, which will be commented on shortly.

European efficiency standards

Under the new EU Merger Regulation, the European Commission does not have unrestricted power to level out restrictions on competition by reference to efficiencies or to the technological progress expected from the concentration.[134] As with the former merger regulation, as a matter of law, the new regulation does not provide an express efficiency defence.[135]

Signs of an underplayed efficiency criterion under the old merger regulation can be found in *MSG/Media Service* (1994).[136] The parties to a full-function joint venture (thus analysed under the merger regulation) pointed out that the venture would promote technical and economic progress in the field of digital television. The Commission replied that, although there is a criterion of technological and economic progress in the Merger Regulation,[137] it 'is subject to the reservation that no obstacle is formed to competition'.[138] In this case, the Commission assessed that the joint venture would seal off the future market and create a dominant position.[139]

---

132 US 1992 Horizontal Merger Guidelines (revised 1997), section 4; US 2000 Competitor Collaboration Guidelines, §3.37: 'As the expected anticompetitive harm of the agreement increases, the Agencies require evidence establishing a greater level of expected cognizable efficiencies in order to avoid the conclusion that the agreement will have an anticompetitive effect overall.'

133 See, however, *FTC v. H.J. Heinz, Co.*, 116 F.Supp.2d 190 (D.D.C. 2000), where the recognition of innovation efficiencies substantially contributed to the District Court's denial of a preliminary injunction.

134 According to the 2004 Merger Regulation, Article 2 (1) (b) the Commission shall, in its appraisal of a merger take into account, *inter alia*, 'the development of technical and economic progress provided that it is to consumers' advantage and does not form an obstacle to competition'.

135 See Camesasca, Peter D., 'The Explicit Efficiency Defence in Merger Control: Does it Make the Difference?' 20 *European Competition Law Review* 14 (1999).

136 Case No IV/M.469 – *MSG Media Service*, OJ L 364/1 (1994)

137 Article 2 (1) (b) of the Merger Regulation.

138 *MSG Media Service*, §100.

139 The Commission nevertheless continued to question whether the alleged technological and economic progress actually would be achieved, which would seem unnecessary if the mentioned reservation was strictly applied.

Yet, in some cases brought under the former regulation, the Commission has made general references to potential positive effects, such as allowing the pooling of 'skills and resources to be a competitive player on worldwide R&D markets'.[140] But more explicit references to R&D efficiencies also seem to have been accepted. In *ABBOTT / BASF*[141] the Commission began the assessment of future products with general references to consolidation and size in the pharmaceutical industry and the achieving of efficiencies thereby. According to the Commission, size 'allows firms to leverage increasing R&D costs across a broader range of products and to spread the risk inherent in every new research project over a large capital base. The greater resources of a larger company can be used to fund additional R&D projects, to devote more resources to long term projects and to increase spending on already advanced projects to accelerate the development process'.[142] In this case Abbott claimed that its larger size would ensure sufficient resources to bring a certain BASF pipeline product to the market, as well as investing in new R&D. This seems to have been accepted by the Commission. Such references are not used as a trade-off in the analysis but give support to the argument that this qualitative kind of approach may have been part of the dominance assessment too.[143]

But whereas the substantial test under the former regulation was occupied with the creation of dominance, the current test is whether a concentration would significantly impede competition. Such a criterion seems more adapted to explicit assessment of the likely anti-competitive and pro-competitive effects, before making an appraisal of the merger. Moreover, in preamble 29 of the new regulation it is stated:

> In order to determine the impact of a concentration on competition in the common market, it is appropriate to take account of any substantiated and likely efficiencies put forward by the undertakings concerned. It is possible that the efficiencies brought about by the concentration counteract the effects on competition, and in particular the potential harm to consumers, that it might otherwise have and that, as a consequence, the concentration would not significantly impede effective competition.

The accompanying EU Horizontal Merger Guidelines set out a policy for implementing efficiency considerations that is almost identical to the one expressed in the US guidelines.[144] The increased attention to efficiencies is

---

140 *Upjohn/Pharmacia* (EU 1995), §25.

141 Case No COMP/M.2312 – *ABBOTT / BASF* (2001).

142 *ABBOTT / BASF* (EU 2001), §38.

143 See Camesasca, *supra*, note 119, pp. 292 *et seq.* for a comprehensive discussion and further examples.

144 EU 2004 Horizontal Merger Guidelines, §§76 *et seq.*

also one of the aspects of the new merger policy that the European Commission is happy to stress.[145] The future will show to what extent this will lead to substantial changes in practice.

Under Article 81, on the other hand, an efficiency analysis is called for and in terms of an efficiency defence. Although an agreement restrictive of competition is prohibited under Article 81(1) and void under Article 81(2), it can be exempted under Article 81(3) if it 'contributes to improving the production or distribution of goods or to promoting technical or economic progress, while allowing consumers a fair share of the resulting benefit'. The exemption is only possible for restrictions that are indispensable to the attainment of the benefits and do not eliminate competition.

But efficiencies at some level often form part already of the assessment whether a transaction is anti-competitive in the first place. In recent years the Community Courts and the Commission have tended to perform a more qualitative test under Article 81(1), which seems to allow for efficiency arguments in the analysis of whether an agreement is likely to restrict competition 'appreciably' (in line with the Merger Regulation). If parties are unable effectively to carry out the relevant R&D or other contemplated operations on their own, or through a substantially less restrictive alternative arrangement, there will not be a restriction of competition by cooperation to this end. Moreover, if a restriction entails pro-competitive efficiencies, such as the prevention of free-riding, the agreement is less likely to be considered restrictive of competition. In addition, since it is relevant to assess potential restrictions of competition in the light of the level of competition which would have existed in the absence of the transaction, certain restraints may be objectively necessary for the existence of the agreement and may therefore be deemed to be outside 81(1). For innovation-related transactions this means that the risk facing the parties when entering the agreement, and the sunk costs incurred can make the agreement fall outside 81(1) entirely.[146] Even if some restriction of competition is likely to follow, the scope for granting exemptions under Article 81(3), on the basis that positive effects outweigh the negative effects, is large. In the Horizontal

---

145 'Let me stress, in particular, that for the first time the Commission has set out levels of concentration as preliminary indicators of anti-competitive effects of mergers and has explicitly indicated that, under certain restrictive conditions, efficiencies will be taken into account to counteract the anti-competitive effect of notified operations' (Mario Monti, *Convergence in EU–US antitrust policy regarding mergers and acquisitions: an EU perspective*, Speech at UCLA Law First Annual Institute on US and EU Antitrust Aspects of Mergers and Acquisitions Los Angeles, 28 February 2004; available at http://www.europa.eu.int/comm/competition/speeches/ (last visited 11 October 2004)).

146 EU 2004 Technology Transfer Guidelines, §§11f, 147. Case 56/65 *Société Technique Minière* [1966] ECR 337; Case 258/78, *Nungesser*, ECR 2015 (1982).

Cooperation Guidelines, the Commission assert that '[i]f considerable market power is created or increased by the cooperation, the parties have to demonstrate significant benefits in carrying out R&D, a quicker launch of new products/technology or other efficiencies'.[147]

As seen in *Pasteur Mérieux/Merck* (EU 1994) and *Corning-Optical Fibres* (EU 1986) the scope for an efficiency defence under 81(3) is wide and explicit. In Pasteur Mérieux/Merck the parties would be able to offer tailored multivalent vaccines, by combining their antigen and vaccine technology portfolios. Apart from saving costs by reducing R&D overlaps this represented a clear qualitative improvement and was likely to speed up the development of future vaccines. Hence dynamic efficiencies played a prominent role.

Efficiencies in innovation analysis

In both jurisdictions it is thus possible to weigh (or at least factor in) efficiencies in the competition assessment. But the authorities are nevertheless restricted by lack of information when weighing innovation efficiencies and future impacts.[148] It is very difficult to forecast and measure dynamic efficiencies in precise terms. Such difficulties could explain why efficiency arguments are not highlighted in more of the innovation market cases. Further considerations relate to the nature of the cases.

First, many of them have involved mergers between large companies, where the innovation market aspect is only a (minor) part of the overall transaction. The transaction as a whole, and the efficiencies the parties presumably plan to realize through it, largely relate to products and markets besides the combination of R&D that triggered this particular analysis. So the parties probably could not present efficiency arguments in favour of this particular aspect of the integration. Probably they have not been motivated to complicate the review process by pushing these issues either. Moreover, if the products are not far from being launched, there is less likelihood that dynamic benefits would be achievable.

Second, the role of efficiencies is likely to be built into the test of whether an arrangement is likely to have anti-competitive effects in the first place, particularly when the efficiencies involved are related to enhanced capabilities of bringing new or improved products to the market. FTC officials have argued that enforcement agencies should use their prosecutorial discretion not to bring cases in the innovation market area, when efficiencies outweigh the

147 EU 2001 Horizontal Cooperation Guidelines, §69.

148 The US 1992 Horizontal Merger Guidelines symptomatically close the efficiency section by stating that '[o]ther efficiencies, such as those relating to research and development, are potentially substantial but are generally less susceptible to verification and may be the result of anticompetitive output reductions'.

anti-competitive effects.[149] This argument is applicable both to merger cases and to other kinds of transactions.

Third, innovation market analysis in mergers typically does not assess competition effects on the margin. It is impossible to assess the net-effects on R&D competition in precise terms, above all because of the lack of appropriate variables such as price/output, used in product market analysis. Interventions founded on reduced innovation competition have instead acted, in a rudimentary manner, to maintain a minimum level of competition and/or to prevent insurmountable entry barriers. Since efficiencies are normally important to the antitrust analysis when the anti-competitive effects are limited, and seldom make a difference when the transaction creates a near-monopoly, the scope for efficiencies allowing these mergers has been limited.

For the same reasons, the importance of efficiencies is much greater when considering joint ventures, licence arrangements or IPR acquisitions directed to a specific R&D programme. The same could apply for other acquisitions of a more limited kind (such as mergers between a large and a small specialized company, as indicated in *Genzyme/Novazyme,* FTC 2004). Anti-competitive effects may be more limited than in a large merger, making it easier to offset them with evidence of efficiencies. Moreover, these transactions are typically formed with the intention of realizing efficiencies related to the particular project. If the main purpose of the transaction centres on the efficiencies achievable by combining R&D assets (including IPRs), know-how and specialized human resources, their role is likely to be central and may thus be essential for allowing a transaction between competitors to be accepted.

Interesting problems will arise in the appraisal of anti-competitive effects and efficiencies. Previously it has been argued that a transaction leading to an R&D monopoly should be accepted if this is considered necessary to enable a resulting product of superior quality. Where the parties are likely to succeed independently in R&D, and are perhaps already conducting relevant R&D or are present on an affected product market, cooperation in large and expensive R&D programmes may limit the number of competing R&D sources, but at the same time improve product quality, cut R&D expenses and possibly shorten R&D time lags. The possibility of less diversity and future product market competition must then be weighed against improved quality and faster market launch.

149 Dahdouh, Thomas N. & Mongoven, James F., 'The Shape of Things to Come: Innovation Market Analysis in Merger Cases', 64 *Antitrust Law Journal* 405, 436f. (1996).

6.2.2 Remedies and Efficiency Considerations

In most merger cases where intervention has been triggered by innovation market analysis, the existence and nature of efficiencies have had an impact on the choice of remedies. As seen from the cases, some mergers were abandoned, but more often they were made subject to conditions. When choosing a remedy, the US authorities in particular explicitly weigh competitive aspects against R&D efficiencies. But similar considerations are also part of EU decision making following the European Commission's notice on remedies.[150]

The nature of the R&D related remedies might be both structural and behavioural. There are great difficulties in establishing a remedy that efficiently restores competition without undermining the incentives of the IPR owners and not demolishing the efficiencies that the transaction may create. Remedies may include divestiture of companies or divisions; licensing of patents, know-how and research; undertakings to support third parties by providing information, training and assisting R&D personnel, or to continue to deliver important inputs.[151] Success in R&D is often contingent on variables such as expertise, knowledge and timing. In order for a licence or divestiture to create a viable competitor in R&D, the licensee's or acquirer's R&D activities may have to be safeguarded by current obligations.[152] Also, firms may be threatened with penalties as an incentive to keep the R&D projects viable and running until the divestiture is completed.[153]

Balancing proper remedies and continued incentives and efficiencies may be a delicate matter. In *American Home Products* (FTC 1995), the majority chose a licensing solution that the minority found inadequate, urging divestiture.[154] Likewise, in *Ciba-Geigy/Sandoz* (FTC 1997), the majority considered that licensing (of patents belonging to both parties) was just as effective as divestiture and more appropriate to remedy the anti-competitive foreclosure. Whereas a divestiture could have created a 'substantial disruption in the parties' research and development efforts', a licensing requirement would allow third parties to develop gene therapy products and replace the lost competition. Competitors and other scientists had confirmed this.[155] The FTC

---

150 Commission Notice on remedies acceptable under Council Regulation (EEC) No 4064/89 and under Commission Regulation (EC) No 447/98, OJ C 68/3 (2001).

151 *Glaxo-Wellcome* (FTC 1995), *Crown Cork* (EU 1995).

152 Baer & Balto, *supra*, note 116, pp. 80f.

153 See, e.g., *American Home Products* (FTC 1995), providing for a $10 000 fine a day if failing to keep the programme running: Dahdouh & Mongoven, *supra*, note 149, p. 440.

154 See separate statement by Commissioner Azcuenaga.

155 Analysis to Aid Public Comment, §7.

thus required the parties to grant non-exclusive licences or sublicences to certain technologies essential for developing and commercializing gene therapy products, to all gene therapy researchers and developers at prescribed low royalties. In *Genzyme/Novazyme* (FTC 2004) reference was made to the unavailability of adequate remedies, which may have affected the outcome. In *Amgen/Immunex* (FTC 2002) an unusually attractive remedy (licensing of blocking patents) was available that would allow all the efficiency gains from the merger but at the same time allow for future entry by a potential competitor.

FTC officials allege that licensing is usually appropriate where the market participants recognize that IPRs are crucial or when the merged entity is strongly committed to continuing R&D.[156] In this way both the new entity and the licensees may benefit from the technology and pursue research along the specific lines. Divestiture is more likely when there is a 'pressing need to expedite the R&D effort', as when commercialized products already exist on the market.[157]

In the US it is also common, when divestiture or licence has been ordered, to follow up with a second remedy in case the party fails to comply, for example when no agreement has been reached within a certain time period. The second remedy is often even less attractive to the parties. For example, in *Hoechst/Rhône-Poulenc* (FTC 2000), a failure to divest Rhône-Poulenc's product in final stages of development could result in divestiture of Hoechst's already FDA-approved product.

According to the European Commission's notice on acceptable remedies, divestiture is normally the preferred remedy to ensure access to key technology.[158] In that way a lasting relationship between competitors is avoided. Nevertheless, licensing arrangements can be accepted as an alternative when current research would otherwise be impeded. Generally, at least outside the pharmaceutical industry, mergers and other agreements with the potential to reduce competition in innovation unduly often involve the combination of unique R&D assets, rather than particular R&D projects. Where these assets relate to IPRs, an appropriate remedy could be to require licences in order to maintain some competition in R&D. In this way the parties may be able to achieve their objectives, but ultimate success will be determined by competition on the merits. At the same time, the Commission's argument in favour of divestiture makes sense, and limits the scope for ex post opportunism by the parties and the need for monitoring.

156 Dahdouh & Mongoven, *supra*, note 149, p. 438.

157 Ibid.

158 Commission Notice on remedies acceptable under Council Regulation (EEC) No 4064/89 and under Commission Regulation (EC) No 447/98, OJ C 68/3 (2001), p. 6.

That the design of the remedy matters and that monitoring of its fulfilment may be necessary is apparent in the aftermath of *Boston Scientific Corp.* (FTC 1995). The parties were forced to license out 'a broad package of patents and technology relating to IVUS catheters'.[159] The FDA approved Hewlett-Packard (HP) as a licensee, and HP and Boston entered into a licence agreement, which was also approved by the FTC. At the time, HP was active in a neighbouring market, but not in the catheter market. However, HP gave up its efforts to enter the catheter market and exited the field altogether in late 1998. In 1999, HP filed a private action against Boston, alleging breach of contract, monopolization and attempted monopolization. This case was settled by the parties and withdrawn from litigation. However, in October 2000, the Department of Justice, on behalf of the FTC, sued Boston for breach of the terms of the order. According to the DOJ's complaint, Boston had failed to provide HP with a licence to a certain patent and a certain device relating to IVUS catheters. Boston had also refused to provide the necessary information for several catheters and to supply a new kind of catheter. The DOJ pleaded that the Court should rule that Boston violated the original order and called for an appropriate civil penalty. In March 2003, Boston was fined $7 million for eliminating competition.

The perspective of the innovation analysis also affects the remedy. If the analysis merely aims at restoring future product market competition, the remedy discussion may overlook aspects relating to the R&D process itself. The European Commission has confirmed that the choice of remedy may differ, depending on whether the aim is to protect competition in future sales of the resulting product or R&D competition to create the product. In *Glaxo/Wellcome* (EU, FTC 1995) 'the FTC considered a horizontal market for R&D for anti-migraine drugs on its own, while the Commission looked at the spill-over effects of R&D in the market for the sales of medicines. The Commission decision therefore provided for the merged company to license one of the two anti-migraine treatments in development and so retain a potential competitor, while the FTC required full divestiture of Wellcome's R&D for this anti-migraine treatment'.[160]

In *Glaxo Wellcome/SmithKline Beecham* (EU 2000), the Commission separated competitive effects on the R&D market from product market effects.

---

[159] See Analysis to Aid Public Comment on the Provisionally Accepted Consent Order.

[160] *Commission report to the Council and the European Parliament on the application of the Agreement between the European Communities and the Government of the United States of America regarding the application of their competition laws*, 1996, §4.21, available at http://europa.eu.int/comm/competition/international/com479_en.html (last visited 11 October 2004).

While R&D competition in the COPD area was thriving, the Commission believed the merger could have anti-competitive effects in one segment of COPD products. The remedy required the parties to license out one of SB's future products in the event that the competing phase III pipeline compounds for this segment should fail. The remedy thereby focused on the product market. It may nonetheless be questioned whether this kind of remedy is appropriate, since it is possible that the merged entity would have reduced incentives to develop the product, facing the risk of a compulsory licence at a later stage.

Moreover, efficiency concerns are further enforced in situations where innovation competition is central and product markets are further away. Under such circumstances, the proper remedies should entertain the hard issues of dynamic efficiencies. If not, the intervention will not be optimal and could in the end do more harm than good. Perspective matters.

6.2.3 Time of Assessment

A difference between mergers and other market practices is that the latter can typically only be subject to scrutiny ex post, upon suspicion or allegation of antitrust violation. Even if the US authorities may challenge mergers falling outside the requirements for pre-merger notification some time after they have been consummated, the majority of cases will be analysed ex ante. The question then arises as to how analysis of transactions varies, depending on when the assessment is conducted.

As a general rule of competition law, the legality of an agreement is a function of its effects on competition. As these may change over time, so may the legality. Therefore an agreement that was legally entered into may become illegal owing to internal and external developments: reorganization, developed cooperation, changed market conditions and so on. In the R&D context this implies that assessments made at an early stage of an uncertain R&D process are often limited to existing markets and innovation markets.[161] Whenever the assessment is made, the plaintiff bears the burden of showing the anti-competitive effects of an agreement. If successful in doing this, the parties may rebut the presumption of unlawfulness, for example by showing efficiencies outweighing the anti-competitive effects.

However, it may be very detrimental to assess the competitive nature of transactions in the innovation process from an ex post perspective. The more successfully the parties perform in innovation, the greater are the chances that

[161] As described above, that is also stated in the EU 2001 Horizontal Cooperation Guidelines, §73.

they will capture substantial market shares, earn high profits and so on. Such success should not be punished. It is with a view to such success that the heavy investments are made in the first place. The American guidelines assert that competitive effects are assessed 'as of the time of possible harm to competition', whether at formation or later. However, it is also asserted that an assessment conducted after the collaboration has been formed must be sensitive to reasonable expectations of the parties whose sunk cost investments have been made in reliance on the agreement, 'before it became anticompetitive'.[162] Hence, although it is unlikely that an anti-competitive R&D agreement will be subject to fines, the question of when the agreement became anti-competitive is still very relevant. If subsequently challenged, it may be essential for the parties to have documented their innovation market assessment and supportive evidence, as of the time of formation and investment. Moreover, if the positive effects of the agreement outweigh the restrictions on competition, and the restrictions are reasonably necessary to the attainment of the benefits, the agreement will not be considered anti-competitive. Although it appears that the authorities will take an ex ante perspective, acknowledging the parties' justified expectations at the time they entered into the agreement, the full extent to which such considerations trump later developments is not evident.

In Europe too, the Commission recognizes that the application of Article 81 must take into account initial sunk investments and the risk facing the parties as well as the time needed and the restraints required to commit and to recoup such investment.[163] Also, the Commission is sensitive to the fact that a restrictive agreement may be irreversible in the sense that the ex ante situation cannot be reinstated, for example when the parties have abandoned their individual R&D projects in favour of a joint project. If such a collaboration does not impede competition at the time of its implementation, because, for example, there is a sufficient number of competing R&D projects, the joint R&D will not become anti-competitive as a result of subsequent failures of competing projects. Nevertheless, the Commission has affirmed the possibility of reassessing reversible parts of the cooperation, such as joint exploitation of the R&D results, to see if they still meet the conditions under Article 81.[164]

At the same time, the Commission maintains that an R&D agreement should be assessed *when it is formed*, even if it includes joint exploitation. This

---

162 US 2000 Competitor Collaboration Guidelines, §2.4.

163 Guidelines on the application of Article 81(3) of the Treaty, §44, OJ C 101/97 (2004). Similarly the EU 2004 Technology Transfer Guidelines, §147, acknowledge that account should be taken of initial risks and sunk investments and the restraints required to commit and recoup such efficiency enhancing investments.

164 Guidelines on the application of Article 81(3) of the Treaty, §45, OJ C 101/97 (2004).

is the practice under the EU R&D block exemption Regulation, where the exemption applies seven years after the introduction of the products to the common market. Also, at the time when agreements not falling under the block exemption were notified to the Commission, the Commission's decision to exempt the cooperation would normally cover both the duration of the R&D and the phase for introducing the product to the market. Since a strong initial market position due to successful R&D and product introduction is seen as a natural consequence of being first on the market, and not as an elimination of competition, this applied irrespective of the market shares that may result on introducing the product.[165]

Consequently, the conditions on signing the agreement are important. Just as in the US, the parties need to be able to provide documentation of the assessment of and considerations and evidence regarding competition at the time of the formation. If the agreement was lawful at the time of its formation and when investments were made, later developments would have to be very severe in order to invalidate the parties' legitimate expectations.

6.2.4 Concluding Observations

Even when considering whether a transaction is likely to result in some anti-competitive effect, efficiency considerations are at the centre of analysis. In merger control in particular, it is the overall effect on competition and consumers that is being analysed. When a transaction does not create a permanently integrated entity, but combines assets and competencies for a particular purpose or project, the realization of specific efficiencies is the purpose of the transaction and thus even more important to the assessment. This is particularly relevant when considering dynamic efficiencies in innovation analysis. Efficiency considerations are also inherent in the choice and design of appropriate remedies for alleviating anti-competitive effects. Finally, the importance of an ex ante perspective in innovation-related competition analysis must be emphasized.

6.3 UNILATERAL CONDUCT

6.3.1 Introduction

One of the most intricate kinds of innovation analysis concerns what a dominant company may do or must do in relation to its competitors. Contrary to the

165 EU 2001 Horizontal Cooperation Guidelines, §73.

situations considered previously, where parties create a dominant position or otherwise limit competition through various contractual means, abuse situations normally relate to unilateral conduct. A dominant company's behaviour may still affect the path, pace and variety of innovation in various ways.[166]

Under neither US nor EU law is it a violation of antitrust law to be dominant, or to keep on competing while being dominant. On the contrary, firms at all levels and sizes are intended to compete vigorously. To deem a conduct abusive involves striking a balance between, on the one hand, encouraging companies to make use of their comparative advantages and efficiencies by competing in the market and, on the other, identifying those strategies of dominant companies that would not constitute competition 'on the merits' but rather destroy opportunities for competition. In *Microsoft III* (D.C. Cir. 2001) the court addressed these difficulties:

> Whether any particular act of a monopolist is exclusionary, rather than merely a form of vigorous competition, can be difficult to discern: the means of illicit exclusion, like the means of legitimate competition, are myriad. The challenge for an antitrust court lies in stating a general rule for distinguishing between exclusionary acts, which reduce social welfare, and competitive acts, which increase it.[167]

Apart from questions regarding the dominance criterion (or possession of monopoly power) which will not be further elaborated here, it is important to consider what may constitute an abuse with regard to innovation, and what can, on the other hand, be objectively justified and rather attributed to effective competition.[168]

Besides possession of monopoly power in the relevant market, the offence of monopolization under §2 of the Sherman Act, requires 'the willful acquisition or maintenance of that power as distinguished from growth or development as a consequence of a superior product, business acumen, or historic

---

[166] As stated in Chapter 5, the treatment of unilateral conduct will not be exhaustive. The factual, legal and economic disparity makes the area impossible to cover in a systematic way within the scope of this book. This presentation is rather intended to complete the picture of innovation analysis in the light of some recent case law.

[167] *Microsoft III* (D.C. Cir. 2001), 253 F.3d 34, 58.

[168] In *Microsoft III* the court offers the following definition of monopoly power under §2: '[A] firm is a monopolist if it can profitably raise prices substantially above the competitive level' (p. 50). In other words, we face a monopoly if a firm has substantial market power in the market. This does not seem far from the EU standard for dominance. The EU standard formulated in *United Brands* – that a firm is dominant if it is able to behave to an appreciable extent independently of competitors, customers and, ultimately, consumers – describes a condition of substantial market power. Otherwise such behaviour would be whittled away by competition: Case 27/76, *United Brands Company v. Commission*, ECR 207 (1978).

accident'.[169] The acquisition or maintenance of such power can thus suffice as an 'injury'. Still, in order to distinguish the attainment or protection of monopoly power through legitimate means, such as superior efficiency, as opposed to anti-competitive conduct, a monopolization offence requires some conduct that is exclusionary in itself.[170] In order to be anti-competitive, the conduct must hurt the competitive process, and thereby consumers. Presumably, when considering innovation-related conduct, to show such harm does not necessarily require concrete proofs in terms of actual reductions in R&D or lessened product diversity. But a requisite harm to competition in itself must be established – not just harm to a competitor.[171]

In Europe, abuse of dominance under Article 82 does not necessarily have to involve conduct that hurts consumers directly, but also includes practices that are indirectly detrimental through their impact on the competitive market structure. In the language of the ECJ in *Hoffmann-La Roche:*

> abuse is an objective concept relating to the behaviour of an undertaking in a dominant position which is such as to influence the structure of a market where, as a result of the very presence of the undertaking in question, the degree of competition is weakened and which, through recourse to methods different from those which condition normal competition in products or services on the basis of the transactions of commercial operators, has the effect of hindering the maintenance of the degree of competition still existing in the market or the growth of that competition.[172]

Moreover, considering the abuse cases handled in Chapter 4, it should be noted that, according to Article 82(b), the abuse prohibition includes 'limiting production, markets or technical development to the prejudice of consumers'.

The application of Article 82 has received a fair share of criticism, often from the point of view that it tends to protect competitors rather than consumers, which would be a consequence of too strong a devotion to market structure. The application of economic analysis has not come so far in helping establish the legal standards under Article 82 as it has with Article 81. The need to reassess its abuse policy in the light of economic thinking is one of the reasons why the European Commission has commenced an overhaul that aims to adopt a more systematic approach in this field, similar to what has previously

---

169 *United States v. Grinnell Corp.*, 384 U.S. 563, 570–71 (1966).

170 Philip E. Areeda and Donald F. Turner consider abusive 'conduct other than competition on the merits, or other than restraints reasonably "necessary" to competition on the merits, that reasonably appear capable of making a significant contribution to creating or maintaining monopoly power' (*Antitrust Law – An Analysis of Antitrust Principles and their Application,* Little, Brown, Boston, 1978, vol. 3, p. 79).

171 See *Microsoft III* (D.C. Cir. 2001), pp. 58f.

172 Case 85/76, *Hoffmann-La Roche & Co. AG v. Commission,* ECR 461 (1979), §6.

been carried out for various classes of agreements under Article 81, and mergers.[173] According to Director General Philip Lowe, economic thinking should be used to evaluate current practices, explain the rationale of the Commission's policy, ensure consistency and allow Article 82 to be applied to new markets and practices.[174] Comprehensive contributions to the possible contents of such a coherent and economically rational policy have also been presented by commentators.[175]

Similarly, the US standards, above all those in §2 of the Sherman Act, have been criticized for being vague and inadequately underpinned from an economic point of view.[176] The lack of clarity and transparency has also led to inconsistent case law, particularly in lower courts. US officials indicate their readiness to discuss and develop the legal standards within this area.[177]

The analysis here will be limited to commenting on recent cases where dominant firms' activities have been evaluated with regard to effects on the innovation process. Although the case law still leaves many questions unanswered, recent cases show that both the US and the EU authorities are prepared to evaluate incentives, abilities and efficiencies in innovation – and to balance the interests of the dominant company and the potential exclusionary effects. Particularly when some efficiency can be attributed to the dominant firm's conduct, inducing or facilitating the development and production of its products, the standards for showing anti-competitive effects and the possibilities of justifying the conduct are crucial. Many of these questions are common to all the treated cases, but the first case particularly highlights the potential need or value of delineating innovation markets here too. The way authorities weighed different innovation effects in *Microsoft* will be analysed second. And, thirdly, further duties of IPR holders to share their assets with innovative competitors will be discussed. This will lead up to some closing observations.

---

173 Lowe, Philip, 'DG Competition's Review of the Policy on Abuse of Dominance', in Hawk, Berry (ed.), *International Antitrust Law & Policy*, 2003 Fordham Corporate Law Institute (2004), p. 165.

174 Ibid., p. 166.

175 Temple Lang, John, 'Anticompetitive Non-Pricing Abuses under European and National Antitrust Law', in Hawk, Berry (ed.), *International Antitrust Law & Policy*, 2003 Fordham Corporate Law Institute (2004), p. 235.

176 See Elhauge, Einer, 'Defining Better Monopolization Standards', 56 *Stanford Law Review* 253 (2003), for an extensive analysis, including policy proposals.

177 Pate, R. Hewitt, 'The Common Law Approach and Improving Standards for Analyzing Single Firm Conduct', Address before the Thirtieth Annual Conference on International Antitrust Law and Policy Fordham Corporate Law Institute, New York, October 23, 2003, available at www.usdoj.gov/atr/public/speeches/202724.htm (last visited 3 March 2005).

6.3.2 The Use of Innovation Markets in Abuse Cases

In *Intel* (FTC 1999) the dominant firm enforced its demand for royalty-free licences from computer manufacturers (OEMs) by ceasing to provide vital pre-launch product information and samples. The company frequently concluded such cross-licences with microprocessor competitors and downstream OEMs.

It seems to follow that Intel was able to monitor, and was allowed free access to, important developments in the industry through these licensing arrangements. Indeed, Intel's action was a reply to the complaining parties invoking their IPRs to seek damages and to enjoin the sales of Intel's products. If Intel kept this access to all relevant patents, the structure of the market could be cemented in favour of this dominant incumbent. Further, if the ability of various actors to attain any technological edge was thereby diminished, competition on the merits could be prevented.[178] At a general level, Intel's conduct suggested some anti-competitive effect, which was also the conclusion of the FTC.

On the other hand, substantial cross-licensing arrangements were a necessity in the industry. Where a single microprocessor could otherwise infringe upon hundreds of dispersed patents, the question thus arises how far the dominant player could go when navigating through the patent thicket. It does not seem easy to determine precisely to what extent Intel's conduct was indeed limiting competition and if this was the case, whether it was justifiable.

Intergraph had left the microprocessor market in 1993 and now used Intel's products for their workstations. In the infringement case they relied on an old (Clipper) microprocessor technology, which they no longer utilized themselves. As they had left the microprocessor market they were uninterested in exchanging patent rights and presumably preferred to exert maximum revenues from the abandoned technology.[179] In such a situation, the decision by the (sued) supplier to stop serving the customer with pre-lease information seems like a justified manoeuvre, needed to eliminate a holdout position by an IPR holder of outdated or otherwise inferior technology. Thus it is likely that Intel's conduct brought efficiencies to its business activities while merely preventing unproductive redistribution to the IPR holder.

Digital was currently selling its Alpha microprocessor and was thereby a competitor to Intel, although a small one. The Alpha processor was considered one of the best performing on the market and upon examination Intel's new Pentium Pro processor (introduced in 1995) was found to infringe its technology.

---

[178] This line of reasoning was also used in *Microsoft III* (D.C. Cir. 2001).

[179] Gilbert & Tom, *supra*, note 10, p. 69.

In this case, the small player's abilities seem threatened if it cannot enforce its property rights, particularly if they relate to top of the line technology. The question nevertheless remains to what extent a player serving 1 per cent of the market should be able to obstruct efficient deliveries of the much bigger supplier, by refusing a cross-licence that was otherwise common in the market. Above all, if the market is characterized by continuous product development, with short product generations, firms might rely on lead-times in innovation in order to appropriate the returns of R&D investments and increase their market shares.[180] If, on the other hand, microprocessor generations are not so short or if, for any other reason, the cross-licence will allow the dominant firm to appropriate substantial benefits from the innovation by rivals (for example through reverse engineering), it seems that the anti-competitive effects are substantial and the conduct hard to justify. Above all, it is a question whether the conduct is likely to improve or diminish efficiency, particularly in innovation. When analysing the likely effects on innovation, an inventory of actors and technologies, economic and competitive conditions, technological trajectories and expected market developments all play key roles.

Compaq's strategy was to differentiate their products from those of their competitors. Through successful innovation they strove to provide more features, greater reliability and lower costs. In this case they were relying on bus patents which they alleged were infringed, not by Intel but Intel's other customers (which Intel now acted to protect). In this situation, it appears important, if one is to maintain competition at the modular level, among computer manufacturers, that the common supplier in the industry does not close off opportunities for gaining advantages through innovation. That would be similar to the situation in *Optical Fibres* (EU 1986). It has been suggested that Intel acted to prevent Compaq from appropriating a larger share of the revenues from computer sales (that is, the combined value of microprocessor and other technologies forming the computer).[181] If the market power of dominance were used to extend the cross-licensing schemes outside the realm of blocking microprocessor technologies, the conduct would be hard to justify on efficiency grounds.

To sum up the Intel case, in an industry where patent rights usually are shared out between the holders, a dominant company must also be able to adopt such a strategy. But it cannot be applied without distinction. It may be abusive to force various actors into royalty-free licences, if the dominant party is thereby able to appropriate innovations to such an extent that rivals effectively lose the ability to compete. Moreover, when the scope of the arrangement goes

---

180 See Chapter 2.

181 Gilbert & Tom, *supra*, note 10, pp. 69f.

outside what is necessary for the dominant company's own product development and sales, there is less countervailing efficiency gain.

It should be noted that the FTC declared the parties to be competitors in innovation, although they were not involved in product sales in the same markets. Intel was therefore alleged to have levered its monopoly power in the sales of microprocessors into the innovation markets for related technologies. Particularly after *Trinko* (US Supreme Court 2004) it is clear that such leverage would be prohibited under §2 only if there was a 'dangerous probability' of monopolization of the second market.[182] Yet, in Intel, if competition was diminished in the innovation market, even if in a manner short of monopolization, that could still have an entrenching effect on Intel's market power in the microprocessor market.[183] Under US standards, the innovation market analysis in such a case must therefore be supplemented by an assessment of the ultimate effect on a relevant technology or product market.

6.3.3 Prevention and Restriction of Competition

In *Microsoft III* (D.C. Cir. 2001), the exclusivity terms included in the dominant company's agreements with manufacturers, its product design (the co-mingling of code and removal of program utilities) and certain deceptive and coercive tactics were found actively to prevent the technological development and establishment of a new software structure that would have threatened current market positions. The DOJ had identified an area of middleware that was of particular strategic value for innovation with the possibility of reshaping much of the PC industry and diminishing dependence on Windows. To the extent that the dominant firm's restrictive practices could not be justified in terms of efficiencies or other pro-competitive advantages to consumers, they were deemed unlawful. Failing to provide such substantiated justifications, Microsoft was found guilty of antitrust violations on many counts.

Nevertheless, while the court made it clear that IPRs give no carte blanche in respect of the antitrust laws, such property rights were treated with some inherent element of justification, probably to protect their underlying function of incentives provider. Consequently, Microsoft was considered justified in protecting itself from drastic alterations in its copyrights when this would only

182 Another question is to what extent the probability of success criterion can be relaxed when applying Section 5 of the FTC Act, which has a wider scope of application and may condemn acts that are contrary to the 'spirit' of the Sherman and Clayton Acts.

183 As seen in Chapter 4, Intel was able to identify a number of firms active in microprocessor innovation, why it can be questioned whether any appreciable innovation market effects occurred.

have marginal anti-competitive effect. Moreover, the court refrained from using certain old standards for evaluating conduct when they were unlikely to take account of possible efficiencies. It thus refused to apply the per se doctrine to the tying of newly integrated software products. Microsoft's decision to physically integrate Windows with Internet Explorer could have created efficiencies, which is why the rule of reason should apply when analysing such conduct.

The European Commission in *Microsoft* (EU 2004) did not hesitate to take on the evaluation of innovation incentives, stating that 'a detailed examination of the scope of the disclosure [of interface information to ensure interoperability with Microsoft's Windows client PC operating system] leads to the conclusion that, on balance, the possible negative impact of an order to supply on Microsoft's incentives to innovate is outweighed by its positive impact on the level of innovation of the whole industry (including Microsoft)'.[184] The Commission also considered compulsory disclosure of interface information less intrusive than *internal* product design (which would mean Microsoft's source code), but in the light of the 'exceptional circumstances' it did not devote too much attention to the question to what extent the information was protected by IPRs or not.[185]

To conquer the group server operating system (server OS) market appears to have been a clear strategy for Microsoft. There is much to suggest that the Commission correctly assessed Microsoft's propensity to use its power in the associated client PC operating system (PC OS) market and the likely harm to consumers induced by the refusal to disclose interface information. Price increases seem likely as a result of Microsoft's expansion into new areas, but, more importantly, it would diminish opportunities for innovation by potential and incumbent providers of server OS, while shaping technological development in a way that benefited Microsoft. In fact, the threat to innovation was the major anti-competitive effect considered by the Commission.

The view that monopolists must be hindered from entering or expanding their market power into adjacent markets has received criticism for neglecting economic insights. It is maintained that a monopolist could not increase its profits by monopolizing a related, previously competitive, market for complementary products.[186] At the end of the day, there will only be one optimal

---

184 *Microsoft* (EU 2004), §783.

185 The distinction between information required for interoperability and information on product design is also clear from Case No IV/29.479 – *IBM* (1984), European Commission, *Sixteenth Report on Competition policy*, 1984, pp. 77, 79. Moreover, Article 6 of the 'Software Directive' (Council Directive 91/250/EEC of 14 May 1991 on the legal protection of computer programs) recognizes the potential need to obtain interoperability information.

186 Bork, *supra*, note 72, pp. 372 *et seq*.

monopoly price charged for the complementary products. The more competitive the second market is, and the lower the price on this market, the higher will the profit-maximizing monopoly price be in the first market. But this is dependent on various preconditions that may not hold in reality. And the Commission also tried to reject such criticism of its leveraging argument.[187] For such an interrelation in price, products must be perfect complements with fixed ratios, which is not the case between the PC and the server operating systems. Microsoft would find it very profitable to become dominant on the second market and this would also give the company control over a market that is of strategic importance for the future development of the software industry and a bridgehead for expanding into other areas of the server industry. It was also contended that Microsoft, by creating and maintaining dominance in the server OS market, could erect barriers to entry and hence preserve the monopoly enjoyed by Windows in the PC OS market. It should be noted that the Commission's major concern was not pricing but various dynamic consequences of reduced competition in the related market, an aspect outside the effects considered in price theory.[188]

Taken together, the different elements indicate that the Commission's analysis of Microsoft's refusal seems apt. The case is about discontinuance of supply of the interoperability information essential for technological innovation – and thus viable competition – by the actors in a separate second market. Microsoft previously furnished the market with such information, but ceased to do so following its own entrance and expansion in the market. This implies that the company was prepared to sacrifice interoperability between its Windows PC OS and others' OS for servers, although this would normally increase the consumer value of the PC OS and thus be valuable to Microsoft (absent a plan to protect and extend its market power). As the Commission notes, it is not the product design as such at stake, but information on how products should function in a network, a kind of information that is normally supplied by non-dominant actors. All parties' property rights seem to be respected and innovation incentives improved. The refusal thereby also seems hard to justify on efficiency grounds, and should be condemned.[189]

For the tying of Windows Media Player (WMP), the Commission chose a case of less strategic importance for innovation than the bundling of Windows and IE (as one in an array of acts intended to eliminate the middleware threat) in *Microsoft III* (D.C. Cir. 2001). Although the decision is concerned about the

---

[187] *Microsoft* (EU 2004), §§764–78.

[188] Cf. Temple Lang, *supra*, note 175, p. 313.

[189] As noted in Chapter 4, according to the settlement between the DOJ and Microsoft, the company faces similar obligations to share (also IPR protected) interoperability information, in the US although in a manner more limited than in Europe.

value for Microsoft of eliminating competition in media players as a further means of entrenching its operating system dominance, intervention in media players seems unlikely materially to affect market developments or the structure of competition at a more general level. Moreover, the anti-competitive effect does not seem as clear as one could expect when intervening in a market characterized by fast technological development. It is not evident that receiving a media player free of charge hurts consumers, or merely Microsoft's competitors. And although the decision claims to take existing case law one step further in showing the true nature of the foreclosed competition, it appears that a very structural approach is taken, based on the difficulties created for competitors in matching the ubiquitous WMP.

It ought to be considered whether a possible tip of the market in favour of WMP (although competing media players in absolute numbers were not threatened with immediate extinction) was due to Microsoft serving the market with a competitive product through a distribution method more efficient than any competitor. That network effects, such as the fact that content providers and complementary software developers favour the likely winner in the media player battle, would further increase such a shift should not force Microsoft into far less efficient means of distribution. Yet, as an example, the decision claims that 'what is critical in a market characterised by network effects is not so much whether downloading allows for widespread distribution of competitors' media players, but whether downloading allows for distribution of competing products which is approximately equal to WMP's'.[190] In the same vein, the remedy, demanding a version of Windows without WMP to be distributed, prohibits Microsoft from favouring the distribution of WMP through Windows, for example by providing a downloadable link (unless such a link is also provided for competitors' products).

It can be argued that Microsoft was able to fix the winner in the media player race, imposing a less attractive product on customers, and tilting the market in its favour. The network effect is a feature of the market that then fortifies the anti-competitive effect of Microsoft's strategy. If it is efficient for the market to choose a standard platform for media players, and hence a winner in the media player war is to be decided, this should be the result of customers' free choice and not the decision of any single producer. This is also the line taken by the Commission, arguing that, under EC competition law, 'an undistorted competition process constitutes a value in itself as it generates efficiencies and creates a climate conducive to innovation'.[191] Therefore, the argument continues, Microsoft cannot rely on 'Windows' historic success in

190 *Microsoft* (EU 2004), §861.
191 Ibid., §969.

the client PC operating system market – and not on the merits of media players' when putting forward network effects.[192]

It should, however, be kept in mind that it is not until the time when Microsoft introduced a technically competitive media player that the Commission considered the bundling an abusive tie.[193] Moreover, although the decision claims that diminished innovation incentives would result if Microsoft was able to continue its bundling, the decision does not contain any profound analysis of past trajectories or expected developments in the technological innovation of media players. This could be compared to the first offence, regarding client PCs and group servers, where the Commission maintained that Microsoft would have a justified competitive advantage by being able to optimize their products with each other with a lead time over its competitors, forcing competitors not only to duplicate Microsoft's features but to be able to offer additional benefits in order to persuade customers to buy their products. The same could apply where Microsoft, through Windows, presents consumers with a media player, while competitors, facing no technological or contractual barriers that prevent their products from being easily installed by end-consumers and OEMs, must rely on technological superiority to compete.

As a matter of policy, if technological efficiencies were created by an integration of Windows and WMP, it is advisable to follow the court in *Microsoft III*. Here Microsoft had developed its own JVM (Java Virtual Machine, allowing for Java applications to run on Windows) which was faster than Sun's existing JVM, but also incompatible with it. This meant that applications written for one of the JVMs could not run on the other. With its faster JVM, Microsoft 'lured Java developers into using Microsoft's developer tools'. Even if the court acknowledged that the development of an incompatible product could violate the antitrust laws if the anti-competitive effect outweighed any pro-competitive justification, the court held that Microsoft's JVM did allow applications to run faster and did not 'itself have any anti-competitive effect'.[194] In other words, if integration technically benefits the

---

192 Similarly, John J. Flynn asserts with regard to the tying of Windows to IE that restraints from tying or bundling can be justified if technologically necessary – thus from an innovation efficiency perspective: 'Allocative efficiency, on the other hand, should not be a justification where there is evidence of market power having the purpose or effect of blocking the entry or use of a competing technology. The value of maintaining open markets so that innovations succeed or fail on the merits should be seen as more important than maximizing short-term allocative efficiencies' ('Antitrust Policy, Innovation Efficiencies, and the Suppression of Technology', 66 *Antitrust Law Journal* 487, 514 (1998)).

193 'The negative impact of tying until 1999 could [. . .] be off-set by media player vendors who provided a product that Microsoft was not able to provide' (§820).

194 *Microsoft III* (D.C. Cir. 2001), 253 F.3d 34, 75.

users, counter-balancing the anti-competitive effects is very difficult to perform, which is why intervention should only be considered where the anti-competitive effects are the principal or only effect.[195]

6.3.4 Further Duties versus Innovative Competitors

The question whether dominant firms must assist rivals does not stop at interface information allowing compatibility. Concerning refusals to deal and, more particularly, refusals connected to IPRs, a highly interesting, but delicate, development of antitrust policy has been initiated by the ECJ. The latest addition, *IMS* (ECJ 2004) is no exception. The Court upheld, and extended, the rule hammered out in Magill,[196] which makes it abusive to refuse to license a product or service that is indispensable for a potential competitor, if (a) the refusal prevents the emergence of a new product for which there is a potential consumer demand; (b) the refusal is not objectively justified; and (c) it is likely to exclude all competition in the secondary market.[197]

Since the key attribute of the property right established by patent law, just like any other property right, is the ability of the property holder to exclude others from using the property, a duty to put the property at the disposal of others, particularly competitors, may come with serious repercussions. Any shift in the policy which broadens or narrows the ability to exclude potential users (be it through the property rules, antitrust rules or other fields of law) affects incentive mechanisms for investing time, money and effort. It is often maintained that antitrust policy should not undermine the incentives created by IPRs. Here, the ECJ accurately continues to hold that the mere refusal to license cannot be abusive. At the same time, as shown in Chapter 2, it is clear that intellectual property rights come at a price, including the possibility of blocking further innovation. It is evident that the ECJ has taken on the task of protecting such follow-up innovation by including the prevention of a new product as a possible additional element making such refusal illegal. Dismissing a prerequisite of two distinctly separate markets, and considering the identification of a potential or even hypothetical upstream market sufficient, also opens up a potential for mandatory supply of inputs. The question is which effect (the erosion or the creation of innovation incentives) is likely to prevail under such a standard.

Antitrust law may properly intervene when market actors extend or main-

---

195 Temple Lang, *supra*, note 175, p. 319; see also Elhauge, *supra*, note 176, pp. 316 *et seq*.

196 Joined Cases C-241/91 P and C-242/91 P, *RTE and ITP v. Commission* ('Magill') (1995).

197 IMS judgment, §§37, 38.

tain their power, for example by extending their IPR portfolio by purchases, entering into restrictive agreements with customers or competitors, or exercising their IPRs in discriminatory ways. Antitrust law may thus be important in identifying and prohibiting strategies that limit competition or create substantial foreclosure. But a compulsory licence is much more questionable in situations where a firm merely has developed and protected a technology and subsequently has done nothing more than rely on this property right for its own production of goods and services. If follow-on innovation by (potential) rivals in the same market is hampered by such an IPR, it would generally be better to change the IP laws than to turn property rules (right to exclude unless the owner consents to the offered price) into liability rules (where others are allowed to use the owner's property as long as a court-determined price is paid).[198]

Interpreting the IMS standard literally, it could have serious negative consequences for ex ante incentives, since the more unique and valuable an innovation turns out to be, the greater the likelihood that the innovator will lose the exclusive rights to commercialize it.[199] At the same time there are elements that will probably limit too stretched an application of the standard. Still, at the margin, the uncertainties are substantial.

First, it is not clear what would constitute a 'new' product or service with a potential consumer demand. In *Magill*, a TV guide comprising the programme listings of all channels was something new and superior for which there was a clear demand, compared to the existing guides each covering only one TV network. The consumers' interest in getting a superior product thereby prevailed over the legitimate interests of the producer of the 'old' product. In *IMS*, the parties' opinions about the novelty of NDC's planned product were at variance, an issue which will be for the German court to decide. In the meantime, it is worth noting that Advocate General Tizzano considered that the licensee must intend to produce goods or services 'of a different nature' which, although competing with existing ones, meet unsatisfied 'specific consumer requirements'.[200] Yet the ECJ chose the words 'new product' and 'potential consumer demand', which seems to open up access for incremental innovation, although excluding situations where the licensee will essentially duplicate existing goods or services.

There is also an issue of the objective considerations that would justify a

198 Elhauge, *supra*, note 176, pp. 303f. See also Eklöf, Dan, *Upphovsrätt i konkurrens – särskilt om tvångslicensiering*, Stockholms universitet, Stockholm, 2004, pp. 339 *et seq*.

199 Temple Lang, *supra*, note 175, p. 296.

200 Case C-418/01 *IMS Health GmbH & Co. OHG v. NDC Health GmbH & Co. KG*, Opinion of Advocate General Tizzano (2003), §62.

refusal to supply the input. It should be noted that *Magill* concerned TV networks' copyrighted programme listings – channel, day, time and title of coming programmes – a natural by-product of producing TV. Thus there was no such justification 'either in the activity of television broadcasting or in that of publishing television magazines'.[201] In *IMS*, where it will be for the German court to decide on the issue, the distinction is not so obvious since the development of a structural basis for collecting, processing and selling data presumably takes some skill, effort and investment. If the court accepted this line of argument for determining objective justifications for refusal, it would, fortunately, be difficult for a potential competitor to rely on the three cumulative criteria in a situation where the incumbent is a research-based company that has developed an IPR-protected (upstream) input (such as a pharmaceutical compound) and enjoys a monopoly in the market for the resulting (downstream) product (the finalized drug). In such a situation the refusal to license seems quite justified, as the request hits at the core of the company's investment and business activity. If that kind of refusal were not to be accepted, antitrust policy would create serious incentive problems for investments and for creating the input in the first place.

The justification could, however, depend on how much the 'new' product will affect the demand for the existing product. If the licensee intends to make a product that is competitively unrelated to existing products, in that it will not render obsolete or affect the demand for existing products, a refusal might be harder to justify.[202]

6.3.5 Concluding Observations

The supervision of dominant companies by antitrust law must be subject to similar limiting principles to those of other fields of competition policy. Innovative success and superior efficiency should not be held against a company, for the simple reason that this would hurt competition and consumer welfare in the long run. If anything, the case law analysis shows how hard it is correctly to identify and remedy dominant firms' potentially anti-competitive behaviour while enabling firms to compete forcefully in the market.

---

201 Advocate General Jacobs considered the copyright protection for the programme listings 'difficult to justify in terms of rewarding or providing an incentive for creative effort': Case C-7/97, *Oscar Bronner GmbH & Co. KG v. Mediaprint*, Opinion of Advocate General Jacobs (1998).

202 Yet another question that arises when reading *IMS*, is what other kinds of circumstances may qualify as 'exceptional'. The ECJ describes the three conditions making a refusal of indispensable inputs abusive as 'sufficient', but does not indicate that they rule out all other conditions.

The analysis seems to suggest that, if a dominant company is using its position to force upon competitors in innovation contractual terms that allow it to take part of the competitors' innovations and thereby both creates disincentives for innovative activity and cements its position, this constitutes a limitation of competition. The extent to which the anti-competitive effect will materialize depends on the conditions for innovation in the industry: the actors, the technologies, the means of appropriation and commercialization, and so on. A structured analysis must be conducted to distinguish between behaviour that furthers the development and distribution of products (*inter alia* by unravelling blocking IPRs and holdout positions) and that which impinges negatively on incentives and the ability to innovate to the ultimate detriment of consumer welfare. This is similar to the analysis of grantbacks in licensing arrangements.

In innovative industries, it may be abusive for a dominant company to withhold information necessary to ensure interoperability with other kinds of products. In competitive markets, the dissemination of such information is in the interest of all parties, and does not constitute any considerable intrusion in the ex ante incentives to product development. At the same time, such information may constitute a bottleneck to innovation in various related markets.

Although 'predatory innovation', in the context of intentionally making a product incompatible with rivals' products on a second market, is a possible antitrust offence, it is crucial not to hold genuine product development against a dominant actor.[203] And even if a balancing of efficiencies and anti-competitive effects is theoretically possible, and called for by the case law, it is virtually impossible on the margin.[204] The relevant test should be whether the case involves a non-marginal foreclosure without any appreciable benefits.

The ECJ has attempted to spur follow-on innovation through its notion regarding refusals to license IPRs. Since liability is confined to instances when a refusal will prevent the emergence of a new product, the court could be interpreted as saying that the standard applies only when the holder of an essential input is an inactive monopolist in the relevant innovation market. Here, an ex ante perspective is a necessity, since liability should not be based on the effects of genuine product development, ex post, on competitors. Net effects on innovation cannot be estimated on the margin, and liability should therefore be confined to reasonably clear cases. It must be ascertained that, all things

---

203 Regarding predatory innovation see e.g. Ordover, Janusz A. & Willig, Robert D., 'An Economic Definition of Predation: Pricing and Product Innovation', 91 *Yale Law Journal* 8 (1981) and discussions in Case No IV/30.979 and 31.394 *Decca Navigator Systems*, OJ L 43/27 (1989) and *C.R. Bard, Inc v. M3 Systems Inc.* 157 F.3d 1340 (Fed. Cir. 1998).

204 Langlois, *supra*, note 112, pp. 220f.

considered, innovation abilities and incentives are stimulated rather than hollowed out. Even if one may agree with the outcome in the individual cases decided by the ECJ, a potential drawback of the judgments in this area is that they relate to a few somewhat peculiar cases, leaving many questions unanswered, which makes it hard to predict the result when applying the tests to other, potentially more mainstream, situations. Even if the 'exceptional circumstances' will be limited to pure exceptions, which can be expected, a 'we know it when we see it' policy may do more harm than good. There is much to suggest that investment in innovation is spurred by transparent and foreseeable property rules. Even Arrow's models, emphasizing superior innovation incentives in competitive markets, presuppose that property rights are enforced.[205] Further clarification and limiting principles are therefore called for.

It is clear that the Commission and the ECJ go further than their American equivalents in the application of antitrust law to this area. DOJ officials maintain that 'it cannot possibly make sense for intellectual property law to recognize as its most valued creation a patent describing an invention essential to the creation of a valuable commercial product, and for competition law to then step in and say that the owner will be required to relinquish exclusive ownership of the patent because it is essential to the creation of a valuable commercial product'.[206] Yet, also in the US, the appropriateness of current IP standards is debated.[207] With reference to that discussion it is therefore noted that 'the intellectual property community must recognize that, if it does not address possible areas for reform, then it should not be surprised to see competition law trying to do so, even if not very well'.[208]

Both in Europe and in the US, antitrust policy seems to be in search of clearer standards. In this regard, it seems appropriate and important that the showing of a prima facie anti-competitive effect should include considerations of the overall economic and technological context, including conditions for innovation. Since dominant firms, to the benefit of the consumers, are supposed to compete vigorously, they cannot be made responsible for, or be forced to provide, efficiency justifications for every restrictive effect their

---

205 Elhauge, *supra*, note 176, pp. 298f. See Chapter 2 for a short overview of Arrow.

206 Pate, Hewitt R., 'Antitrust In A Transatlantic Context – From The Cicada's Perspective'; address at 'Antitrust in a Transatlantic Context' Conference, Brussels, Belgium, June 7, 2004; available at http://www.usdoj.gov/atr/public/speeches/203973.pdf, (last visited 11 October 2004).

207 See, e.g., Federal Trade Commission, *To Promote Innovation: The Proper Balance of Competition and Patent Law and Policy*, Report by the Federal Trade Commission (2003).

208 Pate, *supra*, note 206.

behaviour may have on rivals. Rather, such a responsibility should be saved for the instances where the exclusionary effects are substantial and can only be saved by showing efficiencies, for example of a technological nature, the information on which is typically private.[209]

The ultimate test of an innovation market approach would be an abuse case where no relevant product market exists yet, giving rise to an abuse of a dominant position in innovation. In contrast to the US abuse doctrine (monopolization or attempt of monopolization), in Europe such a case would depend upon the delimitation and assessment of ex ante dominance in a relevant innovation market. To establish such dominance would be delicate. Even if a company is spending vastly more on R&D than the rest of its competitors this does not imply that it is dominant in innovation. Other qualitative factors should be factored in.

Although there are good reasons to caution against such a policy, it could be a way of attacking unilateral anti-competitive behaviour affecting competition at an early stage. For example, if acquisitions of patents and licences can be shown to be anti-competitive in terms of diminished R&D competition and future product market competition, it seems odd to rule out entirely the possibility that a firm that dominates R&D in a particular area could act abusively, merely because no product has yet been introduced to the market. But since that will not entail unilateral conduct, it may be better handled under Article 81.[210] Another possible example would be fraudulent procurement of intellectual property rights.[211] Such behaviour may be part of an R&D-level strategy

[209] This would match the view that if a dominant firm effectively raises its rivals' costs, an inquiry into business justifications is mandated in non-marginal cases. If the foreclosure is small, if alternatives can be developed or if the practice results in substantial efficiencies, the judiciary should favour non-liability. See Hovenkamp, Herbert, 'The Reckoning of Post-Chicago Antitrust', in Cucinotta, Antonio, Pardolesi, Roberto & Van den Bergh, Roger (eds), *Post-Chicago Developments in Antitrust Law*, Edward Elgar, Cheltenham, 2002, pp. 16f.

[210] See Tom, Willard K., 'The 1975 Xerox Consent Decree: Ancient Artifacts and Current Tensions', 68 *Antitrust Law Journal* 967, 976 (2001), criticizing the reasoning by the court in *SCM Corp. v. Xerox Corp.*, 645 F.2d 1195 (2d Cir. 1981), for rejecting the imposition of liability for Xerox patent acquisitions based on the notion that the relevant product market did not exist at the time of the patent acquisitions.

[211] Regarding fraudulent procurement of intellectual property rights, see *American Cyanamid Co.*, 72 F.T.C. 623 (1967), *aff'd sub nom. Charles Pfizer & Co., Inc. v. Fed. Trade Comm'n*, 401 F.2d 547 (6th Cir. 1968). In this case the FTC found that the patents, on which the cross-licensing arrangement was based, had been procured by suppressing material information and by misrepresenting material facts. See also *Summit Technology, Inc. and VISX, Inc.*, Docket no. 9286 (1998). Here an administrative law judge later rejected the complaint concerning fraudulent procurement of patents by VISX. Recently, the European Commission decided to fine

to stifle innovation and competition from others, lacking any pro-competitive business justification. In addition, it has been discussed whether firms can effectively seal off an area from competing R&D and future product market competition by engaging in pre-emptive patenting.[212] But if liability is difficult to determine for powerful firms already incumbent in ordinary product markets, an innovation market-based analysis is even trickier.

AstraZeneca €60 million, *inter alia* for abusing the patent system. According to the Commission, the company provided misleading information to several national patent offices with a view to obtaining supplementary protection certificates (SPCs) for the medicinal product Losec. This practice led to the illegitimate extension of the basic patent protection in a number of EU countries. See press releases, IP/05/737, 'Commission fines AstraZeneca €60 million for misusing patent system to delay market entry of competing generic drugs', 15 June, 2005; IP/03/1136, 'Commission warns AstraZeneca of preliminary findings in Losec antitrust investigation', 31 July 2003.

[212] See, e.g., Audretsch, David B., Baumol, William J. & Burke, Andrew E., 'Competition policy in dynamic markets', 19 *International Journal of Industrial Organization* 613, 631 (2001); Gilbert, Richard J. & Newbery, David M.G., 'Preemptive Patenting and the Persistence of Monopoly', 72 *American Economic Review* 514 (1982).

7. A policy for innovation analysis

7.1 PURPOSE AND PRINCIPLES

All aspects of innovation competition analysis, such as the firms and R&D sources to include in a relevant market, the suspected potential anti-competitive effects, the modus operandi of analysing markets and practices and the difficult efficiency and remedy issues, are crucially dependent on the facts. However, the above analysis of legal prerequisites, doctrinal discussions, indicative conclusions from economic theory and empirical studies, and experiences from authority practices, should make it possible to outline some elements of a rational policy for innovation analysis. In light of the complexity of such analysis, the open-endedness of current legal concepts, and the need for predictability and legal security, an important feature is to identify limiting principles for the use of innovation market analysis. This will also summarize the conclusions and recommendations presented in Chapters 5 and 6. The overriding aim of such a policy would be to maintain a process for the development of new generations of products and technologies that is reasonably open for competition. With the innovation process exposed to (at least potential) competition, static product market concerns can be relatively played down.

Since the relevant market is not an end in itself, but rather a way of identifying the non-trivial constraints on the exercise of market power, its delimitation must vary from case to case. Where innovation is an important feature of competition, a comprehensive analysis should include a structured assessment of trajectories, conditions and forecasts of that dimension. Regulatory frameworks for the assessment market transactions cannot disregard these fundamental features of competition. One should therefore assess whether the market practice substantially reduces the incentives for innovation or artificially decides winners or excludes participants. Strategic actions at the R&D level should not be able to eliminate the uncertainty prevalent on any functioning market.

Any antitrust policy must at the same time include appropriate limiting principles, providing legal security while making the implementation sufficiently transparent. The burden of proving anti-competitive effects is on the authorities; if a sufficient likelihood of such effects is established, the burden of rebuttal is on the parties. Without diminishing the importance of this principle for the rule of law, the practical interpretation of these burdens should result in an efficient allocation of the onus to provide relevant information.

Transactions and practices that enable technological development that would otherwise not have occurred, or which genuinely facilitate such development, are beneficial to competition. To so combine resources furthers technological development and constitutes a means of competing on the merits, and this should consequently be allowed. Hence the resulting benefits should not primarily be seen as part of an efficiency defence, such as an offsetting rebuttal of prima facie illegality due to risks of future product market dominance. If a transaction promotes technological development (for example if the parties were not able to reach the market independently) and does not lead to durable foreclosure of a market (perhaps it even establishes a market) it should be regarded as efficient management, stimulating the market process. Nevertheless, if the practice leads to substantial foreclosures, eliminates innovation competition, risks spillover collusion and so on, it must be considered whether a less restrictive means is immediately available and, if not, whether the benefits still prevail.

7.2 CURRENT MARKETS

Various types of transaction may reduce competitive pressure in an oligopolistic market. Conventional competition law analysis focuses on existing markets for products and technologies and aims to detect whether the parties will raise prices or exercise market power in other dimensions.

Where innovation is an important means of competition in the market, or where the subject matter of the transaction concerns improvements of current products or technologies, a detailed investigation of conditions in the innovation process is called for in order to fully appreciate the level and nature of current and potential competition and thus the likely effect of the transaction. The innovation market concept seems apt, at least *as a method* of analysing R&D potentials and effects, either as part of, or as supplemental to, a product market analysis. The merit of elaborating different market definitions is that this may shed new light both on possible anti-competitive effects and on sources of competition that constrain the parties. A full analysis may require the delineation of product, technology and innovation markets.

The time horizon is important. As an example, if entry within one to two years can be considered within the framework of barriers to entry and potential competition in an ordinary product market analysis, the innovation market concept may provide a way of analysing future developments, which would not normally be considered. At the same time, such an extended analysis must be confined to instances where the characteristics of the innovation process allow for an assessment with a requisite level of certainty. Even if the success of an individual R&D project may be uncertain, the overall conditions for technological change may be susceptible to analysis.

To perform a prospective analysis in relation to the relevant product market, the focus will be on the underlying technologies and capabilities of firms in the market, rather than on the features of current products. This will allow for an evaluation of how the market is likely to evolve, in terms both of current technologies and of the impact and direction of technologies under development.[1] In this way it can be assessed whether past trends are likely to continue and what this would bring about, or whether radically new technology is likely to be introduced which may modify current structures. Moreover, with a focus on R&D developments, rather than on the mere product market, important changes outside the current product market may more easily be factored in.

The authorities ought to be consistent and thorough in characterizing the innovation process of an industry, in investigating any strategic positions held by the parties and the specific assets they control and to state this clearly in the public record.

Anti-competitive effects on innovation may arise when the parties are important innovators in a concentrated market and the transaction would eradicate alternatives in the R&D dimension or eliminate the possibility of the parties outperforming each other through successful innovation. Similarly, the effect of transactions between an incumbent firm and a potential entrant depends on the relative strategic importance of the R&D conducted by the entrant, compared to that of incumbents and other potential entrants.[2] In all these settings, structured innovation analysis may well lessen anti-competitive concerns, both in the innovation and the product market, by finding promising conditions for dynamic competition.

Whereas complex multi-market analysis is often called for in analysing borderline cases, the rationale of block exemptions and safety zones is to single out those agreements which will not pose a threat to competition or which should be exempted because of inherent efficiency enhancement. The European technology transfer block exemption has been criticized for being

---

[1] Europe Economics, *The Development of Analytical Tools for Assessing Market Dynamics in the Knowledge Based Economy*, Report to the European Commission (2003), pp. 41, 47 *et seq*; available at http://europa.eu.int/comm/enterprise/library/lib-competition/doc/analytical_tools_final_report.pdf (last visited 3 March 2005).

[2] Whether the likelihood of such consequences can be assessed may also depend on the possibility to predict the overlap between the two categories of products.

too hard to apply and giving too little attention to the dynamics of the markets where licensing occurs, on the grounds that current market shares in technology and product markets are both difficult to assess at the time of the transaction and a poor proxy for market power. The US IP Guidelines in this respect offer a technology and innovation market 'safe harbour' if four additional, independently controlled, technologies/innovation sources remain. It has been indicated that this 'technology centre' approach is widely relied upon by industry.[3]

As a result of the criticism of the European block exemption and with a view to promoting predictability and confining detailed analysis to instances where real competition concerns are present, a test similar to the American safe harbour was built into the EU Technology Transfer Guidelines. Outside the area of hardcore restrictions, the Commission thus considers it unlikely that Article 81 is infringed where there are four or more independently controlled technologies that may be substitutable for the licensed technology.[4] This creates an important presumption of non-infringement. Conceivably, a similar safe harbour could be accepted with regard to innovation markets. From a policy point of view it would be rational to grant these safety zones increased importance as rules of thumb. The innovation market approach would presumably convey important information on competition. Products and technologies under development may be just as much a restraining factor for licensors of a technology market as are products under development for sellers of goods on a product market.

The risk of collusion in the market should also be addressed. Normally, collusion in relation to innovation will be difficult, since it is an activity where the parties cannot effectively monitor each other. However, in markets where the R&D process is both concentrated and transparent, collusion risks or other kinds of less explicit strategic behaviour may also affect the analysis. With high barriers to entry and transparency in lengthy R&D processes, an increased concentration in a particular area may well lead to coordination in future R&D.[5] For transactions short of mergers, spillover collusion risks

---

3 American Chamber of Commerce to the European Union, *Position Paper on the Commission's Communication of 1st October 2003 on the Application of Article 81(3) to certain categories of agreements and concerted practices*; available at http://www.europa.eu.int/comm/competition/antitrust/technology_transfer_2/59_amcham_en.pdf (last visited 11 October 2004). Note that the equivalent innovation market safety zone in the US 2000 Competitor Collaboration Guidelines requires four R&D sources in total (§4.3).

4 EU 2004 Technology Transfer Guidelines, §131.

5 In the pharmaceutical industry, although reasonably fragmented on an industrial macro level, typically only a small number of firms are active in specific therapy areas: Ben-Asher, Dror, 'In Need of Treatment? Merger Control, Pharmaceutical Innovation, and Consumer Welfare', 21 *Journal of Legal Medicine* 271, 283 (2000).

between the parties are also relevant, particularly those into other currently marketed products.

As to the role of efficiencies, any such assessment is likely to depend on the specificity of the proposed transaction. In full-blown mergers among incumbents, productive efficiencies are likely to be anticipated. Dynamic efficiency may be achieved by joining complementary assets and skills or by achieving an efficient scale and scope in R&D. Explicit accounts of dynamic efficiencies are more likely to be at the centre of analysis when considering joint ventures, licensing agreements or more limited acquisitions of IPRs or specialized (smallish) research-based firms. Such transactions typically aim to achieve these benefits. So, efficiencies should be part of analysing whether innovation competition will be reduced at all. If the parties could not have achieved the relevant R&D objectives in an effective way independently, anti-competitive effects generally do not arise. Even if some anti-competitive effect occurs, transaction-specific efficiencies may prevail.

Under all circumstances, any corrective remedy should be tailored in a way that causes minimum harm to the efficiencies potentially created by the transaction, while maintaining competition on the merits in the innovation dimension. In other words, if a winner does emerge on the product market, this is due to its superiority, and the position is not being upheld by artificial barriers to rivals' innovation.

7.3 POTENTIAL FUTURE MARKETS

This level of analysis is appropriate where a transaction will affect the development of a new product or technology, and will either change current market boundaries or possibly render current products obsolete. It focuses on specific R&D projects aiming at particular new product(s) in the future and, as such, on more drastic innovation. This is the realm of the innovation market approach as set out by American and European authorities in their respective guidelines. Central questions include the following: is the transaction likely to have anti-competitive effects on the scope and pace of R&D; might it lead to an anti-competitive narrowing of the range of products and the lessening of consumer choice; and will it seriously restrict competition in the future product market?

7.3.1 Distant Future Markets

Where competing R&D sources are combined at a stage relatively distant from future product markets, one where the chances of success and the boundaries of future product markets are uncertain, the analysis should assess the conditions of innovation in broader terms. Focusing on the overall R&D structure, long-term R&D incentives and foreclosure of third parties, it should be less dependent on the timing of individual R&D projects, and the relevant innovation market may include R&D pursued on disparate alternative technology lines (although increasing the possibility of imperfect future product match). Which firms or R&D projects are to be considered to have a constraining effect on the merged entity must be assessed in the light of the particular industry and the facts of the specific case, but can be quite broad compared to a product market investigation. Less precision is thus required in identifying the boundaries of the particular future product market at which the individual R&D is directed.[6]

This kind of assessment prompts several considerations. First, in order for an anti-competitive effect to occur in the first place, the arrangement (typically a merger, joint venture or exclusive licence arrangement) must involve firms able to perform the relevant R&D, either independently or through a significantly less restrictive arrangement. Here, the authorities should take a pragmatic and realistic view as to alternative arrangements.[7] For example, if a small firm seeks to develop and market a technology in combination with a large counterpart, it is possible that the most efficient partner in terms of incentives and the ability to carry on the development will be the only known R&D competitor.

Second, in cases where a significant actor would remain in the innovation market after the transaction, the authorities should be able to give clear indications why a reduction or delay in R&D could be expected. Without any such indications the authorities may be just implying that reductions in R&D can be presumed if less than four firms are engaged in competing R&D. Since four remaining firms provide a safety zone (at least for US joint venture cases, though a similar harbour ought to apply in Europe), that number must be considered large enough to create a competitive market. But it does not auto-

---

[6] In the pharmaceutical industry, it may be hard to estimate the exact characteristics and effects a particular future drug will have, implying that different R&D programmes directed at treating a disease could lead to future drugs appealing differently to different consumer segments. As a reference, pharmaceutical R&D in phases I and II could be included even though the success of such R&D is very uncertain. See, e.g., *GlaxoWellcome/SmithKline Beecham* (EU 2000) regarding active competitors on the R&D market for pharmaccines. Without further analysis of the competing R&D projects, their mere existence seems to have been sufficient. This is probably due to the fact that the pipeline products under investigation were so far away from commercialization. Moreover, the parties had no dominance in current markets to reap benefits from.

[7] The guidelines indicate that this is how the authorities will assess the situation. See EU 2001 Horizontal Cooperation Guidelines, §§35, 56, 69; US 2000 Competitor Collaboration Guidelines, §3.36(b).

matically follow that a deviation from this standard must amount to a substantial lessening or significant impediment of competition. Presumption rules based on concentrations ratios as they are used in product market analysis should not be deployed for innovation markets.

Although it cannot be certain that such a combination to monopoly would necessarily lead to anti-competitive reductions in innovation, there seem to be good grounds for presuming that a secure monopoly position in R&D is not conducive to efficient performance.[8] In the absence of case-specific circumstances that alleviate such concerns or the showing of expected efficiencies of considerable magnitude, monopolization of R&D in this broad sense should not be accepted.[9] This holds even if the likelihood that the particular products under development will reach the market cannot be determined. It should be kept in mind that, in Europe, the R&D block exemption may apply to this kind of situation and an authority would then be left with the possibility to withdraw the exemption for the specific agreement. Such a measure is provided for in case the R&D agreement 'would eliminate effective competition in research and development on a particular market'.

In between a monopoly and the safety zone, further evidence should be presented before remedies seeking to reinstate R&D competition are tried. Particular care should be taken if the parties, or some of them, are already dominant on current markets that are likely to be affected by the R&D to be undertaken (the new product may even have the potential of rendering some current products obsolete). In this situation, depending on the level of R&D competition, a combination of projects already at an early stage can imply lessened incentives to maintain efficient R&D efforts, in terms of pace, direction and scope of the product development.

The number of remaining R&D sources required depends on their ability to constrain inefficient behaviour. This may in turn be dependent on their scope, strength and credibility. Access to assets, human resources and funding is important.[10] Although innovation market analysis is typically deployed when relevant entry into the R&D process in the short to medium term is unlikely, possibilities of such entry counteract inefficient conduct by the firms. Such considerations depend mainly on how the relevant R&D capabilities are spread, potential entrants' incentives and the time that would be required for

---

8 See section 6.1.3, above.

9 Relevant efficiencies should include showing that the quality of the resulting products, or the speed and efficiency of R&D, will benefit substantially if the R&D assets are combined or, perhaps more important, that the likelihood of successful product development will increase substantially.

10 See US 2000 Competitor Collaboration Guidelines, §4.3; EU 2001 Horizontal Cooperation Guidelines, §51.

entry.[11] Collusion in relation to R&D between the remaining parties is normally quite difficult, considering the secrecy involved.

Third, both the presumption of negative effects of an R&D monopoly and case-specific findings of anti-competitive effects in a situation between monopoly and the safe harbour should be rebuttable, a presumption being more easily rebutted than a case specific finding.[12] If the parties can show that anti-competitive effects are offset by efficiencies – particularly if the likelihood of product launch increases, enabling superior product quality or substantially enhancing the pace of innovation – it should be determined whether consumers in the end are likely to benefit from the transaction. Since, in Europe, an elimination of competition as a matter of law cannot be exempted under Article 81(3), efficiency arguments in favour of a transaction to R&D monopoly should be directed at rebutting any claimed anti-competitive effect, for example by showing a substantial increase in the likelihood of R&D success or that the transaction enables the development of a clearly superior product.

7.3.2 Imminent Future Markets

Where the R&D process is reasonably predictable, at the time of the transaction, in terms of the likelihood that the R&D will in fact result in a product launch, the characteristics of the future product, the boundaries of its market and the product's attractiveness to consumers, the analysis may increasingly focus on maintaining competition in that future market. For combinations close to product market launch, this is the natural perspective for competition analysis, not least as substantial efficiencies in the innovation process are unlikely to materialize from a combination at this stage. The scope and timing of other products or technologies under development may be essential to the analysis. If the parties are active on some related current markets, such positions also become increasingly influential to the analysis.

At the first level of analysis, it may be a concern that unified control over two new and competing products may result in the likely cancellation or delay in the development of one of them, if competition is too weak.[13] Lacking sufficient competition from current products or from competing R&D, this decision will not be taken with regard to the competitive merits of the products, as much as the maximization of profit on a non-competitive market. That could

[11] See US 2000 Competitor Collaboration Guidelines, §3.35.

[12] Naturally there could also, in an R&D monopoly, be case specific circumstances suggesting anti-competitive effects.

[13] The reason for doing so could be that the product under development would merely cannibalize profits from the parties' other product under development or from currently marketed products.

be regarded as an anti-competitive result of less R&D competition. Variety as a value for consumer welfare could thereby be regarded as the bridge between concerns for efficient performance in innovation and efficient future product markets. If R&D is heavily concentrated and entry is difficult, the parties may maximize profits by dropping, or putting on hold, the development of a product, typically the one that would require more time and investment to bring to the market. Thus a potentially superior product could be dropped or delayed through lack of competition in R&D.[14] Decreased product quality and variety may also result from mere streamlining of the potentially competing products' attributes, or merging the developments into one product.[15] Still, considering the difficulty in distinguishing artificial reductions in product variety from efficient savings of resources, it would be necessary to show that a reduction is likely as a result of anticipated market power.

Apart from lessened product variety, a substantial anti-competitive concern in these cases would be pure price competition in the future product market. The connection to the potential competition doctrine is evident, yet formal differences do not necessarily change the underlying analysis. In order to find an appreciable reduction in potential competition, analysis would have to include the identification of other R&D projects, their timing and competitiveness. Product market effects would depend on the number and significance of remaining products under development as well as the current product market situation. Although it is difficult to predict the future attractiveness of different pipeline products, some kind of estimate may be necessary. This may warrant maintenance of some independent product lines. If anti-competitive effects are considered likely, it must be determined whether efficiencies will offset any harm to customers.

In this respect too, a broader innovation aspect may be distinguished. A competitive product market will leave the market participants with innovation as an important tool to achieve larger profits. This will motivate the quest not only for revolutionary innovation but also for follow-up improvements and developments. Incremental innovation may also have substantive welfare implications for an industry where product development typically goes through an R&D process that is lengthy and expensive.

---

[14] Ben-Asher, Dror, 'In Need of Treatment? Merger Control, Pharmaceutical Innovation, and Consumer Welfare', 21 *Journal of Legal Medicine* 271, 307 *et seq.* (2000), including a discussion on incentives and abilities for pharmaceutical firms to reduce R&D.

[15] See *Sensormatic* (FTC 1995) regarding quality aspects. For pure R&D joint ventures (not extending to joint commercialization) and similar licence agreements at the R&D stage, commenced close to market introduction, variety may be the primary variable at stake.

Even when the effects of a transaction largely relate to a product market, the appropriate remedies may have to include R&D aspects. Full divestitures, rather than licences, could be required in order to create a viable competitor on the future product market. Also behavioural conditions regarding continued R&D efforts, such as support to the acquiring firm in the transition period, should be considered.

7.4 TECHNOLOGY BASES

The innovation market concept, as outlined in the US and EU guidelines, is not a full-blown dynamic concept. Presumably, too much was borrowed from the (static) product market concept and transferred to competing R&D. Thus the orthodox method is appropriate when it is used to prevent monopoly in a particular future market (7.3.2). The same holds when it is used to supplement traditional potential product market competition (prolonging entry analysis from short to medium term) (7.2.) By widening the scope of competing R&D sources and assessing incentives and abilities for continued performance in R&D, dynamic considerations regarding the development of future markets – 'true' competition in innovation – can be assessed (7.3.1). But still, the concept is limited to identifiable R&D sources aimed at potentially substitutable future products. This brings us to the last market level: technology bases.

A transaction that combines technology and know-how may create a bottleneck for research and commercialization of a variety of potential product markets. Where the competitive restraints are not tied to particular R&D projects or identifiable competing future products, a market delineation based on such products is not the adequate basis for analysis. Rather, the focus must be on lessened competition between parties in their quest to develop and commercialize a certain technological area and, more important still, the creation of anti-competitive foreclosure in that area.

An upstream transaction may reduce the level of uncertainty regarding the other party's abilities and strategies and reduce the possibilities for parties outperforming each other through technological development. Moreover, such a transaction could create opportunities for anti-competitive foreclosure of third parties, limiting both actual and potential competition regarding the research that is conducted by the parties, and complementary developments in a broader area.

A central problem is how to draw the boundaries of the technology base. At some level, the competitive restraints – the limits of the bottleneck – will be alternative technologies or assets. Therefore a technology base has much in common with a 'regular' technology market, where the relevant market includes 'the intellectual property right that is licensed and its close substitutes'. If the bottleneck is created through a licence arrangement, the negative effects of availability and licensing terms could presumably be dealt with through a technology market analysis. At the same time, both the creation of the bottleneck and its effect may be different from what is normally considered in a technology market analysis according to the guidelines.

Rather than focusing on the substitutability of a technology for some specified downstream purposes, the analysis is an appraisal of critical technologies, perhaps combined with other assets and capabilities, for continued R&D in a broader research area. An example of upstream activity protected by IPRs could be research tools in biotechnology (for example, sequenced genes predisposed for a certain disease). Another could be where important players, wishing to increase interoperability of products, exclusively share information to this end (for example, software interfaces). Conduct in relation to such bottlenecks can thus have effects for various future technology and product markets. The sequenced genes may be essential to the development of different analytical and diagnostic methods, vaccines, treatments, mapping of gene mutations and so on. And software interfaces may potentially be used for a range of software requiring interoperability with other software. Nevertheless, there must be some particular features of the combined assets that make such an analysis of competitive effects tenable.

The approach taken in analysing the potential effects of patent pools for standards puts the standard to which the patents relate at the centre. A standard is typically used for the development of a range of applications, belonging to different downstream markets. At the same time, a standard may face competing standards at the upstream level. This would, outside the realm of industry standards, be equivalent to the common denominator of the combined technologies and other assets. In *Ciba-Geigy/Sandoz* that would be gene therapy, in *Pasteur Mérieux/Merck* it would be vaccines and vaccine technologies.

Although gene therapy technology may not be a product in itself, the assets may, for the sake of the analysis, be put at the core of the innovation market so that the effects that could materialize can be analysed. If products derived from the combined assets are likely to have different characteristics (basically, unlikely to be close substitutes) from products resulting from alternative inputs, the combination is likely to create a bottleneck.

A possible remedy for overcoming anti-competitive effects could be to take a restrictive attitude towards combination of upstream patents, research tools and information. But, just as in the patent pool cases, the upsides from these exchanges are frequently great. Rather, it is continued third party access that primarily needs to be protected. The merits of conducting this kind of analysis lie in pre-empting the creation of essential facilities *by means of consolidation rather than innovative success*, that may later be used in an anti-competitive way. By the imposing of remedies that are not limited to the protection of competition in the development of a particular product, the availability of critical R&D inputs at a general level is ensured, and the whole area of potential applications can be exploited.

The further merits of such a policy draw on the same logic as does the analysis of ordinary technology markets. In the economic literature it is stressed that the economic effects of the patent system are influenced by the existence of a well-functioning technology market. Such a market allows the patent holder (original inventor) to extract the value of the technology produced, it facilitates dissemination of existing technologies and know-how in society and at the same time it alleviates the blocking effects of IPRs for third parties' R&D. It thus has the much desired effect of spurring initial R&D while allowing further development of improvements and entirely new applications.

Like other kinds of property rights, the legitimate rights (and incentives) provided a holder of intellectual property rights do not extend to a general right to combine with others' assets, if such a combination produces negative net effects on markets. Diminished opportunities for third-party R&D may very well be just as, or even more, detrimental to innovation, than lessened competition between the parties of the transaction. If the transaction affects R&D that does not aim at, or will not necessarily result in, products competing with those being developed by the transacting parties, many applications could be prevented and damage inflicted on several product markets.

7.5 ABUSES

The execution of innovation analysis when examining suspected abuse is slightly different. In abuse cases a firm must be in such a strong position that it can determine market conditions. This position may relate to innovation (for example, key patents) but it may also relate to other variables (such as a strong and protected position in production). In any event, to assess the effects on the innovation process of the allegedly abusive conduct, it is necessary closely to analyse conditions in that process. Only if the company has control of the relevant innovation market or in some way significantly impedes possibilities for competition in innovation, will the action have an appreciable effect on innovation. Typically, such conduct would entrench the dominant position, excluding potentially more efficient rivals to the detriment of consumers.

As stated above (7.4), it is more advantageous to deal with the creation of bottlenecks by anti-competitive means than to try to unravel the effects of dominant firms in themselves. A position acquired through successful product development and internal growth must be considered legal. To oblige firms to share valuable R&D assets, acquired or developed through pro-competitive means, with rivals, could only be considered in very exceptional circumstances. This is not to say that the powerful market actors should not be monitored with a view to protecting the conditions for competition in the innovation process. Where the dominant firm's conduct is not so much a consequence of its internally created efficiencies (such as refusing to share a successful product or component), but rather directly affects the efficiencies of its rivals (as by discrimination, contractual tying or obtaining licences to rivals' IPRs) the scope for intervention is greater. Here, a balance between anti-competitive effects and achieved efficiencies is natural, although with a caveat for intervention in marginal cases.

A careful assessment of underlying market conditions is crucial, as well as analysis as to whether the behaviour may be justified if it is a means of providing attractive products in an efficient manner. Since dominant companies are common in high-tech industries, it is vital that antitrust law does not impede the possibilities for these companies themselves to compete. Superior efficiency must not be held against any company.

8. Concluding remarks

A dynamic market character spurs competition on various levels. To be successful in many types of industry, firms must offer customers new and improved products and services, based on modern and efficient technologies. Older or inferior products will be disregarded by customers or only sellable at low prices. But the causal relation works both ways: dynamic competition stimulates technological development and leads to efficiencies. The conditions in the innovation process affect both market structures and corporate strategies and decision making. These conditions consequently influence the execution of competition law too. An important role of competition policy, as guardian of consumer welfare, is to safeguard a dynamic competitive process, rather than focusing on competition in static terms in the sales of current products.

This book has examined the legal standards for the protection of competition in the innovation process, evaluating the legal content and its underlying economic rationale. At the centre of the study has been the innovation market concept, the most notable legal framework for this kind of antitrust analysis. Various situations have been addressed, in which a transaction could restrict competition in the R&D process by limiting market participants' incentives and abilities for continued product development and future competition. Another very important dynamic dimension, though mainly outside the scope of this work, concerns the way in which rich opportunities for innovation affect the standards for competition in product markets. An overall question, then, is to what extent antitrust policy should relax static (price) competition concerns in reliance on innovation and dynamic competition.

As expressed in the model of innovation market analysis developed by Gilbert and Sunshine, the US authorities were aiming high when they introduced the concept. They sparked off an intense debate and critics of the new approach probably had good cause to worry about it. There was concern that it would be implemented indiscriminately when the authorities wished to incorporate dynamic considerations into the analysis of transactions in the knowledge-based economy. Critics pointed especially to the dangers of delineating and assessing innovation markets rather than focusing on regular product markets. It was held that the approach took a static concept from product market analysis and applied it to R&D in an inappropriate way. For example, neither theory nor empirical data support the existence of strong links between market structure and innovation; and R&D expenditure may be a bad proxy for innovation output. In other words, to uphold some given number of actors in R&D may not improve R&D incentives but merely result in wasteful investments and forgone dynamic efficiencies. Summing up ten years later, the critique probably did its job in limiting too enthusiastic an application of the new approach.

More recent criticism of the innovation market approach reiterates the arguments of the mid-1990s. It is claimed that the potential competition doctrine should be preferred to the innovation market approach, 'because the potential competition doctrine, unlike the innovation market approach, focuses on the effects in an output market of reduced competition (i.e., price, quality, speed of introduction) instead of the more general and harder to predict effect of reduced R&D on unspecified future products'.[1] Yet this critique is not particularly sensitive either to the definition of the innovation market in the antitrust guidelines or to the case law where it has been applied.

In spite of the lack of theoretical and empirical underpinnings for determining optimal market structures and R&D investment levels, the application of antitrust law in R&D intense markets must include a thorough analysis of this dimension. Dynamic competition depends on an innovation process that is reasonably open, where incumbents face a threat of potential competition, so as to have incentives to keep on developing both their existing products and new ideas. But also where innovation is an important means of actual and potential competition, substantial entry barriers may be present. In markets where product performance and quality are major means of competition, large sunk costs, strategic patents and other unique R&D assets, extensive R&D cycles and acquired lead times, network effects as well as other obstacles at the product market level, may all diminish the competitive threat and increase the scope and effectiveness of anti-competitive strategic behaviour in the innovation process. Such behaviour will ultimately harm consumers in the downstream market for resulting goods.

As seen in the case law analysis, negative effects on innovation have been predicted where the analysis was not restricted to competition between current products but also considered the parties' unique position and highly concentrated capabilities in R&D. Even where the transaction could have been contested from a traditional product market perspective alone, the innovation perspective allows for a comprehensive analysis of competitive effects and appropriate remedies. In the review of transactions between incumbents and

---

1 Carlton, Dennis W. & Gertner, Robert H., *Intellectual Property, Antitrust and Strategic Behavior*, NBER Working Paper, No 8976 (2002), p. 17; available at www.nber.org/papers/w8976 (last visited 11 October 2004).

potential entrants with important products under development, it is apparent how the analysis of competing R&D was directed at assessing incentives for the speedy and efficient introduction of products in an output market, as well as competition in this market.

Where a transaction relates to R&D regarding products or technologies which will not fit into existing markets, the innovation market is the adequate relevant market. And it was particularly in these situations that the innovation market critics feared too summary an approach. But competing R&D is still determined by the expected products and a significant concern in these situations has been competition in the future product market. The connection to potential competition doctrines is evident, and many 'innovation market cases' could arguably have been analysed under a (developed) potential competition doctrine. But doctrinal labelling does not necessarily change the underlying analysis. In order to find an appreciable reduction in potential competition for a future market, the analysis would have to include identification of R&D actors and projects, their timing and overall competitiveness.

An innovation market analysis may also include assessment of negative effects that relate more directly to the innovation process, for example lessened incentives and foreclosure effects. Here, analysis starts from the parties' position in the R&D process, the relevant actors' assets and capabilities and the features and strengths of their R&D projects and the presence of current products to find out whether the parties would have the incentive to narrow down, close or delay their R&D efforts owing to the absence of competition, and not for 'normal business motives'.[2] Even if innovation and future market developments (including new entry) never can be entirely foreseen, firms' behaviour will be determined by the information available, estimating the costs, benefit and likelihood of different future scenarios. In a few cases, the innovation market analysis has been used to protect the development of 'unspecified future products'. This is typically to prevent the monopolization of a relevant technology base, where the parties have critical R&D assets and capabilities which, if joined, will afford them the possibility of controlling development in a broader area. When applied in this context, intervention has been limited to cases where the effects, not least in terms of third-party foreclosure, have been immediate and clear.

Based on its practical implementation, the innovation market approach should not be regarded as a reverse Schumpeterian campaign. The primary competitive effects identified by an innovation market analysis (competition in innovation or future competition in technology and product markets) always

---

[2] Scherer, Frederic M. & Ross, David, *Industrial Market Structure and Economic Performance*, Houghton Mifflin, Boston, 1990, pp. 160–67.

depend on the particular circumstances. And the analysis has its merits primarily as a supplementary method, useful for appreciating the R&D aspects of a situation.

On the whole, the innovation market approach, as applied in practice, is not in conflict with current economic thinking. It effectively constitutes the extended potential competition doctrine often advocated by innovation market critics themselves. When going beyond potential product markets in the strict sense, and considering anti-competitive effects associated with the innovation process, a careful case-by-case analysis is deployed to determine effects on innovation abilities and incentives. It is not based on generalizations about anti-competitive 'concentration' in R&D, and it does not prescribe some level of R&D expenditure.

At the same time, case law is sparse and partly inconsistent, and it tends to leave out information that would have been helpful for fully comprehending the underlying analysis. Substantial uncertainties thus remain. It is, for example, unclear to what extent the delimitation of competing R&D efforts (constituting 'the market') could depend on the stage in the R&D process the parties are in. It is also unclear how the authorities will determine the likelihood of success in R&D and how that assessment affects the possibility of establishing anti-competitive effects on R&D and in future markets. Based on economic considerations and case law analysis, the model presented in Chapter 7 outlines some elements of a doctrine that would protect consumer welfare through competition and efficiency in the innovation process. It is hoped that this model can be used to fill some of the gaps and contribute to increased coherency and to the better understanding of the problems at stake. But it is not intended as a complete policy proposal. Rather, the need for further discussion among lawyers and economists must be emphasized.

The need for practicable antitrust standards for analysing R&D competition is growing. Many types of transactions, such as mergers involving small research-based firms, joint venture agreements and various licensing arrangements, will not be reviewed ex ante by the authorities. The legal appraisal of transactions in specialized, international markets where unique R&D abilities are decisive for competitiveness is thus left to the parties. Where inter-firm combinations of complementary and alternative resources and capabilities in R&D are growing in importance, so must the legal standards governing them.

Bibliography

Abramovitz, Moses, 'Economics of growth', in Haley, Bernard F. (ed.), *A Survey of Contemporary Economics*, vol. II, Richard D. Irwin Inc., Homewood, 1952.

Aghion, Philippe, Bloom, Nicholas, Blundell, Richard, Griffith, Rachel & Howitt, Peter, 'Competition and innovation: an inverted U relationship', *NBER Working Paper*, No 9269, 2002; available at http://www.nber.org/papers/w9269.

Ahlborn, Christian, Evans, David S. & Padilla, Atilano Jorge, 'Competition policy in the new economy', 22 *European Competition Law Review* 156 (2001).

Ahn, Sanghoon, 'Competition, innovation and productivity growth: a review of theory and evidence', *Economics Department Working Papers*, No. 317, OECD, 2002.

Ahn, Sanghoon & Hemmings, Philip, 'Policy influences on economic growth in OECD countries: an evaluation of the evidence', *Economics Department Working Papers,* No. 246, OECD, 2000.

American Chamber of Commerce to the European Union, Position Paper on the Commission's Communication of 1st October 2003 on the Application of Article 81(3) to certain categories of agreements and concerted practices; available at http://www.europa.eu.int/comm/competition/antitrust/technology_transfer_2/59_amcham_en.pdf.

Andrews, Lori B., 'Genes and patent policy: rethinking intellectual property rights', 3 *Nature Reviews Genetics* 803 (2002).

Areeda, Philip & Kaplow, Louis, *Antitrust Analysis: Problems, Texts, Cases*, 5th edn, Aspen Law & Business, New York, 1997.

Areeda, Philip E. & Turner, Donald F., *Antitrust Law – An Analysis of Antitrust Principles and their Application*, Little, Brown, Boston, 1978.

Arrow, Kenneth J. 'Economic welfare and the allocation of resources for inventions', in Nelson, R. (ed.), *The Rate and Direction of Inventive Activity*. Princeton University Press, Princeton, 1962.

Audretsch, David B., Baumol, William J. & Burke, Andrew E., 'Competition policy in dynamic markets', 19 *International Journal of Industrial Organization* 613 (2001).

Azcuenaga, Mary L., 'Antitrust and intellectual property: recent highlights and uncertainties', Remarks before the American Law Institute–American Bar Association Boston, Massachusetts April 24, 1997; available at www.ftc.gov.

Baer, William J. & Balto, David A., 'New myths and old realities: recent developments in antitrust enforcement', 2 *Columbia Business Law Review* 207 (1999).

Baer, William J. & Balto, David A., 'Antitrust enforcement and high-technology markets', 5 *Michigan Telecommunication Technology Law Review* 73 (2001).

Bain, J.S., *Barriers to New Competition*, Harvard University Press, Cambridge, USA, 1956.

Baker, Jonathan B., 'A preface to Post-Chicago antitrust', in Cucinotta, Antonio, Pardolesi, Roberto & Van den Bergh, Roger (eds), *Post-Chicago Developments in Antitrust Law*, Edward Elgar, Cheltenham, 2002.

Balto, David A., 'Standard setting in a network economy', Address at Cutting Edge Antitrust Law Seminars International, February 17, 2000; available at http://www.ftc.gov/speeches/other/standardsetting.htm.

Balto, David A. & Sher, Scott A., 'Refining the innovation focus: the FTC's *genzyme* decision', 18(2) *Antitrust* 28 (2004).

Barney, Jay B., 'Competence explanations of economic profits in strategic management: some policy implications', in Ellig, Jerry (ed.), *Dynamic Competition and Public Policy,* Cambridge University Press, Cambridge, 2001.

Barton, John H., 'Patents and antitrust: a rethinking in light of patent breadth and sequential innovation', 65 *Antitrust Law Journal* 449 (1997).

Barton, John H., 'Antitrust treatment of oligopolies with mutually blocking patent portfolios', 69 *Antitrust Law Journal* 851 (2002).

Baumol, William J., *The Free-market Innovation Machine: analyzing the growth miracle of capitalism*, Princeton University Press, Princeton, 2002.

Baumol, William J. & Ordover, Janusz A., 'Antitrust: source of dynamic and static inefficiencies?', in Jorde, Thomas M. & Teece, David J. (eds.), *Antitrust, Innovation and Competitiveness,* Oxford University Press, New York, 1992.

Baxter, William F., 'The definition and measurement of market power in industries characterised by rapidly developing and changing technologies', 53 *Antitrust Law Journal* 717 (1985).

Beeney, Garrard R., 'Pro-competitive aspects of intellectual property pools: a proposal for safe harbor provisions', Submission to the DOJ and FTC Hearings on Competition and Intellectual Property Law and Policy in the Knowledge-Based Economy (2002).

Bellamy, Christopher W. & Child, Graham D., *Common Market Law of Competition*, Sweet & Maxwell, London, 1993.

Ben-Asher, Dror, 'In need of treatment? Merger control, pharmaceutical innovation, and consumer welfare', 21 *Journal of Legal Medicine* 271 (2000).

Benowitz, Steve, 'French challenge to BRCA1 patent underlies European discontent', 94:2 *Journal of the National Cancer Institute* 80 (2002).

Bergman, Mats, *Potential Competition: theory, empirical evidence and legal practice*, The Swedish Competition Authority, 2002.

Bork, Robert H., *The Antitrust Paradox – a policy at war with itself*, The Free Press, New York, 1978/1993.

Brodley, Joseph F., 'The economic goals of antitrust: efficiency, consumer welfare, and technological progress', 62 *New York University Law Review* 1020 (1987).

Brunell, Richard M., 'Editor's Note', *64 Antitrust Law Journal* 1 (1995)

Cameron, Gavin, 'Innovation and growth: a survey of the empirical evidence', Nuffield College, Oxford, 1998, p. 4; available at http://hicks.nuff.ox.ac.uk/users/cameron/papers/empiric.pdf.

Camesasca, Peter D., 'The explicit efficiency defence in merger control: does it make the difference?' 20 *European Competition Law Review* 14 (1999).

Camesasca, Peter D., 'European merger control: getting the efficiencies right', Intersentia-Hart, Antwerp, 2000.

Carlin, Wendy, Schaffer, Mark E., & Seabright, Paul, 'A minimum of rivalry: evidence from transition economies on the importance of competition for innovation and growth', *CEPR Discussion Paper* No. 4343, London, Centre for Economic Policy Research, 2004; available at http://www.cepr.org/pubs/dps/DP4343.asp.

Carlton, Dennis W. & Gertner, Robert H., 'Intellectual property, antitrust and strategic behavior', *NBER Working Paper*, No. 8976 (2002), p. 10; available at www.nber.org/papers/w8976.

Chang, Howard F., 'Patent scope, antitrust policy, and cumulative innovation', 26 *Rand Journal of Economics* 34 (1995).

Charles River Associates, *Report on Multiparty Licensing*, Report to the European Commission (2003); available at http://europa.eu.int/comm/competition/antitrust/legislation/multiparty_licensing.pdf.

Chin, Andrew, 'Analyzing mergers in innovation markets', 38 *Jurimetrics Journal* 119 (1998).

Choumelova, Dessy 'Competition law analysis of patent licensing arrangements – the particular case of 3G3P', 1 *Competition Policy Newsletter* 41 (2003).

Clark, Jeanne, Piccolo, Joe, Stanton, Brian & Tyson, Karin, *Patent Pools: A Solution to the Problem of Access in Biotechnology Patents*, United States Patent and Trademark Office, 2000; available at www.uspto.gov/web/offices/pac/dapp/opla/patentpool.pdf.

Cohen, Seth A., 'To innovate or not to innovate, that is the question: the functions, failures, and foibles of the reward function theory of patent law in relation to computer software platforms', 5 *Michigan Telecommunication Technology Law Review* 1 (1998).

Cohen, Wesley M. & Levin, Richard C., 'Empirical suggestions of innovation and market structure', in Schmalensee, Richard & Willig, Robert D. (eds), *Handbook of Industrial Organization,* North-Holland, Amsterdam, 1989.

Cohen, Wesley M., Nelson, Richard R. & Walsh, John P., 'Protecting their intellectual assets: appropriability conditions and why U.S. manufacturing firms patent (or not)', *NBER Working Paper,* No. 7552 (2000); available at http://papers.nber.org/papers/W7552.pdf.

Cook, C.J. & Kerse, C.S., *E.C. Merger Control,* 3rd edn, Sweet & Maxwell, London, 2000.

Cooter, Robert & Ulen, Thomas, *Law and Economics*, 3rd edn, Reading, Mass., Addison-Wesley, 2000.

D'Aspremont, Claude & Jacquemin, Alexis, 'Cooperative and noncooperative R&D in duopoly with spillovers', 78(5) *American Economic Review* 1133 (1988).

Dahdouh, Thomas N. & Mongoven, James F., 'The shape of things to come: innovation market analysis in merger cases', 64 *Antitrust Law Journal* 405 (1996).

Dalpé, Robert, Bouchard, Louise, Houle, Anne-Julie & Bédard, Louis, 'Watching the race to find the breast cancer genes', 28 *Science, Technology, & Human Values* 187 (2003).

Dasgupta, Partha & Stiglitz, Joseph, 'Uncertainty, industrial structure, and the speed of R&D', 11(1) *Bell Journal of Economics* 1 (1980).

Disner, Eliot G. 'The Chicago School meets the real world', 25-Mar *Los Angeles Lawyer* 14 (2002).

Dolmans, Maurits, 'Standards for standards', Joint DOJ/FTC hearings on Competition and Intellectual Property Law and Policy in the Knowledge-Based Economy, May 22, 2002; available at http://www.ftc.gov/opp/intellect/020522dolmans.pdf.

Eisenberg, Rebecca, 'Public research and private development: patents and technology transfer in government-sponsored research', 82 *Virginia Law Review* 1662 (1996).

Eklöf, Dan, 'Upphovsrätt i konkurrens – särskilt om tvångslicensiering', Stockholms universitet, Stockholm, 2004.

Elhauge, Einer, 'Defining better monopolization standards', 56 *Stanford Law Review* 253 (2003).

Eliasson, Gunnar, 'Business competence, organizational learning, and economic growth: establishing the Smith–Schumpeter–Wicksell (SSW) connection', in Scherer, Frederic M. & Perlman, Mark (eds), *Entrepreneurship, Technological Innovation, and Economic Growth – Studies in the Schumpeterian Tradition,* The University of Michigan Press, Ann Arbor, 1992.

Ellig, Jerome, 'Industrial organization', in Boettke, Peter J. (ed.), *The Elgar Companion to Austrian Economics*, Edward Elgar, Aldershot, 1994.
Europe Economics, *The Development of Analytical Tools for Assessing Market Dynamics in the Knowledge Based Economy*, Annex to Draft Final Report: Literature Review (2003); available at http://europa.eu.int/comm/enterprise/library/lib-competition/doc/analytical_tools_annex.pdf.
Europe Economics, *The Development of Analytical Tools for Assessing Market Dynamics in the Knowledge Based Economy*, Report to the European Commission (2003); available at http://europa.eu.int/comm/enterprise/library/lib-competition/doc/analytical_tools_final_report.pdf.
European Commission, 'Commission report to the Council and the European Parliament on the application of the Agreement between the European Communities and the Government of the United States of America regarding the application of their competition laws', 1996; available at http://europa.eu.int/comm/competition/international/com479_en.html.
European Commission, *First Report on Competition Policy*, 1972.
European Commission, *Tenth Report on Competition Policy*, 1981.
European Commission, *Eleventh Report on Competition Policy*, 1981.
European Commission, *Sixteenth Report on Competition Policy*, 1984.
Evans, David S. & Schmalensee, Richard, 'Some economic aspects of antitrust analysis in dynamically competitive industries', *NBER Working Paper*, No. 8268, 2001.
Federal Trade Commission, 'Anticipating the 21st century, competition policy in the new high-tech, global marketplace', Staff Report, 1996.
Federal Trade Commission, 'FTC antitrust actions in pharmaceutical services and products', May 2000; available at www.ftc.gov/bc/rxupdate.pdf.
Federal Trade Commission, 'FTC antitrust actions in pharmaceutical services and products', October 2003; available at http://www.ftc.gov/bc/0310 rxupdate.pdf.
Federal Trade Commission, 'To promote innovation: the proper balance of competition and patent law and policy', Report by the Federal Trade Commission (2003).
Feinstein, Richard A., Pender, David R. & Meier, Markus H., 'FTC antitrust actions in health care services and products', Health Care Services and Products Division, Bureau of Competition, Federal Trade Commission Washington, DC, June 29, 2001; available at http://www.ftc.gov/bc/hcindex/hcaindex.htm.
Fisher, Franklin M. & Rubinfeld, Daniel L., 'United States v. Microsoft – an economic analysis', 46 *Antitrust Bulletin* 1 (2001).
Flynn, John J., 'Antitrust policy, innovation efficiencies, and the suppression of technology', 66 *Antitrust Law Journal* 487 (1998).
Fox, Eleanor M. 'Post-Chicago, Post-Seattle and the dilemma of globalization', in Cucinotta, Antonio, Pardolesi, Roberto & Van den Bergh, Roger

(eds), *Post-Chicago Developments in Antitrust Law*, Edward Elgar, Cheltenham, 2002.

Freeman, Chris, 'The economics of technical change', 18 *Cambridge Journal of Economics* 463 (1994).

Gellhorn, Ernest & Kovacic, William E. *Antitrust Law and Economics,* 4th edn, West, St. Paul, 1994.

Gerla, Harry S., 'Restoring rivalry as a central concept in antitrust law', 75 *Nebraska Law Review* 209 (1996).

Gilbert, Richard J., 'Antitrust for patent pools: a century of policy evolution', 2004 *Stanford Technology Law Review* 3 (2004).

Gilbert, Richard J. & Newbery, David M.G., 'Preemptive patenting and the persistence of monopoly', 75 *American Economic Review* 514 (1982).

Gilbert, Richard J. & Sunshine, Steven C., 'Incorporating dynamic efficiency concerns in merger analysis: the use of innovation markets', 63 *Antitrust Law Journal* 569 (1995).

Gilbert, Richard J. & Sunshine, Steven C., 'The use of innovation markets: a reply to Hay, Rapp, and Hoerner', 64 *Antitrust Law Journal* 75 (1995).

Gilbert, Richard J. & Tom, Willard K., 'Is innovation king at the antitrust agencies? The intellectual property guidelines five years later', 69 *Antitrust Law Journal* 43 (2001).

Glader, Marcus, 'Research and development cooperation in European competition law', *CFE Working Paper Series*, No. 6, 2000; available at http://www.cfe.lu.se/CFEWP/WP.html.

Glader, Marcus, 'Innovation economics and the antitrust guidelines on horizontal co-operation', 24 *World Competition – Law and Economics Review* 513 (2001).

Grossman, Gene M. & Helpman, Elhanan, *Innovation and Growth in the Global Economy,* MIT Press, Cambridge, Mass., 1991.

Grossman, Gene M. & Helpman, Elhanan, 'Endogenous innovation in the theory of growth', 8 *Journal of Economic Perspectives* 23 (1994).

Grossman, Gene M. & Shapiro, Carl, 'Research joint ventures: an antitrust analysis' 2 *Journal of Law, Economics and Organization* 315 (1986).

Gutterman, Alan S., *Innovation and Competition Policy: A Comparative Study of the Regulation of Patent Licensing and Collaborative Research & Development in the United States and the European Community*, Kluwer Law International, London, 1997.

Hamel, Gary, 'Competition for competence and interpartner learning within international strategic alliances', 12 *Strategic Management Journal* 83 (1991).

Hart, David, M., 'Antitrust and technological innovation', 15(2) *Issues in Science & Technology* 75 (1998/99).

Hay, George A., 'Innovations in antitrust enforcement', 64 *Antitrust Law Journal* 7 (1995).

Hayek, Friedrich A., *Individualism and Economic Order,* Routledge and Kegan Paul, London, 1949.

Heller, Michael A. & Eisenberg, Rebecca S., 'Can patents deter innovation? The anticommons in biomedical research', 280 *Science* 698 (1998).

Hoerner, Robert J., 'Innovation markets: new wine in old bottles?', 64 *Antitrust Law Journal* 49 (1995).

Hovenkamp, Herbert, 'The reckoning of post-Chicago antitrust', in Cucinotta, Antonio, Pardolesi, Roberto & Van den Bergh, Roger (eds), *Post-Chicago Developments in Antitrust Law*, Edward Elgar, Cheltenham, 2002.

Jacquemin, Alexis, 'Theories of industrial organisation and competition policy: what are the links?', Working paper, European Commission, Forward Studies Unit, 2000.

Jensen, Michael C., 'The modern industrial revolution, exit, and the failure of internal control systems', 48 *Journal of Finance* 831 (1993).

Jorde, Thomas M. & Teece, David J., 'Innovation and cooperation: implications for competition and antitrust', 4(3) *Journal of Economic Perspectives* 75 (1990).

Jorde, Thomas M. & Teece, David J., 'Innovation, cooperation, and antitrust', in Jorde, Thomas M. & Teece, David J. (eds), *Antitrust, Innovation, and Competitiveness,* Oxford University Press, New York, 1992.

Jorde, Thomas M. & Teece, David J., 'Introduction', in Jorde Thomas M. & Teece, David J. (eds), *Antitrust, Innovation, and Competitiveness,* Oxford University Press, New York, 1992.

Kattan, Joseph, 'Antitrust analysis of technology joint ventures: allocative efficiency and the rewards of innovation', 61 *Antitrust Law Journal* 937 (1993).

Kattan, Joseph, 'Antitrust considerations in innovation-driven markets', 21 *Canada–United States Law Journal* 115 (1995).

Kattan, Joseph, 'After the IP guidelines: trends in intellectual property antitrust enforcement', 11 *Antitrust* 26 (Summer, 1997).

Kattan, Joseph & Arp, D. Jarret, 'Trends in intellectual property antitrust enforcement', 566 *Practising Law Institute – Patents, Copyrights, Trademarks, and Literary Property Course Handbook Series* 401 (1999).

Katz, Michael L., 'An analysis of cooperative research and development', 17 *Rand Journal of Economics* 527 (1996).

Kirzner, Israel M., *How Markets Work: Disequilibrium, Entrepreneurship and Discovery*, Institute of Economic Affairs, London, 1997.

Kitch, Edmund W., 'The nature and function of the patent system', 20 *Journal of Law and Economics* 265 (1977).

Klein, Joel I., 'A stepwise approach to antitrust review of horizontal restraints', Address before the American Bar Association, Washington, D.C. November 7, 1996; available at www.usdoj.gov/atr/public/speeches/jikaba.htm.

Kolasky, William J. and Dick, Andrew R., 'The merger guidelines and the integration of efficiencies into antitrust review of horizontal mergers', 2002; available at http://www.usdoj.gov/atr/hmerger/11254.pdf.

Korah, Valentine, *R&D and the EEC competition rules. Regulation 418*, ESC, Oxford, 1986.

Korah, Valentine, 'The interface between intellectual property and antitrust: the European experience', 69 *Antitrust Law Journal* 801 (2002).

Kulbaski, James J., 'Comments on patent pools and standards for Federal Trade Commission hearings regarding competition & intellectual property'; available at http://www.ftc.gov/opp/intellect/020417jamesjkulbaski.pdf.

Lande, Robert H., 'Proving the obvious: the antitrust laws were passed to protect consumers (not just to increase efficiency)', 50 *Hastings Law Journal* 959 (1999).

Lande, Robert H., 'Consumer choice as the ultimate goal of antitrust', 62 *University of Pittsburgh Law Review* 503 (2001).

Landman, Lawrence B., 'Competing in the global pharmaceutical industry: innovation and future potential competition', 2 *The Journal of Biolaw & Business* 29 (1998).

Landman, Lawrence B., 'Innovation markets in Europe', 19 *European Competition Law Review* 21 (1998).

Landman, Lawrence B., 'The economics of future goods markets', 21 *World Competition – Law and Economics Review* 74 (1998).

Landman, Lawrence B., 'Innovation and the structure of competition', 81 *Journal of the Patent and Trademark Office Society* 728 (1999).

Langlois, Richard N., 'Technological standards, innovation, and essential facilities', in Ellig, Jerry (ed), *Dynamic Competition and Public Policy*, Cambridge University Press, Cambridge, 2001.

Leahy, Dermot & Neary, J. Peter, 'Public policy towards R&D in oligopolistic industries', 87(4) *American Economic Review* 642 (1997).

Levin, Richard C., Klevoric, Alvin K., Nelson, Richard R. & Winter, Sidney G., 'Appropriating the returns from industrial R&D', *Brookings Papers on Economic Activity* , No. 3 783 (1987).

Lidgard, Hans Henrik, *Parallellhandel: Konsumtion av immaterialrätt i Europa och USA*, Norstedts Juridik, Stockholm, 2002.

Lopatka, John E. & Page, William H., ''Obvious' consumer harm in antitrust policy: the Chicago School, the Post-Chicago School and the courts', in Cucinotta, Antonio, Pardolesi, Roberto & Van den Bergh, Roger (eds), *Post-Chicago Developments in Antitrust Law*, Edward Elgar, Cheltenham, 2002.

Lopatka, John E. & Page, William H., 'Monopolization, innovation, and consumer welfare', 69 *George Washington Law Review* 367 (2001).

Loughran, Mary, Parplies, Kay & Schade, Roosmarijn, 'Merger control: main developments between 1st January 2003 and 30th April 2003', *Competition Policy Newsletter* 2 (70) (2003).

Lowe, Philip, 'DG competition's review of the policy on abuse of dominance', in Hawk, Berry (ed), *International Antitrust Law & Policy*, 2003 Fordham Corporate Law Institute (2004).

Lutz, Alyssa A. & Stiroh, Lauren J., 'The relevant market in intellectual property/antitrust litigation', 658 *Practising Law Institute – Patents, Copyrights, Trademarks, and Literary Property Course Handbook Series* 75 (2001).

Mason, Edward S., 'Price and production policies of large scale enterprises', 29 *American Economic Review* 61 (1949).

Merges, Robert P. & Nelson, Richard R., 'Market structure and technical advance: the role of patent scope decisions', in Jorde, Thomas M. & Teece, David J. (eds), *Antitrust, Innovation, and Competitiveness,* Oxford University Press, New York, 1992.

Merges, Robert P., 'Institutions for Intellectual Property Transactions', University of California at Berkeley, 1999.

Merges, Robert P., 'Intellectual property rights, input markets, and the value of intangible assets', University of California at Berkeley, 1999.

Merges, Robert P. & Nelson, Richard R., 'On the complex economics of patent scope', 90 *Columbia Law Review* 839 (1990).

Metcalfe, Stan, 'The economic foundations of technology policy: equilibrium and evolutionary perspectives', in Stoneman, Paul (ed), *Handbook of the Economics of Innovation and Technological Change*, Blackwell Publishers, Oxford, 1995.

Mises, Ludwig von, *Human Action,* Yale University Press, New Haven, 1949.

Monti, Mario, 'Convergence in EU–US antitrust policy regarding mergers and acquisitions: an EU perspective', Speech at UCLA Law First Annual Institute on US an EU Antitrust Aspects of Mergers and Acquisitions Los Angeles, 28 February 2004; available at http://www.europa.eu.int/comm/competition/speeches/.

Monti, Mario, 'European Competition policy for the 21st century', Speech at The Fordham Corporate Law Institute, 28 Annual Conference on International Antitrust Law and Policy, October 20, 2000; available at http://www.europa.eu.int/comm/competition/speeches/.

Morse, Howard M., 'The limits of innovation markets', 2(1) *Antitrust and Intellectual Property* 22 (2001).

Morse, Howard M., 'Product market definition in the pharmaceutical industry', 71 *Antitrust Law Journal* 633 (2003).

Muris, Timothy J. 'Improving the economic foundations of competition policy', Remarks at George Mason University Law Review's Winter Antitrust Symposium, Washington, DC, January 15, 2003; available at http://www.ftc.gov/speeches/muris/improveconfoundatio.htm.

Muris, Timothy J., 'The FTC and the law of monopolization' 67 *Antitrust Law Journal* 693 (2000).

Nam-Hoon Kang & Kentaro Sakai, 'International strategic alliances: their role in industrial globalisation', *STI Working Paper* 2000/5, OECD, Paris, 2000.

Nelson, Richard R., 'The agenda for growth theory: a different point of view', 22 *Cambridge Journal of Economics* 497 (1998).

Newberg, Joshua A., 'Antitrust for the economy of ideas: the logic of technology markets', 14 *Harvard Journal of Law and Technology* 83 (2000).

Newberg, Joshua A, 'Antitrust, patent pools, and the management of uncertainty', 3 *Atlantic Law Journal* 1 (2000).

North, Douglass, *Institutions, Institutional Change and Economic Performance*, Cambridge University Press, 1990.

OECD, Competition Policy and Joint Ventures, Paris, 1986.

OECD, 'Competition policy and efficiency claims in horizontal agreements', Roundtable in November 1995, Paris, 1996.

OECD, 'Application of competition policy to high tech markets', *OECD Working Papers,* Series Roundtables on Competition Policy No. 9, Paris, 1997.

OECD, Globalisation of Industrial R&D: Policy Issues, Paris, 1999.

OECD, *A New Economy?: The Changing Role of Innovation and Information in Growth*, Paris, 2000.

OECD, 'Competition and regulation issues in the pharmaceutical industry', Roundtable in June 2000, Paris, 2001.

OECD, Merger Review in Emerging New Innovation Markets, Paris, 2003.

OECD, 'OECD Global Forum on Competition – Preventing Market Abuses', 2004; available at www.oecd.org/dataoecd/13/42/27892500.pdf.

OFT, *Innovation and Competition policy*, Economic Discussion Paper 3, Report prepared for the Office of Fair Trading by Charles River Associates, 2002.

Ordover, Janusz A. & Willig, Robert D., 'An economic definition of predation: pricing and product innovation', 91 *Yale Law Journal* 8 (1981).

Pate, R. Hewitt, 'The common law approach and improving standards for analyzing single firm conduct', Address before the Thirtieth Annual Conference on International Antitrust Law and Policy Fordham Corporate Law Institute, New York, October 23, 2003; available at www.usdoj.gov/atr/public/speeches/202724.htm.

Pate, R. Hewitt, 'Antitrust in a transatlantic context – from the cicada's perspective', Address at 'Antitrust in a Transatlantic Context' Conference, Brussels, Belgium, June 7, 2004; available at http://www.usdoj.gov/atr/public/speeches/203973.pdf.

Pate, R. Hewitt, 'The common law approach and improving standards for analysing single firm conduct', in Hawk, Barry E. (ed), *International*

Antitrust Law & Policy, 30 Fordham Corporate Law Institute 2003, New York, 2004.

Petit, Maria Luisa & Tolwinski, Boleslaw, 'R&D cooperation or competition?', 43 *European Economic Review* 185 (1999).

Porter, Michel E., *Competitive Advantage: creating and sustaining superior performance*, Free Press, New York, 1985.

Posner, Richard A., *Antitrust Law,* The University of Chicago Press, Chicago, 2001.

Rai, Arti K., 'Fostering cumulative innovation in the biopharmaceutical industry: the role of patents and antitrust', 16 *Berkeley Technology Law Journal* 813 (2001).

Rapp, Richard T., 'The misapplication of the innovation market approach to merger analysis', 64 *Antitrust Law Journal* 19 (1995).

Romer, Paul M. 'Increasing returns and long-run growth', 94 *Journal of Political Economy* 1002 (1986).

Romer, Paul M., 'Endogenous technological change', 98 *Journal of Political Economy* S71 (1990).

Romer, Paul M., 'Beyond classical and Keynesian macroeconomic policy', *Policy Options*, July-August 1994; available at www.stanford.edu/~promer/policyop.htm.

Romer, Paul M., 'New goods, old theory, and the welfare costs of trade restrictions', 43 *Journal of Development Economics* 5 (1994).

Romer, Paul M. 'The origins of endogenous growth', 8 *Journal of Economic Perspectives* 3 (1994).

Rubinfeld, Daniel L. & Hoven, John, 'Innovation and antitrust enforcement', in Ellig, Jerry (ed.), *Dynamic Competition and Public Policy,* Cambridge University Press, 2001.

Scherer, Frederic M., *Industrial Market Structure and Economic Performance*, Rand McNally, Chicago, 1980.

Scherer, Frederic M., 'Antitrust, efficiency, and progress', 62 *New York University Law Review* 998 (1987).

Scherer, Frederic M. & Ross, David, *Industrial Market Structure and Economic Performance,* Houghton Mifflin, Boston, 1990.

Schmookler, Jacob, *Invention and Economic Growth,* Harvard University Press, Cambridge, 1966.

Schumpeter, Joseph A., *The Theory of Economic Development: an inquiry into profits, capital, credit, interest, and the business cycle*, Harvard University Press, Cambridge, Mass., 1934.

Schumpeter, Joseph A., *Capitalism, Socialism, and Democracy,* 2nd edn, Harper & Brothers, New York, 1947.

Scotchmer, Suzanne, 'Standing on the shoulders of giants: cumulative research and the patent law', 5 *Journal of Economic Perspectives* 29 (1991).

Scotchmer, Suzanne, 'Protecting early innovators: should second-generation products be patentable?', 27 *Rand Journal of Economics* 322 (1996).

Shapiro, Carl, 'Navigating the patent thicket: cross licenses, patent pools, and standard-setting', University of California at Berkeley, 2001; available at http://faculty.haas.berkeley.edu/shapiro/thicket.pdf.

Shapiro, Carl, 'Competition policy and innovation,' *STI Working Paper* 2002/11, OECD, Paris, 2002.

Solow, Robert, 'A contribution to the theory of economic growth', 70 *Quarterly Journal of Economics* 65 (1956).

Solow, Robert, 'Technical change and the aggregate production function', 39 *Review of Economics and Statistics* 312 (1957).

Starek, Roscoe B., 'International cooperation in antitrust enforcement and other international antitrust developments', Prepared Remarks before 'Antitrust 1997' Conference, 1996; available at www.ftc.gov.

Sung, Lawrence M., 'Greater predictability may result in patent pools' , Submission at US DOJ and FTC hearings 'Competition and Intellectual Property Law and Policy in the Knowledge-Based Economy'; available at http://www.ftc.gov/opp/intellect/020417lawrencemsung1.pdf.

Sylos-Labini, Paolo, 'Capitalism, socialism, and democracy and large-scale firms', in Scherer, Frederic M. & Perlman, Mark (eds), *Entrepreneurship, Technological Innovation, and Economic Growth – Studies in the Schumpeterian Tradition,* The University of Michigan Press, Ann Arbor, 1992.

Temple Lang, John, 'European Community antitrust law: innovation markets and high technology industries', 20 *Fordham International Law Journal* 717 (1997).

Temple Lang, John, 'Anticompetitive non-pricing abuses under European and national antitrust law', in Hawk, Berry (ed.), *International Antitrust Law & Policy*, 2003 Fordham Corporate Law Institute, 2004.

The Economist, 'The New Enforcers', article, October 7, 2000.

Tirole, Jean, *The Theory of Industrial Organization,* MIT Press, Cambridge, Mass., 1988.

Tom, Willard K., 'Licensing and antitrust: common goals and uncommon problems', Address before the American Conference Institute, 9th National Conference on Licensing Intellectual Property (1998); available at www.ftc.gov.

Tom, Willard K., 'The 1975 Xerox consent decree: ancient artifacts and current tensions', 68 *Antitrust Law Journal* 967 (2001).

Tom, Willard K. & Newberg, Joshua A., 'Antitrust and intellectual property: from separate spheres to unified field', 66 *Antitrust Law Journal* 167 (1997).

U.S. Department of Justice, 'Antitrust enforcement and the consumer'; available at www.usdoj.gov/atr/public/div_stats/1638.htm.

Valentine, Debra A., 'Abuse of dominance in relation to intellectual property: U.S. perspectives and the Intel cases', Address before the Israel International Antitrust Conference, November 1999; available at www.ftc.org.

Van Cayseele, Patrick & Van den Bergh, Roger, 'Antitrust law', in Bouckaert, Boudewijn & de Geest, Gerrit (eds), *Encyclopedia of law and economics, Volume II. Civil Law and Economics,* Edward Elgar, Cheltenham, 2000.

Van den Bergh, Roger, 'The difficult reception of economic analysis in European competition law', in Cucinotta, Antonio, Pardolesi, Roberto & Van den Bergh, Roger (eds), *Post-Chicago Developments in Antitrust Law*, Edward Elgar, Cheltenham, 2002.

Varney, Christine A., 'Antitrust and the drive to innovate: innovation markets in merger review', 9 *Antitrust* 16 (Summer 1995).

Viscusi, W Kip, Vernon, John M. & Harrington Jr., Joseph E., *Economics of Regulation and Antitrust,* MIT Press, Cambridge, Mass., 1995.

Whish, Richard, *Competition Law,* 4th edn, Butterworths, London, 2001.

Wickelgren, Abraham L., 'Innovation, market structure and the holdup problem: investment incentives and coordination', 22 *International Journal of Industrial Organization* 693 (2004).

Widnell, Nicholas A., 'The crystal ball of innovation market analysis in merger review: an appropriate means of predicting the future?', 4 *George Mason Law Review* 369 (1996).

Williamson, Oliver E., 'Antitrust policy', *The New Palgrave – A Directory of Economics,* Stockton Press, New York, 1987.

Wilson, Bruce B., 'Patent and know-how license agreements: field of use, territorial, price and quantity restrictions', Address Before the Fourth New England Antitrust Conference (1970).

Wolfram, Richard, 'Entering European innovation markets: antitrust implications of innovation markets and intellectual property licensing – a U.S. perspective', conference paper on 'Entering European Innovation Markets', February 3–4, 2000, Lund University, Sweden.

Index